The Complete HOME RESTORATION MANUAL

An Authoritative, Do-It-Yourself Guide to Restoring and Maintaining the Older House

ALBERT JACKSON & DAVID DAY

Introduction by GORDON BOCK, Editor, *Old House Journal*

SIMON & SCHUSTER

NEW YORK • LONDON • TORONTO • SYDNEY • TOKYO • SINGAPORE

SIMON & SCHUSTER
Simon & Schuster Building, Rockefeller Center,
1230 Avenue of the Americas, New York, NY 10020

**THE COMPLETE
HOME RESTORATION MANUAL**
was created by

INKLINK,
1-3 HIGHBRIDGE WHARF, GREENWICH, LONDON SE10 9PS

First published in 1992 by
HarperCollins Publishers
London

TEXT ·
Albert Jackson, David Day

EXECUTIVE ART DIRECTOR
Simon Jennings

DESIGN & ART DIRECTION
Alan Marshall

EDITOR
Peter Leek

US CONSULTANT
Hugh Howard

ILLUSTRATIONS
Robin Harris, David Day

LOCATION PHOTOGRAPHY
Shona Wood

STUDIO PHOTOGRAPHY
Neil Waving

ADDITIONAL ILLUSTRATIONS
Brian Craker

For HarperCollins:

EXECUTIVE EDITOR
Polly Powell

PUBLISHING DIRECTOR
Robin Wood

ISBN 0 671 73798 8

TEXT SET IN PALATINO & GARAMOND BY
Inklink, London

IMAGESETTING BY
Blackheath Publishing Services, London

COLOUR ORIGINATION
HarperCollins Publishers Ltd, Hong Kong

PRINTED & BOUND BY
HarperCollins Publishers Ltd, Glasgow

10 9 8 7 6 5 4 3 2 1

Library of Congress Cataloging-in-Publication Data
Jackson, Albert, 1943-
    The complete home restoration manual : an authoritative, do-it-yourself
guide to restoring and maintaining the older house/Albert Jackson and David
Day ; introduction by Gordon Bock ; [illustrations, Robin Harris, David Day].
    p. cm.
    Includes bibliographical references and index.
    ISBN 0-871-73798-8
    1. Dwellings--Remodeling--Amateurs' manuals. 2. Historic buildings--
Conservation and restoration--Amateurs' manuals.
I. Day, David, 1944- . II. Title. III Title: The complete home restoration manual.
IV. Title: Complete home restoration manual.
TH4816.J33 1992
643'.7--dc20   92-7122
                                                                   CIP

INTRODUCTION

ONCE YOU START RESTORING AN OLD HOUSE, rehabilitating it with a sensitivity to its original architectural concept, you'll soon find it is a project that draws on the whole universe of construction arts. Inevitably, some old-house ills are unique and the cures are cooked-up for the occasion. However, after a while you'll notice that a large measure of the most effective restoration work is really based on time-tested repair techniques. Traditionally, each of the building trades had methods worked out for the periodic upkeep of the carpentry, masonry and plasterwork that went into a house – methods all but forgotten in our no-maintenance age. It is these techniques that form the backbone of house restoration today and are spelled out, craft by craft, in this manual.

You will also see that restoring a house means more than just putting the roof, siding, and windows – the "weather envelope" – back in order. The working parts of the building, including staircases, fireplaces, bathrooms and the kitchen will probably need attention as well. Most important, though, restoring means reviving the rich decorative surfaces such as plaster cornices, wood paneling, or ceramic tile that "make" an older house. The twenty-one chapters presented here each focus on a particular building fabric or house part, and together cover the common problem areas you are likely to encounter.

Finally, you will realize that having clear, accurate information right at hand about the architecture and construction of houses is one of the most valuable restoration tools. The at-a-glance format of this book is ideal for its role as a manual, combining overviews of each subject with a thorough selection of repair and design alternatives. Like any good tool, it is easily handled and well-suited for the job.

Gordon Bock, Editor
Old-House Journal.

CONTENTS

CONTENTS

DIRECTORY OF SUPPLIERS

ARCHITECTURAL SALVAGE YARDS

Architectural Salvage Warehouse
337 Berry St, Brooklyn, NY 11211
(718) 388-4527

The Bank Architectural Antiques
1874 Felicity St, New Orleans,
LA 70113
(800) 2-SHUTTER

Berkely Architectural Salvage
2741 Tenth St, Berkeley, CA9410
(510) 849-2025

Sylvan Brandt
653 Mail St, Lititz, PA 17543
(717) 626-4520

Great American Salvage Co.
34 Cooper Sq, New York, NY 10003
(212) 505-0070

Lost City Arts
275 Lafayette St, New York, NY 10012
(212) 941-8025

Materials Unlimited
2 West Michigan Ave, Ypsilanti,
MI 48197
(313) 483-6980

Nostalgia Architectural Antiques
307 Stiles Ave, Savannah, GA31401
(912) 236-8176

Renovation Concepts
213 Washington Ave North,
Minneapolis, MN 55401
(612) 333-5766

Urban Archaeology
285 Lafayette St, New York, NY 10012
(212) 431-6969

Urban Artifacts
4700 Wissahickon Ave,
Philadelphia, PA 19144
(800) 621-1962

Dennis C. Walker
PO Box 309, Tallmade, OH 44278
(216) 633-1081

DOORS AND WINDOWS

American Heritage Shutters, Inc.
2345 Dunn Ave, Memphis, TN 38114
(800) 514-1186; (901) 743-2800

Andersen Corporation
100 Fourth Ave North, Bayport,
MN 55003-1096
(612) 439-5150

Architectural Components
26 North Leverett Rd, Montague,
MA 01351
(413) 367-9441

The Atrium Door & Window Co.
PO Box 226957, Dallas, TX 75222-6957
(214) 634-9663

S.A. Bendheim Co., Inc.
61 Willet St, Passaic, NJ 07055
(800) 221-7379; In NJ: (201) 471-1733,
Fax: (201) 471-3475

Blenko Glass Company
Box 67, Milton, WV 25541
(304) 743-9081

Grand Era Reproductions
PO Box 1026, Lapeer, MI 48446
(313) 664-1756

Historic Windows
PO Box 1172, Harrisonburg, VA 22801
(703) 434-5855

Hope's Landmark Products Inc.
PO Box 580, 95-99 Jamestown Ave,
Jamestown, NY 14702-0580
(716) 665-6223

Kenmore Industries
One Thompson Sq, PO Box 34,
Boston, MA 02129
(617) 242-1711

Lamson-Taylor Custom Doors
3 Tucker Rd, Sth Ackworth, NH 03607
(603) 835-2992

Marvin Windows
Warroad, MN 56763
(800) 346-5128; (800) 552-1167

Morgan Products Ltd
Oshkosh, WI 54903
(800) 766-1992

Ramase Old Building Supplies
266 Washington Rd, Woodbury,
CT 06798
(203) 263-3332

Shuttlecraft
282 Stepstone Hill, Guilford, CT 06437
(203) 453-1973

Touchstone Woodworks
PO Box 112, Ravenna, OH 44266
(216) 297-1313

Velux-America Inc.
PO Box 3268, Greenwood,
SC 29648-9968
(803) 223-3149

The Old Wagon Factory
PO Box 1427, Clarksville, VA 23927
(804) 374-5787

The Woodstone Company
Patch Rd, PO Box 223, Westminster,
VT 05158
(802) 722-4784

FIREPLACES AND STOVES

Danny Alessandro, Ltd
Edwin Jackson, Ltd
1156 Second Ave, New York,
NY 10021
(212) 421-1928; (212) 759-8210

Bryant Stove Works, Inc.
Box 2048, Rich Rd, Thorndyke,
ME 04986
(207) 568-3665

Buckley Rumford Fireplace Co.
PO Box 21131, Columbus, OH 43221
(614) 221-6131

The Country Iron Foundry
PO Box 600, Paoli, PA 19301
(215) 296-7122

Draper and Draper, Ltd
200 Lexington Ave, New York,
NY 10016
(212) 679-0547

Elmira Stove Works
22 Church St, Elmira, Ontario,
N3B 1M3, Canada
(519) 669-5103

Fourth Bay
10500 Industrial Drive, Garrettsville,
OH 44231
(800) 321-9614; (216) 527-4343

Rais and Wittus, Inc.
Hack Green Rd, Pund Ridge,
NY 10576
(914) 764-5679

FLOORS

Aged Woods
First Capital Wood Products, Inc.
147 West Philadelphia St, York,
PA 17403
(800) 233-9307; (717) 843-8104

Albany Woodworks
PO Box 729, Albany, LA 70711
(504) 567-1155

American Olean Tile Co.
1000 Cannon Ave, PO Box 271,
Lansdale, PA 19446-0271
(215) 855-1111

The Italian Tile Center
Italian Trade Commission,

499 Park Ave, New York, NY 10022
(212) 980-1500

Chevalier, Inc.
11 East 57th St, New York, NY 10022
(212) 750-5505; Fax: (212) 750-6234

Doris Leslie Blau
15 East 57th St, New York, NY 10022
(212) 759-3715

J.R. Burrows and Co.
818 Centre St, Jamaica Plain,
MA 02130
(617) 524-1795

Carlisle Restoration Lumber
Route 123, Stoddard, NH 03464
(603) 446-3937

Edward Fields Carpetmakers
232 East 59th St, New York, NY 10022
(212) 310-0400

Designs in Tile
PO Box 358, Mt Shasta, CA 96067
(916) 926-2629

Good and Co.
Salzbury Sq, Rt.101, Amherst,
NH 03031
(603) 672-0490

Goodwin Lumber Company
Rt.2, Box 119-AA, Micanopy, FL 32667
(800) 336-3118; (904) 373-9663

Harris-Tarkett, Inc.
PO Box 300, 333 East Maple St,
Johnson City, TN 37605-0300
(615) 928-3122

The Joinery Co.
PO Box 518, Tarboro, NC 27886
(919) 823-3306

Kentucky Wood Floors
4200 Reservoir Ave, Louisville,
KY 40213
(502) 451-6024

Mountain Lumber
PO Box 289B, Ruckersville, VA 22986
(804) 985-3546

Sandy Pond Hardwoods
921-A Lancaster Pike, Quarryville,
PA 17566
(717) 284-5030

Tiresias, Inc.
PO Box 1864, Orangeburg, SC 29116
(803) 534-8478

Thos. K. Woodard
835 Madison Ave, New York,
NY 10021
(212) 988-2906

GLASS

Jennifer's Glass Works
6767 Peachtree Industrial Blvd,
Norcross, GA 30092
(404) 447-4878

HARDWARE

Anglo-American Brass Co.
PO Box Drawer 9487, San Jose,
CA 95157-9487
(408) 246-0203; (408) 246-3232

The Antique Doorknob
Maudie Eastwood, 3900 Latimer Rd,
N, Tillamook, OR 97141
(503) 842-2244

**The Antique Doorknob Museum
and Shop**
St Peters, PA 19470
(215) 469-0970

The Antiques Hardware Store
RD#2, Box A, Route 611,
Kintnersville, PA 18930
(215) 847-2447

Ball and Ball
463 W. Lincoln Highway, Exton,

PA 19341
(215) 363-7330

Monroe Coldren and Sons
723 East Virginia Ave, West Chester,
PA 19380
(215) 692-5651

Colonial Restoration Products
405 East Walnut St, North Wales,
PA 19454
(215) 699-3133

Crawford's Old House Store
301 McCall, Rm 907, Waukesha,
WI 53186
(800) 556-7878; (414) 542-0685

Elephant Hill Ironworks
Rt 1, Box 168, Tunbridge, VT 05077
(802) 889-9444

The Farm Forge
6945 Fishburg Rd, Dayton,
OH 45424
(513) 233-6751

**Gainsborough Hardware
Industries, Inc.**
PO Box 569, Chesterfield, MO 63017
(314) 532-8466

P.E. Guerin
21-23 and 25 Jane St, New York,
NY 10014
(212) 243-5270

Historic Housefitters Co.
Farm to Market Rd, Brewster,
NY 10509
(914) 278-2427

**Kayns & Son Custom Forged
Hardware**
76 Daniel Ridge Rd, Candler,
NC 28715
(704) 667-8868

Brian F. Leo
7532 Columbus Ave, South
Richfield, MN 55423
(612) 861-1473

Newton Milham
672 Drift Rd, Westport, MA 02790
(617) 636-5437

The Renovator's Supply
Millers Falls, MA 01349
(413) 659-2231

Trmont Nail Company
8 Elm St, PO Box 111, Wareham,
MA 02571
(617) 295-0038

Virginia Metalcrafters
1010 East Main St, PO Box 1068,
Waynesboro, VA 22980
(703) 949-8205

Williamsburg Blacksmiths
PO Box 1776, Williamsburg,
MA 01096
(413) 268-7341

Woodbury Blacksmith & Forge Co.
PO Box 268, Woodbury, CT 06798
(203) 263-5737

LIGHTING

Authentic Designs
The Mill Rd, West Rupert,
VT 05776-0011
(802) 394-7713

B and F Lamp Supply, Inc.
McMinnville, TN 37110
(615) 473-3014/3016

Bradford Consultants
PO Box 4020, Alameda, CA 94501
(415) 523-1968

Colonial Metalcrafters
5935 South Broadway, PO Box 1135,
Tyler, TX 75710
(214) 561-1111

DIRECTORY OF SUPPLIERS

Conant Custom Brass
PO Box 1523T, Burlington, VT 05402
(802) 658-4482
Hammerworks
6 Fremont St, Worcester, MA 01603
(508) 755-3434
Hurley Patentee Lighting
R.D.7, Box 98A, Kingston, NY 12401
(914) 331-5414
Iron Apple Forge
Routes 263 and 413, PO Box 724,
Buckingham, PA 18912
(215) 794-7351
Just Bulbs
938 Broadway, New York, NY 10010
(212) 228-7820
King's Chandelier Company
Highway 14, PO Box 667, Eden
(Leaksville), NC 27288
(919) 627-0071
Gates Moore
River Rd, Silvermine, Norwalk,
CT 06850
(203) 847-3231
Nesle
151 East 57th St, New York,
NY 10022
(212) 755-0515
Rambusch
40 West 13th St, New York,
NY 10011
(212) 675-0400
Rejuvenation Lamp & Fixture Co.
901-E North Skidmore, Portland,
OR 97217
(503) 249-0774
Roy Electric Co. Inc.
1054 Coney Island Ave, Brooklyn,
NY 11230
(800) 366-3347; (718) 434-7002
The Saltbox
3004 Columbia Ave, Lancaster,
PA 17603
(717) 392-5649
Victorian Lighting Works
251 South Pennsylvania Ave, PO
Box 469, Centre Hall, PA 16828
(814) 364-9577

METALWORK

AA Abingdon Affiliates, Inc.
2149 Utica Ave, Brooklyn, NY 11234
(718) 258-8333
Architectural Iron Company
Box 126, Rte 6 West, Milford,
PA 18337
(717) 296-7722; (212) 243-2664
Cassidy Bros. Forge, Inc.
US Rte 1, Rowley, MA 01969-1796
(508) 948-7303
Chelsean Decorative Metal Co.
9603 Moonlight Drive, Houston,
TX 77096
(713) 721-9200
Monte Haberman
1202 East Pine St, Placentia,
CA 92670
(714) 993-4766
Mike Shaffer, Blacksmith
Mountain Forge, 1155 Dantel Court,
Stone Mountain, GA 30083
(404) 469-2680
W. F. Norman Corp.
PO Box 323, Nevada, MO 64772
(417) 667-5552; (800) 641-4038
Robinson Iron
Robinson Rd, Alexander City,
AL 35010
(205) 329-8486

Steptoe and Wife Antiques Ltd
322 Geary Ave, Toronto,
Canada M6H 2C7
(416) 530-4200
Stewart Iron Works Co.
20 West 18th St, Covington,
KY 41012-2612
(606) 431-1985
Wind and Weather
The Albion Street Water Tower, PO
Box 2320, Mendocino, CA 95460
(800) 922-9463; (707) 937-0323

PLUMBING

American-Standard
PO Box 6820, Piscataway, NJ 08855
(800) 821-7700; (213) 595-8824
Eljer Plumbingware
901 Tenth St, Plano, TX 85086-9037
(800) 988-1030
Kohler Co.
Highland Drive, Kohler, WI 53044
(800) 4 KOHLER
Sherle Wagner, International
60 East 57th St, New York,
NY 10022
(212) 758-3300

WALL COVERINGS

Bradbury and Bradbury
PO Box 155-C, Benicia, CA 94510
(707) 746-1900
Brunschwig and Fils
979 Third Ave, New York,
NY 10022
(212) 838-7878
Cowtan and Tout
979 Third Ave, New York,
NY 10022
(212) 753-4488
Eisenhart Wallcovering Co.
400 Pine St, Hanover, PA 17331
(717) 632-5918
Evergreene Painting Studios, Inc.
635 West 23rd St, New York,
NY 10011
(212) 727-9500
Greeff Fabrics
200 Garden City Plaza, Garden City,
NY 11530-3301
(516) 741-9440
Nolan Studios
1290 Oak Point Ave, Bronx,
NY 10474
(212) 842-4077
Old-fashioned Milk Paint Co.
Box 222, Groton, MA 01450
(508) 448-6336
Osborne and Little
979 Third Ave, New York,
NY 10022
(212) 751-3333
Paxwell Painting Studios
223 East 32nd St, New York,
NY 10016
(212) 725-1737
Pratt and Lambert
75 Tonawanda St, PO Box 22,
Buffalo, NY 14240
(716) 873-6000
San Francisco Victoriana
2245 Palou Ave, San Francisco,
CA 94124
(415) 648-0313
Arthur Sanderson and Sons
979 Third Ave, New York, NY 10022
(212) 319-7220

Scalamandré
950 Third Ave, New York, NY 10022
(212) 980-3888
F Schumacher and Co.
79 Madison Ave, New York,
NY 10016
(800) 523-1200; (212) 213-7900
The Sherwin-Williams Company
101 Prospect Ave, Cleveland,
OH 44115
(800) 321-1386
Trend Lines
375 Beacham St, Chelsea, MA 02150
(617) 884-8882
Tromploy Inc.
400 Lafayette St, New York,
NY 10003
(212) 420-1639
Tania Vartan Studio
970 Park Ave, New York, NY 10028
(212) 744-6710

WALLS, CEILINGS AND MILLWORK

Anthony Wood Products
PO Box 1081, Hillsboro, TX 76645
(817) 582-7225
Architectural Paneling, Inc.
979 Third Ave, New York, NY 10022
(212) 371-9632
Arvid's Historic Woods
2820 Rucker Avenue, Everett,
WA 98201
(800) 627-8437; (206) 252-8374
Bendix Moldings, Inc.
235 Pegasus Ave, Northvale,
NJ 07647
(800) 526-0240
Joseph Biunno
129 West 29th St, New York,
NY 10001
(212) 629-5636
Blue Ox Millworks
Foot of X St, Eureka, CA 95501
(800) 24-VICKY
Chadsworth, Inc.
PO Box 53268, Atlanta, GA 30355
(404) 876-5410
Craftsman Lumber Company
436 Main St, Box 222J, Groton,
MA 01450
(508) 448-6336
Cumberland Woodcraft Co., Inc.
PO Drawer 609, Carlisle, PA 17013
(800) 367-1884
Decorators Supply Corp.
3610 South Morgan St, Chicago,
IL 60609
(312) 847-6300
Driwood
PO Box 1729, Florence, SC 29503
(803) 669-2478
Empire Woodworks Co.
PO Box 407, Johnson City, TX 78636
(512) 868-7520
Raymond Enkeboll Designs
16506 Avalon Blvd, Carson,
CA 90706
(213) 532-1400
Eureka Woodworking Co.
121 East 2nd St, Mineola, NY 11501
(516) 747-0888
Fisher and Jirouch Co.
4821 Superior Avenue, Cleveland,
OH 44103
(216) 361-3840
Gold Leaf Studios
PO Box 50156, Washington,
DC 20004
(202) 638-4660

Haas Wood and Ivory Works, Inc.
64 Clementina, San Francisco,
CA 94105
(415) 421-8273
Hicksville Woodworks Co.
265 Jerusalem Ave, Hicksville,
NY 11801
(516) 938-0171
Hyde Park Fine Art of Moldings, Inc.
47-9 30th St, Long Island City,
NY 11101
(800) 843-3015; (718) 706-0504
Dimitrios Klitsas, Fine Wood Sculptor
705 Union St, Springfield, MA 01089
(413) 732-2661
Mad River Woodworks
PO Box 1067, 189 Taylor Way, Blue
Lake, CA 95525-1067
(707) 668-5671
Mendocino Millwork
Box 669, Mendocino, CA 95460
(707) 937-4410
Moyner & Shepherd Joyners, Inc.
122 Naubuc Ave, Glastonbury,
CT 06033
(203) 633-2383
Orac Decor
Outwater Plastic Industries, 4
Passaic St, Dock No. 1, Wood-Ridge,
NJ 0775
(800) 888-0880; (201) 340-1040
Pagliacco
PO Box 225, Woodacre, CA 94973
(415) 488-4333
Garry R. Partelow
PO Box 433, 34 Lyme St, Old Lyme,
CT 06371
(203) 434-2065
A.F. Schwerd Mfg Co.
3215 McClure Ave, Pittsburgh,
PA 15212
(412) 766-6322
Sheppard Millwork, Inc.
21020 70th Ave W., Edmonds,
WA 98020
(206) 771-4645
Silverton Victorian Millworks
PO Box 2987, Durango, CO 81302
(303) 259-5915
W.P. Stephens Lumber Company
22 Polk St, PO Box 1267, Marietta,
GA 30061
(404) 428-1531
Stromberg's Architectural Stone
3200 Stonewall, Greenville,
TX 75401
(214) 454-0904
Sunshine Architectural Woodworks
Route 2, Box 434, Fayetteville,
AR 72703
(501) 521-4329
Vintage Wood Works
513 South Adams, Fredericksburg,
TX 78624
(512) 997-9513
J.P. Weaver Co.
2301 West Victory Place, Burbank,
CA 91506
(818) 841-5700
The Woodfactory
901 Harvard, Houston, TX 77008
(713) 863-7600
Worthington Group, Ltd
PO Box 53101, Atlanta, GA 30355
(404) 872-1608

PHOTOGRAPHS & ILLUSTRATIONS

Inklink are grateful to the following companies and individuals for additional photographs and illustrations:

Photographs

Peter Aprahamian/Traditional Homes Magazine
Pages 209BR; 212C

**B. C. Sanitan Ltd.
(C. P. Hart & Sons Ltd.)**
Pages 241BR; 243

C. D. (UK) Ltd.
Page 239

Chris Challis/Traditional Homes Magazine
Pages 210; 242

Paul Chave
Pages 14C; 155B

Classical Concrete Ltd.
Page 150TC

Crown Berger Ltd.
Page 174T

John Cullen Lighting
Page 233T

Michael Dunne /EWA
Page 231BL; 232

Bruce Greenlaw/Fine Homebuilding Magazine
Pages 58C; 85

Tony Herbert
Pages 147BR; 154CR; 155TL

John Heseltine/Traditional Homes Magazine
Pages 146CL; 190T; 213BL; 231BR; 240TL

Hugh Howard
Pages 11CR; 13T; 39TL; 219L

Hygrove Kitchens
Page 235BL

Inklink
Pages 18; 19; 20; 21

Albert Jackson
Pages 11C, BL, BR; 12; 13; 15C; 16; 17; 23BL, C, TR; 24; 25R; 26; 27; 28L; 31TR, BR; 32; 34BL; 38CR; 40C, BL; 42; 55BC, BR; 56; 60CL

Simon Jennings
Pages 14T; 15TL; 23TL; 25TL; 43TR; 57TR; 60CR, B; 62; 83TC; 86CR; 99TL; 108; 114BR; 116B; 203L

Ken Kirkwood
Pages 145; 246CR

Tom Leighton/EWA
Page 233B

Richard Littlewood/Traditional Homes Magazine
Page 190B

Alan Marshall
Page 156

Alison Needler/Traditional Homes Magazine
Page 238BC

Michael Nicholson/EWA
Page 234

Old Sturbridge Village
Page 236TR

Ian Parry/Traditional Homes Magazine
Pages 28R; 146C, CR; 148; 189; 197; 212BL, BR; 220BR; 222T; 237BL; 238BR; 240TR; 241BL; 244

Rentokil Ltd.
Page 195

Traditional Homes Magazine
Page 147TL

Vernon Tutbury
Page 245CR

Adele Bishop/Carolyn Warrender Stencil Designs
Page 198

Neil Waving
Pages 9R; 119BR; 140; 162; 173; 203

Winther Browne & Co. Ltd.
Page 81

Historical illustrations

B. T. Batsford Ltd.
Pages 9T; 10B

Bexley Library & Museums Department
Page 15CL

Chiswick Library
Page 9BL

Mary Evans Picture Library
Pages 10T; 30TL; 55T; 145T; 146T; 235T

Ironbridge Gorge Museum Trust
Pages 6L; 6BR; 7L; 23T; 24CL; 33T; 37TL; 56TL; 69T; 105CL, TR; 107TR; 125TR; 135; 159T; 199T; 208L

Warwick Leadlay
Page 10C

Frank Lloyd Wright Foundation
Page 15C

Marflex International Ltd.
Pages 219T; 220T; 221T

Twyfords Bathrooms
Pages 245TR, B

John Vince Collection
Page 236CL

Mark Wilkinson Furniture
Pages 235BR; 237BR; 238TL

KEY TO CREDITS
T=TOP, B=BOTTOM, L=LEFT, R=RIGHT, TL=TOP LEFT, TR=TOP RIGHT, C=CENTRE, TC=TOP CENTRE, CL=CENTRE LEFT, CR=CENTRE RIGHT, BL=BOTTOM LEFT, BR= BOTTOM RIGHT, BC=BOTTOM CENTRE.

RESTORATION MATERIALS

Inklink are indebted to the following companies and individuals who generously supplied samples or products for photography:

STONEWORK
The Carving Workshop, Cambridge, Cambridgeshire

DOORS AND WINDOWS
The Antique Hardware Store, Frenchtown, NJ, USA
Ball & Ball, Exton, PA, USA
Clayton-Munroe Ltd., Totnes, Devon
Comyn Ching Ltd., London, EC1
Peter Cornish
Dorset Restoration, Wareham, Dorset
Forgeries, Winchester, Hampshire
GKN Crompton Ltd., Wigan, Lancashire
Joseph Tipper Ltd., Wednesbury, W. Midlands

ORNAMENTAL GLASS
Lamont Antiques Ltd., London, SE10
Sam Towers (Coeur de Lion Stain Glass Ltd.)

PLASTERWORK
E. J. Harmer & Co., London, SE21

TILING
Chris Blanchett
H. & R. Johnson Tiles Ltd., London, W9
Dennis Ruabon Ltd., Wrexham, Clywd

WALL PANELING
Desfab, Beckenham, Kent
Winther Browne & Co. Ltd., London, N18

DECORATIVE WOODWORK
Cumberland Woodcraft Co. Inc., Carlisle, PA, USA

DECORATIVE METAL
R. Bleasdale (Spirals), London, N1
Britannia Architectural Metalwork & Restoration, Alton, Hampshire
County Forge Ltd., Frome, Somerset

FIREPLACES
Westcombe Antiques, London, SE3

HELPFUL ORGANIZATIONS

The Center for Historic Houses
The National Trust for Historic Preservation
1785 Massachusetts Avenue
Washington, DC 20036
(202) 673-4025

The National Trust for Historic Preservation
1785 Massachusetts Avenue
Washington, DC 20036
(202) 673-4000

HELPFUL PUBLICATIONS

* **Preservation News** and **Historic Preservation** (published by The National Trust for Historic Preservation)

* **Old House Journal**
* **Victorian Homes**
* **Fine Homebuilding**

CHAPTER ONE

DECORATIVE STYLES

WE ARE BECOMING MORE SENSITIVE *to the importance of protecting our heritage. Yet over the past few decades many old houses were subjected to indiscriminate assault, with relatively little protest.*

During that period many house owners discarded unfashionable details or finishes in the belief that they were increasing the market value of their homes. But this proved to be an illusion. "A period property retaining all its original features" still has a unique appeal, and many of us who own old houses that have not been completely ruined now make every effort to restore them.

This book seeks to encourage well-conceived restoration by suggesting ways of maintaining and repairing the type of house that has been most at risk – the family home built between Colonial times

and the start of the Second World War. Often these houses require extensive repairs and improvements, such as the installation of new wiring or plumbing, and insulation. But such considerations seldom dissuade us from acquiring a period house that attracts us. What we find so enticing are those elegant façades with their perfectly proportioned windows, the carved wood and stonework, the delightful plasterwork, stained glass and moldings – all those decorative elements that our forebears were able to fashion with such consummate skill and confidence, and which give every old house its special character.

Preserving or re-creating such features can give a great deal of satisfaction – and it is with these, the most enjoyable and rewarding aspects of house restoration, that this book is primarily concerned.

A lithograph of 1882 depicting the London suburb of Bedford Park

Thoughtful conservation has preserved Bedford Park for over 100 years

9

THE COLONIAL AND THE CLASSICAL
From the medieval to the Grecian

WHEN THE EARLIEST SETTLERS *arrived on American shores in the seventeenth century, they were confronted with a primeval forest. So they cut down trees and used the wood to build houses, employing the many skills and tools they had brought with them from Europe.*

The colonies, as a result, were dominated by wooden houses, many built in medieval English styles. As the process of adaptation proceeded, the classic Cape Cod house, the "Saltbox," and other forms evolved. In Dutch-dominated regions, masonry houses were more common, while the Spanish colonies tended to use a combination of timber and masonry.

In the early eighteenth century, the influence of the classicism that by then dominated in Europe began to be felt and the more opulent Georgian style came into vogue. The Georgian house was larger, grander, and more self-conscious than previous styles. There were more chimneys, taller rooms, larger windows, and more decorations. All of which were a reflection of the growing mercantile success of the Colonies – and the continuing debt to European styles.

The Saltbox house in all its elegant simplicity

The classical orders of architecture

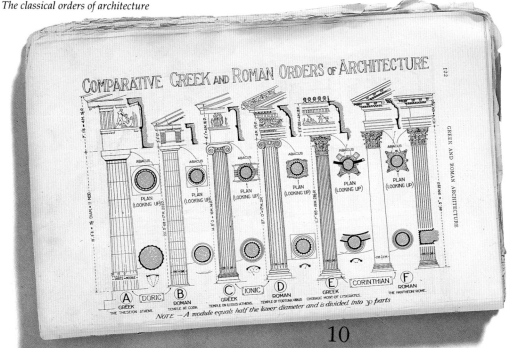

PALLADIANISM AND PROPORTION

The Georgian style got its name from the English kings who reigned for much of the eighteenth century, but its inspiration was the classical Roman monuments, and its translator Italian architect Andrea Palladio (1508-80).

The birth of the Georgian style was in part the result of Palladio's *Quattro Libri Dell-Architettura (The Four Books of Architecture)*, first published in England in 1715. It was a detailed study of the ruins of ancient Rome, interpreting style and proportion in terms of the five classical orders of architecture: the Tuscan, Doric, Ionic, Corinthian, and Composite.

The orders embodied a set of guidelines and rules that enabled an architect or builder to determine the proportions of a building with confidence. Once the key dimensions were established the rest could be calculated with ease. Thus, the early Georgian buildings – most in England, a few in this country – were conceived like an ancient Greco-Roman façade.

This literal interpretation, however, was too much for average houses. Generally they were built on a smaller scale than large public buildings. Yet certain of the same principles of proportion still applied – the use of columns or pilasters (flattened columns) or quoins on the corners and an elaborate center doorway. The door surround usually featured a pediment, often with columns and other classical motifs.

The Georgian façade is balanced, two stories tall, and topped with a gable or hip roof and one or two pairs of chimneys. On the first story, an elaborate center doorway is flanked by evenly spaced pairs of windows. Above are five windows aligned with the openings below. This configuration constitutes the paradigm for the oft-imitated "colonial" design.

An eighteenth-century house in the Dutch style

Grand stone-built façade based on Graeco-Roman architectural concepts

THE FEDERAL STYLE

After the Revolution, the Georgian style – being English – fell quickly from popularity. It was replaced by the Federal style, a somewhat simplified version of the Georgian that, despite an apparent rejection of things English, nonetheless drew upon the English designers Robert and James Adam.

The American interpreters of the brothers Adam, primarily Charles Bulfinch and Asher Benjamin, designed houses that featured thinner, more delicate moldings, most often of wood. While classically inspired decorations like swags and urns were used, the style tended to be simpler than the Georgian.

Most characteristic of the Federal style is its front door. The elliptical fan sash over the door is the hallmark, most often in combination with flanking sidelights. In many examples, another feature is a portico with classical orders (columns, full frieze, and cornice) that stands before the doorway.

Inside, the decoration was more attenuated, too, with decorated mantels, window and door frames, and even ceilings, featuring rosettes, swags, and garlands along with classically inspired orders. Wood and plaster were used, and the proportions were thinner and longer.

THE GREEK REVIVAL

While the Georgian and Federal styles were found along the eastern seaboard, the next architectural fashion arrived in a land whose borders were reaching further west. Thus, handsome Greek Revival style houses, most built between 1830-1850, are found along the paths of the western migration.

The Greek Revival style, too, came from the emerging archeological studies of ancient Greece. Its typical dwelling has the shape of a classical temple, its gable-end façade decorated like the Parthenon. However, the American Greek style was translated into virtually all shapes. The traditional box shape of the Cape Cod house is among the most common.

The roof had a shallower slope than earlier styles, its lower ends usually connected, forming a triangular pediment which was supported by columns or pilasters.

The style also grew more simplified with fewer moldings and more porches. Doorways with pilasters on the side and elaborate headpieces. The interior was almost spartan. The parlor often had a heavy cornice and decorations, but the rest of the house had only simply molded architraves and plaster walls.

The Federal-style house featured quite delicate wooden decorations

Greek Revival, with its bold use of classical architectural elements

THE VICTORIAN PERIOD
Confident opulence

THE VICTORIAN AGE, *like the Georgian period, was an era named after an English monarch. It is perhaps most often remembered as an age of decorative excess, yet Victoria's reign (1837-1901) also saw immense changes, in building styles and in the economic and social fabric of life. The steam engine and the railroads made the Industrial Revolution possible, and an essentially rural and agricultural society gave way to one in which a plethora of disparate architectural influences were to be seen – influences from the Middle Ages, the Renaissance, France, Italy, Germany, England, and America. Perhaps most importantly, the machine age produced a stream of factory-made products to construct, adorn, and improve even quite average houses.*

Richly decorated Italianate house, featuring the characteristic cornice brackets

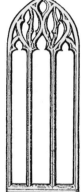

A large family house with Gothic-Revival features

THE GOTHIC REVIVAL

This style developed at roughly the same time as the Greek Revival (its examples most often date from the years 1840 to 1875), but its impact was less widespread. Like the Greek style, it was an adaptation of an earlier architectural era, namely the medieval European Gothic styles. Again, though, an English revival – in the eighteenth and early nineteenth centuries – produced the American version of the style.

Gothic stone cathedrals soared to great heights, and Gothic Revival houses share the tendency to direct the eye skyward, although American Gothic houses are typically one-and-a-half or two stories high. The roofs are steeply pitched, their gables often topped with finials. The windows and doorways very often sweep upward to a characteristic pointed-arch shape, another of the hallmarks of Gothic style. Single-story porches were common; and, for the first time in American architectural history, the floor plan in many Gothic houses was asymmetrical.

The term "gingerbread" describes the wooden decorative elements found on Gothic Revival houses, sawn and chiseled shapes on bargeboards or vergeboards or standing up from rooftops. American Gothic houses were most often built of wood, but brick and stucco are also found.

THE ITALIANATE STYLE

This imensely popular style is known under a variety of names: Italianate, Italianate Villa, and American Bracket styles. "Italianate" alludes to the original inspiration of the style; the brackets are its most distinctive architectural detail.

Andrew Jackson Downing and Alexander Jackson Davis worked in this style, which was popular from about 1840 to roughly 1880. Two or three stories tall, houses in this style have a low pitched roof with a broad overhang supported by the characteristic brackets. Along with the Gothic Revival style, the bracket house was influential in the move in American housing away from the strictly symmetrical: many, though not all, Italianate houses had asymmetrical features like towers, ells, bay windows, balconies with balustrades, and verandas. Almost all examples had porches.

Double entrance doors are common and, for the first time, glass was incorporated into the door itself (rather than in transom or sidelights). Tall, narrow windows are the rule, often with arched or curved tops and carved or molded crowns. Window sashes are usually two-over-twos. Bay windows are common, as are adjacent pairs of round-headed windows.

THE OCTAGON STYLE

The idiosyncratic octagon-style house was conceived by one Orson Fowler, an eccentric. He thought the circle was nature's perfect building form, and the octagon shape was as close as he could get to it using the dominant American building material, wood. Within the minimum of exterior wall surfaces, his houses contain the maximum interior space.

Fowler advanced his ideas in 1848 in a book, *A Home for All*. His designs were built across the country until the Civil War slowed domestic construction. Octagon houses are identifiable by their shape (when viewed from above, they are symmetrical, eight-sided structures), but their details varied considerably. Some feature Greek or Gothic trim, while many had Italianate brackets or other decorations. Usually two stories tall, many octagonal houses featured a cupola on top.

Inside, the octagonal house is equally unique, as its floor plan was, necessarily, riddled with oblique angles. Often the major rooms were rectilinear, with the closets and less important areas consigned the peculiar angles.

An elaborate paint scheme emphasizes the details of this Stick-Style house

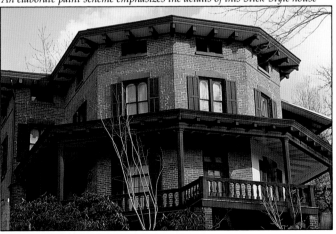

Orson Fowler's richly imagined Octagon house

AFTER THE CIVIL WAR

In the decades following the Civil War, a middle class was emerging in and around the industrial cities. It provided a ready market for sales of manufactured construction goods. Increasingly, that meant that houses constructed almost anywhere in the land were similar to many others elsewhere since, often, the parts came from the same factories, having been delivered by rail.

On the other hand, there was also a taste for architectural experiment, an interest in diverse styles and colors. In fact, the last third of the nineteenth century proved to be a time of ferment in American housing, as styles came and went.

THE STICK STYLE

The Italianate style remained popular after the Civil War, but it was shortly joined by others, like the Second Empire, Queen Anne, and Shingle styles (see page 140). Another style was the so-called Stick style, a manner that was at once an echo of the Gothic Revival and a reinterpretation of a dimly remembered mode of medieval German construction.

The Stick style featured many horizontal, vertical, and diagonal wooden pieces applied to its wall surfaces. Characteristic of the style is decorative trusswork at the peak of the inverted V of the gable. In theory, the style was to echo the medieval half-timbered houses whose façades featured the faces of the timber frame with the area between infilled with plaster or stucco. In fact, the Stick style is more of an expression of sheer wonder on the part of its builders at the wealth of material that was available to them.

THE SECOND EMPIRE STYLE

The mansard roof is the key characteristic of the Second Empire house. The style got its name from the reign of Napoleon III (1852-1870) in France, the so-called "Second Empire," and was popular from about 1860 until 1890.

Typically an urban style, the tall Second Empire house fit comfortably on narrow, in-town lots where light and space were limited. The roof has two pitches on each of its four sides. (Most examples have a rectangular or square plan, though some are L-shaped and many have a tower at center front.) From the peak, the roof line slopes at an almost flat pitch, then suddenly becomes nearly vertical when it approaches the eaves. The roofs were frequently decorated with ornate iron work and decorative slate shingling. Most often two stories tall, Second Empire houses usually have dormers that make the attic essentially a third floor. Brackets typically decorate the wide eaves.

The Shingle-style house is a refreshing blend of interior and exterior spaces

Imposing Second Empire house with a fine tower and typical Mansard roof

THE QUEEN ANNE STYLE

Anne was queen of England from 1703 to 1714, and the architectural style of her reign saw a revival in England in the nineteenth century. While the Queen Anne style here owes its name and inspiration to those sources, the American Queen Anne house – popular from around 1870 till 1900 – is but a distant cousin.

The American Queen Anne house has steeply pitched roofs, often in irregular configurations blending varied roof lines, dormers, gables, turrets, and tall, multiple chimneys. At the first-floor levels, asymmetrical porches add to the overall effect, as do bay windows, in some examples, that are found on both the first and second floors. The single, front-facing gable that usually dominates the Queen Anne façade is generally the only aspect of the style that is likely to be symmetrical.

There is often a mix of different materials and textures. There can be shingles, clapboards, moldings, half-timbering, terra-cotta panels, and porches with spindles, brackets, finials, and all kinds of ornamentation. The windows, too, vary greatly: Palladian, double hung, round head, oculus (round), six-over-ones, bays, and others. And then the paint: bold, bright and rich colors were used to handsome effect.

THE SHINGLE STYLE

The Shingle style never attained the national popularity of the Italianate or the Queen Anne, yet it proved to be an important transition between the styles of the late nineteenth century and the Colonial Revival. Most examples were built between 1880 and 1900, though a new interest in the style in our time has seen many houses constructed that owe a debt to the century-old Shingle style.

The style was the result of a new consciousness of early American architectural styles and the grace and simplicity of such houses and the materials used in them. In particular, the unpainted siding – the wooden shingles – represented to the Shingle style's innovators a refreshing contrast to the ornateness of the prevailing styles, especially the Queen Anne.

The Shingle style house – as designed by such luminaries as H. H. Richardson, Stanford White, and Frank Lloyd Wright – were usually two or three stories tall, with a steep, gabled roof, often with porches and dormers. The interior spaces tended to be open, as the divisions between different spaces and rooms were beginning to fade. Such open plans and the willingness to look to the past presaged much that was to come in the following decades.

14

TWENTIETH CENTURY
Revivals and new innovations

STANFORD WHITE AND FRANK LLOYD WRIGHT *represent two of the dominant modes of architectural thinking at the turn of the century in America. White and his firm, McKim, Mead, and White, pioneered the Colonial Revival style, in which America's architectural past was mined for forms, shapes, details, and inspiration. The result was the emergence in popularity of new Georgian Colonial houses, along with Cape Cods, Dutch Colonial, and other houses loosely based on eighteenth-century originals. In some sense, these styles have been in vogue ever since, though as the century wore on the resemblance to early American houses gave way to contemporary changes in material and workmanship.*

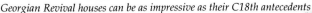

Georgian Revival houses can be as impressive as their C18th antecedents

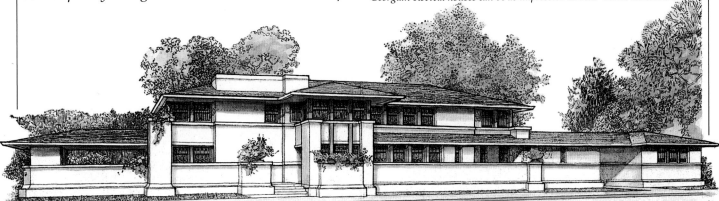

A Frank Lloyd Wright house, as long and low as prairie

THE PRAIRIE STYLE
Frank Lloyd Wright on the other hand, was working on the broad flat plains of the Middle West. Unencumbered with visions of local early buildings, Wright imagined a new style, the Prairie style, which featured long overhangs deriving from the terrain and climate of its setting. A popular manifestation of the Prairie style was the foursquare, which was widely constructed in the first quarter of the century.

THE BUNGALOW
Another key architectural influence of the time is personified by Gustav Stickley. A furniture-maker, designer, theorist, and publisher of *The Craftsman*, Stickley had traveled to England and been influenced by William Morris and others involved in the Arts and Crafts movement of the nineteenth century. Their credo was a reaction against the perceived tyranny of the machine, and attempt to reintroduce high-quality, handmade goods. Stickley preached the same gospel, and designed houses to fit the philosophy.

The immensely popular bungalow was one result. Usually constructed in one- or one-and-a-half-story configurations, the bungalow featured broad overhangs and open porches. Often – though not always – small in size, the bungalow fit neatly on small suburban lots. The open-plan interior gave a sense of openness uncharacteristic of the usual small house.

EUROPEAN INFLUENCES
Peculiarly American houses were finally emerging, yet the influence of Europe was by no means entirely absent. English Tudor and Spanish Revival style houses were introduced after the turn of the century, and the International Style made an appearance here between the wars. Art Deco and Art Moderne styles, as well, were to be seen in domestic architecture, though largely in urban apartment buildings. The melting pot immigrant tradition produced an integration of a remarkable variety of houses.

15

COST-EFFECTIVE RESTORATION

BEFORE THE PRESERVATION MOVEMENT *came into being in the wake of the Bicentennial celebration, relatively few Americans regarded ownership of an old house as a great asset. Countless antique houses in rural areas were allowed to deteriorate, and sound and desirable housing stock in urban areas was often poorly maintained, was rented at reduced rates, and attracted few house-proud tenants.*

Victorian housing, in particular, was regarded as, at best, peculiar; more often, Victorian styles were thought of as grotesque and hopelessly out of date. Today the situation has been reversed, for Victorian houses and a whole range of older American homes.

Rising prosperity engendered new confidence in the long-term benefits of home ownership. This in turn led to a profound change of attitude, and we now take it for granted that improving a house can be financially advantageous. Nevertheless, opinion is divided as to exactly what constitutes worthwhile improvement and what should be the limits to restoration.

ABOVE: *Residing an individual house in poorly matched materials destroys the integrity of a streetscape*

RIGHT: *Drastic refurbishments have all but obliterated the original character of these Victorian houses*

WORTHWHILE IMPROVEMENTS

Unless you are intent on creating a living museum, it makes sense to take advantage of modern technology. In theory we might enjoy the romance of candlelight, but few of us would now seriously contemplate forgoing modern lighting or hesitate to install labor-saving laundry and kitchen appliances. And, although accommodating radiators discreetly in an old house may take ingenuity, central heating has become a welcome and universally accepted advance. Today we consider hygienic, functional bathrooms plumbed with hot and cold water a necessity, and would scarcely entertain the notion of doing without a bathroom.

Provided that the work is carried out tastefully and to a good standard, all these improvements not only add to our own comfort and wellbeing but also have a positive effect on the value of our house. On the other hand, it pays to think twice before spending large sums of money on what are at best fashionable whims. Cladding the exterior of a house with colorful fake stone, for example, or pebble-dashing what was intended to be exposed brickwork are irreversible measures that have limited appeal. Apart from the visual disruption they cause to a row or group of buildings, the costs are unlikely to be recoverable when it comes to selling a house once such treatments have fallen from favor – and they may detract from the house's value. It makes even less sense to spend money on replacing doors or windows when the originals can be repaired, or even remade with improved draftproofing, at no extra cost. No one is likely to refrain from buying a house because it has authentic windows in good condition, whereas the same cannot necessarily be said of a house with vinyl-clad or aluminum replacements.

TAKING STOCK

THE LIMITS OF RESTORATION

Provided it's structurally sound, it is generally preferable to buy a house that has not been modernized, even if it is in poor condition. You will have the satisfaction of owning an authentic, unspoiled period house, and will find that restoring dilapidated features is almost always cheaper than having to locate and install suitable replacements.

Nevertheless, basically sound, untouched period houses are now scarce, and most people in search of an old house have to settle for one that is not only in need of some repair but has also been stripped of at least some of its original features. In today's market it still makes financial sense to

Colorful but inappropriate paintwork may not appeal to prospective buyers

reinstate them, so long as the "improvements" made by the previous owners don't inflate the purchase price unduly and you resist the temptation to spend more on restoration than is warranted by the house's market value. To attempt to enhance its status by introducing uncharacteristically ornate fittings or decorative elements is as inappropriate as ripping out original features in the name of modernization.

Each type of house within a given locality has a maximum value and no one, especially an experienced realtor, is going to be fooled into paying an inflated price for a house that is pretending to be something it isn't. A shrewd investor will put back only what was there in the first place, while insuring that all repairs and restoration work are done to the highest standard. That way, the house will command the best price in return for the minimum investment.

*B*EFORE BUYING ANY HOUSE, *especially an old one, it is essential to have it inspected professionally in order to ascertain its true value and insure that there are no unforeseen problems. A full structural inspection, for example, will include everything from the state of the foundations and roof to the condition of the interior decoration. At first sight most inspector's reports make depressing reading – until you can put it all into perspective and decide which repairs to tackle first.*

ASSESSING REPAIRS

If you are applying for a mortgage, a bank may well insist that you carry out any essential repairs highlighted in the inspector's report before they advance the entire sum you have applied for. And they will almost certainly demand that the repairs are carried out by a contractor who is prepared to furnish long-term guarantees.

Very often this is just the beginning, and it pays to make your own list of other repairs in order to decide which of them you can do yourself. Even if you have been living in a house for years, a similar exercise will help you plan a program of regular maintenance.

Houses are built primarily from three materials – wood, stone, and brick. Also, some brick houses are finished in stucco. Each of these materials deteriorates in a certain way, and this determines how well a house is able to stand up to natural weathering. No two houses are precisely the same, but knowing where to look and what to look for will help you spot potential problems before

they develop into something more serious. The illustrations on the following pages will serve as a guide to analyzing the condition of your house and preparing a plan of action.

The fees for professional labor and advice constitute the largest proportion of house-restoration costs. It is therefore not surprising that the do-it-yourself trade has mushroomed dramatically over the past three decades or so in order to serve the ever-growing numbers of amateur builders, plumbers, electricians, and decorators. Nevertheless, inexperienced newcomers, perhaps buying their first home, may need to take advantage of expert advice. And no matter how enterprising you are, there will always be some aspects of house restoration where it is expedient to hire contractors simply because they can do a job better, safer, and faster than someone who is not a skilled professional.

To help you decide on the most appropriate approach to restoring your own house, where relevant throughout the book keyed illustrations have been included indicating which repairs are so straightforward that even a beginner can achieve satisfactory results, which ones require a reasonable level of competence, and which are best left to a professional.

Loose shingles
Rusted nails allow shingles to slip.
● Tap back and renail (page 54).

Split shingles
Dry weather can make shingles split along the grain.
■ Replace shingles (page 54).

Damaged chimney
Exposed chimneys are susceptible to weathering.
◆ Repair or rebuild (pages 65-8).

Flaking paintwork
Weathering makes paint flake from south-facing walls.
● Scrape and repaint (page 52).

Rotted clapboards
Exposed end grain absorbs rainwater.
■ Insert new section of board (page 52).

Split clapboards
Shrinkage can make boards split lengthwise.
■ Glue split boards (page 52).

Overpainted woodwork
Layers of old paint obscure details.
● Strip paint (pages 75-6).

Woodboring insects
Insect larvae consume wood.
● Treat minor outbreaks with preservative (page 194).
▲ Replace seriously infested timber (page 194).

WOODEN HOUSE

Houses built with a structural wood framework are among the oldest still in use. The exterior walls are frequently sided with horizontal planks known as clapboards or, especially in this country, with shingles.

Rot and woodboring insects are perhaps the most serious natural threats to a wooden house. Also, gusts of wind can rip away clapboards or shingles that have worked loose as a result of long-term neglect.

ASSESSING REPAIRS
● Easy even for beginners.
■ Fairly difficult. Good practical skills required.
▲ Difficult. Hire a professional.
◆ Various levels of skill required.

18

Decaying stone
Pollution destroys stonework.
▲ Badly affected stone may need expert treatment (pages 41-2).

Broken carvings & moldings
Accidental damage leaves chipped stonework.
■ Patch or reglue broken components (pages 41-2).

Loose slates
Corroded fixings allow slates to slip out of place.
■ Reinstate or replace individual slates (page 36).

Dirty stonework
Pollution stains pale stone.
● Scrub with water (page 36).
▲ Use a chemical or abrasive cleaner (pages 36-7).

Rusty or broken metalwork
Corrosion is the most common cause of metal deterioration.
◆ Paint, repair or replace shoddy metalwork (pages 199-208).

Poorly maintained joinery
Doors and windows are frequently in need of attention.
◆ Repair or rebuild in period style (pages 76-9 and 95-118).

Delaminating stone
Poorly laid stone can flake.
■ Patch with mortar (page 42).
▲ Consolidate with epoxy resin (page 42).

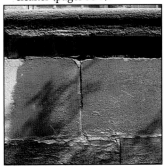

Loose pointing
Brittle cement mortar tends to crack and fall out.
■ Repoint rubble walling (page 37).
▲ Repoint ashlar (page 37).

STONE HOUSE

For centuries stone has been used for building every type of dwelling, from modest cottages to imposing town houses and country mansions. Although stone is such a durable material, some stone building blocks are particularly prone to erosion, especially if they have been laid incorrectly.

Pale-colored stonework that has been subjected to years of urban pollution can become so stained and discolored that cleaning is imperative to prevent further deterioration.

ASSESSING REPAIRS
● Easy even for beginners.
■ Fairly difficult. Good practical skills required.
▲ Difficult. Hire a professional.
◆ Various levels of skill required.

Dirty & stained brickwork
Airborne dirt and pollutants
stain brickwork.
● Wash with water (page 25).
● Apply a poultice (page 26).

Deteriorated pointing
Mortar erodes and falls out
from joints.
■ Repoint wall (pages 28-30).

Deteriorating wooden trim
Decorative woodwork is often
broken or missing.
◆ Repair or replace damaged
items (pages 177-88).

Spalled brickwork
Frosty conditions can cause
bricks to flake.
■ Insert replacements for spalled
bricks (page 30).

Cracked brickwork
Obtain an inspector's opinion.
■ Repoint or replace bricks
(pages 28-30).
▲ Have an expert treat extensive
cracking (pages 30 and 32).

Efflorescence
White salts are drawn out from
damp masonry.
● Brush from surface (page 26).

Porous bricks
Brick that has become porous
allows rainwater to penetrate.
■ Treat with a clear repellent
(page 26).

Painted brickwork
What was intended to be
exposed brick is often painted.
▲ Remove paint from brickwork
with stripper (page 26).

BRICK HOUSE

A most attractive and durable building material, brick is
found in modest and fancy homes alike. All but the softest
brickwork lasts indefinitely provided that the pointing is
sound. However, once the mortar joints deteriorate,
rainwater may penetrate the masonry, causing the bricks to
flake and promoting damp and rot and eventually loose
brickwork. Door and window openings are weak points
where cracks in brickwork are particularly likely to occur.

ASSESSING REPAIRS
● Easy even for
beginners.
■ Fairly difficult.
Good practical
skills required.
▲ Difficult. Hire a
professional.
◆ Various levels of
skill required.

Damaged roof tiles
High winds can dislodge loose
roof tiles.
■ Replace broken or missing tiles
(page 61).

Blown pebble-dash
Rainwater gets behind pebble-
dash and causes it to flake.
■ Repair with fresh stucco and
pebbles (page 45).

Poorly maintained flashing
An inappropriate repair
deteriorates rapidly.
▲ Have an expert replicate the
original flashing (page 64).

Missing ornamentation
Damaged ornamenation is
often removed and discarded.
■ Cast and replace (page 48).

Broken stucco
Large areas of stucco become
loose and fall from wall.
■ Patch holes (page 44).

Damaged rustication
Rusticated stucco deteriorates
like plain finish.
■ Patch and re-create rustication
(page 48).

Cracked stucco
Shrinkage and movement
causes stucco to crack.
● Fill with mortar (page 44).

Mold growth
Organic growth proliferates in
damp conditions.
● Treat with a solution of bleach
(page 26).

STUCCO

Stucco, a cement-like coating, has been used since ancient
times to finish the exterior walls of houses. Cracked stucco
must be repaired as soon as it is detected. If rainwater is able
to penetrate and collect behind the facing, it soaks through
to the interior of the house and eventually causes large areas
of stucco to burst from the wall. As stucco moldings aren't
as hard-wearing as carved stone, old stuccoed houses often
look dilapidated, with broken cornices and architraves.

**ASSESSING
REPAIRS**

● Easy even for
beginners.
■ Fairly difficult.
Good practical
skills required.
▲ Difficult. Hire a
professional.
◆ Various levels of
skill required.

LEGAL PROTECTION FOR OLD HOUSES

GIVEN THAT SO MANY PERIOD HOUSES *have been subjected to such appalling treatment in the recent past, one could be forgiven for thinking that there is nothing to prevent owners doing what they like with their houses. In fact, that is more or less the truth in most American communities. Unlike in Great Britain and some other European countries – where there is legislation that protects buildings of special architectural or historical interest and where every household is obliged to obtain approval before carrying out alterations or developments that might alter the structure of such buildings – the United States has no national body of law protecting a wide range of old buildings of merit or importance.*

On the other hand, there are local ordinances that, in some instances, help assure the continued survival and preservation of antique buildings, and various organizations that, though lacking in enforcement capabilities, have served to raise awareness of some important properties.

HISTORIC DISTRICTS

Beginning in 1931 in Charleston, South Carolina, a movement developed on a community-by-community basis to protect and preserve buildings of cultural, historical, and architectural merit. Individual houses, public buildings, and even whole neighborhoods were declared historic, and were, by local ordinance, provided some degree of protection.

In some places, this protection is considerable and virtually inviolable. For example, the Supreme Court ruled in a case involving the Landmarks Preservation Commission of New York City (established 1964) that "...states and cities may enact land-use restrictions or controls to enhance the quality of life by preserving the character and desirable aesthetic features of a city." In practice, that meant that once a building is designated a landmark in New York, it is to be protected forever, unchanged at least on its exterior. Some interiors, as well, are specially designated.

THE NATIONAL REGISTER

The National Register of Historic Places was created under the 1966 National Historic Preservation Act. It is the official list of the nation's historic districts, sites, buildings, and objects that are significant in American history,

architecture, archaeology, engineering, and culture. Candidates for the Register are nominated, then documented and evaluated according to the criteria established by the Secretary of The Interior. When listed on the National Register, a landmark is eligible for various kinds of federal help, ranging from grants for preservation and tax benefits to protection from surface coal mining.

LOCAL ORDINANCES AND RESTRICTIVE COVENANTS

Many communities today have regulations on the books that require review and approval of renovations to those houses which are designated as historic or that are within historic districts. Find out what your requirements are first, before you embark upon any restoration or renovation work.

An increasing number of houses also come complete with restrictive covenants. Though such covenants are most common in new developments, in some instances older houses that have been laboriously restored by non-profit organizations also have restrictions as to what kinds of changes can be made to the fabric of the houses. The rules vary widely, some specifying historically appropriate colors, others the size and nature of additions or changes that are to be allowed.

Again, find out first what will be required of you, before you plan in detail the work you want to do.

BUILDING REGULATIONS

Even if your town has no local landmark ordinance in effect and your deed carries no covenants, you will probably have to file for approval for any structural alterations. The regulations are designed to insure that adequate construction and health and safety standards are observed.

You are obliged either to supply full plans showing all constructional details or to complete a form called a building notice obtainable from your local Building Inspector. Scale drawings have to accompany a building notice, but they need not be as detailed as the ones required for a "full plans" application.

It is advisable to apply for approval well in advance so that you have time to discuss your proposals with the Building Inspector. He or she can also advise on relevant local legislation and tell you whether you need to approach other authorities concerning sanitation, fire escapes, and so on. So that the Building Inspector can arrange an inspection, you must give at least 48 hours' notice before starting work and 24 hours' notice before covering foundations or laying drains. You must also let the Inspector know that the work has been finished.

CHAPTER TWO

BRICKWORK

STURDY, HANDSOME, AND PRACTICAL *brick was used early in Colonial America and has had a continued appeal. Handmade brick gave way to* machine-manufactured brick with the Industrial Revolution, but brick has long been used in houses of impressive size and design, as well as in simpler freestanding homes and rowhouses built for people of average means.

In the southern United States, brick was more likely to be used in the impressive Georgian mansions of the eighteenth century, but by the Victorian age brick was increasingly commonplace in the North and South alike.

The ways in which the bricks were

used – *the various joint styles, the many bonding patterns and methods of adding interest to the surface through decorative detailing – reveal much* about the character and era of a particular brick structure.

Better-quality houses often boast fine ornamental brickwork, with molded tiles, decorative coursing, and finely gauged arches. Yet with its subtle colors and texture enhanced by age and weathering, even plain bonded brickwork is often a delight to the eye.

These are qualities well worth preserving. They are all also difficult to recover if brickwork is defaced by inept renovation or clumsy repairs.

A classically inspired brick façade

Victorian molded-brick tiles

Care and attention was often lavished on the smallest of brick houses

Beautifully detailed brick almshouse

Fine early C18th rubbed brickwork

COLORS & TEXTURES

BEFORE THE INDUSTRIAL REVOLUTION *made mass production feasible and transportation easier, bricks were produced for a particular locality, using the clays which occurred there. These clays often lent a distinctive color to the brickwork.*

Handmade bricks feature distinct variations in shape and finish, reflecting the fact that they were "struck" by hand from molds made of wood, often onto a straw-covered surface. It is this very imprecision which lends them character.

With improved transportation systems in the nineteenth century it became possible to buy bricks made at the other end of the country or even the other side of the world. The ready availability of different-colored bricks brought to an end clearly defined regional characteristics. It also contributed to the spread of the spectacular polychrome brickwork sometimes featured in Victorian architecture.

BRICK MANUFACTURING
Although the local clay gave a brick its distinctive color, the subtleties of shape and hue were to a large extent determined by the method of manufacture.

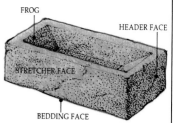

A typical handmade brick

Hand-molded bricks
Although there were early attempts at mechanization, before the mid nineteenth century all bricks were made by hand in individual wooden molds. The clay was "pugged" (mixed with water and kneaded to a smooth, even consistency), often in a horse-driven pug mill.

Sand, or sometimes water, was sprinkled into open-top molds to prevent the clay from sticking to them. The molds were filled, and the clay leveled with a steel or wooden straightedge. After the "green" bricks had been turned out of the molds, they were stacked between layers of straw to dry naturally before being fired.

Pressed bricks
Bricks with sharper arrises (edges) and a smoother surface texture were produced mechanically by pressing semi-dry clay into molds. Since they were dense and hard-wearing, pressed bricks were frequently employed as facing bricks for Victorian façades.

Wire-cut bricks
The other common mechanized method of production was to extrude a long bar of clay and use wires to slice it into bricks.

Wire-cut bricks do not have the distinctive recesses known as "frogs" often found on pressed or hand-molded bricks. The recess fills up with mortar, thus keying the brick into the wall, and also reduces the brick's weight. Some pressed or handmade bricks have a recess in the top face only; others also have a frog in the bedding face. Wire-cut bricks can be made with holes passing through them that perform a similar function.

The mottled colors of old handmade bricks

Patterned polychromatic brickwork

Colorful brickwork incorporating projecting headers

An impressive Gothic-revival façade built from colored bricks and stone

CLEANING & WEATHERPROOFING

BEFORE EMBARKING *on an ambitious and irreversible cleaning program, it is worth pausing to consider why you should want to clean the brickwork of your house at all. There's every reason to remove stains, spilled paint, and graffiti, but it would be disastrous to lose the mellow character of nicely weathered brickwork in the pursuit of total renovation. Harsh methods of cleaning that involve sandblasting or powerful chemicals have the most detrimental effects and they tend to leave brickwork looking unpleasantly raw.*

An overcleaned individual house looks bad enough. It is even worse to spoil the appearance of an entire row of houses by cleaning an individual dwelling.

Yellow English brickwork showing the dramatic results of a cleaning

Firing bricks

Once the clay had dried out, the bricks had to be baked to make them hard enough for building purposes. The earliest method of firing bricks was to pile them in rows in a stack or "clamp." Channels left between the rows were filled with timber (or, later, with coal or coke), and the entire stack was surrounded with previously fired bricks daubed with clay. The whole clamp was then set alight and was left to burn, sometimes for weeks. The method produced unevenly fired bricks that varied in color according to their position within the clamp.

Handmade bricks specifically produced for matching old brickwork were fired in clamps until fairly recently.

Brick-built kilns tended to produce bricks of a more consistent hardness and color, so kiln firing became the preferred method of production. The early kilns were tiny compared with modern continuous kilns. They normally consisted of a simple brick chamber with an opening at one end that was sealed before firing.

BRICK CLASSIFICATION

Modern firing techniques are designed to produce bricks with specific characteristics – but with earlier methods the bricks from a single firing varied in quality and had to be sorted according to their properties.

The most regular bricks (the ones that were most evenly fired) were classified as "facings" or face bricks. These attractive, weather-resistant bricks were generally used for building exposed exterior walls.

The less uniform, poorly-fired bricks were designated as common bricks and were normally used for constructing walls that were to be covered with plaster or stucco.

Overburned bricks, from the hottest parts of the clamp or kiln, were reserved for flue linings.

WASHING BRICKWORK

An old brick house in any environment will eventually become discolored to some extent due to airborne dirt and pollution. This "natural" weathering simply reflects the history of the building. However, if you are really bothered by the appearance of your brickwork, it is often possible to wash off surface grime with water.

The safest though most laborious way to clean brickwork is to scrub it by hand.

Starting at the top of a wall, wet an area of bricks with a garden hose and scrub the brickwork with a stiff-bristle brush. Clean the wall in horizontal bands, gradually working your way down to the bottom. Scrub heavy deposits with a bucket of water containing half a cup of household ammonia, then rinse the wall with the hose.

See CLEANING STONEWORK for other methods of cleaning masonry.

STRIPPING A PAINTED WALL

Most brickwork in good condition doesn't need painting, stuccoing or any other form of weatherproofing – but sadly there are plenty of houses with once beautiful brickwork hidden beneath layers of paint. Probably unnecessary in the first place, the paint is now expensive to remove.

Houses with soft or inferior brickwork were often painted when they were built. To strip this protection may lead to serious deterioration. It is therefore best to determine the softness of the material used before stripping painted walls.

Stripping painted brickwork

There are several reasons why it may be advisable to get a reliable professional company to strip paint from brickwork. First of all, it is usually necessary to erect scaffolding, perhaps around an entire building that is several stories high. Then experience of applying and removing stripper is needed to remove all the paint from a deeply textured surface. In addition, paint stripping on this sort of scale can be a messy business, involving the use of toxic materials that have to be handled with care and disposed of safely.

To determine whether the outcome is likely to be satisfactory, ask the company you are thinking of hiring to strip an inconspicuous patch of brickwork, using the chemicals they recommend for the job. The results may indicate that it is better to repaint. In that case, choose a good-quality masonry paint that will let moisture within the walls evaporate effectively.

Alternatives to painting

The best option is to prevent moisture permeating a wall by repointing or by repairing or replacing cracked and spalled bricks. But there are situations where a whole wall has become porous due to natural erosion or because the brickwork has been subjected to coarse abrasive cleaning. Some contractors will recommend painting or even skin-coating the wall to prevent its becoming saturated by rainwater. However, it is possible to preserve the appearance of your brickwork by painting it with a colorless water repellent. Some repellents contain a fugitive dye that makes it easier to see whether the wall has been coated evenly (the color fades rapidly after application).

Water repellents can penetrate as much as $1/2$in (12mm) into masonry and are applied either by brush or sprayed onto the wall. It is usually necessary to make two applications, but read the maker's instructions to be sure. Wear protective clothing, a face mask, and breathing apparatus when handling or using a water repellent, as recommended by the manufacturer.

Choose a reputable brand of repellent that is specifically designed for use on brickwork, and always carry out repointing or any other repairs that may be necessary before treating a wall. Because some repellents subtly alter the color or tone of the brickwork, it is advisable to treat at least one whole wall rather than apply the repellent in patches.

Mask surrounding woodwork and all other materials that you are not planning to waterproof. Also, take careful precautions against overspray that might drift into a public area or a neighbor's property. This is normally achieved by rigging up screens of plastic sheeting around the work area, but if that is difficult or impossible you may be best advised to hire a company to carry out the waterproofing.

Heavy organic growth on brickwork should be treated with bleach

REMOVING STAINS

Tar, grease and oil can normally be softened by applying mineral spirits, paraffin, or a grease solvent. Since there is a slight risk that the softened stain will be spread further as you attempt to wash it from the surface, apply a poultice to absorb the oil or grease. To make a poultice, saturate any convenient absorbent material (such as whiting, fuller's earth, sawdust, or even talcum powder) with solvent. Follow the maker's recommendations when handling and disposing of solvents. It is also advisable to wear protective gloves.

Dampen the stain with the solvent, then immediately cover it with a layer of poultice about $1/2$in (12mm) thick. Tape a sheet of plastic over the poultice, and leave it to dry out and absorb the stain. When the poultice is dry, use a wooden or plastic spatula to lift it off the wall. Finally, scrub the bricks with water and a bristle brush.

EFFLORESCENCE

A white crystalline deposit that commonly appears on brickwork, efflorescence is caused by soluble salts within the masonry migrating to the surface. This occurs as saturated masonry gradually dries out. Locate and cure the cause of the dampness within the wall (such as a failed damp-proof course), then brush the crystals from the bricks with a stiff-bristle brush. You may also have to brush the wall periodically as the masonry dries out.

REMOVING ORGANIC GROWTH

You occasionally encounter owners of a masonry house who encourage growth of colorful lichens by painting the walls with washes of liquid manure or vinegar.

Nevertheless, molds and lichens tend to grow in moist conditions. So if they occur naturally, their presence may indicate a source of damp that needs to be eradicated.

To remove heavy organic growth from a wall, scrape it from the bricks with a non-metallic spatula; then apply a sterilizing solution of 1 part household bleach and 4 parts water (preferably on a sunny day) to kill remaining spores. Paint on a generous application of the solution, starting at the top of the wall. After a couple of days, brush off the dead growth and apply a second wash.

BRICK BONDS

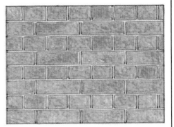
English bond

Mortar, *though strong under compression, has practically no tensile strength. If a wall were built by stacking bricks one directly above the other, creating continuous vertical joints, movement within the wall would tend to pull the joints apart and seriously weaken the structure. Bonding (staggering the vertical joints) ties the bricks together and spreads any load over a wide area. Brick bonding is primarily functional, but the patterns created by staggering the joints are most attractive.*

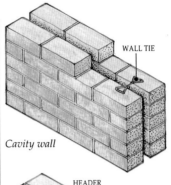
Cavity wall

WALL TIE

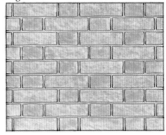
Flemish bond

TRADITIONAL BRICK BONDS

Modern cavity walls consist of two separate stacks of masonry that are separated by a gap spanned by metal ties. Most frequently, the outer layer consists of brickwork built with a stretcher bond. In contrast, up to at least the end of the nineteenth century, since most brick walls were solid, they were constructed with a variety of traditional bonding patterns that utilized different combinations of stretchers and headers. Stretchers are the bricks that run parallel with the face of the wall; headers run from front to back, tying the stretcher courses together.

In the eighteenth century, façades were frequently only one brick thick. These façades were tied to the structural brickwork of the building with true headers in every fifth or sixth course; the rest of the "headers" were simply half-bricks.

There is no real evidence to suggest that one bond is significantly stronger than another. It must therefore be assumed that the popularity of any particular style was primarily due to its visual appeal. English bond, Flemish bond, and English garden-wall bond were all developed in Europe by the sixteenth century, and have been used for solid-brick walls ever since. The header bond was especially popular in Georgian times.

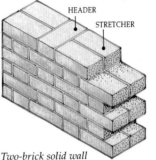
HEADER
STRETCHER
Two-brick solid wall

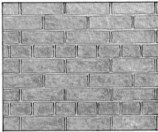
English garden-wall bond

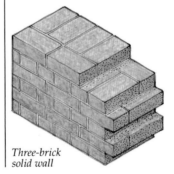
Three-brick solid wall

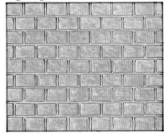
Header bond

DECORATIVE BONDS

Purely decorative bonds were used to relieve large areas of unbroken brickwork, typically in the form of basketweave or herringbone panels.

Traditional diaper work (which used dark headers to produce diamond patterns against paler brickwork) is just one example of how bricks of contrasting color or tone were incorporated into a decorative bond. Similar patterns were also created by allowing headers to project slightly from a wall so that they would cast attractive shadows.

Nineteenth-century diamond-pattern brickwork

A combination of basketweave and herringbone panels

27

REPOINTING BRICKWORK

SKILLED BRICKLAYERS *have always taken pride in their ability to build regular bonds with precise joints. Much relies on the consistency of the mortar. It must be neither so firm that it prevents the bricklayer from tapping each course into alignment nor so soft that it slumps under the weight of the bricks. In addition, each mortar joint must be shaped to complement the style of the building and the type of bricks used in its construction. The collective name for these shaped joints is pointing.*

Early-C18th tuck pointing used to simulate rubbed brickwork

Eroded pointing weakens the wall

Portland-rich mortar may crack

WHEN TO REPOINT

Repointing is a laborious job that is expensive if you hire a bricklayer to do the work and time-consuming if you do it yourself. Consequently, it is advisable only to repoint when necessary and to limit repairs to as small an area as possible, matching the old pointing in shape, color and texture. Within a fairly short time, the new and old pointing will be practically indistinguishable, provided the work is done properly. But if say three quarters of the pointing has decayed, then it makes sense to rake out what's left and repoint the entire wall – or, if need be, the whole building.

If recent repointing is too unsightly to ignore, there may be a case for raking out the mortar and starting again. Otherwise, look for signs of deterioration likely to lead to penetrating damp or to the disintegration of the bricks themselves.

Natural erosion

Under the combined assault of wind and driving rain, soft mortar tends to erode, especially on the windward side of exposed buildings. Erosion can lead to deep crevices in the pointing that not only allow rainwater to soak deeply into the wall but may eventually lead to loose brickwork.

Damp and frost

Excessive damp caused by leaking gutters and down-pipes can exacerbate the effects of erosion, and the action of frost tends to make matters even worse.

Cracked mortar

As often as not, cracked mortar is the result of using an inflexible Portland-rich mortar that is unable to absorb the slightest movement within the masonry. In a relatively short time, cracked mortar falls out, leaving vulnerable open joints.

JOINT STYLES

Unless it is leading to deterioration of the brickwork, it is best to copy the existing style of joint when repointing a small area of wall. However, if complete repointing seems inevitable, choose the style most appropriate for the age of the house and the condition of the brickwork.

The joints described below are probably those most often used for the brickwork of old houses. If you have walls pointed with one of the less common styles (such as beaded or V-shaped pointing) that may be original, then it is worth finding a bricklayer able to replicate them.

Flush joint

Before the second half of the nineteenth century most brickwork was pointed with flush joints. In practice, many so-called flush joints are slightly recessed or concave to allow for the rounded arrises of old handmade or worn bricks.

Weatherstruck joints

This joint was rarely used until the 1850s or 1860s. It sheds water efficiently and enhances the appearance of bricks with sharp arrises. It is not suitable for repointing very old brickwork.

Tuck pointing

Tuck pointing was used, in the eighteenth century especially, to simulate the exactness of rubbed brickwork (see OPENINGS IN BRICKWORK).

The joints were filled flush, using mortar colored to match the brickwork. Fine grooves, scored along the centers of the joints, were filled with a slightly projecting strip of lime putty. This was normally white and was sometimes mixed with silver sand. Less commonly, soot was used to stain it black. When repairs are necessary, it pays to hire a bricklayer with experience of replacing tuck pointing.

Ruled-joint pointing

As proper tuck pointing was expensive, bricklayers often made ruled joints, sometimes called penny-round pointing. Although a narrow groove was scored along each joint (presumably with a coin), to save money the lime putty was omitted.

1 Flush joint   *2 Weatherstruck*   *3 Tuck pointing*   *4 Ruled joint*

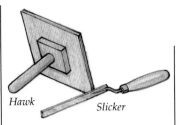

Hawk   *Slicker*

PREPARING THE WALL

Rake out the old mortar to a depth of about ¾ to 1in (18 to 25mm), using a piece of wood that has been shaped to fit the joints.

If necessary, chop out hard mortar using a cold chisel with a suitably narrow blade. Take care not to damage the edges of the bricks. Never use a power tool, such as a chain saw or an angle grinder.

Brush out all loose material, then hose the wall lightly so that the new mortar will not dry too quickly.

Chop out hard pointing

FILLING AND SHAPING THE JOINTS

Many builders use a small pointing trowel to push mortar into the open joints, but an amateur may find it easier to use a narrow margin trowel (also called a jointer or slicker) to fit between the bricks. Carry a small quantity of mortar to the wall on a hawk (a hand-held board with a handle underneath). Holding the hawk against the wall, fill each joint flush with mortar, compacting it with the margin trowel (1). Try not to smear mortar onto the faces of the bricks. Leave the mortar to stiffen until it will retain a clear impression of your thumb, then shape the joints as appropriate. As soon as the pointing has set, use a dry scrubbing brush to clean any specks of mortar from the faces of the bricks.

Flush joints
Flush joints need no further shaping, but if the finish left by the margin trowel looks smoother than the old mortar, stipple the joints with a stiff-bristle brush to expose the sand aggregate (2).

Weatherstruck joints
Use a margin trowel to shape the mortar, leaving each joint with a sloping profile. The vertical joints, which should be shaped first, can slope to either right or left – so look at the original pointing and make the new weatherstruck joints consistent.

Bricklayers remove excess mortar from the base of the joints using a tool called a Frenchman that has a blade with a right-angled tip. You can make one from a narrow strip of thin metal.

Use a wood straightedge to guide the Frenchman's blade. Nail plywood scraps to the straightedge to serve as spacers that leave a gap through which the excess mortar can drop as you draw the tool along the joints (3).

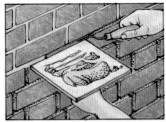

1 Use a margin trowel to fill joints

2 Stipple flush joints with a brush

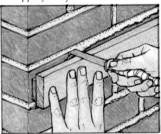

3 Scrape off mortar with Frenchman

MORTAR

Old brickwork was built using mortar made by mixing approximately 1 part lime with 3 parts sand in water. Even when set, this mortar was flexible enough to withstand slight movement in a wall without cracking. Also, being relatively weak, lime-based mortar allowed moisture within the wall to evaporate harmlessly. When strong Portland-based mortar is used to repoint soft brickwork, it prevents evaporation except through the bricks themselves. This results in the surfaces of the bricks flaking, or "spalling," leading to a general disintegration of the wall.

Lime mortar
The one drawback of lime mortar is the time it takes to set. Consequently, repointing is usually carried out with a lime mortar that contains a little cement to shorten the setting time. A mixture of 1 part Portland cement, 1 part lime and 6 parts sand is ideal for brickwork that is in an exposed position, but you can use an even weaker mix of 1:2:9 for soft bricks in a sheltered location.

You can buy hydrated (pre-slaked) powdered lime from a builders' supplier. Alternatively, buy a ready-mixed lime mortar that simply requires "gauging" (mixing) with cement just before it is used. A range of colored mortars is available.

Matching color and texture
To match existing pointing it is necessary to choose the ingredients of the new mortar carefully. Sand varies a great deal in color, but the fact that mortar was often made with local materials helps to limit the options. Perhaps even more critical is the grade of sand. Old pointing often contains sand of a relatively coarse grade.

To adjust the color add powdered pigments, sold at masons' supply stores. To lighten the tone, use a white Portland cement instead of the standard gray variety.

Even with the right materials, it is difficult to make a precise match unless you prepare some test samples of the mortar and allow them to dry thoroughly.

Mixing mortar
Thoroughly mix the dry ingredients on a flat board, then scoop a well in the center of the mound. Pour some clean water into the hollow, then shovel the dry materials from around the edges into the center until the water is absorbed. Blend the ingredients, then once again make a well and add water until the mortar has the consistency of soft butter.

Mortar containing cement sets in a couple of hours, so don't mix too much at a time. Wear gloves, goggles, and a face mask when you're handling hydrated lime.

REPAIRING BRICKWORK

EXTENSIVELY CRACKED BRICKWORK *and bulging walls should be inspected by an engineer to ascertain the cause of the damage and to determine whether the structure has stabilized. Even serious faults such as defective foundations, broken lintels, or detached bonding can be corrected, but the remedial work should always be carried out by an experienced contractor.*

You may find that the engineer's report indicates minimal movement, and it is always possible that the movement may have been arrested by a previous householder. In such cases, you will probably be able to repoint or replace the damaged bricks yourself.

REPLACING SPALLED BRICKS

In freezing conditions the expansion of water trapped just below the surface of bricks often causes spalling, or flaking, since the moisture cannot evaporate evenly.

If spalling is widespread, the only practical solution is to repoint the brickwork with lime mortar and apply a clear water repellent (see CLEANING & WEATHERPROOFING) that will protect the wall while allowing it to breathe.

More often, spalling affects only a small area of the wall, so individual bricks can be cut out and replaced. Cracked bricks can be renewed in a similar way. There's a limit to the number of bricks you can take out without a wall collapsing. So if more than two or three bricks have to be removed, ask a builder for advice before proceeding with the repairs.

Cutting out a spalled brick

Rake out the mortar joints around a spalled brick. If necessary, loosen the mortar by boring into it with a masonry drill (1) and chop out what remains with a narrow cold chisel. After removing the brick, clean the dust from the cavity then dampen the inside.

1 Loosen mortar with a drill

Inserting a replacement

Spread mortar on the bottom of the cavity and up one side. Wet the replacement brick, spread mortar on top of the brick and on one end, then insert it into the cavity (2). Compact the mortar and, once it begins to get firm, shape the joints to match the rest of the pointing.

2 Insert a mortared brick

POINTING WORN BRICKS

As soft mortar is eroded the corners and arrises (edges) of the bricks are exposed to the elements, and eventually they will become worn and rounded. If worn bricks are pointed so that the mortar is flush with their stretcher faces, the joints look much wider than intended. Also, the mortar presents weak feathered edges that quickly deteriorate (1).

When you are repointing worn bricks, recess the joints to retain their original width. Recessed joints look best if they are slightly concave (2). Special tools are made for shaping concave joints, but you can improvise with a short length of bent copper tubing. Finally, stipple the mortar with a brush to match weathered pointing.

 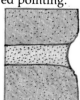

1 Flush joint with weak edges   *2 Recessed joint is preferable*

FINDING REPLACEMENT BRICKS

Finding replacement bricks that will blend with period brickwork is not easy. With their clean, sharp edges, mass-produced bricks are usually too perfect; they are also unlikely to be the same size as the ones that you are replacing. On the other hand, you can have hand-molded bricks made to any specification you require, although you will need to track down a specialist brick manufacturer operating in your part of the country.

Most people restoring old brickwork try to acquire second-hand bricks (seconds) from a building of a similar age and style that has undergone extensive alterations or partial demolition. Whenever possible, avoid buying seconds that have been repointed with Portland-rich mortar. It usually has to be hacked off with a cold chisel, which often results in bricks being broken.

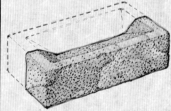

Cut bricks lengthwise for economy

If you are repairing a small area of brickwork, you can make your supply of second-hand replacement bricks go twice as far by cutting them in half with a power brick saw fitted with a masonry blade. This provides you with two half bricks that you can back up with mortar and fit into the wall with their good faces outward.

Similarly, if you are able to remove a spalled brick without breaking it, you can turn it around, so that the flaking face is hidden and the intact face exposed, then mortar it back in place.

OPENINGS IN BRICKWORK

*T*HE BRICKWORK *above window and door openings has to be supported in some way, otherwise the wall would collapse. Very often this is achieved by the insertion of a stone, metal or even wooden lintel, but frequently a brick arch is used instead. The two methods are also sometimes combined, a lintel being concealed behind a brick arch.*

Brick arches are invariably carefully designed and constructed, and they contribute significantly to the character of row houses and individual façades. The effect is enhanced when openings are given additional embellishment in the form of colored-brick jambs.

Late C18th semi-circular brick arch

Exquisite elliptical-arched doorway

BRICK ARCHES

A true arch is composed of a number of tapered bricks that support each other as weight is applied from above, transmitting the load to the brickwork on each side of the door or window opening.

Purpose-made shaped bricks are now used to construct arches, but better-quality structures were once made from soft bricks that were individually cut and ground to shape on an abrasive stone. A skilled bricklayer could shape these "rubbers" so accurately that the joints between them were no more than 1/8in (2 to 3mm) wide. Superior-quality "gauged" (rubbed-brick) arches were pointed with lime mortar. For cheaper work, ordinary bricks were cut to a tapered shape or, alternatively, uncut bricks were built into the arch with tapering mortar joints.

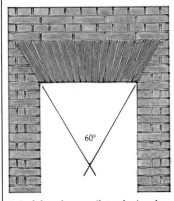

1 Arch based on equilateral triangle

2 Joints aligning with center of sill

Skewback arch

An elegant skewback arch is a pleasing feature of some eighteenth-century straight-head windows.

The lower edge of this type of arch has to be raised with a slight curve in order to counteract an optical illusion – if it was perfectly straight, the arch would

appear to sag in the middle.

Each brick in a skewback arch is a different shape. The joint lines radiate from the apex of an imaginary inverted equilateral triangle plotted below the arch **(1)**. Alternatively, they align with a point in the center of the window sill **(2)**.

Segmental arch

A segmental arch is built with identical tapering bricks, known as voussoirs, once again centered on the apex of an equilateral triangle. Although there are notable exceptions, few segmental arches seem to have been built with the same care lavished on most skewbacks and they are frequently constructed with whole or crudely cut bricks.

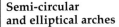

Segmental arch with equal voussoirs

Semi-circular and elliptical arches

Semi-circular arches were used not only for spanning windows but also doorways with fanlights. The elliptical arch is more subtle in shape and consequently requires a variety of accurately made rubbed voussoirs for its construction. It is generally used to span fairly wide openings.

Pointed arch

The pointed arch, sometimes picked out in soft red bricks, became popular during the Gothic-revival period.

Soldier arch

The soldier arch (or "brick lintel") is nothing more than a row of upright standard bricks. The structure, which is inherently weak, is usually supported from below by a sturdy angle iron or a flat metal bar.

Classic Gothic-revival pointed arch

POINTING RUBBED BRICKWORK

The extremely fine joints in rubbed brickwork cannot be repointed in the usual way. The process described below demands patience and care, but it will insure that the bricks are not smeared with lime mortar.

Make a batch of putty by sprinkling hydrated lime into a bucket containing clean water. Stir the putty to the consistency of thick cream and leave it covered for 24 hours. At this stage you can add fine sand if needed to match the texture of the original pointing.

Improvise a narrow steel jointing tool that will fit snugly between the bricks.

Rake out loose pointing with a hacksaw blade, taking care not to damage the edges of the very soft bricks, and dampen the open joints.

Sandwich some lime mortar between two strips of waxed paper or plastic sheeting. Use a piece of wood to press the sandwich flat until it will slide into a joint with an exact fit (1).

Holding the putty in place with the jointing tool, carefully extract each piece of paper or plastic (2). Trim off excess putty with a knife, then compact the joints with the jointing tool.

A pair of skewback arches composed of soft red rubbed bricks

1 Insert a lime-mortar sandwich

2 Pull out strips of paper or plastic

REPAIRING BRICK ARCHES

Cracks tend to develop at the corners of the window and door openings whenever there is a structural failure of a building's foundations. If this happens, the integrity of the window or door arch is compromised and there is a danger that the voussoirs will fall out. This is a situation that must be remedied without delay.

Get an experienced builder to correct the original cause of the collapse. It will then be possible to insert a beam through the wall above the arch to support the brickwork while the arch itself is dismantled. Rubbers should be handled with care, as they are easily chipped or broken.

The builder will erect a timber-and-plywood form to support the arch while it is being rebuilt. This should not be removed until the mortar has set hard.

SHAPED BRICKS

BRICKLAYERS *were adept at constructing decorative detailing from ordinary bricks. Dentil courses beneath the eaves or dogtooth brickwork created by laying bricks at an angle to the face of the wall are typical of the ornamentation found on even the humblest of Victorian workers' cottages. However, much more elaborate embellishments were possible using special-purpose shaped bricks and molded-brick tiles.*

Special-purpose brick voussoirs

Doorway with molded-brick panels

SPECIAL BRICKS

Rubbed brickwork, which was extremely laborious to produce, gradually gave way to factory-made shaped bricks. By the second half of the nineteenth century, brick manufacturers were offering a vast selection of profiles and "specials" for creating all manner of plinths, cornices, chamfered borders, brick arches, and molded jambs.

There is still a wide range of special-purpose bricks in production from which you may be able to select suitable replacements for damaged originals. But if it proves impossible to find appropriate substitutes, then it is generally preferable to live with ornamentation that is in less than perfect condition rather than allow a builder to cut away or skim-coat original decorative brickwork.

MOLDED BRICKWORK

The Victorians frequently used molded-brick tiles or slips to make cornices, string courses, and other classical-style moldings. Much of the detailing was extremely elaborate, making it possible to create extravagant ornamentation that was previously only possible with expensive hand carving.

Purely decorative panels, composed of soft pinkish-red abstract or figurative brick tiles, are a familiar feature of better-quality Victorian and turn-of-the-century housing. If such decorative tiles have been hacked away in the course of insensitive refurbishment, it may be possible to find modern reproductions of molded brickwork that will enable you to recreate perfectly acceptable period-style paneling.

CHAPTER THREE

STONEWORK

Because we are accustomed *to seeing impressive public buildings and gentrified houses constructed from dressed stone, many of us tend to equate stonework with quality, permanence, and wealth. And yet in some areas where stone is plentiful, it was in earlier centuries commonplace for practically every house, cottage, workshop, and barn in the vicinity to be built of local stone. But this in no way diminishes the importance of stone as a building material. Being built from indigenous stone, using local methods of construction, vernacular architecture becomes virtually part of the landscape – an admirable quality.*

Despite the seemingly endless variety of colors and textures used for domestic stonework, limestone or sandstone is the most common material. The catch-all term "field stone" describes a range of rubblestone dwellings. A relatively small number of houses incorporate hard red or gray granite, and perhaps even rarer are the distinctive cobblestone buildings. Native and imported marbles have always been costly, so tend to be reserved for decorative elements or internal features.

Dressed and carved stone has always been expensive. Builders and clients were therefore often not averse to substituting cast imitation stone. Some early examples look so authentic that only an expert can tell them from the real thing.

A charming rubble-built cottage

Squared rubble makes for precision

Sophisticated carved stone doorway

Mellowed limestone masonry in the neo-classical manner

C19th surround with transom lights

RUBBLE & DRESSED STONE

NOWADAYS MACHINERY AND POWER TOOLS *take much of the hard labor out of the quarrying of stone. Until the mid nineteenth century, however, quarrying had hardly changed since ancient times. Although the harder building stones would have been extracted by controlled blasting, huge slabs of softer stratified rocks were still being split from the bed using metal wedges driven into the rock. These slabs were then split or sawn into building blocks, which perhaps received a surface dressing depending on the requirements of the builder or mason.*

Solidly built Second Empire style mansion constructed in squared rubble

FLINT WALLING

In England, nodules of flint have long been dug out from soft chalk deposits or collected for use as the main constituent of this delightful form of rubble walling. When quarried, a nodule is covered with a pale-gray crust of lime. It's only when the stone is split that the glassy black flint core is revealed.

The smoother flint cobbles are selected for building purposes and are laid in courses with their rounded ends projecting from the face of the wall. Alternatively, the cobbles are snapped in half to expose the black core. For best-quality work, snapped cobbles are then knapped (dressed) on all four sides to make building blocks, approximately 4in (100mm) square, which are laid in bonded courses with very fine joints.

Although flint facing is extremely hard-wearing, an all-flint wall is not particularly strong and it's impossible to build one with accurate square corners. Consequently, most flint buildings have brick or stone quoins at each corner, usually tied together at regular intervals with narrow lacing courses and piers of brick, stone, or tiles. Though relatively rare in America, flint-built houses are a delightful blend of colors and textures, with the various structural elements creating attractive geometric patterns.

Typical flint and brick combination

Square-knapped flintwork

RUBBLEWORK

Although the name might suggest otherwise, rubble walls are not shoddy structures. Even with random rubblework **(1)**, the irregular stones must be carefully selected and arranged to build stable masonry walls with staggered joints. In addition, transverse stones that extend for at least two thirds of the thickness of a wall are incorporated in order to bond the masonry securely.

For slightly better-quality work, the stones are laid in courses **(2)**, typically creating a level bed every 1ft 6in (450mm) or so.

Random-rubble walling is frequently finished at the corners with quoins of dressed stone.

Random rubblework is most often found in rural areas, but occasionally better-quality housing, in town features squared rubble **(3)**. This type of rubblework is composed of split blocks, which are sometimes roughly dressed with a hammer or steel chisel. With squared rubble it was possible to construct masonry with regular courses **(4)** that are constant in height although the stones themselves vary in length.

1 Random rubblework

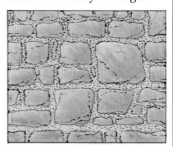

2 Coursed random rubble

3 Squared rubblework

4 Regular-coursed squared rubble

Surface dressings
1 Tooled finish
2 Punched
3 Picked
4 Furrowed
5 Vermiculated
6 Rock-faced

ASHLAR

Ashlar is the name given to masonry constructed from accurately cut and jointed blocks of stone. Usually, each block is sawn on all sides and the face (the outer exposed surface) is sometimes polished to a flat finish.

Ashlar walls are almost always laid to regular courses, and are frequently built with an accurate bond resembling brickwork. Due to the high cost of ashlar, dressed blocks were often used as a facing backed by rubble or bricks. This type of construction is known as veneer walling.

Joints

The majority of ashlar blocks are flush-faced and butted together, with lime mortar used as a bedding material (**1**). The mortar joints are very narrow – normally no more than 1/8 to 3/16in (3 to 4mm) wide. However, stonework is often "rusticated" to emphasize the joints, the edges of each block either being chamfered to form V-jointing (**2**) or rebated to create channeling (**3**).

1 Square-cut flush-faced ashlar

2 V-jointed rustication

3 Deep rebates cut in the edges of each ashlar block form chaneled joints

Surface dressings

Masons cut a variety of textures into the face of building stones by hand in order to draw the eye to features such as doors and windows, or to give a building the impression of strength and solidity at street level.

One of the simplest textures comprises little more than a hand-tooled flat surface covered with fine, closely packed lines made with the edge of a chisel (**1**). A punched texture (**2**) or the even finer picked dressing (**3**) are made with a pointed tool, and a gouge is used to incise a furrowed dressing with 1/4 to 3/8in (6 to 9mm) parallel flutes (**4**). Deeply carved vermiculation (**5**), which is supposed to look like worm tracks, is often employed to lend visual emphasis to openings and quoins. Rock-faced masonry (**6**) is deliberately left rough, usually in contrast to smooth margins carved around the edges of each block of stone.

CLEANING STONEWORK

MANY PRESERVATION *organizations and professionals concerned with period buildings normally advise against cleaning stonework unless it is absolutely necessary. This advice is primarily intended to prevent irreversible damage caused by insufficiently skilled operatives or use of unnecessarily harsh cleaning methods. There are also those who feel that cleaning stonework reduces its aesthetic appeal by eliminating all those subtleties of color and tone that have developed over the years.*

However, there are some stone houses, particularly in urban areas, that would undoubtedly benefit from cleaning in order to remove disfiguring black staining caused by pollution. Even more important, in some cases cleaning is essential to prevent or halt physical deterioration of the stone itself.

Partly cleaned limestone demonstrates the advantages of expert treatment

SELECTING THE BEST METHOD

It is important to select the appropriate treatment for a particular type of stone. If you are concerned about the condition of your house, it pays to get expert advice before you make a decision. The principal risk of employing the wrong contractor or using inappropriate techniques to clean your stone house is that permanent damage can be done if too harsh an abrasive or chemical agent is used, affecting the appearance and durability of the stone. Seek out preservation architects or engineers practicing in your part of the country who offer advice on the cleaning of stone.

Having established that cleaning would be beneficial, it is vital to find a reputable company that will undertake the task. Again, local preservation experts may be able to direct you to professionals who can recommend the most appropriate treatment and give you an estimate of the cost. Fees tend to be high, but vary considerably depending on the treatment and the status of the company concerned.

The principal methods currently available for cleaning masonry are outlined here. Together with the recommendations of your professional advisers, they will serve as a guide to selecting the most suitable process for your house.

WASHING STONEWORK

Dirty limestone, especially, generally responds well to washing with water. In fact, it is possible to clean a fairly small house yourself, using a stiff-bristle brush and a garden hose (see WASHING BRICKWORK). However, scrubbing stone by hand is very hard work and professionals usually resort to some form of high-pressure spraying.

The gentlest method used by professionals involves rigging up a series of spray heads that direct a fine mist of droplets onto the surface of the stone to soften the dirt before it is scrubbed from the masonry with bristle brushes or ones made from phosphor-bronze. Steel-wire brushes should not be used for cleaning stone.

A jet of water forced under pressure from a hand-held lance is often extremely effective, but experience is needed in order to avoid damaging mortar joints and soft stonework.

Steam cleaning is sometimes recommended for removing oily stains, but in practice it is not much more effective than hosing down the stonework with water.

Whichever method of cleaning you decide on, it is essential to take measures to avoid oversaturation of the stone and to prevent water from penetrating joints between joinery and masonry.

Water should not be used on stonework if there is any likelihood of frost.

CHEMICAL CLEANING

Chemical cleaners must only be applied to stonework under the supervision of an expert. This is especially important since careless use of chemicals can cause local environmental damage. Moreover, it is necessary to ascertain the effects of a particular chemical in order to avoid staining, discoloration, and even disintegration of the stone.

Acidic cleaning agents, for example, are recommended for cleaning granite and most sandstones, but are not suitable for calcareous or chalky sandstone and would probably dissolve limestone, or marble. You therefore need to make sure that a professional conducts a test before applying a cleaner to a wide area of stone. Even a few drops of diluted hydrochloric acid causes soluble stone to bubble and foam.

Alkali or caustic cleaners are employed for heavily soiled terracotta, limestone and marble. Chemical cleaning may be recommended for these materials when there's a danger that washing the stonework down with water might result in oversaturation.

The normal procedure for chemical cleaning involves spraying the grimy masonry with water before the chosen cleaner is either brushed or sprayed onto the surface. Once the dirt has been dissolved, the stone is washed down with low-pressure jets.

REPOINTING STONEWORK

Traditional mason's handtools

ALTHOUGH MOST GOOD BUILDERS *know how to repoint brickwork, they often lack experience of similar work on stone-built houses. This is evident from the many examples of walls where mortar has been spread over the edges of the stones or where the joints project beyond the face of the masonry, creating what is known as ribbon or strip pointing. Both methods spoil the appearance of a wall by emphasizing the joints at the expense of the stones.*

Whether a wall is built of ashlar or rubble, the mortar should be as close to the color of the stone as possible and maybe very slightly lighter in tone. It also should be slightly gritty in texture.

It's a mistake to be too eager to repoint an old wall. Even slightly recessed pointing is acceptable, provided the original mortar has not become soft and friable. If there are obvious signs that the pointing is being eroded, leaving deep open joints, carefully rake out and replace the loose mortar.

Ribbon pointing is unsightly

Well-executed recessed pointing

USING ABRASIVES

Indiscriminate sandblasting and the use of power tools fitted with wire brushes or grinders have been responsible for serious damage to old stone and brickwork. As a result, it is rarely recommended that abrasives be used on such masonry buildings. In the hands of a careless operator, harsh abrasives can totally destroy carved or molded detail and may leave the surface of soft stone permanently pitted and scoured.

However, for a number of years conservators have been cleaning valuable stone sculpture with extremely fine abrasive particles that can be used for removing surface dirt only. Some companies are developing this "microparticle" system on a commercial scale for cleaning dirty buildings without most of the hazards of abrasive cleaning or the risk of staining and discoloration associated with other techniques. Nevertheless, it must be stressed that all abrasive materials have to be adequately controlled and contained in order to safeguard the health not only of the operator and the occupants of the house but also of other people working or living nearby.

MORTAR FOR REPOINTING

Old masonry was invariably constructed with a weak lime mortar that was plastic enough to absorb any slight movements within the structure. A modern Portland-rich mortar, which is often misguidedly employed for repointing stonework, has little flexibility. As a result, it cracks easily, leading to the ingress of water and eventually to the disintegration of the masonry. And there is no advantage in using such a strong mortar, even for hard stone.

When repointing a rubble wall that is in an exposed situation, use a mortar comprising 1 part white Portland cement, 1 part hydrated lime and 6 parts aggregate (sand or crushed stone) mixed with water. For stonework that's in a sheltered position, use a weaker 1:3:12 mix. See REPOINTING BRICKWORK for how to mix mortars to match the original pointing.

Ashlar walls are normally repointed using a lime mortar made by mixing hydrated lime with an equal amount of crushed stone.

REPOINTING RUBBLE WALLING

Using either a pointed stick or a smooth steel tool that will not damage the stones, rake out the joints to a depth that equals their width. Wet the wall, in order to reduce its suction, then press fresh mortar between the stones, leaving the joint very slightly recessed (see POINTING WORN BRICKS). When the mortar begins to stiffen, stipple the joints with a stiff-bristle brush to expose the texture of the aggregate.

REPOINTING ASHLAR

Repointing a finely jointed ashlar wall would tax the patience of most amateurs. The joints are filled flush with lime mortar which, to keep the stones clean, is sandwiched between two strips of waxed paper that are removed once the mortar is in place (see POINTING RUBBED BRICKWORK).

REPOINTING FLINT WALLING

Cobbles can be repointed in the same way as rubble walling. However, the joints between square-knapped flints are sometimes so fine that they have to be pointed like ashlar – a job that is best left to a skilled professional.

GALLETING

Wide mortar joints were sometimes filled with small stones or flint flakes. Known as galleting, this is not just an attractive detail – it also helps the mortar to resist weathering. When repointing galleted work, collect the small stones and rebed them while the new mortar joints are still soft.

CARVED STONEWORK

VERNACULAR STONE HOUSES AND COTTAGES *have a charm and character that relies more on skillful construction and the colors and textures of the natural materials than on unnecessary embellishment. But this was not so with the average urban dwelling – for even when a town house was constructed mainly from brick, stonemasons and carvers were frequently employed to create decorative features in the form of classically inspired moldings or elaborately carved door and window surrounds.*

Traditional hand skills still continued to be used even on quite humble dwellings well into the twentieth century, but from the eighteenth century genuine carved stone had already begun to be rivaled by cast artificial-stone enrichments.

Typically Victorian entrance with deeply carved foliage and bird motifs

DOOR AND WINDOW OPENINGS

The stone components used in the construction of door and window openings were not simply decorative linings. Each element has a specific structural function and was shaped and installed accordingly.

Nevertheless, typical of builder craftsmen, stonemasons decorated practically every stone-built opening to some extent, even if only with chamfers to relieve the sharp edges. Much of the carving was done at the mason's own yard then later transported to the building site. Very little carving was actually done *in situ*.

Window and door openings have to be made precisely in order to accommodate the necessary joinery. Consequently, rubble-built houses normally incorporate dressed-stone openings. Brick houses are also frequently built with stone lintels above the windows and doors, and some even have complete surrounds of carved stonework.

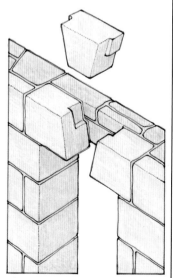

Carved stone lintels and mullion

An unusual form of vermiculation

Lintels

A lintel is a beam that spans an opening, supporting the weight of the masonry above a window or door.

Stone lintels are normally cut as a single block. However, if there was a risk that a long lintel might crack under load, it would be made from three separate blocks joined with sloping joggle joints (which are designed to tighten as weight is applied to them). This type of lintel is also known as a flat arch.

The lintels even on fairly modest row houses, particularly in the Victorian era, are frequently decorated, if only with shallow carvings.

Three-part joggle-jointed lintel

Arches

An arch is the alternative method of spanning window or door openings. It is constructed from accurately cut tapering stones, called voussoirs, that support each other and transfer the load to the section of wall on each side of the opening.

The voussoir at the center of the arch, which locks the other stones in place, is known as the keystone and is usually singled out for special decorative treatment. Very often keystones are embellished with a carved "mask" representing a minor classical deity or an animal. Alternatively, the stone may simply be vermiculated to distinguish it from the other voussoirs.

A relieving arch is built into the masonry above an opening when it is necessary to deflect the load away from a lintel that is too slim to bear the weight without support. Relieving arches are not always visible on the outside of the house.

Sometimes the presence of a relieving arch is incorrectly assumed to be evidence that the shape of an opening has been altered. But don't be tempted to remove the lintel, since the arch may not be strong enough on its own.

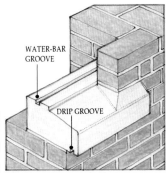

WATER-BAR GROOVE

DRIP GROOVE

Weathered stone subsill

Sills

A stone sill (or, strictly speaking, subsill) is used to cap the section of wall at the base of a window. The wooden window frame sits directly on the stone sill and the joint is weatherproofed with a metal water bar fitted into a groove in each component. The ends of a stone sill are normally built into the brick or stone wall on both sides of the window. The top surface is sloped to drain water away from the wooden window frame. In addition, a drip groove cut along the underside causes rainwater to drop to the ground before it can run back to soak the wall behind. Drip grooves should be raked out periodically to insure that they do not become bridged by paint, moss, or lichen.

Jambs

The stone jambs flanking door and window openings are usually constructed from quoins (alternate headers and stretchers of dressed stone). These are particularly obvious when they are built into rubble walls or when picked out with distinctive surface dressings.

The jambs in ashlar walls, in particular, are sometimes lined with narrow dressed stones that form reveals. Sometimes called upstarts, these stones often project slightly from the face of the wall and are carved to create decorative architraves.

Jambs may be splayed to provide more natural light.

Mullions and piers

Stone mullions are used to divide a window opening in order to accommodate two or more individual windows and provide additional support to the lintel above. Larger vertical supports, such as those at the corners of a bay window, are called piers. Piers and mullions are frequently decorated with ornamental carvings.

New York brownstone surrounds

Stone courses contrast with brick

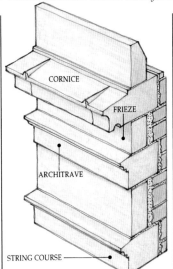

Painted stone arch with carved keystone and capitals

STONE COURSES

Many stone-built or brick façades are broken by horizontal molded bands of stone that project beyond the face of the wall. As well as dividing a building into aesthetically pleasing proportions, these stone courses have a more prosaic function. Like a window sill, stone courses are sloped so that they shed rainwater, which would otherwise saturate or stain the wall.

Cornices

A cornice is normally situated just below the parapet at the top of a house. Often the junctions between the individual blocks of stone were saddled (raised) to encourage water to flow away from the actual joints; alternatively, the top of the entire cornice was protected with a lead flashing.

Architraves

An architrave is a similar but smaller molding situated just below the cornice. The section of wall between the two is known as a frieze.

String courses

A string course is a narrow horizontal band of molded stones. A square-faced one is called a band course.

CORNICE

FRIEZE

ARCHITRAVE

STRING COURSE

Horizontal stone courses

COPINGS

A coping is a row of capping stones designed to shed rainwater from the top of a brick or stone wall. Coping stones, which may be either saddled or sloped, are wider than the wall itself and have drip grooves on the underside.

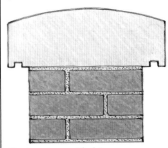

Coping stone with drip grooves

39

ARTIFICIAL STONE

WE TEND TO REGARD IMITATIVE MASONRY *as a relatively modern phenomenon restricted to garden paving and cast-concrete walling. However, by the mid nineteenth century artificial cast stonework was already fairly commonplace as a cheaper alternative to hand carving and the earliest experiments in processing artificial stone were carried out perhaps a century earlier.*

In the eighteenth century in England, the public was intrigued by artificial-stone products, not just because of their natural appearance but also because of the mystery surrounding their manufacture. Richard Holt, who took out a patent for artificial stone in 1722, went so far as to claim that he had rediscovered a lost formula possessed by our ancestors long ago, who used it for manufacturing building materials for such well-known monuments as the pyramids of ancient Egypt and the megaliths of Stonehenge.

COADE STONE

The artificial-stone market was potentially so lucrative that processes and exact compositions were jealously guarded secrets. However, recent scientific analysis has revealed that Coade stone, perhaps the most famous of all artificial stones, was composed of nothing more exotic than china clay mixed with finely ground aggregates and linseed oil.

Founded in the 1760s, the Coade Company in Great Britain established a reputation for manufacturing artificial stonework of the highest quality, and time has proved its durability. Coade's output included copies of well-known classical stonework, but most of their products were designed specially for their catalog. The company produced a vast range of cast architectural features, including their now familiar door surrounds complete with masked keystone and vermiculated quoins. Even though Coade-stone artifacts were made in quantity, the more intricate castings were finished by hand – which is perhaps why it is sometimes difficult to tell Coade-stone castings from genuine stone.

The Coade family and their associates traded successfully for about seventy years, eventually exporting their products to America and other countries as well.

A Coade-stone door surround incorporating quoins and masked keystone

Vermiculated window opening

Terracotta is rich and colorful

TERRACOTTA

Terracotta arguably has more in common with brick so far as its composition and manufacture are concerned. Nevertheless, for architectural purposes it is generally classified as an artificial stone. It had already been in use for centuries when the Victorians took to terracotta and its glazed version "faience" with their characteristic enthusiasm for ornamentation, exploiting the potential of industrial production to full advantage.

We are perhaps used to thinking of terracotta as a decorative facing for large public buildings and department stores, but it was also used in better-quality houses to embellish entrances and for sculptured panels, cornices, and other moldings. Manufacturers experimented with different colors, but castings for both commercial and domestic buildings were mostly brick red or beige.

Normally made as hollow blocks, terracotta and faience in particular are extremely durable unless water is able to seep behind them, rusting steel or iron fixings, which eventually expand and crack the castings. It is possible to order replacement castings, although the cost is likely to be prohibitive. However, depending on the nature of the damage, you may be able to repair cracked terracotta with epoxy adhesive.

REPAIRING DEFECTIVE STONE

DESPITE ITS REPUTATION FOR DURABILITY, *stone is surprisingly susceptible to wear and decay. In addition to the more obvious defects resulting from accidental breakages, stonework can be eaten away by atmospheric impurities caused by the coal fires and furnaces of the past or today's acid rain. Occasionally the erosion is very gradual and may be acceptable, even attractive, but when stone begins to flake, the disintegration can be rapid, and urgent treatment may be essential.*

In most cases, especially when you are dealing with carved stonework or ashlar, professional skills are required to produce a sound and inconspicuous repair. However, most of the better-known stone-restoration companies are used to working on public buildings, such as city halls or churches, and their fees are correspondingly high. There are both individual masons and carvers and small groups that are happy to undertake domestic commissions, but they are not always easy to find. The best way to track down suitable repairers is to contact local preservation organizations or to look at the advertisements in trade or specialist house-restoration magazines.

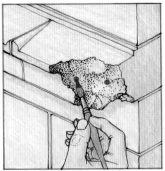

1 Mark pin positions with paint

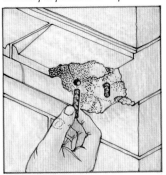

2 Insert keyed and glued pins

MECHANICAL REPAIRS

If a fragment of stone breaks away – from a carving or molded course, for example – glue it back in place with epoxy adhesive. This type of glue only begins to set once its constituents have been mixed. Low-viscosity epoxy glues are available, but most suppliers stock a standard two-part adhesive that can be thinned sufficiently by warming the tubes briefly in direct sunlight or on a radiator. Add some titanium dioxide (available from pharmacists) to the mixed adhesive to prevent a yellow glue line from showing when it sets. Large pieces of stone need to be reinforced with non-ferrous metal pins.

Regluing broken stone

Make the reinforcing pins by cutting stainless-steel or brass rod into short lengths. File notches along each pin to form keys for the glue. Mark the position of the pins on one half of the repair with small spots of paint **(1)**. Reposition the broken piece of stone to transfer the spots.

Dismantle the repair again and use a masonry drill to bore holes in each half of the repair that are slightly larger in diameter than the pins. Make a dry assembly with the pins in place to insure that the joint fits snugly.

Scrub the mating surfaces with mineral spirits, then glue the pins into one half **(2)**. Spread a thin layer of glue on the other half and onto the projecting pins. Assemble the joint, rocking the stone slightly to squeeze out excess glue, then wipe it off immediately with a rag dampened in clear mineral spirits. If possible, bind the repair with wire, string, or self-adhesive parcel tape until the glue has set hard.

THE EFFECTS OF INCORRECT BEDDING

Sedimentary rocks, such as sandstone and limestone, are the products of materials that have been deposited in geological beds (strata) by water or wind. As a result, when cut or split blocks are laid, erosion may be exacerbated by failure on the part of the mason to allow for the effect of this bedding.

When a block of stone is laid with its strata horizontal **(1)**, the weight of subsequent masonry prevents the block from delaminating. Laying stones in this way is known as "natural bedding." It is the method that should be used in most situations.

When a stone block is face-bedded **(2)**, with the strata on edge and parallel to the face of the wall, the action of spalling tends to shear flakes from the surface – rather like shedding individual playing cards from a deck. Gradually the disintegration eats deeper and deeper into the wall till it seriously compromises the stability of the masonry.

Courses, such as cornices, that project from a wall should be constructed from edge-bedded stones **(3)** in order to prevent delamination. For the same reason, stone lintels above window and door openings should also be edge-bedded.

Even skilled stonemasons sometimes have difficulty in identifying the direction of the bedding on a newly cut block. The direction is therefore normally marked on the stone itself, either at the quarry or once the block has been sawn roughly to size.

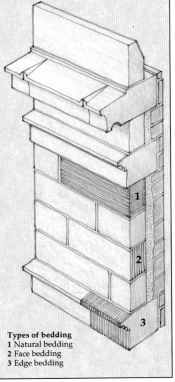

Types of bedding
1 Natural bedding
2 Face bedding
3 Edge bedding

Face-bedded stone that begins to delaminate can be consolidated by an expert

Gluing delaminating stone

It is possible to consolidate flaking face-bedded stones by injecting a thin epoxy adhesive into holes drilled through the laminations. Reinforcing pins are then introduced into the same holes. However, this is a skilled repair best left to a professional.

Indenting

Indenting is the process of replacing damaged stone with new blocks. Unless it is possible to cannibalize stone from some inconspicuous part of the same building, it is difficult even for an experienced mason to guarantee an exact match of color and texture. As a result, you may find that it is preferable to live with slightly blemished stonework rather than risk having a repair done that could prove more noticeable than the blemish itself.

One stone at a time can be cut out and replaced without propping, but if a number of adjacent blocks are affected, the surrounding masonry should be supported while the work is in progress.

An entire facing stone can be removed with a hammer and chisel, but it is in fact

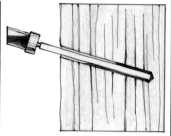

Injecting glue consolidates stone

only necessary to cut back a header by 4in (100mm) or so in order to make sufficient room for a shallow block to be mortared in place.

Unless the stonework has been face-bedded, it may be possible to dismantle an eroded section and turn the blocks around so as to expose an undamaged face.

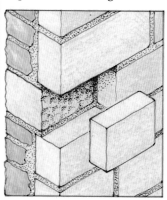

Use shallow blocks to repair headers

PLASTIC REPAIRS

Patching stonework with mortar is simpler and cheaper than having to cut out and replace damaged stones. In fact, as long ago as the early nineteenth century builders used Roman cement for such repairs. Provided that the damaged stones have a simple profile, it is possible to undertake "plastic" repairs yourself – however, since it is notoriously difficult to obtain an exact match, it pays to hire a professional mason unless the stonework is painted.

Depending on the nature and color of the original stonework, a mason will probably select fine sand or even crushed stone as the aggregate for a suitable repair mortar. Some masons include lime and cement in the mortar. Others prefer to use white Portland only, especially for sandstone. Local knowledge is essential; it therefore pays to consult an experienced architect practicing in the area. One mix often recommended is 1 part cement, 2 parts hydrated lime, and 9 parts aggregate.

Preparing the masonry

The decayed stone should be cut back by at least 1in (25mm) to sound material. Cut a regular shape with undercut edges, except for the bottom edge which should be left square **(1)**. Treat each individual stone separately, using strips of wood to form appropriate joints in the mortar until it has set (the strips are then removed and the joints repointed in the usual way).

Reinforce the repair by gluing non-ferrous pins or wire into holes drilled in the stone **(2)**. Brush off loose material and wet the stone to reduce suction.

Applying the mortar

Apply a coat of mortar $1/2$ to $3/4$in (12 to 18mm) thick and scratch the surface to provide a key. Two to four hours later, apply a second coat and smooth its surface with a wooden float. Once the top coat has begun to get firm, stipple it with a damp sponge or a bristle brush in order to expose the aggregate. When repairing cornices and other molded courses, you can use a running mold to shape them (see STUCCO MOLDINGS).

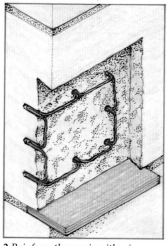

1 Cut a recess in decayed stone

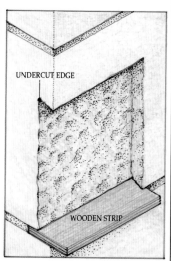

2 Reinforce the repair with wire

CHAPTER FOUR

STUCCO

ONCE USED TO DESCRIBE PLASTERWORK in general, the term "stucco" owes its origin to Italian plasterers, or stuccatori, who introduced the craft to northern Europe. Nowadays, it is normally used to distinguish external cement finishes from internal plasterwork.

The primary function of stucco was to weatherproof the exterior walls of a house. It was also useful for hiding indifferent brickwork. However, its undisputed popularity in the late eighteenth and nineteenth centuries stemmed from the fact that stucco could be used as a cheap yet convincing substitute for stone facings – the façade of a house being coated with stucco incised to look like stone blocks or molded in imitation of carved stonework. Although the illusion was frequently reinforced by painting stucco to resemble nicely weathered masonry, there was also considerable competition to produce stuccos that would dry naturally to match the colors of familiar building stones. Stucco was to remain popular through to the Colonial Revival era.

Toward the end of the nineteenth century an earlier type of stucco, chiefly associated with rural buildings, was to become fashionable – especially in the form of coarsely textured wall panels between the timbers of mock-Tudor houses. Known as roughcast, the top coat of this material is mixed with a high percentage of gravel.

Pebble-dash is similar in composition, but a dry aggregate is thrown onto the wet surface so that it remains exposed. The unfortunate use of pebble-dash to obliterate earlier Victorian brickwork has given it a bad reputation, but when used appropriately it can be an attractive finish.

Painted stucco contrasts with brick

Plain-stuccoed porch

Fully stuccoed early-C19th house with rusticated ground floor

Unpainted stucco with white details

Freely applied Californian stucco

PLAIN STUCCO

APPLYING STUCCO *involves the same basic techniques that are employed for plastering interior walls. A plasterer's steel trowel is used for applying the material, but the characteristic sandy texture of stucco is achieved by smoothing the surface with a wooden float.*

Although extensive stuccoing is a job for a professional, any reasonably competent amateur can patch holes and repair cracks in stucco. However, it is not easy to disguise a patch repair unless you intend to repaint the entire wall.

FILLING CRACKS
Rake out large cracks with a cold chisel, undercutting the edges where possible. (If you discover that the brickwork behind is cracked too, seek professional advice.) Clean out loose debris with a stiff-bristle brush, then wet the crack and fill it flush with cement mortar, as described below. Apply a layer of concrete bonding agent first.

PATCHING HOLES
If you neglect to repair cracked stucco, rainwater gradually penetrates and soaks the wall behind. Being unable to dry out efficiently, the masonry retains moisture which tends to expand at freezing temperatures, causing patches of weak stucco to separate from the wall.

Preparing the wall
Tap the wall in the vicinity of obvious damage with a wooden mallet, listening for the hollow sound that indicates loose stucco.

Use a bolster chisel and a heavy hammer to hack off loose stucco. Cut the edges straight, to avoid a patchy appearance, and try to align them with features of the building that will disguise joints between old and new stucco. Undercut all but the bottom edge, which should be left square. Rake out the mortar joints between bricks to a depth of about 5/8in (16mm), then brush all loose material from the wall.

Applying the stucco
Thoroughly wet the area that is to be patched and use a plasterer's trowel to apply the first layer of stucco. Sweep the render onto the wall with upward strokes of the trowel, using fairly firm pressure **(1)**, then smooth it out to a depth of between 3/8 and 1/2in (10 and 12mm). As the stucco begins to set firm, scarify the surface to form a key for the next coat and leave it till the following day to set.

Depending on the thickness of the original stucco, repeat the procedure – adding a second layer of stucco approximately 3/8in (10mm) thick – before applying a 1/4in (6mm) finishing coat.

Before you trowel on the finishing coat, wet the keyed surface of the previous layer. Use a wooden straightedge to scrape the stucco flush **(2)**, working with a zigzag action from the bottom upward, then fill any low spots with fresh stucco.

Finally, smooth the finishing coat with a wooden float, using circular and figure-of-eight strokes.

INGREDIENTS OF STUCCO
Before the latter part of the eighteenth century exterior stuccoing was carried out with a mixture of lime and sand that set slowly, drying out over a period of days while the lime absorbed carbon dioxide from the atmosphere. Binders, such as a combination of eggs, milk, and grated cheese, were sometimes added when moldings were required in stucco, but the demands for a faster-setting stucco led to experiments aimed at developing a more durable and water-resistant cement.

These developments culminated with the patenting, in England in 1824, of Portland cement. Cement sets by a chemical reaction that begins as soon as it is mixed with water. As a result, stucco containing cement sets hard in hours and continues to gain strength over a period of weeks, making it possible to create elaborate imitations of stone facings.

For general restoration purposes use a cement-lime-sand mix for the first two layers mixed in the proportions 1:1:6, then finish with a slightly weaker mix of 1:2:9 for the top coat. In most circumstances ordinary Portland cement is ideal, especially if the render is to be painted – but you may need to use either white or colored Portland cement to match an unpainted stucco. Hydrated (preslaked) lime is available from builders' suppliers as a dry powder. Use plasterer's sharp sand to give bulk to the mixture.

Well-mixed stucco retains ridges

Mixing cement stucco
The simplest way to make cement stucco is to add the lime to the cement powder first, then thoroughly mix all the dry ingredients. Form a well in the center of the pile and pour in some water. Shovel the dry ingredients from around the edges of the well into the water until it has been absorbed, then gradually turn the mixture over until the consistency is even. If necessary, add water till the stucco retains marks left by the shovel without slumping or crumbling.

Wear a face mask, goggles, and gloves, when handling hydrated lime.

1 Trowel on first layer of stucco

2 Scrape level with a straightedge

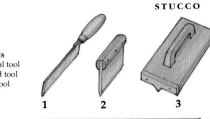

1   2   3

Late-Victorian roughcast

PATCHING PEBBLE-DASH AND ROUGHCAST

The method for patching a hole in a pebble-dash wall is the same as for plain stucco – but while the top coat is still soft, pick up some 1/4in (6mm) washed pebbles on the toe of your plasterer's trowel and flick them onto the stucco **(1)**. Spread a dust-sheet at the foot of the wall to catch fallen pebbles. When you have filled the patch evenly, tap the pebbles lightly with a float to bed them into the stucco **(2)**.

When patching roughcast, mix equal parts of sand and 1/4in (6mm) crushed-stone aggregate into the top-coat stucco, using slightly more water than normal. Soak the keyed undercoat and flick the roughcast mixture onto it, covering the patched area evenly so as to match the surrounding wall.

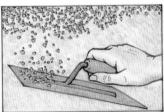

1 Flinging pebbles with a trowel

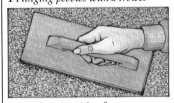

2 Bed them in with a float

RUSTICATION

ON CLOSER EXAMINATION, *what appear to be ashlar (dressed stone) blocks making up the ground floor of a nineteenth century house often prove to be nothing more than an illusion created by a plasterer drawing a tool through wet stucco in an attempt to disguise less impressive brickwork.*

The horizontal and vertical joints of closely fitting ashlar blocks are frequently represented in the stucco-work of the period. Alternatively, pronounced grooves are incised – often as banded rustication, which does not include vertical joints. When executed by a skilled plasterer, it is difficult to distinguish rusticated stucco from genuine stonework unless part of the stucco has broken away to reveal a telltale brick background.

VERMICULATION

Some plasterers went to even greater lengths to deceive the eye by reproducing vermiculation – a deep irregular texture, similar in appearance to worm tracks, which was a traditional stonemason's surface dressing. Vermiculation was most commonly used to decorate door or window surrounds and to create fake quoins on the corners of buildings.

Half-stuccoed late-Georgian houses with banded rustication

RE-CREATING VERMICULATION

If you are sufficiently skilled, it is possible to cut vermiculation by hand in wet stucco, using modeling tools or old chisels. However, it is easier to take an impression from an identical "stone" and to cast vermiculated blocks in sand-and-cement stucco (see CASTING VERMICULATION).

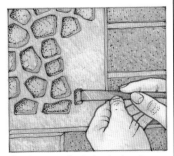

Cutting vermiculation by hand

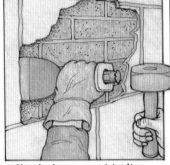

1 Chop back to nearest joint lines

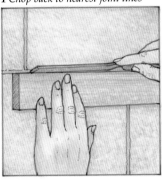

2 Rule lines with a jointing tool

RESTORING RUSTICATION

Square-cut ashlar rustication was created by marking stucco with a steel jointing tool, but there's no need to buy special tools. You can make a jointing tool of your own from wood; and to re-create deep V-grooves you can screw an improvised wooden template to the end of a float.

Use a bolster chisel and a hammer to cut loose rusticated stucco back to the nearest joint lines in sound stucco **(1)**. Fill flush with fresh stucco and finish the surface with a wooden float.

Using a straight batten as a guide, slowly draw a jointing tool through the stucco **(2)**. For the time being leave any specks of stucco that are dragged out onto the surface, then carefully rub them off with a float when the stucco begins to harden.

STUCCO MOLDINGS

STUCCO REALLY COMES INTO ITS OWN *when it is used to simulate the moldings and other enrichments associated with carved stonework. The façades of some Georgian houses were covered with ornamental stucco, whereas the Victorians tended to favor the contrast of brickwork with stucco details.*

Classically inspired stucco cornice and string course

Decorative molding and pediment

Stucco architrave with keystone

RESTORING MOLDINGS

Classically inspired cornice moldings running just below the parapet of a house or near the top of a porch are designed to shed water clear of the face of the wall. Their top surfaces are therefore sloped to insure that rainwater drains away from the masonry. Similar, though smaller, moldings known as string courses are used to provide horizontal emphasis and improve the visual proportions of a façade. Architraves in stucco often surround window openings, and many a doorway is flanked with stucco pilasters.

Moldings were either fabricated directly on the wall or cast on a bench then fixed to the building once they had set. As with internal plasterwork, stucco moldings frequently include beds for accommodating separately molded decorative features.

RUNNING MOLDINGS ON THE WALL

It is normally easier to work on a horizontal bench than on the vertical surface of a wall. However, there are times when it makes more sense to repair moldings *in situ* – for example, when a molding is built around an integral support of brick or tile corbeling (1), or only a short section of a long molding is damaged, or a molding is simply too large to be lifted into place.

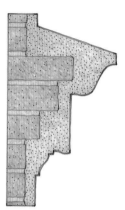
1 Brick-corbeling reinforcement

The running mold

A stucco molding is shaped by using a metal template screwed to a running mold. This is made in a similar way to the molds used for making interior plaster cornices (see RUNNING A PLAIN CORNICE). Wooden battens, known as rules, are nailed to the masonry to guide the running mold (2).

2 Running mold with fixed rules

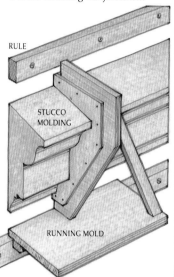

RULE

STUCCO MOLDING

RULE   RUNNING MOLD

EMPLOYING PROFESSIONALS

You should seriously consider whether it is worth attempting to restore stucco moldings yourself or whether it would be wiser to employ a professional plasterer. Considerable skill is required to restore some moldings, especially those that have to be run *in situ*, and there are inherent risks in working at the height at which some of these features are located. Expensive scaffolding is required to provide a safe working platform for the duration of the work, and as you are likely to take longer to complete the job than a skilled professional the saving on scaffold rent makes at least some contribution toward the cost of paying a plasterer.

However, there is a degree of satisfaction in restoring one's own house that cannot be measured in financial terms – and provided that you can reach damaged stucco from a low platform constructed from rented slot-together scaffold frames, there is no practical reason why you shouldn't tackle the work yourself.

Fabricating a molding

Every professional plasterer has a favorite recipe for the stucco he or she likes to use for moldings. Some add lime to the mixture, others prefer to use a modern plasticizer. However, a mixture of 1 part Portland cement, 1 part hydrated lime and 2½ parts stucco sand is generally suitable.

After the masonry background has been dampened, the approximate shape of the molding is built in stucco. A professional plasterer would use a gauging trowel – a tool shaped like a bricklayer's trowel but with a round-tip blade. However, a pointing trowel can be used instead. The running mold is then slid along the rules, scraping the stucco to create the profile of the finished molding (1). Any slight blemishes are smoothed out with a wooden float. All miters and returns must be shaped by hand as the work progresses.

Deep moldings are built up gradually in layers approximately ½in (12mm) thick by making several runs with smaller templates in advance of running the finished-profile template. Several templates of increasing size may be needed in order to build a large molding.

Each layer is scratched to provide a key for the next (which is normally applied about 24 hours later), the keyed surface having first been dampened with water.

Some plasterers prefer to apply a subsequent coat while the previous one is slightly wet – when it's still "green." This is possible if you make one run early in the morning and a second run sometime after lunch.

Creating a stonelike texture

To create a stucco molding with a convincing stonelike texture, mix roughly equal proportions of dry sand and cement together – then while the finished molding is still wet, flick the dry mixture onto the surface of the stucco with a plasterer's trowel.

When you see the mixture change color as it absorbs moisture from the molding, make one final pass with the running mold.

Including reinforcement

Repairs to deep moldings are sometimes reinforced with metal rod and wire bent into a suitable armature (2). Choose non-ferrous metal and use an epoxy adhesive to glue the rods into holes drilled in the masonry. Before gluing them, file the ends of the reinforcement rods in order to provide a key for the adhesive.

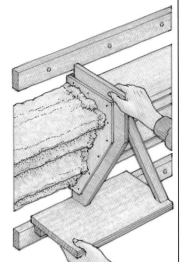

1 Slide the running mold sideways

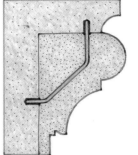

2 Bent-metal reinforcement

MAKING MOLDINGS ON A BENCH

The alternative method for making moldings was to cast them on site then apply them to the walls. The same procedure can be used when replacing damaged sections or to re-create entire cornices or other moldings. When installing replacement moldings, it pays to attach them to the wall with strong fixings such as expanding-anchor screws.

Making a reverse mold.

A replacement molding is cast in a reverse mold (1) run in plaster of Paris (see RUNNING A PLAIN CORNICE).

Traditionally, once the plaster of Paris has set, the reverse mold is sealed with three coats of shellac.

However, to produce a casting with a better surface finish, seal the mold with a coat of bonding agent then paint a film of cooking oil over it. If the bonding agent should stick to the stucco, it will peel off easily, due to the presence of the oil, without harming the surface of the casting.

Casting the molding

Make a semi-dry mixture of 1 part cement and 3 parts sand. Add just enough water for a ball of stucco squeezed in your hand to retain the impression of your fingers.

Evenly cover the inside of the mold with stucco to a depth of about 1in (25mm), then use a piece of wood to tamp it into all the crevices. Lay longitudinal reinforcement in the mold (such as galvanized-metal rods or expanded-metal lath), then fill the mold with more well-tamped stucco.

Push lengths of wooden dowel through the stucco to form clearance holes for fasteners (2). Next day, lift the casting out of the mold and leave it on the bench for 48 hours or so to harden. Spray it with water from time to time to prevent cracking.

Installing the molding

You will probably need at least one assistant when installing a stucco molding. It also helps if you nail a wooden batten to the wall to support the molding (3).

Countersink the clearance holes, then drill through them into the wall. Insert and tighten the fasteners before removing the batten.

Depending on the style of stuccowork, either stucco to the molding or fill gaps between the molding and the wall with a mortar paste. Also, cover the screwheads with mortar.

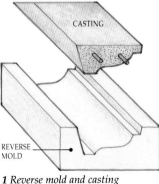

1 Reverse mold and casting

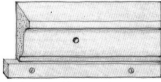

2 Make clearance holes for fixings

3 Support molding on a batten

CASTING ORNAMENTS IN STUCCO

BROKEN OR MISSING CONSOLES, *scrolls, and other ornaments cast in stucco can be reproduced by taking an "impression" from an original that is still intact. A flexible mold made from cold-cure silicone rubber is normally used, but it is possible to reproduce simple textures such as vermiculation using plaster of Paris alone.*

Decorative painted-stucco gable

Ornamental lintel in painted stucco

USING A FLEXIBLE MOLD

Brush loose dust off the original ornament and spray it with the release agent supplied. Mix the silicone rubber following the manufacturer's directions, including if possible an additive that enables the material to cling to vertical surfaces without slumping. Build a 1/8in (3mm) layer of silicone rubber, embed a light scrim and add a further layer of rubber about 1/8in to 1/4in (3 to 6 mm) thick. Leave it to set for 12 hours or so.

An unsupported silicone-rubber mold is often too flexible and tends to distort when filled with stucco. Consequently, you usually need to apply a fairly thick layer of reinforced plaster of Paris to the outside of the flexible mold while it is still in place. Remove the plaster backing once it has set hard, then peel the flexible mold off the wall.

Making the casting

Reunite the flexible mold with its plaster backing and lay them on a workbench. Brush a fairly liquid mixture of 1 part cement to 3 parts sand onto the inside face of the mold, then fill it to the brim with more stucco.

Heavy castings may need reinforcing with expanded metal, and they should be attached to the wall with screws or expanding bolts. Disguise the screw or bolt heads with mortar.

Classical Revival-style pilasters with ornate capitals

CASTING VERMICULATION

To re-create vermiculation, first brush the original clean then paint it with cooking oil to facilitate the release of the mold. Coat the stone with a 1 1/4in (30mm) layer of plaster of Paris, including some scrim to reinforce it. When the plaster has set, ease the mold off the wall and lay it flat on a bench. Coat the inside of the mold with the oil.

Half-fill the mold with stucco. Then place a strip of expanded metal lath on top and cover with more stucco, filling the mold to the brim. Leave the stucco to set hard, then remove the casting and screw it to the wall. Finally, fill the edges and cover the screwheads with mortar.

Impeccably restored vermiculated arches and dentil cornice

PAINTING STUCCO

Traditionally, stucco was painted with limewash (a paint made from slaked lime, linseed oil, and colored pigments). Limewash is still used, not purely for the sake of authenticity but also because it allows damp masonry to breathe. It is possible to make your own limewash, but it is easier to buy it ready-made from a specialist paint supplier.

Providing the building has an efficient damp-proof course, good-quality modern masonry paints are often recommended, especially for Victorian and later houses.

A variety of historically appropriate colors are now commercially available.

48

CHAPTER FIVE

WOOD SIDING

WOOD-FRAME HOUSES are among the earliest buildings still standing. The familiar clapboarded and shingled wooden houses are more common in the United States, but the earliest wooden houses on these shores featured the half-timbered style transplanted from England, with its exposed framing infilled with bricks or a mix of mud and sticks ("wattle and daub"). As the more demanding climate in North America took its continuing toll, building practices changed, and shingles and clapboards replaced the infills that were rapidly broken down by the cycles of freezing and thawing.

Fire risk and the climate led to a gradual decline in the use of clapboards and shingles in Britain, except for decorative purposes such as siding gable ends and bay windows. In America, however, where wood has always been plentiful, wooden wall sidings transposed from Europe by the early colonists were enthusiastically adopted for grand and humble houses alike. Clapboards tended to remain a functional though attractive means of insulating a house from the elements, but shingle siding developed into something of a folk art form. Various textures were created by juxtaposing plain shingles, but their impact was negligible compared with the seemingly limitless decorative possibilities afforded by the shaped shingles that became available in America from the mid nineteenth century.

An early clapboarded house that has been maintained in perfect condition

Simple but pleasing textures can be created from standard cedar shingles

CLAPBOARDS

Clapboarding *is essentially a means of sealing a house effectively against the weather – and perhaps it is this honest "no-frills" appearance, with its neat horizontal shadow lines, that we find so appealing. There are plenty of examples of houses clad from eaves to ground level with clapboard siding; but another common practice in certain areas was to use wood siding for the second floor only, which was supported by a lower story of brick or stone, and siding is sometimes nailed to battens to protect substandard brickwork. This combination of painted wooden clapboards and natural-colored masonry is particularly handsome.*

Since the earliest times, softwoods such as white pine, hemlock, and spruce were used for clapboarding. It was not until the turn of the century that red cedar, perhaps today's most fashionable wood for exterior siding, became widely available.

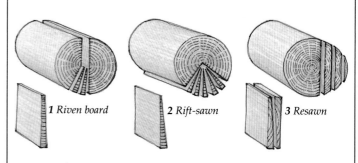

1 Riven board   *2 Rift-sawn*   *3 Resawn*

CLAPBOARD PROFILES

The earliest clapboards were beveled planks, which were riven from logs like slicing a cake. The result was a more-or-less symmetrical feather-edged board **(1)** with the grain running directly across its thickness. By the late nineteenth century similar boards were being produced by machine. Turned logs, suspended above a circular saw, were rotated fractionally between cuts, producing rift-sawn boards **(2)**. Due to the orientation of the grain, riven and rift-sawn boards are relatively stable and are rarely susceptible to the splitting and warping that often result from shrinkage. Riven boards were seldom more than 4in about (100mm) in width. Much wider boards were cut by machine. Rift-sawn boards were typically 5 to 6in (125 to 150mm) wide, but widths of 9in (225mm) or more were possible.

Another method for producing feather-edged clapboards was to saw logs into thick planks, which in turn were resawn to make two beveled boards **(3)**. The grain direction varies with this type of clapboard, and the worst effects of shrinkage are common.

Riven and sawn boards were usually planed on one face. At the same time, some clapboards were machined with a molding along their bottom edges **(4)**.

Rebated shiplap boarding **(5)** has been popular since the late nineteenth century. Tongue-and-groove boards **(6)**, used since the 1920s, were often machined with a profile that made a wide board look like two narrower ones, thus halving the time it took to side a house.

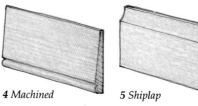

4 Machined   *5 Shiplap*   *6 T & G board*

C18th clapboarded house in the Georgian style

Typical British combination of painted clapboards and red bricks

NAILS FOR CLAPBOARDING

In the eighteenth century, clapboards were fixed in place with handmade iron nails which had large raised heads. Although most iron nails will have rusted away by now, it is usually preferable when replacing clapboards to use reproduction rose-head nails with their characteristic heads that stand out from the siding's surface. However, it is generally more practical to use modern galvanized nails for repairs, or other non-ferrous nails that will not corrode. Ring-shank nails with their superior grip are good for fixing clapboarding, too.

FIXING CLAPBOARDS

There is some debate about the best way to fix clapboarding. Traditionalists follow the time-honored method, whereas others favor an approach that is designed to cope with the vagaries of modern mass-produced clapboards.

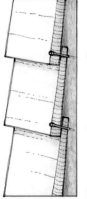
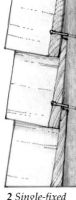

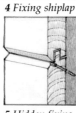

4 Fixing shiplap

1 Double-fixed   *2 Single-fixed*   *3 Blind-nailed*   *5 Hidden fixing*

CORNERS AND EDGE DETAILS

In theory it is possible to miter the ends of clapboards where they meet at a corner, but such detailing requires skillful carpentry. And even when boards are fitted perfectly the joints are likely to open up in time, which is not only unsightly but exposes the vulnerable end grain to wet rot.

Corner boards

The most common method of finishing the siding both at internal and external corners is to butt the ends of the clapboards against a vertical wooden corner board nailed to the underlying framework. An internal-corner board is simply a square board **(1)**. Two strips of wood are nailed together at right angles to cap an external corner **(2)**.

Nailing procedures

Feather-edged boards overlap by about 1 to 1½in (25 to 38mm). Traditionally, nails were driven right through the overlap, pinning both boards to the framework **(1)**. Because riven and rift-sawn boards tend to shrink and swell across their thickness only, fixing them rigidly in this manner leads to few problems.

The modern practice is to hammer each nail through one board only, just missing the board below **(2)**. This permits the boards to move unrestrictedly and prevents splitting if the timber shrinks across its width. However, even some professional installers are of the opinion that driving nails in this way is likely to cause a board to cup (bend across its width), which is in itself sufficient to promote a split.

With "blind nailing" each board is nailed along the top edge only so that the overlap hides the fixings **(3)**. This method has the advantage of being neat in appearance, but there's nothing to stop the lower edges of the clapboards bowing or twisting.

It is normal to fix shiplap siding with a single row of nails for each board **(4)**. Hidden fixings are more usual when nailing tongue-and-groove boards **(5)**.

Drip moldings

Some early clapboard houses have siding running right down to the ground – an unsatisfactory solution that inevitably leads to rotting timber. The clapboarding on later houses, which were normally built on masonry foundations, begins just above the ground with some kind of drip molding to shed rainwater. This may be nothing more than a wooden starter strip nailed under the first clapboard to hold the bottom edge away from the wall **(3)**, but better-quality houses often have purpose-made drip moldings **(4)**.

Fascia boards

At the eaves, the siding is lapped by a flat fascia board. Occasionally, the top clapboard is tucked into a rebate planed along the bottom edge of the fascia board.

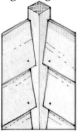
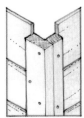

1 Internal

2 External

Clapboards bent around a corner

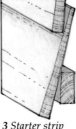

3 Starter strip

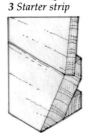

4 Watertable

Drip molding fixed above windows

Fascia boards lap painted siding

REPAIRING CLAPBOARDS

EXPERIENCE HAS PROVED *that provided a wood-sided house is maintained regularly it can last for centuries. What is perhaps even more encouraging is the fact that few if any of the repairs that may be necessary are beyond the skills of any reasonably competent carpenter. The repairs described below refer mainly to beveled clapboarding, but you can adapt the techniques for other varieties of horizontal wooden siding.*

ROUTINE MAINTENANCE

You will find that it pays to inspect clapboarding annually and also after prolonged periods of high winds or storms. If you can spot potential problems early enough, they need never develop into costly or time-consuming repairs.

Old iron nails are bound to corrode, until eventually they are too weak to hold the clapboards securely. Look out for loose boards and tap back and renail any that have dropped before the wind does further damage. Check to see if it is time to recaulk around window and door frames and along the butt joints between clapboards and corner boards. If need be, apply fresh caulk to keep out rainwater.

REPLACING A ROTTED SECTION

The end grain of any piece of timber is particularly prone to wet rot. As a result, it is quite common to find that an otherwise sound length of clapboard has rotted at one end. Rather than discard a perfectly serviceable piece of siding, replace the rotten section only with new wood.

Pry up the bottom edge of the board above the one that has rotted, then make a sawcut over the nearest stud so you can remove the rotten section (1). Keep the saw upright and make the last few strokes with the point of the blade only, in order to avoid damaging the board below.

Use a chisel to split out the decayed wood (2), which you can remove piece by piece. Don't drive the chisel too deep or you will tear the building paper that usually lies beneath the siding.

A strip of wood still held by the nails under the edge of the clapboard above is now all that remains of the rotted section. Slide a hacksaw blade up behind the board to cut through the nails, then pry out this last piece of wood. If necessary, patch any building paper that is torn. Next, cut a new

1 Open split and apply adhesive

2 Clamp glued split with nailed block

REPAIRING SPLIT BOARDS

A crack running along the centre of a clapboard can be caulked or filled to prevent water getting in behind the siding, but if a split occurs near the end of a board it is best to repair it with glue. Prise the split apart carefully (1) and apply an exterior wood glue to the exposed edge. To clamp the split together, temporarily nail a

piece of clapboard to length. Treat both sides of the board with a primer sealer (coating the end grain thoroughly) before you tap the new piece into place, using a block of wood to protect the edge (3). Since you will have to nail very close to the ends of the new piece of clapboard, drill pilot holes first in order to insure that you don't split the wood. If the rest of the siding is fixed with hidden nails, drive the new fixings just below the surface and cover their heads with either exterior wood filler or putty before you paint the timber.

block of wood against the underside of the damaged clapboard (2). You may have to slip a hacksaw blade up behind the board to cut the nails so that the section below is free to move. Wipe excess glue from the surface of the siding. Then, once the glue has set, remove the block and if necessary renail the repaired board.

PAINTING CLAPBOARD

If you fail to paint a wood-sided house regularly, sooner or later you will be faced with serious deterioration.

Siding that has been thickly overpainted can be stripped with chemicals (see STRIPPING DOORS), although you may be tempted to hire a professional to tackle a large job. Alternatively, this could be the one situation where it pays to use a blow torch, though you may be able to do much of the work with an electric hot-air gun.

Fortunately, when exterior paint deteriorates it tends to dry out and flake, so all you need do is scrape it off and rub down the woodwork with sandpaper. Areas of sound paintwork may simply need washing down with a solution of household cleaner.

After sealing bare timber with a wood primer, apply two coats of good-quality exterior paint to all surfaces.

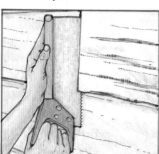

1 Cut off rotted section of clapboard

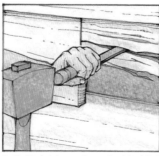

2 Split out decayed wood with chisel

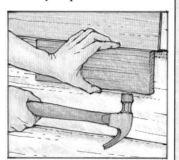

3 Tap new clapboard in place

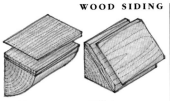

1 *Rift-sawn* **2** *Flat-sawn*

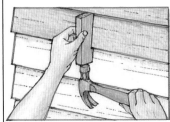

Keep overlap constant with a spacer

REPLACING SEVERAL BOARDS

If there are several rotten or split clapboards together in one area, it is probably better to replace complete boards rather than finish up with a patchwork of short pieces. If perhaps a quarter of the boards are suspect, it may be time to reside the wall or even the entire house.

Complete residing will give you the opportunity to install thermal insulation between the studs, which may be some consolation for the cost and labor involved. Choose rolls or batts of insulating material with an integral vapor barrier. The insulation should fit snugly between the studs, and the vapor barrier should face the interior of the house.

At the same time, you can paint the underlying framework with a primer sealer and install new building paper.

To remove several boards, pry up the first sound clapboard above a damaged section and cut through the nails with a hacksaw blade. Now lever up each damaged board, using a bolster chisel and hammer, and remove it. Pull out all remaining nails with a claw hammer.

Treat new clapboards with a primer sealer before installing them by tapping each one under the edge of the board above, using a wood-block spacer to keep the overlap constant. Fix each board with nails as the work progresses. If need be, join lengths of board by butting their ends together over a stud. Stagger joints in adjacent courses.

SHINGLES

SHINGLES *are rectangular and tapered, and nowadays are usually sawn from the log. Originally all shingles were split by hand, using a tool called a froe, but in recent times riven shingles have become known as shakes.*

TEXTURES AND PATTERNS

Provided that the installer is reasonably competent, it is practically impossible to construct an unattractive shingled wall. The subtlety of texture and color of the wood as it matures naturally to muted grays is in itself appealing, but particularly in America craftsmen and builders delighted in exploiting the decorative potential of shingling to the full. Thanks to the advances in woodworking machinery brought about by the Industrial Revolution, in Victorian times it became possible to manufacture decorative shingles on an economic scale. As a result, the character of shingling altered radically. Fashionable houses soon became a riot of pattern as builders competed with one another to conceive ever more ingenious and imaginative compositions, using the extensive range of fancy shingles offered for sale.

HOW SHINGLES ARE MANUFACTURED

The best-quality shingles are rift-sawn **(1)** so that the grain of the wood runs more or less across their thickness. Although flat-sawn shingles **(2)** are cheaper to produce, they are more susceptible to splitting and warping.

A minimum of 1ft 4in (400mm) in length, shingles are cut to random widths and taper from 3/8in (10mm) at their thickest or "butt" end to about 1/8in (3mm) at the other. Nowadays cedar is the timber normally employed for shingle production (or occasionally pine), but oak and elm were also used for shingles in the past.

Old shingles mellow to a pleasant muted gray

Fancy painted shingles are used to side this upper story

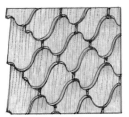
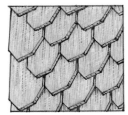
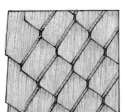

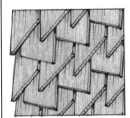

Typical decorative-shingle patterns

1 Single coursing   *2 Double coursing*   *3 Woven corner*

NAILING SHINGLES

Shingles in Britain were nailed to horizontal battens fixed to masonry or across the studs of a wood-frame house. Building paper is usually sandwiched between the battens and the background. Similarly, American shingles are sometimes fixed to battens, but in America due to the abundance of cheap wood a wood-frame house is normally sheathed completely in planks before being covered with shingles.

Single coursing

Traditionally shingles were nailed in rows with each course overlapping the one below by about half the length of the shingles **(1)**. A gap of approximately 1/8 to 1/4in (3 to 6mm) was left between adjacent shingles to allow for expansion. In order to make the siding weatherproof, the gaps were deliberately not aligned with the ones in the course below. For the same reason, the bottom course was always two shingles thick.

Most shingles were fixed with two nails, which were concealed by the next overlapping course. Shingles more than 8in (200mm) wide usually needed a third nail for security.

Double coursing

To provide more effective weatherproofing, shingles were sometimes applied in

Shingles are ideal for a round tower

pairs – with inferior-grade shingles used to back up better-quality ones **(2)**. As a rule, the butt ends of the exposed shingles would overlap the ones underneath them by about 1/2in (12mm). Double-coursed shingling is regarded as particularly handsome because of the deep shadow lines that are cast by the extra thickness.

The additional weatherproofing afforded by double shingling meant that the overlap between the courses could be reduced. As a result, the nail heads are normally visible.

Finishing at the corners

Corner boards like those used for clapboarding were fixed to shingled houses, too. Otherwise, the shingles were "woven" by lapping the courses alternately at the corners of the building **(3)**.

REPLACING SHINGLES

ONE OF THE ADVANTAGES *of shingle siding is the fact that individual shingles can be replaced without having to disturb neighboring ones. Consequently, provided you don't allow the siding to deteriorate needlessly, shingle maintenance is not the tiresome chore it might be.*

Unless they are painted, it can be difficult to match the color of weathered shingles. It therefore often pays to replace damaged shingles on the front of the house with ones taken from part of the building where new shingles will be less noticeable.

REPLACING INDIVIDUAL SHINGLES

From time to time you may find that perfectly sound shingles have dropped out of alignment because the nails that once held them have corroded away. These shingles can be tapped back into place and refixed with galvanized nails.

You will need to replace any shingles that have split lengthwise, and may well have to cut through the nails that are still holding the two halves in place. Because these fixings are very often inaccessible, you need to use a tool known as a shingle puller or slater's ripper, which releases nails holding damaged roof slates. You are unlikely to find a shingle puller in the average hard-

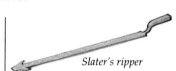

Slater's ripper

ware store, but they are still sold by good tool suppliers, some of which do business primarily by mail.

The puller has a long flat blade with two sharp hooks at the tip. Pass the blade up between the shingles, locate one of the hooks over the appropriate nail, and sever it by giving the handle of the tool a sharp blow with a hammer **(1)**. Pull the pieces of split shingle from beneath the overlapping course. If necessary, plane the replacement shingle to fit between its neighbors **(2)**. Tuck it under the course above and face-nail it securely.

1 Strike puller with a hammer

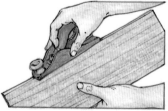

2 Plane a replacement shingle to fit

REPLACING A ROW OF SHINGLES

When a number of adjacent shingles have to be replaced, remove them using the method already described, then sort the replacements to make sure that the joints between them will not align with the ones in the course above.

Temporarily nail a guide batten to the wall to help you to align the butts of the new shingles – or, alternatively, stretch a length of string between a pair of nails.

CHAPTER SIX

ROOF COVERINGS

I N THE DAYS OF RUDIMENTARY TRANSPORTATION, most building supplies except portable finish materials like hardware and glass were likely to have a distinctly local character. Only a few coastal cities with busy ports could boast materials from abroad or other regions. The average householder had to wait for the arrival of the railroad to use, for example, slate on his roof. With the spread of cheaper machine-made materials following the Industrial Revolution and the growth of the railroads, goods from other regions became more common during the course of the nineteenth century.

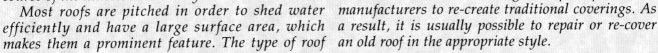

Most roofs are pitched in order to shed water efficiently and have a large surface area, which makes them a prominent feature. The type of roof covering is therefore important to the character of the building. Like brickwork, most roof coverings are made up from small units that together form an aesthetically pleasing pattern. Roof coverings have a naturally attractive quality of color and texture, which like other building materials, mellow with age to enhance the appearance of a house.

Roofs require sympathetic maintenance to preserve their original character. Original materials for repair work can be acquired from architectural-salvage companies. Also, the resurgence of interest in old buildings has prompted some manufacturers to re-create traditional coverings. As a result, it is usually possible to repair or re-cover an old roof in the appropriate style.

Decorative C19th mansard roof

An impressive 1920s hipped and gabled plain-tiled roof

Plain-tiled roof with dormer window

Slate roofing harmonizes with stone and stuccoed walls

Gable roof with tile-hung walls

TYPES OF ROOF

T HE FUNCTION OF THE ROOF *is to shelter the fabric and contents of a building from the weather. The shape of the roof and the type of surface material used are usually the result of both local historical precedent and changing tastes in a given era.*

ROOF SHAPES
The shape of a roof is important not only to its function but also to the architectural style of the house. A flat roof affords good shelter from wind and sun, but is not very efficient for shedding rain. Pitched roofs are more common, as they are better able to withstand rain or snow. The pitch can vary considerably, depending on the type of covering used and the complexity of the roof shape.

The simplest form of pitched roof is the single-pitched type, but the most common in most regions is the gable roof. Hipped roofs, which are a variant of the latter, have one or both ends pitched as well as the front and rear slopes. Various combinations of these two types are frequently used.

The Mansard roof, which originated in France, is a variation of the pitched roof incorporating two angles on each side in order to create a greater volume of habitable space within the roof area.

Conical, hexagonal, pyramidal, or octagonal roofs are all used for capping decorative turrets. Some pitched roofs have dormers, projecting structures that usually include a window to allow light into the attic space.

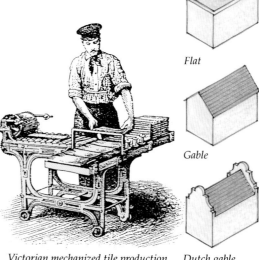
Victorian mechanized tile production

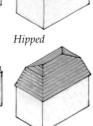
Flat   *Single-pitch*

Gable   *Hipped*

Dutch gable   *Mansard*

Decorative slate-covered tower

Functional needs
The design of a roof must take into account the exposure of the site, the architectural style of the building, and the loading on the structure. The roof load is not restricted to the static load of the covering alone. Wind forces apply pressure on the windward side and suction on the lee side, so adequate covering and fasteners are important. Weight of snow may need to be taken into account, and thermal movement caused by extremes of temperature in different seasons. The fire resistance of the covering has to be considered, too.

When it comes to repairing or renewing an existing roof, most of these factors will already have been established by the original design and the performance of the roofing materials over the years. However, if you are planning modifications or a change of roof covering, then it is best to obtain advice from an experienced roofing specialist and it may be necessary to seek approval from your local building department. While maintenance and non-structural repair work on an old roof are not usually restricted, a new roof or major alterations have to comply with building regulations and may require planning approval.

Components of a pitched roof
The terminology that is used to describe the individual parts of a roof can become quite complex when different elements are combined in its construction. The principal terms used in the roofing trade are illustrated here.

ASSESSING REPAIRS
● Easy even for beginners.
■ Fairly difficult. Good practical skills required.
▲ Difficult. Hire a professional.

Tiled roofs
Tiles can fracture, spall, or fasteners can fail.
● Check the condition of the fasteners (page 60).
■ Replace damaged or dislodged tiles (page 61).

Wooden shingles
Shingles can split, fall out, or decompose.
● Keep the roof clear of debris and mosses (page 59).
■ Replace loose or damaged shingles (page 59).
■ Repair hips and ridges (page 59).

Slate roofs
Cracked or missing slates can allow water to enter.
■ Remove and replace broken slates (page 63).
▲ If nails fail, have slates in good condition stripped and relaid (page 62).

Ornamental features
Damaged or missing details mar the integrity of a roof.
■ Renail or replace loose or damaged ridge tiles (page 63).
▲ Have damaged or missing details replaced (page 63).

Metal roofing
Corrosion and thermal movement can weaken sheet-metal roofs.
● Keep the roof clear of debris and moss (page 64).
● Check condition of flashings regularly (page 64).
▲ Get a specialist to carry out repairs promptly (page 64).

Roof terminology

1 Roof covering
2 Ridge
3 Gable end
4 Verge
5 Bargeboard
6 Eaves
7 Fascia
8 Soffit
9 Hip
10 Hipped end
11 Valley
12 Stepped flashing
13 Back gutter
14 Apron
15 Dormer window
16 Flat roof
17 Parapet

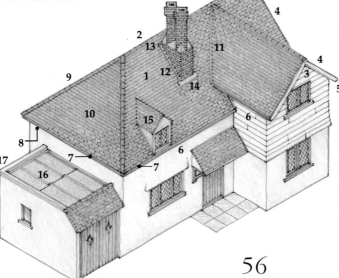

ROOF COVERINGS

Traditional roof coverings which are still in use today include clay tiles, slates, wooden shingles, metal sheeting, and, in a few places, thatch. Their durability, cost effectiveness, and fitness of purpose have been responsible for their continued use. Appearance, too, has played a part in the survival of these roof coverings.

All too often, however, a more economical but less durable substitute has been introduced, typically asphalt shingles. These shingles are inexpensive to buy and relatively easy to install, since few tools and only very basic skills are required. However, it is rare indeed that they look appropriate on a period house.

Steep-pitched plain-tiled roof c.1911 *Beautifully crafted English thatch*

Weathered terracotta pantiles complement the old stone walls

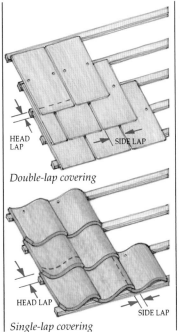

Wood-shingled gable roofs provide an interesting stepped roofline

Roof pitch

The type of covering must be suitable for the pitch of the roof, which is determined by the exposure of the site and the local weather conditions.

The pitch of tiled and slate roofs depends on the size and overlap of the individual tiles or slates. Small plain tiles or slates are typically pitched at 40 to 45 degrees, though they can be used on steeper slopes and even on vertical surfaces. Roofs with large slates or with wooden shingles or profiled single-lap tiles need a pitch of no more than 30 degrees.

Thatch needs a steep angle to shed rainwater quickly.

Flat or shallow-pitched roofs require a continuous covering, such as metal or asphalt. A recent alternative that may be suitable for certain flat roofs where the surface is not visible from below is a plastic membrane that comes in a single sheet.

Double-lap coverings

Shingles, slates, and plain tiles are known as double-lap coverings. They are laid in "broken-bond" courses – staggered so that, with a slate roof, for example, the vertical joints between slates are centered over the slates in the row below. As a result, the "head" of each slate is partly overlapped by the two courses above. In this way, the nail heads are covered and the gaps between the exposed parts of the slates are always backed up by a whole slate, thus rendering the covering waterproof.

Double-lap covering

Single-lap covering

Single-lap coverings

Single-lap roof coverings are made of specially shaped tiles. The profile of each tile is designed to overlap or interlock at the sides to stop rainwater from penetrating the vertical joints. Some are made to interlock at the head and tail in order to provide a barrier between the courses.

Each course only has to lap the one below, and in most cases the vertical joints are not staggered. Single-lap coverings are comparatively quick and economic to fit, though the material itself is expensive and, in most regions, unusual.

Single-lap coverings were traditionally made of clay, but there are also modern types made of concrete and finished in various colors.

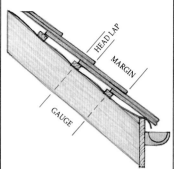

Spacing of battens determines lap

Lap and gauge

If double-lap and single-lap coverings are to perform properly, the head-lap must fall within certain limits. The minimum lap dimensions that suppliers recommend depend on the size of the unit, the pitch of the roof, and the degree of exposure.

The lap is adjusted by the spacing or "gauge" of the battens to which the roof covering is fixed. With modern materials, the maximum specified gauge is usually given in the manufacturer's literature. The exposed part of the tile or slate is called the margin and is the same dimension as the gauge.

SAFETY

- Roof work is hazardous, so every care must be taken to insure that safe working platforms are erected and barriers provided to prevent tools and materials falling or being knocked off the work area.
- For routine repair work, use a stable scaffold tower and a roof ladder – a special lightweight ladder that hooks over the ridge.
- For major work, rent full scaffolding and erect it around the perimeter of the roof. Roofing contractors will provide safe working platforms and will either put up scaffolding themselves or arrange for it to be erected by a scaffolding firm.

SHINGLED ROOFS

SHINGLES ARE WOODEN TILES *used for roof and wall coverings. Oak-shingled roofs were in use in medieval England – but, although they performed well, because of the climate and dwindling supplies of timber they were superseded by other types of roof covering. This was not the case in the United States, where shingles were introduced by early settlers and, thanks to a plentiful supply of suitable wood, have remained popular ever since.*

The proportions, detailing, and wood species used for shingling followed regional styles. White pine, oak, elm, cypress, redwood, and red cedar were all used. Shingle roof coverings were often replaced by fire-resistant materials such as clay tiles, slate, or metal roofing in urban areas, but never lost their popularity in rural ones. The latter part of the nineteenth century saw the American "Shingle style" revival, and traditional shingled roofs (and sidewalls) have remained fashionable in North America to this day.

Amazing "shingle thatch" roofing

The texture of the shingled roof is set off by the formal masonry

Moss can cause shingles to decay

WOODEN SHINGLES

Traditional wood shingles were relatively smooth and thin, and were usually cut to a taper. The length varied between 14in (355mm) and 36in (915mm), and the width between 3in (75mm) and 8in (200mm). The earliest shingles were split by hand to produce stable quarter-cut units (see WALL SIDING). Only the tougher heartwood was used, as the softer sapwood was not as weather-resistant. Each shingle was "dressed" with a drawknife or plane to create a smooth surface. This was to give them a fairly uniform section so they would fit tightly.

Mass-produced uniform shingles became available in the nineteenth century when steam-powered sawmills were introduced. Modern sawn shingles and shakes, as split shingles are now called, are still made in various woods for new roofs and refurbishment work. However, western red cedar is the most common. Both oak and red cedar are very durable and weather to an attractive silver-gray color.

Commercially available shakes are generally thicker than the traditional split shingles and, with their rustic rough surface, are inappropriate for repairing or renewing an old roof unless worked with a plane. Very often modern sawn versions are acceptable when making patch repairs to a traditional sawn-shingle roof.

1 Traditional regular courses

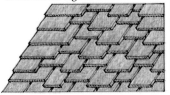

2 Staggered shingles

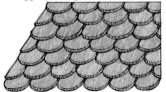

3 Fancy-butt shingles

Textures and patterns

Like slates and plain tiles, wooden shingles are a form of double-lap roof covering that requires staggered vertical joints. Most shingles are rectangular in shape, with the thick butt (bottom) end cut square. These are generally sold in bundles containing a variety of widths. The random widths give shingles laid in regular courses an interesting texture **(1)**. This is sometimes exaggerated by staggering the overlap on alternate shingles in each course **(2)**.

Fancy-butt shingles, which formed a pleasing patterned ornamental roof covering **(3)**, were also produced.

Another type of decorative treatment peculiar to North America was the "shingle thatch" covering, which was introduced in the late nineteenth century. This was a reinterpretation of the traditional thatched roof using wood shingles instead of reeds or straw thatch. The butt ends were usually cut to form a wavy edge on each course, and the shingles at the eaves, valleys, and gables were steam-bent to form a rolled contour to imitate the shape and thickness of traditional thatched roofs.

MAINTENANCE

Depending on the quality of the material, shingled roofs can last up to 40 years or more if well maintained. Inspect the condition of the covering, both inside and out, and also the flashings and guttering. Keep the roof free of debris, particularly if trees are close by.

Mosses and lichen can add an attractive quality to an old shingled roof, but they hold moisture that can cause the wood to deteriorate. A seasonal scraping and brushing down with a bristle brush should help keep the build-up under control. A dilute solution of bleach applied with a brush will kill off the spores.

Replace loose or damaged individual shingles before penetrating moisture produces more widespread problems. Roofs that require more than 20 per cent of repair work are likely candidates for replacement. This is a job for a roofing specialist with experience of installing shingled roofs.

MAKING REPAIRS

The roof details at hips, ridges, and valleys can vary according to regional styles. Before undertaking repairs or replacing a shingle roof, it is worth recording how the covering is applied, using photographs and drawings. For a satisfactory job, always use good-quality matching materials cut to the right size and apply them in the appropriate way.

Replacing a shingle

Wood reacts to weather conditions by expanding and contracting – either cupping or twisting, depending on the direction of the grain. If it is restricted by tight nailing, this natural movement can cause shingles to split.

To remove a split shingle, extract the nails holding it, using a tool sometimes called a slater's ripper (see REMOVING A BROKEN SLATE). Cut the new shingle to length and width. The width needs to allow a 1/8in (3mm) gap on each side when in position. Tap the new shingle in place until the butt is about 3/4in (18mm) from the course line. Drive in two roofing nails at 45 degrees to the face, close to the overlapping course **(1)**. Do not use copper nails for installing red cedar, as the wood can be stained and the nails degraded by a chemical reaction with the wood. For the same reason, don't use iron nails with oak.

Place a scrap-wood block against the butt and drive the shingle into place **(2)**. Or, use a metal-strip fastening (see FITTING A SLATE).

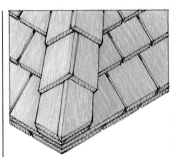

Capped hip detail

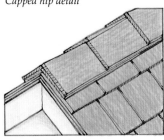

Capped ridge detail

Repairing hips and ridges

The hip and ridge details can vary on shingled roofs, but all are designed to make a weathertight covering where the sloping surfaces of the roof meet. One of the more common types is the capped hip and ridge. This consists of pairs of narrow shingles, with one of them overlapping the angled long edge of the other. The overlap alternates with each course up the hip or pair along the ridge.

If part of the covering breaks, it should be stripped out and replaced. Cut a shingle to width and plane the long edge to the required angle. It will not be possible to fix the new part with hidden nails as originally, so apply a bed of caulk at the nailing points. Fit the new piece, and nail in place through the face.

1 Drive in two roofing nails

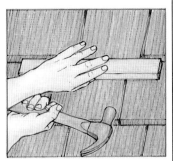

2 Hammer the shingle into place

Fit and nail new shingle in place

TILED ROOFS

CLAY TILES, *which have been in use for centuries, had their origins in the great civilizations of the East and the Mediterranean. The latter had the greater influence in the countries of Europe, and subsequently in their colonies.*

Until labor-saving mechanization was introduced in the nineteenth century, plain and profiled tiles were made by hand. Today there is a resurgence of interest in the qualities of the original materials – and, though they never completely died out, handmade tiles are once more available for those who can afford them.

Glazed colored profile tiles on a C20th hipped roof

Decorative-tiled gable roof

Verge detail of swept valley

PLAIN TILES

Like traditional wooden roofing shingles, plain tiles make up a double-lap covering that produces a similar overall texture to the wooden version. Historically, the color, character, and durability of clay tiles soon became recognized and they began to be used as a fireproof alternative in areas where wooden shingles had predominated.

The small size and overall regular pattern, albeit with some variation due to their handmade nature, produced an attractive covering that mellowed with age and looked equally at home on rural houses and barns and on sophisticated town houses.

Handmade   Machine-made

Types of plain tile

Made from processed clay, plain tiles are mostly made to a standard size of 10½in (265mm) by 6½in (165mm) by ½in (12mm). This size was established in Britain in the fifteenth century and has changed little since, although larger and special tiles are made.

The tiles are simple rectangles molded with a slight curve or "camber" from head to tail. Early handmade tiles also had a cross-camber that gave roofing an attractive texture and a measure of ventilation, while shedding rainwater efficiently. Modern versions, especially machine-made ones, are made without a cross-camber. This can make it difficult to match old plain tiles for repairs.

Fixing methods

Early handmade plain tiles were punctured with two square holes close to the top edge or head, through which oak pegs were fitted. The pegs hooked over riven tiling battens, and the tiles were generally known as peg tiles **(1)**. Later versions had nibs of clay formed in the top edge **(2)**, although nail holes were provided for extra security in exposed situations. Sometimes the head laps were sealed on the inside with lime mortar known as "torching."

Tile-hung walls, which were quite common in Great Britain **(3)**, also required nail fixings. In this case, every tile was twice-nailed, whereas in roof work it was usual only to nail the perimeter tiles at the eaves, verge, and ridge and at every fourth course.

Shaped tiles

During the earlier part of the nineteenth century shaped versions of the simple plain tile began to appear. These were used to create attractive repeat-pattern tile-hung walling as well as decorative roof coverings.

On walls, as with some ornamental roofs, shaped tiles were often laid with alternating courses of plain tiles or tiles of a different color to produce interesting decorative treatments.

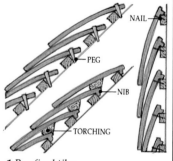

NAIL
PEG
NIB
TORCHING

1 Peg-fixed tiles
2 Nibbed tiles with torching
3 Nail-fixed wall-hung tiles

Decorative tile-hung walling

Colored tiles

Although red-toned tiles are the most common in many parts of the country, other colors, such as blues and beige, were produced from clays of different regions. These were sometimes combined to create diamond patterns or other polychrome designs. If you are fortunate enough to own such a feature, take photographs of it in case it should have to be stripped for renovation purposes in the future.

Hips and valleys

Tiled roofs have the benefit of specially shaped tiles for hips and valleys which are laid to bond neatly with each course. However, one of the most attractive features of a plain-tiled roof is the swept valley, where the tiles are cut to a tapered shape so that the courses can be run around in a curve (1). A less expensive alternative is the laced valley where the tiles are not cut but laid to butt up to wide tile-and-a-half tiles set diagonally (2). Although even a laced valley is quite costly to reproduce, it is worth the expense in order to preserve the style of an old tiled roof. Hire the services of a specialist roofing company familiar with historic craft practices to help maintain the roof's original features.

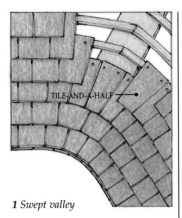

1 Swept valley

2 Laced valley

REPLACING TILES

Although clay tiles are very durable, they can fracture if struck or if undue pressure is applied to them; and if they become porous, they may suffer frost damage. Also, it's inevitable that with time the nail fixings will fail.

Traditional peg-tiled roofs are rare, but if pegs break or perish they can be replaced and the tiles refitted.

If nibbed tiles are broken or fall from the roof due to being dislodged by gusts of wind, replacements can be hooked onto the tile battens. Use copper, aluminum-alloy, or silicon-bronze roofing nails to fix those that can be nailed. Slide the tiles of the last course into position, while using wooden wedges to lift the course above. If the tiles do not have nibs, use a wire or sheet-metal hook (see FITTING A SLATE).

A modern fixing method for old roof coverings uses a plastic glue or foam coating that is applied to the underside of the tiles. The glue type is applied across the lap in much the same way as a traditional cement torching. The foam type of coating is sprayed between the rafters and covers the tiles and battens. Care must be taken that ventilation to the roof space is not restricted. If the treatment is not carried out properly, then it can lead to trapped-moisture problems. Neither type allows the covering to be easily reused.

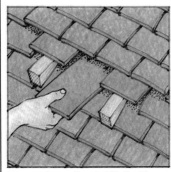

Use wooden wedges to lift the tiles

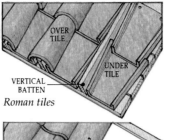

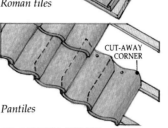

Roman tiles

Spanish tiles

Pantiles

CUT-AWAY CORNER

French tiles

INTERLOCKING EDGES

PROFILED TILES

Profiled tiles are single-lap coverings that are shaped to overlap or interlock with one another. The principal traditional types are Roman tiles, Spanish or mission tiles, pantiles and French or Marseilles tiles. These coverings, which in most cases are laid in unbonded courses, produce a boldly textured roof.

Roman tiles

Roman-tiled roofs are made up of flat "under" tiles and half-round barrel-shaped "over" tiles. Most are tapered from head or tail so that they nest together along their side edges and between courses. The under tiles are nailed flat on tiling battens or close boarding, while over tiles are nailed to vertical battens run between them.

Spanish tiles

Spanish or "mission" tiles (so called because they were introduced into the southern states of America by Spanish missionaries) are similar in principle to the Roman type. The main difference is that the under tile of the Spanish type is concave. The under tiles are nailed sideways into the vertical battens on each side, and the over tiles are single-nailed to the top of the battens.

Pantiles

The pantile is a simpler variation of the Spanish tile, the trough of the under tile being combined with the curve of the over tile to produce an S-shaped profile. The opposite diagonal corners are cut away to allow

Multi-colored Spanish tiles

the tiles to fit together in the same plane where the head and tail meet between courses. The tiles are located on tiling battens by a single wide nib at the head and are fixed with a single nail.

French tiles

The French tile is one of many machine-made interlocking tiles that became widely used in the early part of the twentieth century. It provides an efficient and visually pleasing roof covering that is fairly easy to install.

Most French tiles were a natural terracotta red, but some were colored and glazed. They were hung on tile battens and rarely nailed, as their interlocking shape helped keep them in place.

SLATE ROOFS

SLATE ROOFING *provides a highly durable and relatively maintenance-free roof covering. This type of roofing uses naturally occurring fissile stone that can be converted into thin slabs or sheets.*

True slate (as opposed to the sedimentary limestone or sandstone slabs used in some regions) is a hard metamorphic rock formed from clay sediments. Due to immense pressure millions of years ago, it has a laminated structure that enables it to be readily split into sheets. This type of stone has been quarried or mined for centuries.

Smooth blue-gray slate from Wales is perhaps the best known slate in Britain, since, with the advent of the Industrial Revolution, it was produced in great quantities and transported to all parts of the country and exported abroad. America even imported Welsh slate until improved transport systems developed in the mid nineteenth century made the native slate from quarries in Vermont, Pennsylvania, and Virginia more affordable. The slate industry has diminished in this century, but there are still functioning slate producers in each of these areas; the roofing slates they produce vary widely in color, texture, and durability. Slate is among the most expensive roofing surfaces, though perhaps the longest-lasting.

Traditional slate roof laid in diminishing courses

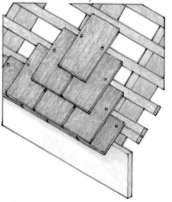

1 *Center-nailed slates*   2 *Counterbattens on boarded roof*

SHAPED SLATES

After splitting, the edges of each slate are cropped to bring the slate to the finished length and width. This process is known as dressing. The dressed edge gives the characteristic beveled finish to the face of natural-slate roofing. Slates were cut and dressed by hand but are now mostly machine-processed.

Most are cut to standard rectangular sizes, although sometimes the tail of the slate is shaped to form a decorative pattern when laid.

Slates that cannot readily be worked and thick stone slates are sometimes sold as "random sizes" for thickness grading and sorting by the roofer. This roofing is laid with the largest slates at the eaves and the smallest at the ridge. As it takes skill to install, it is expensive.

COLOR AND TEXTURE

The color and texture of slate vary according to its origin. The surface of some slates is smooth; others have a distinct riven texture to the face. The colors can vary from cool greens, blues, and grays to warmer purples and russet reds in a range of tones. Some are variegated, with stripes or mottled patterns, while others are plain. In most cases just one type of slate was used, giving a pleasing natural color and texture to the roof. However, in the late nineteenth century different-colored slates were sometimes combined to create a decorative effect.

If you need to replace old slates, take a sample slate or fragment to an architectural-salvage company or roofing-material supplier to help you match the color.

FIXING METHODS

Slate roofing is a double-lap covering laid in bonded courses. Usually each slate is fixed with two nails, though very occasionally slates were simply located on battens with wooden pegs.

The holes for the nails are punched through by hand or machine from the underside. This produces countersunk holes on the face of the slate in which the the nailheads sit. Slates are sometimes head-nailed, but are more commonly center-nailed to prevent them from being lifted by the wind (1).

Slates may be fixed to battens or to close boarding. If the roof is boarded, in some regions the practice is to fix vertical counterbattens up the slope of the roof to raise the horizontal battens clear of the surface (2). This allows any penetrating moisture to drain down freely.

Many old slate roofs were fixed with iron nails, though more durable copper nails were used on better-quality houses. Good slates will last for generations, but a slate roof covering can fail due to corroded fixings.

Whenever carrying out repairs or having your roof re-covered, make sure good-quality galvanized or copper roofing nails are used. The nails should be $3/4$in (20mm) to 1in (25mm) longer than the thickness of the slate. Galvanized nails should be used for the battens. If the fixings perish but the slates are still in good condition, have the roof stripped and re-laid with the original slates.

1 Cut fixing nails   *2 Nail strip to batten*   *3 Bend tail of strip*

Decorative shaped and colored slates on a mansard roof

REPAIRING A SLATE ROOF

Before tackling the work, you will need to find a supply of matching slates with which to make the repair. You can buy new slates or use secondhand ones from an architectural-salvage company. If they are to function properly and look right, the thickness must be the same as that of the original. If they are too thick, the overlapping courses will not lie flat. The overall size is less of a problem, as a slate that's too large can be cut to the required dimensions. The width should allow a gap of about $1/8$in (3mm) between each vertical joint.

Removing a broken slate

Nail-fixed slate roofing is laid in such a way that each course covers the fixings of the course below. In order to remove an individual slate it is necessary to release the hidden fixing. This is done with a special tool called a ripper or shingle remover.

Slide the end of the tool under the damaged slate and hook it onto one of the nails. Give the hilt of the handle a sharp tap with a hammer to cut or pull out the nail **(1)**. Remove the second nail in the same way. If you aren't able to find a slater's ripper, cut the nails with a hacksaw blade. You should now be able to pull the broken part of the slate free.

Fitting a slate

Cut a strip of copper or zinc sheet approximately 1in (25mm) wide. The strip should be 2in (50mm) or so longer than the head lap of the roofing. If the roof is shallow-pitched, a lead strip can be used. Nail the strip to the fixing battens or boarding between the slates of the course below, just clearing the head of the next course down **(2)**. Slide the new slate into place and bend the tail of the strip over the edge to form a hook **(3)**.

Cutting to size

If you need to cut a slate that is not too thick, hold it face down on a straight board, with the edge of the slate overhanging by the amount that is to be trimmed off. Use the edge of a bricklayer's trowel to chop off the waste, working toward you, using the edge of the board as a guide **(4)**.

4 Cut slate with a trowel

ORNAMENTAL FEATURES

The roofs of many Victorian houses were embellished with decorative metal cresting and terracotta ridge tiles and finials. Sadly many of these are now missing – but you can still buy originals from architectural-salvage companies, and replicas are available from roofing-tile manufacturers.

For any major repairs to an ornamental cresting, call in a roofing company. If you're used to working at heights, you may be able to fix loose ridge tiles yourself. Lift off the loose tiles and chisel off the old weak mortar. Mix a bedding mortar of 3 parts sharp sand to 1 of Portland cement, if necessary adding a pigment powder to color the mortar. Lay a band of mortar on each side of the ridge and at each end. Set the tile into the mortar and bed it down. Remove excess mortar, taking care not to smear the surface of the roof.

Lay mortar carefully in bands

Cast-iron cresting decorates the ridge of a roof

METAL ROOFS

LEAD AND COPPER SHEETING *have been used as roof coverings for generations. Both metals are soft, malleable, and highly durable, and were principally used for important public buildings.*

In the domestic context, lead was most commonly used for covering roofs, doorhoods, and porch or balcony canopies where other traditional coverings were unsuitable because of the pitch or shape of the roof. Lead sheeting is manufactured by a rolling or casting process. Cast lead is considered to be the best, but is more expensive than rolled-sheet lead.

TYPES OF METAL ROOFING
Metal expands and contracts with changes in temperature. To overcome movement problems, sheet roofing is made up from panels of metal. Where the panels meet on vertical edges they are joined by weathertight rolled or flat seams; on horizontal edges they are joined by lapped or drip joints. In both cases, the joints are formed by hand.

Sheet iron began to be used for roofing in the eighteenth century. Corrugated iron, patented in England in the early nineteenth century, was in common use for commercial buildings by the middle of the century. It was also used for colonial domestic buildings and outhouses.

Lightweight tin-plate roofing was in use in the eighteenth century, and became popular in the United States toward the end of the nineteenth century with the introduction of embossed interlocking machine-made tin-plate tiles.

FLASHINGS
Flashings are used to weatherproof the junctions between the roof covering and wall abutments, chimneys, or other elements that interrupt the roof surface. These junctions, which may either be mortar fillets or strips of metal, are often the most vulnerable part of the roof. They therefore require regular inspection, and prompt attention if repairs are needed. Metal flashings are superior and mostly made *in situ* to suit the type of roof covering. If they are beyond repair, get a specialist to replicate the original pattern.

Double-lap covering
The abutment flashings for double-lap coverings, such as tiles, slates, or shingles, are made up with stepped cover flashing **(1)**. Thin sheets of metal are turned up at right angles and fitted under each tile. The top edge generally hooks over the head of the tile to keep the soaker securely in place.

The step flashing is made from a 6in (150mm) strip of lead, no more than 5ft (1.5m) long. This is cut into a stepped shape to follow the pitch of the roof and is tucked into the mortar joints. The flashing is then fixed in place by filling the masonry joints with mortar.

Single-lap covering
Flashings for single-lap coverings, such as profiled tiles, are made using wide step-and-cover flashing, then the extra width is formed into the contour of the roofing **(2)**.

MAINTAINING METAL ROOFING
In time all metal roofing deteriorates, mainly due to fatigue or chemical action. The latter may occur as a result of atmospheric pollution or contact with corrosive substances in other materials or in organic matter. Corrosion can also take place when dissimilar metals are used together (for example, when copper sheeting is fixed with iron nails). It is therefore advisable to use compatible materials – such as copper nails for fixing copper or lead sheeting, galvanized fixings for galvanized iron.

Repairs to lead and copper sheeting require the services of a metal-roofing specialist. Pinholes in lead caused by corrosion can be patch repaired; so can splits caused by thermal movement. It is not usually necessary to have the entire covering stripped and replaced. Splits can be welded successfully using oxy-acetylene (known as lead burning), or a patch of matching material can be let in using the same technique. Lead burning allows the repair to expand and contract at the same rate. Stringent fire precautions must be followed when this process is being used.

Caulking and repair tapes are rarely successful, even as a temporary repair, and can make a permanent repair to metal roofing more difficult.

Always keep flat roofs free from debris and build-up of mosses – both can reduce water flow, and the latter causes corrosion. If organic growth is a persistent problem on a lead roof, apply a chemical treatment available from builders' suppliers. Copper will not sustain organic growth. Wear soft shoes when walking over a flat roof, and take care not to damage the surface when brushing or scraping the covering.

Iron-based roof coverings will rust if the protective galvanizing or tin plating breaks down, so keep them well painted to prolong their working life.

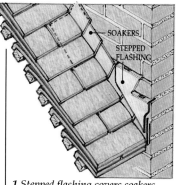

1 Stepped flashing covers soakers

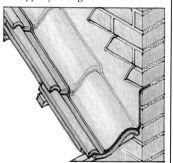

2 Step-and-cover single-lap flashing

CHIMNEY FLASHING
A flashing round a chimney is more complex than other roof flashings, as it has to be waterproof on four sides. This is done with an apron flashing at the front **(1)**, step flashing at the sides **(2)**, and a back gutter at the rear **(3)**.

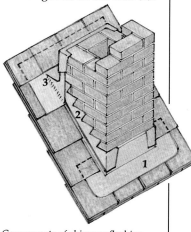

Components of chimney flashing

CHAPTER SEVEN

CHIMNEYS

Before chimneys existed *the smoke from fires simply escaped through a central hole or vent in the roof. Funnel-shaped hoods of* lime-plastered timber were used in houses when fireplaces began to be sited against walls. Eventually the hood evolved into the brick or stone chimney, built onto the outside of the wall or projecting inside the room to form a chimney breast. Nevertheless, the centrally placed fire continued in some houses with the introduction of massive brick or stone single or back-to-back fireplaces that divided the house.

The chimney became an important feature of domestic architecture in Tudor times, when the roofs of palaces and manor houses were graced with magnificent molded-brick examples. But in America the chimney more often had a utilitarian aspect. In the North, it tended to be a massive stack at the center of the house, serving as many as five or more fireplaces. In the South, the chimney was more likely to be located on an end wall, and was often set apart from the house in order to dissipate heat. (The fireplace remained the main cooking area until cook stoves came into general use in the nineteenth century.)

In the Victorian age, chimneys became smaller and regained some decorative function, especially in some English-inspired revival styles that featured chimney pots and elaborate masonry.

An exterior brick-built chimney on a timber-frame house

Imposing random-rubblework chimney with elegant brick-built stacks

CHIMNEY STYLES

CHIMNEYS *are generally constructed of brick, although stone was used for grand houses and in areas where it was a common local material. Often, the only visible part of a chimney is the chimney stack protruding from the roof. However, some chimneys show as imposing monoliths, rising majestically on the outside of the house.*

Stone chimneys are occasionally built of smooth ashlar (dressed-stone) blocks, although rusticated and rubble stone with ashlar quoins are more usual. In elaborate examples, the upper part is molded in the manner of a plain column; or the top is castellated.

Brick chimneys, like stone ones, may be square, octagonal, rectangular, or round in plan, although the brick types tend to be more ornamental. The Victorian revival movements produced some impressive decorative structures based on Tudor models. The flanks of towering brick-built chimneys were often relieved by recessed brick panels and brick strapwork, while corbeled, cantilevered courses added decorative relief at the top. If this was not enough, colored-brickwork patterns were sometimes included, too.

Castellated dressed-stone stacks

Decorative brickwork chimney

CHIMNEY CONSTRUCTION

Single-story dwellings require only a simple chimney. In early country houses this took the form of a massive fireplace with a proportionally large straight flue. The chimneys of houses with more than one floor were more complex. The plan of Georgian and Victorian town houses had the fireplaces of individual rooms built against the side walls so that the flues could be grouped into single chimney structures.

The interior masonry of each chimney was corbeled or "gathered over" above the fireplace to form a funnel shape leading into the flue. In order for the flue of the lower fireplace to circumvent the fireplace in the room above, it had to be bent to one side. Although theoretically a long straight flue is the most efficient, it was found that the bend stopped rain falling on the fire. It was also, erroneously, believed that bends reduced down drafts. Even flues that had no need to avoid obstacles above were therefore built with bends too.

Where the flues converged in the chimney stack, they were separated by brick or stone divisions known as withes or midfeathers. The insides of the flues were "parged" or covered with a $\frac{1}{2}$in (12mm) lining of mortar. This helped seal each flue and make a smoother passage for the smoke.

At the point where the chimney stack emerged through the roof a fillet of mortar or a dressed-lead flashing provided a waterproof seal around the base. The top of the stack may be finished with shaped brick or stone, or each flue may terminate with a chimney pot bedded in an angled fillet of mortar known as a cap.

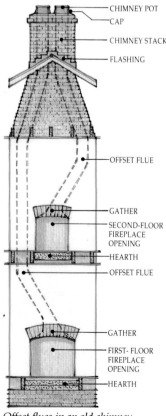
CHIMNEY POT
CAP
CHIMNEY STACK
FLASHING
OFFSET FLUE
GATHER
SECOND-FLOOR FIREPLACE OPENING
HEARTH
OFFSET FLUE
GATHER
FIRST-FLOOR FIREPLACE OPENING
HEARTH

Offset flues in an old chimney

CHIMNEY REPAIRS

Because of their exposed position, chimneys are particularly susceptible to the effects of wind, rain and frost – including deteriorating stonework, brickwork, eroded pointing, cracked mortar caps, damaged pots, and leaking flashing.

They are also susceptible to sulfate attack from inside. Water vapor, given off as a by-product of burning fuel, condenses on the cooler upper regions of the flue and combines with other products of the combustion process to form sulfuric acid and other corrosive chemicals. These acids cause masonry, mortar joints, and parging to decay.

In some cases the condensation is concentrated on the windward side of the flue, resulting in uneven erosion of the lining and mortar joints – which makes the chimney lean in the direction of the prevailing wind. Repointing may arrest the problem, or it may be possible to stabilize the structure by reinforcing it with a concrete liner. Failing this, the chimney can be rebuilt, using the original masonry plus a new liner – which is often the best solution.

Acid attack also causes erosion of the withes, leading to cracks in the structure, bulging, or poor draft due to leakage between the flues.

Erosion of masonry
Badly deteriorating bricks or stone blocks may have to be cut out and replaced. Try to match the original material, and point new brickwork in the appropriate style. If you have difficulty finding suitable replacement material, use a color-matched mortar to fill the surface (see REPAIRING DEFECTIVE STONE).

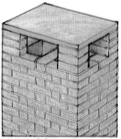

Wire binding   *Stone-slab capping*   *Ridge-tile capping*

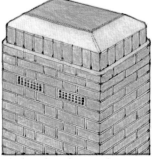

Flush roofing-slate capping   *Terracotta chimney-pot inserts*

CHIMNEY POTS

CHIMNEY POTS *generally started to transform the appearance of chimneys in the eighteenth century, although earlier examples existed. However, a wide range of decorative patterns did not become available until the nineteenth century. Made of terracotta, an unglazed fired clay that has excellent durability and resistance to heat, they were used to improve the efficiency of the chimney.*

You can still buy chimney pots made using traditional methods and patterns. The shapes are produced either by hand on a potter's wheel or by pressing kneaded clay into plaster molds. The molding is removed while the clay is still workable, then finished by hand and left to dry out before being fired in a kiln.

Cracks in brickwork

Differential settlement or erosion of the mortar joints may result in cracks opening up in the stack. Where these follow the joints, they can be raked out and repointed. If the bricks themselves are cracked, have them replaced.

Small brick-built chimneys that have suffered cracking can be reinforced by binding them with stainless-steel wire. This entails raking out the horizontal joints around the upper part of the chimney in order to receive the wire, which is then discreetly hidden with new pointing.

If the old lime mortar is badly deteriorated and the brickwork is in a poor state, you may have to have the chimney rebuilt. Should that be necessary, it is important that the original details are recorded before the stack is dismantled, so they can be reproduced. Have reusable bricks re-laid, preferably with the weathered face showing, using a 1:2:9 mortar mix of sulfate-resistant cement, lime, and sand. Use a 1:1:6 mix for the mortaring around replaced chimney pots and the top edges of corbeled courses.

Damp chimneys

Since chimneys are open to the elements, rain is able to enter them. When the chimney is in use, the heat from the fire normally keeps the system relatively dry. So to some extent does the through draft when the fire is not alight.

A stone slab set on brick piers is a traditional form of capping for a large working stack that provides ventilation when the chimney is not in use. Disused chimneys should be capped in a way that prevents the ingress of water while allowing ventilation. Half-round ridge tiles bedded in mortar can be used. Where the chimney would look better with a flush top, roofing slates can be mortared in place and an airbrick built into opposite sides of the stack to provide the necessary ventilation. A variety of terracotta tops and hood inserts are available that provide ventilated covering for chimney pots.

In all cases, air must be allowed to enter at fireplace level to provide a through draft. If the fireplace opening has been sealed off, fit a vent in the form of an airbrick or grill.

CHIMNEY POT REPAIRS

Although terracotta is fairly durable, it can decay (especially if underfired in manufacture) and, being relatively brittle, it cracks quite easily. However, it is worth trying to preserve old chimney pots even on a chimney that is disused.

Chimney pots are surprisingly large when seen close up, and need careful handling. Although it may be feasible to carry out repairs *in situ*, it is often safer to remove the pot from the stack and either work on it on a securely constructed scaffold platform or lower the pot by rope to the ground.

Repairing cracks

Fix cracks with a two-part epoxy-resin adhesive. Reinforce the repair by binding the pot with fine stainless-steel wire. Twist the ends of the wire together with pliers to tighten it and fold the twisted end back against the face. Position the wire to lie in a groove or under a bead to disguise its presence.

Weathered pots

You may be able to prolong the life of a decaying pot by refitting it so the eroded side faces in a sheltered direction. If it has to be replaced, try to match the style and color. Architectural-salvage firms generally have a variety of pots in stock and you may be lucky enough to find one that is naturally weathered.

Otherwise, try a company that sells new pots – or if you are really dedicated, have a replica made to order.

Fitting pots

Chimney pots must be well seated and securely fitted. The method will depend on the size of the pot and the shape of the base. Tall pots should be set into the top courses of the brickwork to make them less vulnerable to high winds. The top of the stack is then finished with a mortar cap sloped to shed water. Although short pots are very often set in the mortar caps, they are better built into the brickwork, too.

Terminals and inserts

A selection of terminals and inserts is available today, mostly in terracotta or metal. They are designed to assist performance or prevent rainwater entering the flue. Bird guards are available, too.

When fitting a pot or insert, check with the supplier that the design won't restrict smoke flow from the flue.

FLUE LINERS

I F A FLUE IS INEFFICIENT *that can lead to erosion of the mortar joints, causing potentially dangerous fumes and tars to escape. It also boosts the build-up of soot and creosote, increasing the risk of fire.*

All new chimneys now have to be built with a flue lining to protect the masonry from harmful flue gases. The lining is usually made of refractory concrete or impervious clay. It has long been realized that a flue lining improves the flow of combustion gases, and it was not uncommon for old flues to be lined with lime mortar parging as the chimney was erected. However, many were not lined at all.

A modern flue liner can replace deteriorated parging in an old flue, reduce the size of the flue in order to make it more efficient, or add stability to a frail chimney structure. A specialist installer will advise you about the most suitable and cost-effective type of liner.

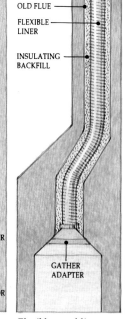
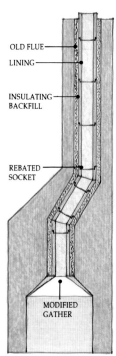
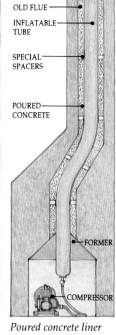

OLD FLUE
LINING
INSULATING BACKFILL
REBATED SOCKET
MODIFIED GATHER

OLD FLUE
INFLATABLE TUBE
SPECIAL SPACERS
POURED CONCRETE
FORMER
COMPRESSOR

CLOSING PLATE
CLAMP
OLD FLUE
FLEXIBLE LINER
INSULATING BACKFILL
GATHER ADAPTER

Rigid sectional liner   *Poured concrete liner*   *Flexible metal liner*

RIGID SECTIONAL LINERS

This type of liner, which may be made of ceramic, light-weight pumice or refractory concrete, is well established because of its durability and is commonly used for new installations. It is suitable for all types of fuel.

Manufactured in short round or square lengths of various sizes, these liners are installed in sections, which are then mortared together. Ideal for straight flues, they can be adapted to offset ones by either cutting the ends to an angle or using standard elbow sections. Usually the meeting edges of the parts simply interlock, the rebated socket always being placed uppermost, but some types have a locating collar too.

The chimney pot has to be removed in order to reline a flue using this method. Also, holes have to be made at key points in the chimney wall, particularly at bends, in order to gain access to the flue. For a straight chimney this may only be at the bottom of the flue, where a support is needed for the liner and insulating backfill.

The sections are lowered down the flue from the top of the chimney. The top joint of each piece is coated with mortar to receive the next section as it is lowered down the flue. Once the openings have been rebuilt, the void around the new liners is usually backfilled with light-weight concrete, although this is not always needed as sectional liners have good insulation properties. The chimney pot and capping are finished in the normal way.

POURED CONCRETE

This fairly recent innovation for lining old chimneys uses a lightweight concrete that is pumped into the flue around an inflatable tube. The concrete is specially formulated to provide a fire-resistant insulating lining that seals the old brickwork while reinforcing the structure.

First of all, the contractors will clean and inspect the chimney. Where bends are located, an opening is made so the former can be centered using special spacers. The toughened-rubber former is passed down the flue and inflated to suit the size of the appliance or fireplace. Then, after all the openings have been sealed, the concrete mix is pumped into the chimney from the top to fill the void around the tube.

When the mix has set, the former is removed, leaving a smooth, efficient cylindrical flue that can be used for all types of fuel. Once installed, it is virtually permanent. It is a good lining for single flues but may not be suitable for a multi-flued system, as the dividing masonry may be too weak to bear the weight of the poured concrete.

FLEXIBLE METAL LINERS

Of the three basic kinds of chimney lining, flexible stainless-steel liners are the simplest to install. The best is the spirally wound double-skinned type. Made of stainless steel, which is resistant to corrosion as well as heat, it has a smooth inner surface and can be used for appliances that burn coal, wood, oil, or gas as well as for open fires. Made as a continuous length, it can be fitted easily to both straight and offset chimneys.

A rope, which is passed down the flue, is attached to the liner by a nose cone. The liner is then fed down the chimney and carefully pulled through from below. The bottom end is sealed and secured into a flue-pipe adaptor, for connecting to an appliance, or a gather-type adaptor (a funnel-shaped hood) for an open fire. At the top of the chimney the liner is cut to length and fitted with a clamp and a closing plate, after back-filling the old flue with a lightweight insulation such as perlite or vermiculite. The closing plate is finished with a cement mortar cap, into which a chimney pot may be set. Gas boilers require an approved flue terminal, which can be set inside the chimney pot.

Single-skin flexible steel liners are usually designed for use with gas-fired boilers or room heaters only. They should never be used with solid-fuel or wood-burning fires or stoves.

CHAPTER EIGHT

DOORS

THE FRONT DOOR OF A HOUSE *is much more than a means of entry or a barrier against intrusion. The porch or doorway becomes the* focus of attention as visitors approach the house, and the door itself creates a first impression of the building and its occupants. And while the visitor waits to be admitted, there's time to admire the decorative moldings and ornamental glass or fine metalwork of the door and its surround.

The front door is usually designed to impress and is singled out for special treatment. This may take the form of nothing more than a bold splash of color in an otherwise plain façade. More often, even in comparatively modest houses, a great deal of money is lavished on embellishing the door and its surround.

Imposing columns and canopies, classically inspired pediments, and elaborate hoods and porches have all been used at one time or another to enhance the visual impact of the main entrance. To "modernize" or remove such important features detracts from the character of a house and may even reduce its monetary value.

Although interior doors are generally less ostentatious, they make an equally valuable contribution to the character of a building. Yet it is disturbingly common to find that they have been spoiled or superficially disfigured by ill-advised attempts to modernize the décor. However, doors are sturdy pieces of joinery that are rarely prone to serious deterioration and they are relatively easy to repair.

Perfectly matched door and surround

Georgian taste and elegance

Porches are designed for relaxation   *It is difficult to imagine a more impressive approach to any house*   *A bold and sturdy entrance*

BATTEN DOORS

T HE BATTEN DOOR *dates from the Middle Ages, but the design is so practical and aesthetically pleasing that it has been employed in one form or another, especially in country houses and cottages, right up to the present day. Batten doors were fitted in internal as well as external doorways; oak and other hardwoods have been used, but more often batten doors were made from softwoods.*

As more sophisticated designs became fashionable, a batten front door was sometimes relegated to the rear entrance of the house or cut down to fit an attic or cellar doorway. Consequently, some batten doors have been in continuous use for centuries.

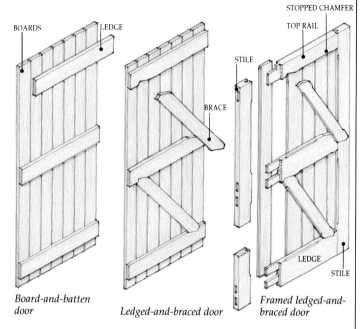

Board-and-batten door

Ledged-and-braced door

Framed ledged-and-braced door

BOARD-AND-BATTEN DOORS

The simplest and earliest type of batten door was made from vertical boards approximately 3/4 to 1 1/4 in (18 to 30mm) thick nailed to three horizontal rails known as battens or ledges.

Stronger doors, primarily for the main entrance of a house, were sometimes made with an internal skin of horizontal boards instead.

LEDGED-AND-BRACED DOORS

In the nineteenth century the construction of batten doors was improved by the addition of wooden braces to prevent sagging. To be effective, a brace must run diagonally downward toward the hinged edge of the door. Preferably, each end of the brace should be notched into the ledges and secured with a nail.

FRAMED LEDGED-AND-BRACED DOORS

An even more sophisticated form of construction was used for better-quality work, the facing boards being surrounded by substantial framing in order to present a flush surface on the outside of the door. The top rail is joined to the vertical stiles with mortise-and-tenon joints, and the stiles and rail are rebated or grooved on the inner edges to hold the boards. Two ledges run behind the boards and are joined to the stiles with pairs of barefaced mortise-and-tenon joints. The braces, as on the simpler versions of the door, run diagonally downward toward the hinged edge of the door. As a decorative feature, stopped chamfers were sometimes planed on the inside of the frame and along the ledges and braces.

BOARD JOINTS

On early batten doors square-edged vertical boards were simply butted together, the joints being covered on the outside with strips of wood to keep out drafts (1). Alternatively, the boards could be rebated to create weatherproof joints (2).

The Industrial Revolution was responsible for the widespread use of machine-cut tongue-and-groove joints. Tongue-and-groove boards often had both edges chamfered to form a V-joint (3), or a bead (4) was cut along one edge. These details were designed to mask the effects of shrinkage, which could result in unsightly gaps opening up between the boards.

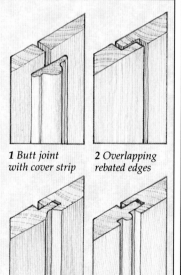

1 Butt joint with cover strip

2 Overlapping rebated edges

3 Tongue-and-groove joint

4 Beaded edge disguises joint

Turn-of-the-century houses frequently incorporated batten doors

PANELED DOORS

PANELED DOORS, *constructed in a similar way to the wooden wall paneling of the time, were made in relatively small numbers in England as early as the sixteenth century. However, it took a further 200 years for the style to gain widespread acceptance. By the middle of the eighteenth century the paneled door had become commonplace; and although from time to time whims of fashion have dictated changes in appearance, its basic construction has remained unaltered to the present day.*

C18th fielded-panel door

Simple English Georgian door

An impressive combination of beveled-glass lights and bolection moldings

PANEL ARRANGEMENTS

The basic design comprises a frame of rails, stiles, and muntins infilled with thin panels of solid wood. The classic Georgian front door had six rectangular panels **(1)**, although various arrangements of five or seven panels were also used by Georgian architects.

Most Victorian doors, especially interior ones, were of the four-panel type **(2)** still widely used today. Panels were sometimes arched **(3)** or circular **(4)**, in which case they were usually surrounded by heavy wooden moldings.

After the First World War paneled doors became simpler in appearance, and there was a tendency to dispense with moldings in favor of solid-wood or plywood panels **(5)**.

1 Six panel

2 Four panel

3 Arched

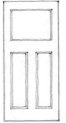
4 Circular

5 Plywood

Unusual Victorian studded door

Paneled door of the 1920s or 1930s

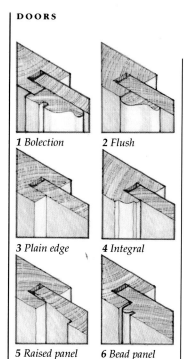

1 Bolection *2 Flush*

3 Plain edge *4 Integral*

5 Raised panel *6 Bead panel*

MOLDINGS & PANELS

The joints between panels and the surrounding frame were often masked with applied moldings. These are nailed to the frame, never to the panels, and are always mitered at the corners.

Bolection moldings were applied moldings rebated to cover the edge of the frame **(1)** and disguise the effects of shrinkage. Flush moldings **(2)** that do not project beyond the face of the frame were also popular, especially for internal doors. The inside face of a door for a cupboard or minor bedroom was frequently left plain, without any moldings **(3)**. Other doors were made with integral moldings cut on the inside of the frame members **(4)**.

Door panels are usually flat on both sides, but sometimes, particularly in the eighteenth century, raised-and-fielded panels **(5)** were used. On entrance doors the bottom panels were often made to be flush with the frame and were edged with a small bead molding **(6)**. These panels were stronger than the raised-and-fielded type and tended to shed rainwater more efficiently.

Springing hinges
Badly fitted hinges prevent the door closing properly.
● Fit correct-size screws (page 78).
● Pack out hinge leaf (page 78).

Creaking hinges
Hinges often creak loudly when dry or under strain.
● Apply oil (page 77).
■ Realign hinges (page 77).

Loose hinges
A door will drop if hinge screws work loose or knuckle joints wear.
● Refill screw holes (page 76).
● Swap hinges (page 77).

Bowed moldings
Moldings can bow because of uneven shrinkage, creating unsightly gaps.
● Renail moldings (page 79).
■ Replace moldings (page 79).

Wet rot
If rainwater can run under the door, the wood rots around end grain.
● Treat with wood preservative (page 108).
■ Fit base of door with door sweep (page 79).

Components of a paneled door
1 Stile
2 Top rail
3 Bottom rail
4 Lock rail
5 Frieze rail
6 Muntins
7 Mortise and tenon
8 Wedges
9 Panel
10 Groove
11 Molding

Loose joints
Shrinkage or failed glue can cause gaps to open up along shoulders of joints.
■ Reglue joints (page 77).

Warped door
A warped door is difficult to close.
● Move doorstops (page 78).
■ Flatten the door (page 78).

ASSESSING REPAIRS
● Easy even for beginners.
■ Fairly difficult. Good practical skills required.
▲ Difficult. Hire a professional.

Split panel
If a solid-wood panel is not free to move, it may split.
■ Repair panel (page 79).

Rattling door
A door may rattle if it is not held firmly against its stops.
● Fit weather stripping.
■ Move catch or striker plate (pages 89 and 90).

Sticking door
A door will jam in its frame if the wood swells or the edge of the stile is caked with paint.
● Shave door with plane (page 77).
● Strip paint from edge (page 75).

HOW PANELED DOORS WERE CONSTRUCTED

Hardwoods such as oak and mahogany have been used at various times for making paneled doors. But more often they are constructed from softwood, which is almost invariably painted.

A typical paneled door has a vertical stile **(1)** on each side. The one that is hinged is known as the hanging stile, the other as the closing or lock stile.

Between the stiles are the top rail **(2)**, bottom rail **(3)**, and middle or lock rail **(4)**. The fourth rail of a six-panel door is known as the frieze rail **(5)**. Running down the center of the door are vertical muntins **(6)**.

The frame is constructed using mortise-and-tenon joints **(7)** throughout, and those that pass right through the stiles are secured with wedges from outside **(8)**. The panels **(9)** are held loosely in grooves **(10)** cut along the inside edges of all the frame members. In order to avoid splitting when the wood shrinks, the panels are not glued or fixed in any way.

On most types of paneled door, moldings **(11)** are used to cover the joints around the panels. They also disguise any shrinkage.

GLAZED DOORS

THE FANLIGHT *above the front door that became a feature of Georgian and Federal architecture was designed to admit light to the hall. For the same reason, narrow windows were sometimes incorporated in the surround. Only later was the front door itself glazed, although the two upper panels were sometimes replaced with glass in earlier doors.*

DECORATIVE GLASS PANELS

From Victorian times glass panels became widely used for all sorts of doors and were especially popular for entrance doors, where acid-etched or stained glass could be employed to impressive decorative effect.

Glazing was generally restricted to the upper half of the door. Often it took the form of a single large panel; but sometimes several small panes were used, divided by wooden glazing bars. A common alternative was to insert glass instead of wood in one of the conventional door-panel arrangements.

Traditional batten doors were never glazed, but many of the country-style "revival" houses that were popular after the First World War have a small rectangular or diamond-shape window placed in the center of the upper half of batten doors.

SAFE GLASS FOR DOORS

Before modern safety standards were introduced, doors were glazed using whatever thickness of glass suited the glazier or the client. However, for greater safety, if you have to replace glass in a door, you should use safety glass. (This does not mean you are obliged to replace old glass that is still intact – for example, when you remove a panel from a door in order to carry out extensive repairs to the woodwork.)

Provided that there is more than one pane of glass in the door or a single pane does not take up the greater part of the door's area, you can install ordinary (annealed) glass, which must be at least 1/4in (6mm) thick. However, this stipulation regarding thickness does not apply to leaded lights because even a large leaded window is constructed from relatively small pieces of glass held in a lead or copper lattice – and the lattice tends to buckle under impact, which reduces the risk of injury from shattered glass.

Recommendations regarding fully glazed doors are particularly stringent, and you may have to fit toughened glass. For more detailed advice about fully glazed doors, contact a local glass dealer.

Glazed cottage door with side lights

Early-C20th glazed entrance door

Glazed lobby doors admit light to a Victorian hallway

Glazed doors frequently incorporate painted lights

FLUSH DOORS

A GREAT MANY OLD HOUSES *have been spoiled by replacing original paneled doors with modern plywood or hardboard flush doors. But, thankfully, thoughtless vandalism of that kind is no longer encouraged and, apart from more modern uses, flush doors are now only considered appropriate for certain apartments and houses built in the 1920s and 1930s.*

When they made their first appearance, flush doors were considered extremely smart and fitted perfectly with fashionably stark Art Deco styling. The cheaper, plywood-faced doors were painted, but flush doors were also frequently finished with hardwood veneer.

HOW FLUSH DOORS WERE CONSTRUCTED

Earlier flush doors were often made by gluing strips of solid wood together **(1)** then applying a plywood sheet **(2)** to each face. Solid edge strips **(3)** along the edges protected the surface veneer from damage.

Framed flush doors

Framed flush doors were developed in order to reduce the overall weight. The outer frame comprises softwood top **(1)** and bottom **(2)** rails joined to vertical stiles **(3)**. Narrow regularly spaced intermediate rails **(4)** form the core, with heavier blocks of wood **(5)** inserted at strategic points in order to accommodate a mortise lock and, in the case of external doors, a letter plate. A plywood skin **(6)** on each side adds rigidity to the door. Slots **(7)** cut across the intermediate rails ventilate the core to prevent changes of atmospheric pressure bowing the plywood skins and disperse moisture-laden air. As on the earlier flush doors, hardwood edges j**(8)** protect the plywood veneer from wear and tear.

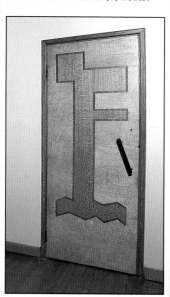

Veneered flush door from the 1930s

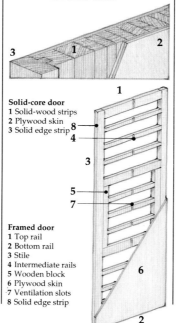

Solid-core door
1 Solid-wood strips
2 Plywood skin
3 Solid edge strip

Framed door
1 Top rail
2 Bottom rail
3 Stile
4 Intermediate rails
5 Wooden block
6 Plywood skin
7 Ventilation slots
8 Solid edge strip

HOW DOORS WERE FITTED

T RADITIONALLY, THE DOOR OPENING *was lined with a wooden frame within which the door was hung. Although the structure of the wall itself varied considerably, the door linings were generally very similar.*

INTERNAL DOORS

The lining of an internal door opening is known as the doorframe. It comprises two vertical jambs **(1)** joined by barefaced housings to the headjamb **(2)**, which runs across the top of the opening. The door hangs from one of the side jambs. Sometimes the doorframe was rebated to create a doorstop, but more often the doorstop took the form of separate strips of wood nailed to the jambs **(3)**. An architrave **(4)** was nailed all around to cover the joints between casing and wall.

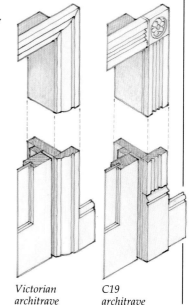

Door-casing components
1 Side jamb
2 Head jamb
3 Doorstop
4 Architrave

Architrave details

Victorian architraves usually take the form of tapered moldings that extend down to the floor on each side of the door and are mitered at the top corners. The baseboards butt against this type of molding. Frequently nineteenth-century doorways were graced by fluted rectangular-section architraves. These had separate decorated square blocks nailed into the top corners. Baseboard blocks were fitted each side of the door to finish the foot.

Wide door casings

Wide framed casings were used to line door openings in thick internal walls.

Victorian architrave

C19 architrave

STRIPPING DOORS

1 *Strip moldings with a shavehook*

2 *Protect glass with a heat deflector*

EXTERNAL DOORS
Door-surround designs vary enormously, but in principle an external door was hung from a substantial wooden frame comprising a header **(1)** across the top, a stud **(2)** on each side and, sometimes, a wooden threshold **(3)** at the bottom. A transom **(4)** was included if there was a fanlight above the door. The studs and header or transom were usually rebated to form a doorstop **(5)**. If the wooden threshold was omitted, a metal dowel was sometimes used to attach the bottom end of each post to the stone doorstep.

Usually, the frame was fixed to the surrounding structure by nails. In stone or brick houses, alternatively, bent metal lugs **(6)** screwed to the outside of the frame were bedded in mortar joints as the wall was being built. Like window frames, doorframes were often fitted in a recess built in the surrounding masonry.

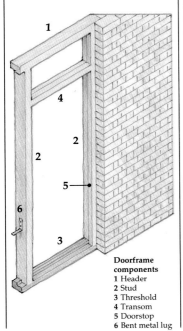

Doorframe components
1 Header
2 Stud
3 Threshold
4 Transom
5 Doorstop
6 Bent metal lug

A FTER REPEATED REDECORATION *woodwork becomes coated with so many layers of paint that attractive details such as moldings and carving are obscured. Clumsy application can also spoil the appearance of woodwork, leaving unsightly runs and sagging paint. Although it is possible to rub down these blemishes with wet-and-dry paper, it often pays to strip the old paint and start again.*

Although this section concentrates on the stripping of doors, most of the information is also relevant to stripping other items of woodwork. For professional industrial stripping, they need to be portable and small enough to be immersed in a tank.

FINISHING STRIPPED PINE DOORS
Nowadays stripped pine doors are often finished with clear varnish or oil. Although originally all softwood was painted, a clear finish does no permanent harm – and the door can always be repainted if the next owner insists on authenticity.

USING HEAT TO STRIP PAINT
Burning the paint off with a propane torch used to be the normal way to strip wood, but apart from a few professional decorators hardly anyone uses this method today. Unless you are fairly experienced, it is easy to scorch areas of woodwork and there is always the risk of causing a fire. Also, torches vaporize the lead contained in old paints, so you could find yourself breathing toxic fumes. A modern electric hot-air stripper is not only safer, it is also easier to handle and there is less risk of scorching. Although these strippers will lift paint while operating at a relatively low temperature, you should still wear a respirator when burning off old lead paint.

Hold the nozzle of a hot-air stripper about 2in (50mm) from the surface and move it from side to side until the paint begins to blister. As soon as it does so, remove the softened paint with a flat scraper,

or with a shavehook if you are stripping a molding **(1)**. When working on a door, it is usually best to strip moldings first then the flat areas. If you use a hot-air stripper close to a window, fit a heat deflector to avoid cracking the glass **(2)**.

If you plan to repaint a door, there's no need to extract the specks of paint trapped in the pores of the wood. Just rub down the stripped wood lightly with a medium-grade sandpaper, then redecorate. If you intend to use a clear finish, however, remove the residue of paint with small balls of fine steel wool dipped in chemical stripper. Rub the wood in the direction of the grain only, then wash the surface with mineral spirits or water to neutralize the stripper.

STRIPPING WITH CHEMICALS
Chemical strippers soften old paint until it is liquid enough to be scraped and washed from the surface. Thick gel-like strippers are

ideal for doors because they are stiff enough to cling to vertical surfaces. The average chemical stripper will dissolve old oil-based and modern water-based paints, but there are also specific varnish strippers that are formulated to remove tough polyurethane varnishes.

Chemical strippers are potentially hazardous, so they must be handled with caution and the maker's recommendations observed very carefully. Wear vinyl gloves and protect your eyes with safety spectacles or goggles. Many strippers emit unpleasant fumes – it is therefore essential to ventilate the area in which you are working and wear a face mask. Never smoke in the vicinity, and keep pets and children away from all chemical strippers. If you splash stripper on your skin, wash it immediately with plenty of cold water. If it gets in your eyes, rinse them thoroughly under running water and seek medical advice without delay.

Safer all-purpose strippers have been developed that are fume-free and will not burn your skin, although they may take a little longer to soften the paint. Read the manufacturer's instructions before you buy one, to make sure it is not one of the more common caustic strippers.

Using chemical strippers
The procedure described below will serve as a guide to using chemical strippers safely and efficiently, but always follow the detailed recommendations supplied by the manufacturer.

Lay a polyethylene dust sheet under the door, then brush on a liberal coat of stripper. Work the gel into moldings to make sure all surfaces are covered. Leave it for 10 to 15 minutes, then scrape a small section to see if the paint is soft enough to remove easily. If the paint is still resistant, apply more stripper – but this time work it into the whole area, so the chemicals come into contact with all the still-unsoftened paint.

Five minutes later, scrape off the paint, wrap it up in newspaper, and dispose of it appropriately, if possible at a facility equipped to process such toxic material.

Unless the wood is oak, use steel-wool balls dipped in fresh stripper to remove stubborn patches of paint and clean up moldings. For oak, use coarse burlap, since steel-wool can stain the wood and detract from its appearance.

Finally, wash the surface with water or mineral spirits, depending on the maker's recommendations. Allow the wood to dry thoroughly before rubbing down and repainting.

INDUSTRIAL STRIPPING
Most people derive great satisfaction from stripping paint from a beautiful door and revealing the natural wood beneath. But faced with the prospect of having to strip perhaps half a dozen doors, many people turn to industrial stripping.

The cheapest method involves dipping a door in a tank of hot caustic stripper, which then has to be washed off by hosing the wood with water. The combination of heat and water can be detrimental and, although most doors emerge from the process relatively unscathed, occasionally solid-wood panels split, joints open up, veneer may peel, and moldings distort.

Another drawback is that hot dipping always raises the grain, leaving a furry surface that has to be rubbed down before you can refinish the wood.

To avoid most of these problems, you need to go to a company that dips wood in cold chemicals only. Cold dipping does not discolor the wood and it is ready for refinishing after 24 hours, whereas after hot dipping it may not be ready for weeks. With cold chemicals the grain may be raised slightly, but you are unlikely to be faced with the worst side effects of hot dipping. The only disadvantage is that, because the chemicals are expensive, you have to pay more for cold dipping.

Most firms will collect a door and deliver it back to you after stripping. If you're having a front door stripped, same-day service is essential. Never submit a veneered door to industrial stripping unless the company can guarantee that the veneers will not delaminate.

CURING MINOR DOOR PROBLEMS

SOME DOORS HAVE TO BE *shouldered open, others catch on the floor or doorframe whenever you use them. These irritating problems can occur for a number of reasons, so you need to check the door carefully to determine the appropriate course of action.*

CURING LOOSE HINGES
If the screws holding the top hinge work loose, the door sags and its top corner binds against the frame. Open the door partially and lift it by the closing stile. If you can see the hinge moving, examine it more closely.

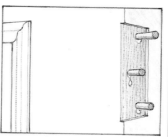
1 Leave dowels until glue sets

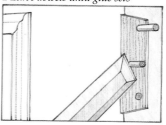
2 Then pare them flush with a chisel

Tightening loose screws
If the screw heads are protruding, try tightening them with a screwdriver; and if that's successful, check whether the screws in the other hinges need tightening, too.

You may find the screws are loose because repetitive movement has caused the screw threads to tear the wood and loosen their grip. If the door has a substantial frame or the screws have worked loose from the door itself, it may be possible to substitute longer screws of the same gauge.

However, the jambs of most interior doorframes are too thin for this solution to work. In this case, remove

the screws and fold the hinge out of the way. Use a sharp knife to whittle softwood strips into tapered dowels that will fit the screw holes. Glue the dowels and tap them into the holes. Leave them untrimmed **(1)** until the glue sets, then cut them off and pare them flush with a chisel **(2)**. Finally, fold the hinge back, drill pilot holes for the screws, and replace them.

Swapping worn hinges
The hinges may be screwed firmly in place, yet when you lift the closing stile you may still be able to detect movement. This is probably due to wear on the hinge pins and knuckles. Since the weight of the door puts uneven strain on the top and bottom hinges, it is sometimes possible to correct the fault by simply swapping the top and bottom hinges, thus reversing the wear on the pins.

REMOVING THICK PAINT
If the closing stile binds regularly against the frame, along its entire length, it is probably due to a build-up of paint over the years. If you are planning to strip the door entirely for some other reason, the problem will be solved in the process. Otherwise, use a hook scraper to remove paint from the edge of the door.

REPAIRING LOOSE JOINTS

Wood shrinks considerably during very dry hot spells, then swells again when wet weather returns. This movement can break down the glue in the joints of a door. If the mortise-and-tenon joints of a paneled door work loose and the securing wedges fall out, the joints can gradually open up until the door is fractionally too wide for its opening.

Check carefully for gaps along the shoulders of the joints (they may have been filled in the past). If necessary, strip the paint around the joints and rake out any debris lodged between the shoulders. Pull out any wedges that remain in a through mortise and tenon. Inject carpenter's glue between the shoulders and into the ends of the joints **(1)**. Tap the joints home, using a mallet and protective softwood block **(2)**, or hire a large clamp with which to pull them together. Glue and insert overlength wedges, tapping them in with a hammer **(3)**. When the glue has set, trim the wedges flush with a chisel.

If a door is made with stopped mortise and tenons, it may be impossible to inject sufficient glue between the shoulders to secure the joints. Having closed the glued joints with a clamp, insert a locking dowel **(4)** and trim it flush when the glue has set.

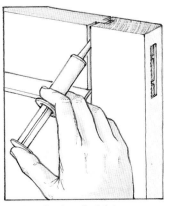

1 Inject glue into the joint

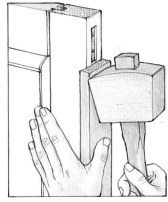

2 Tap the joint home with a mallet

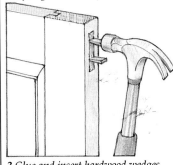

3 Glue and insert hardwood wedges

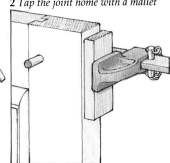

4 Secure stopped tenon with a dowel

CREAKING AND RATTLING DOORS

Most people find creaking doors annoying, and doors that rattle with the slightest draft can be positively infuriating to live with. As well as removing a source of constant irritation, it pays to rectify these relatively minor faults before wear on the door hardware increases.

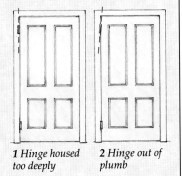

1 Hinge housed too deeply

2 Hinge out of plumb

Stopping a door from creaking

In most cases a creaking door can be cured with a drop of oil on the hinges. Place the oil on the top of the hinge pins, then swing the door gently back and forth so that the lubricant works down into the hinge.

Occasionally, oiling fails to silence the creaking. In this case, examine both hinges carefully to see if their pins are out of line with each other. Use strips of thin cardboard to pack out a hinge housed too deeply in the wood **(1)**. To align a hinge pin that is out of plumb **(2)**, pare the bottom of the hinge housing with a chisel.

Stopping a door from rattling

The easiest way to cure a rattling door is to attach fabric, plastic, or metal weather stripping to the doorstops. If fitting this would make the door difficult to close, you can pry off the stops and reposition them closer to the door. Alternatively, move the striker plate of the lock slightly so that the latch fits snugly (see LOCKS).

DEALING WITH EXPANSION

If a door only sticks during humid weather or after a lot of rain, the cause of the problem is probably the swelling of the wood. The answer is to trim the edge of the closing stile while the weather is still wet. Don't wait for dry weather to return, or the door will shrink and you won't be able to judge how much wood to remove.

Take the door off its hinges and support it on edge, with the closing stile at the top. Remove the latch or lock, and trim the edge of the door with a plane. You may find that it is necessary to adjust the fit of the lock when you replace it.

STOPPING A DOOR FROM CATCHING

People often fit rising butt hinges (which lift the door as it swings open) to stop a door from catching on an uneven floor or thick carpet. However, there are other causes that can make a door catch – and other solutions worth considering before you go to the expense of fitting new hinges.

Detecting a loose bottom hinge

When a door normally opens and closes smoothly, you may well not suspect that it has a loose bottom hinge. However, once the door swings past a certain point, a loose bottom hinge tends to dislocate, allowing the bottom of the door to drag on the floor.

Check whether the screws are loose or the bottom hinge is worn – and, if necessary, either tighten the screws or swap or replace the hinge (see opposite page).

Adjusting the bottom hinge

If the bottom edge of a door is jamming on a bump in the floor, you can sometimes overcome the problem by adjusting the position of the lowest hinge. Open the door and remove the screws from the hinge leaf fixed to the frame. Move the leaf sideways, away from the doorstop, so that the hinge pin projects slightly further from the frame than the pin of the hinge above does. Replace the screws to hold the hinge in its new position. To prevent the door from creaking, you may have to adjust the top hinge slightly, so that both hinge pins are at the same angle.

Trimming the bottom

You may have no option but to trim the bottom of a door that is catching, especially if it is already fitted with rising butt hinges.

Professional carpet layers use a special power saw with a horizontally mounted circular blade that can trim a specified amount off a door *in situ*. However, in order to do the job yourself you have to take the door off its hinges and either plane the bottom edge or trim it with an ordinary circular saw.

You can use a sharp bench plane, with the door held in the vice jaws of a folding workbench – but there is a

lot less effort with a portable power planer. Whichever type of plane you use, work from both ends towards the middle to avoid splitting the end grain.

Trimming the top

You may find that a door fitted with rising butt hinges scrapes the frame above as it opens. To provide the necessary clearance, plane a shallow bevel on the corner of the door.

Plane a shallow bevel on the door

Support a door with a folding bench

INSURING A DOOR CLOSES PROPERLY

You should be able to close a door without having to apply force. There are several problems that can make a door keep springing open, but they are mostly fairly easy to resolve.

Relieving springing hinges

A door that resists closing just before it latches is most probably "hingebound." As a result, it tends to spring open again as you release pressure against it. If that is happening, check whether the hinges are being levered out of their housings by the act of pressing on the door.

It may be that projecting screw heads are stopping the leaves of the hinges closing properly (1). Try driving the screws home; or if someone has inserted screws that are too large, swap them for ones with smaller heads that nestle flush with each leaf.

Inaccurately fitted hinges are another possible cause. If one or more of the leaves have been housed too deeply in the wood (2), unscrew them and place strips of thin cardboard behind each hinge to pack it out flush.

If both the hinges appear to have been fitted correctly, try scraping or stripping any thick paint from the edge of the hanging stile and, if need be, from the doorframe, too.

Easing tight doorstops

You may find a door won't latch properly because the stops and perhaps the door as well are caked with

layers of paint. If scraping the closing face of the stops fails to cure the problem, strip the frame and, if need be, the door itself.

Firm draft-excluding strips sometimes prevent a door from closing properly, in which case, either substitute soft-plastic or foam strips or move the doorstops slightly to accommodate the existing draft excluders.

Flattening a warped door

Temperature variation on each side of a door can dry the timber unevenly. As a result, the door may twist or warp so that it will no longer rest against its stops without being forced shut. Leaving a door to dry in the sun after industrial stripping can also cause warping.

Strip the paint from a warped door and soak both sides with water. To reverse the effects of warping, place the door on the floor with a block of wood under one corner then load the door with heavy weights. After 24 hours remove the block, but leave the weights in place for a similar period.

A much simpler, though less satisfactory, solution is to move the doorstops to accommodate the warping.

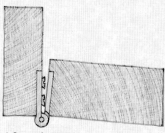

1 Screw heads prevent hinge closing

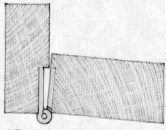

2 Deeply housed leaf has same effect

REPAIRING DOORS

R EPAIRING THE FABRIC OF A DOOR *often requires considerable exertion and skill, but the high cost of an authentic replacement or acceptable replica more than compensates for the effort involved.*

CORRECTING BOWED MOLDINGS
When the moldings on a paneled door bow, unsightly gaps are left between the moldings and the stiles, rails, and muntins **(1)**.

To get rid of the gaps, nail the moldings back against the framework, working from the middle of each length of molding. Drive the nailheads below the surface with a nail set **(2)** and fill the holes before redecorating.

With luck, the miter joints at the corners of each panel will close up as you renail the moldings. If the moldings have shrunk, leaving open miters, you can buy replacement moldings from a do-it-yourself store or builders' suppliers. Alternatively, if you want something special, choose a molding from the catalog of a specialist joinery supplier or ask the joiner to make a replica of the original.

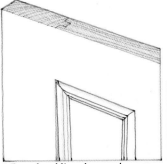

1 Bowed moldings leave ugly gaps

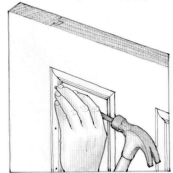

2 Sink nailheads with a nail set

Settlement can distort a doorframe

REPLACING A DOOR SWEEP

Molded door sweeps are occasionally fixed to external doors to shed rainwater away from the threshold. A drip groove machined along the underside of the door sweep prevents water from running back to the base of the door and rotting the wood.

In the past, many a householder found it expedient to discard a damaged or rotted door sweep rather than repair or replace it. In houses without a protective storm door, be sure to replace the decayed door sweep.

Measure the width of the opening between the doorstops and cut the door sweep molding to this length. Plane the end near the latch side of the door to a slight angle, so that it clears the stop when the door swings open **(1)**.

To make a weatherproof seal between the molding and the door, paint the back of the door sweep with a thick coat of primer. While the paint is still wet, screw the door sweep to the door **(2)**. Fill or plug the screw holes, then prime and paint the molding.

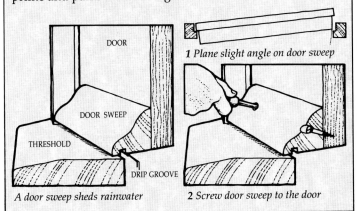

DOOR

DOOR SWEEP

THRESHOLD

DRIP GROOVE

A door sweep sheds rainwater

1 Plane slight angle on door sweep

2 Screw door sweep to the door

REPAIRING SPLIT PANELS
If a solid-wood door panel has been fixed inadvertently with nails or glue, there's a chance that it will split if the wood shrinks. Incompetent industrial paint stripping can also cause splitting. You may be able to reglue a split panel *in situ* (see REPAIRING PANELING). If not, you will have to dismantle the door to remove and repair the panel. Having chopped out any securing wedges, steam the door joints with a kettle to soften the glue. Then tap them apart with a hammer, using a block of softwood to protect the components from damage.

Fixed door panels tend to split

FILLING AN UNEVEN GAP
One characteristic indication of building settlement is the distortion of doorframes, resulting in a tapering gap between the top of the door and the head or jamb. If the settlement is recent consult an engineer, who may recommend under-pinning the foundations to restore the building to an even keel. However, an old house may have settled years ago then restabilized, albeit in a less-than-perfect condition. In this case, the simplest solution is to cut a softwood wedge to fill the gap and screw it to the top of the door. Plane the wedge flush with the door before repainting.

DEALING WITH DECAY
Doors are less susceptible than windows to decay. However, if a door is neglected and its finish is allowed to deteriorate, water can penetrate and soften the fibers, especially around areas of end grain.

For methods of treating decay, see DEALING WITH ROTTED WINDOWS.

REPLACING DOORS

WHATEVER *the cost of repair or maintenance, it pays to do everything you can to retain the doors that were installed when the house was built. They were made to fit openings that almost certainly do not conform to modern notions of standardization and they are, of course, authentic in style.*

However, not everyone holds the same opinion. For example, it was once fashionable to install a brand-new front door in the mistaken belief that it would increase the value of a property; and paneled doors, which were considered old-fashioned, were frequently replaced with mass-produced flush doors. As a result, many home owners are now faced with the task of reinstating old doors in order to restore the character of the building.

With luck you may be be able to buy an old door from a local architectural-salvage company exactly like one that once hung in your home, but the further afield you have to search the less chance there is of obtaining a perfect match. Alternatively, you may be able to find a similar door and then plane or cut it to fit the opening, though there is a limit to the amount of wood you can remove without weakening the structure of the door or spoiling its proportions.

Another option is to buy a modern reproduction door, but it is extremely difficult to find a mass-produced door that is entirely suitable for an old house. However, there are millwork companies that specialize in making doors to order, using traditional methods and authentic styles, including external doors, interior room doors, and a variety of doors with glazed panels. Although custom-made doors are relatively expensive, they are usually made to the highest standards.

REMOVING AN OLD DOOR

First, secure the door in an open position by tapping a wedge under it **(1)**. If the doorframe is painted, uncover the screw heads that hold the hinges to the frame by scraping off the paint. It is important to dig out paint clogging screw slots before you attempt to turn the screws. Place a corner of a screwdriver tip at one end of each slot and tap the screwdriver sideways with a hammer to cut out the paint **(2)**. With the tip in position, tap the end of the handle with the hammer to break the paint seal around the screw head, then extract the screw. Remove all but one screw from each hinge, then get an assistant to support the door while you extract the last screws.

If a screw slot becomes so badly damaged that it is impossible to engage it with the blade of a screwdriver, drill out the head in stages, using progressively larger bits. Lift off the hinge and remove the remains of the screw by turning its shank with a plier wrench.

1 Drive a wedge under the door

2 Clear slots with a screwdriver

HANGING A NEW DOOR

New doors are sometimes supplied with extended stiles, known as horns, to insure that the corners are not damaged during transportation. You need to saw off the horns before fitting the door in its opening.

A custom-made door may need nothing more than a light trimming with a plane, but other doors may have to be cut down with a saw in order to obtain a perfect fit. Ideally, there should be a 1/8in (3mm) clearance at the top and sides of a door and a gap of at least 1/4in (6mm) at the bottom. A gap of up to 1/2in (12mm) may be needed to accommodate a thick carpet. When planing the top or bottom of a door, always plane inward toward the middle to avoid splitting the end grain.

Mark the position of the hinges on the door, using the existing housings in the doorframe as a guide. Cut hinge housings in the door (see HINGES).

Hang the door with a single screw holding each hinge to the doorframe, and check the swing and fit of the door. Make any adjustments that may be needed, then insert the other screws. Finally, fit the lock and other hardware (see DOOR FURNITURE).

Saw the horns off a new door

1 Mark the height of the architrave

2 Mark the length of the top member

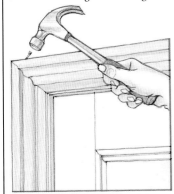

3 Nail the molding to the casing

4 Drive a nail into the miter joint

REPLACING ARCHITRAVES

REPLACING *door or window architraves that are damaged or unsightly is a very straightforward procedure. Standard architrave moldings in softwood can be obtained from hardware stores and lumberyards. If you want a more elaborate or wider-than-average molding, choose one from the stock of a specialist millwork supplier. A good millwork supplier will also make a replica of a molding for you.*

REMOVING AN ARCHITRAVE

To remove a damaged easing or architrave, drive a bolster chisel behind each component until you can lever it off with a claw hammer. Pull out any nails left in the doorframe.

Picture rails and baseboards often butt against an architrave. If the new architrave is wider than the one you are replacing, trim the ends of the picture rail or baseboards with a backsaw. If you are unable to saw a skirting *in situ*, you will need to lever it off the wall (see BASEBOARD REPAIRS).

INSTALLING AN ARCHITRAVE

Hold one slightly overlength upright in position approximately 1/4in (6mm) from the face of the jamb. Mark its length with a pencil, allowing for the width of the top member and 1/4in (6mm) clearance **(1)**. Cut a 45-degree miter on the marked line; then, using a spirit level to keep the upright vertical, nail it to the casing with 2in (50mm) finishing nails at intervals of about 1ft (300mm) or so. Don't drive the nails all the way home at this stage, in case you have to move the architrave. Install the second upright using the same procedure.

Rest the top member upside down on the ends of the uprights and mark its length **(2)**. Cut a miter at each end and nail the molding between the uprights **(3)**. Drive a nail through the edge of the top member into the miter joints at each end **(4)**. Drive all nailheads below the surface with a nail set, then fill the holes and joints before priming and painting the woodwork; if you plan to varnish the architrave, use a colored wood filler instead.

Fitting an architrave to an out-of-square frame

If your doorway is not quite square, 45-degree miter joints will not fit snugly. Instead, hold each component in position against the wall and draw a pencil line against each edge where the joints will occur **(1)**. Mark the miters where the lines cross **(2)** and transfer these points onto the architrave members. Cut the miters and fit the components as described above.

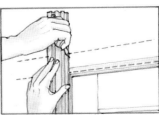

1 Draw alongside each component

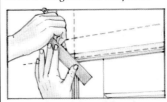

2 Mark the positions of the miters

Reproduction period architrave

FITTING AN ARCHITRAVE USING CORNER BLOCKS

Door casings in a number of styles incorporated fluted moldings with a decorative block at each corner and a block at the base of each upright.

Draw the position of the uprights and top member on the wall. Nail the baseboard blocks in place, in the center of each upright **(1)**. Nail both uprights to the jambs; pin a corner block above each **(2)**. Hide the nailheads in the decorative design. Then, cut the top member to length and nail it between the corner blocks.

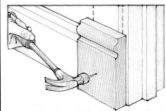

1 Nail baseboard blocks in place first

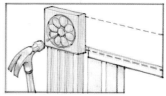

2 Pin corner blocks above uprights

DOORCASES & DOORHOODS

MEDIEVAL BUILDERS *in Europe began the practice of setting dripstone moldings into the masonry above doors and windows in order to divert rainwater to each side of the opening, where it could drip harmlessly to the ground.*

By the eighteenth century, such practical aspects were joined by aesthetic considerations, and the elaborate center doorway became the principal decorative element of the façade. In North America, from the mid-eighteenth century until the mid-nineteenth century, the Georgian style and the Federal and Greek revival styles all incorporated doors that featured classical elements like columns, pilasters, and pediments. The columns and pilasters were frequently fluted, and the pediments set off with elaborate friezes and architraves. Most often the elements were shaped out of softwood such as pine.

Wooden doorcases are often extremely elaborate, mimicking styles originally intended for stonework. The restoration of masonry and stucco surrounds is described elsewhere in the book; only wooden hoods and doorcases are included here.

PILASTERS AND COLUMNS

Narrow pilasters, running from headpiece to ground level on each side of the opening, were frequently used to give doorcases an impression of strength and solidity and add to the splendor of the façade.

Pilasters were to become increasingly complex, often resembling fluted piers that appeared to support a classically inspired entablature, often surmounted by a triangular or curved pediment. A pilaster of this sort might include a carved capital and a molded base.

Some doorcases had semicircular staved-timber columns constructed the same way as a barrel. On larger houses, the canopy above the front door might project sufficiently to form a shallow porch supported by freestanding columns. A second pair of columns, which were semicircular, would usually flank the door opening itself.

As an emphasis on ornamentation took over from strictly functional design, these columns and pilasters became more decorative than structural. When painted, doorcases constructed from separate wooden elements could be difficult to distinguish from the genuine stone surrounds that inspired them.

CONSOLES

In some Georgian houses, the doorcase brackets are vertical wooden consoles that appear to support narrow cornices or pointed pediments. Consoles were often elaborately carved and even pierced.

DOORHOODS

Most common in the early Victorian age, doorhoods consist of wooden frames, often with deep molded edges, supported on pairs of braces projecting from the wall. The exposed part of each brace was typically carved into a decorative scroll, creating what appears to be a bracket on each side of the door.

The shallow sloping "roof" of the hood had a sheet-lead or copper covering which, in order to prevent rainwater from running behind the hood, was formed into a flashing against the wall, and was folded over the edges of the hood. The door opening below the hood was usually surrounded by a relatively simple wooden architrave.

In many doorhoods the brackets are purely decorative and frequently made from separate, deeply carved elements.

Carved brackets support a doorhood

Vertical wooden consoles

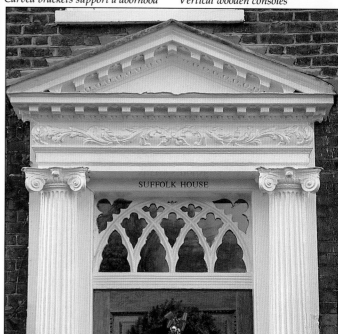

SUFFOLK HOUSE

Beautifully proportioned doorcase with fluted Ionic columns

REPAIRING DOORCASES

T HE BEAUTIFULLY *proportioned doorways of eighteenth-century houses are a delight to the eye. Unfortunately, it is also true that any wooden structure that has stood in the open for a couple of centuries is bound to have suffered from the effects of weathering. Usually, the greatest harm is inflicted by the ingress of water, which can in turn lead to decay. Damaged flashings allow rainwater to run behind hoods and canopies; open joints between a doorcase and the wall or between wooden components also provide routes for water to penetrate; and rising damp in masonry walls can saturate the timbers from behind.*

Simple pilasters with pediment

C18th engaged wooden columns

Freestanding staved columns support this substantial portico

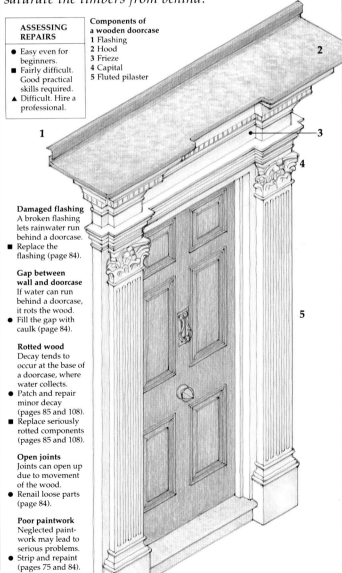

ASSESSING REPAIRS	Components of a wooden doorcase
● Easy even for beginners.	1 Flashing
■ Fairly difficult. Good practical skills required.	2 Hood
	3 Frieze
	4 Capital
▲ Difficult. Hire a professional.	5 Fluted pilaster

Damaged flashing
A broken flashing lets rainwater run behind a doorcase.
■ Replace the flashing (page 84).

Gap between wall and doorcase
If water can run behind a doorcase, it rots the wood.
● Fill the gap with caulk (page 84).

Rotted wood
Decay tends to occur at the base of a doorcase, where water collects.
● Patch and repair minor decay (pages 85 and 108).
■ Replace seriously rotted components (pages 85 and 108).

Open joints
Joints can open up due to movement of the wood.
● Renail loose parts (page 84).

Poor paintwork
Neglected paint-work may lead to serious problems.
● Strip and repaint (pages 75 and 84).

REGULAR MAINTENANCE

If an old doorcase has survived unscathed, it has probably been maintained regularly throughout its life. However, sound paintwork many layers thick can obscure decorative details well worth the effort of stripping and restoration.

If paintwork is beginning to flake, craze, or crack, attend to it before it deteriorates further and lets in water to rot the wood. Except for very minor blemishes that can be rubbed down, filled, and repainted, it is probably best to strip the doorcase down to bare wood, which will allow you to make good any defects and redecorate with a superior finish.

A partially stripped doorcase in the process of being restored

STRIPPING A DOORCASE

Most period doorcases are too elaborate to be stripped using a hot-air gun alone, so the only practicable solution is to use a chemical stripper. However, what looks like low-relief carving on panels, brackets, and pilasters may in fact be molded plaster, which could be damaged by the scrapers and steel wool used for removing softened paint from wood.

To be on the safe side, it is best to scrape a small area of paintwork with a very sharp blade. If you detect plaster below the paint, use the type of chemical stripper recommended for painted plaster ceilings.

Treating and painting the wood

Once you have exposed the wood, treat the whole door-case with clear preservative in order to protect it from rot in the future.

Renail any open joints or loose components using galvanized nails. Sink the nailheads, using a nail set, and fill the holes before you repaint the doorcase.

WEATHERPROOFING A DOORCASE

Take whatever measures are required to prevent water from saturating a wooden doorcase. If possible allow the doorcase to dry out thoroughly before further treatment.

Filling open joints

If nailing doesn't close up a joint satisfactorily, fill it with a flexible exterior wood filler before painting. Use flexible caulk to seal gaps between the doorcase and wall. You can buy it in tube form and inject it into the gap with a gun (**1**) or as a strip sealant that you press into place with your fingers (**2**).

Renewing the flashing

A doorhood or canopy has a metal covering, which is turned up against the wall. A strip of flashing is inserted in a mortar joint just above the canopy and bent down to cover the top, forming a weatherproof joint.

Chop out the mortar joint to a depth of 1in (25mm) and remove any scraps of flashing that remain. Buy a strip of flashing of the same material (probably copper) if possible. Use tinsnips to cut it to width so that it reaches from the canopy to the mortar joint, plus 1in (25mm). Clamp the flashing between two wooden battens, leaving a 1in (25mm) strip projecting (**1**). Bend this over to form a

right-angle lip and gently hammer it flat, using another batten to protect the metal (**2**). Insert the lip in the mortar joint above the canopy and wedge it in place with small rolled strips of lead (**3**). Use a soft hammer to tap the flashing against the upstand, shaping it to fit against the wall snugly. Finally, repoint the mortar joint.

Pointed pediments require stepped lead flashings that are best replaced by a skilled professional roofer.

If the house is wood-framed, loosen the clap-boards above the doorway and slide the flashing beneath, at least 5in (125mm) up the wall.

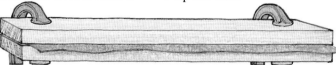

1 Clamp lead strip between battens

1 Inject caulk into the gap

2 Or introduce a strip sealant

2 Hammer strip over to form a lip

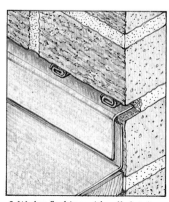

3 Wedge flashing with rolled strips

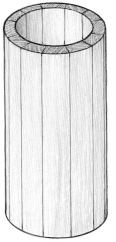
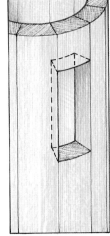

A wooden column is staved like a barrel

1 Cut a hole beveled on all four sides

2 Tap an oversize plug into the hole

REPAIRING COLUMNS

Due to their shape and construction, columns are particularly difficult to repair. Most of them are hollow, comprising a number of narrow strips of wood or staves with beveled edges glued together then shaped on the outside. A staved column is fairly stable, but unless the joints are reinforced with splines they tend to open up as a result of glue failure or shrinkage.

Having supported a porch roof, it is possible to remove an entire column and close a reglued joint with heavy-duty strap clamps. However, this type of repair work is best left to a professional restorer who has the experience to judge whether clamping a joint is likely to create additional strains and splits in the column.

Filling a split column

A vertical split or gaping joint in a semicircular doorcase column would be difficult to repair using the method described above, but provided the wood is relatively stable it is possible to fill a narrow gap with a sliver of softwood.

If necessary, open up the split with a power jigsaw. Shape the sliver with a sharp plane so that it will fill the gap. Plane a shallow bevel on both sides of the sliver to form a wedge, then glue it in place with waterproof exterior adhesive. Tap it home firmly with a hammer (but not too hard, or you may expand the column). Leave enough of the wedge projecting to plane once the glue has set, so that it will fit flush following the curve of the column.

Inserting a plug

An isolated patch of decay in a column can be cut out and replaced with a tapered plug of matching timber.

After drilling an insertion hole, insert the blade of a power jigsaw and cut out the rotted wood, leaving a rectangular hole beveled on all four sides (1).

Make a plug of wood with the grain running vertically, shaping it so that it fits the hole but protrudes slightly from the column (2).

Apply waterproof exterior adhesive to the edges of the plug, then tap it into the hole with a hammer. Either use a strap clamp to hold the plug in place or nail it with long finishing nails, driving them below the surface with a nail set. Once the glue has set, plane the plug to match the shape of the column.

TREATING WET ROT

Decay most frequently occurs near the end grain of timber, where water is able to penetrate more easily. It also often occurs near the base of columns and pilasters, where water tends to collect. Check for decay by pressing the wood with the tip of a screwdriver. Rotted wood is soft and spongy when wet, and becomes dry and crumbly during warm weather.

DECAY

To preserve, harden and fill areas of decay see DEALING WITH ROTTED WINDOWS. Badly affected wood has to be cut out and replaced. Because a doorcase is an assembly of several separate pieces of wood, it is feasible to replace individual components with preservative-treated wood. It is also possible to splice wood onto a component to replace a short section of rotted board.

Period-style reproduction doorcase

REINSTATING DOORCASES AND COLUMNS

Don't be tempted to buy scaled-down mock-classical door surrounds designed to enhance modern townhouses. A good specialist joiner is capable of making accurate replica doorcases and freestanding columns, using traditional materials and methods of construction. However, it is essential to employ a professional who is conversant with period proportion and detailing.

DOOR FURNITURE

DOOR FURNITURE *is the collective name used for hardware made for both external and internal doors. Each piece of hardware is primarily functional – yet for the past 250 years or so, being specifically designed to enrich the main entrance and principal rooms of our homes, much door furniture has been exceedingly handsome. Attractive and sometimes costly materials were used for period door furniture, and as a rule it was expertly crafted.*

Finding and renovating door hardware is perhaps one of the most pleasurable activities associated with restoring old houses. Antique hardware and good-quality reproductions are both widely available, and the level of skill required to fit, clean, and finish just about any piece of door furniture is well within the capabilities of any homeowner with the slightest practical experience.

A pair of cast-iron knockers complements this ornate Victorian door

Suitably dignified brass fittings

Iron fittings are perfect for a cottage

CHOOSING DOOR FURNITURE

With such a wealth of products to choose from, it is not always easy to decide which is the right hardware for a particular door.

The heaviest (and usually most expensive) hardware was normally reserved for the main entrance of the house. However, one should always respect the age, style, and character of a building and select the door furniture accordingly.

A country house with batten doors looks best with simple wrought-iron fittings, whereas a Victorian house can take more elaborate cast-iron or brass door furniture without appearing over-ornamented. Similarly, it makes sense to reserve heavily ornate hardware for the principal rooms and install more modest fittings in what would perhaps have been the servants' quarters in earlier times.

You can learn a great deal about period styles from contemporary magazine advertisements and trade catalogs. However, it pays to exercise a little caution before replacing what at first sight appear to be historically inappropriate additions or modifications.

Whereas few would argue against replacing a 1950s plastic handle added to a turn-of-the-century door, it makes little sense to discard a good-quality Victorian mortise lock on an early-Georgian door simply because it is not "authentic."

Our predecessors were just as keen to improve their homes and take advantage of the latest advances in technology as we are – and, provided an item has been fitted properly, looks good, and is still in working order, there's a great deal to be said for retaining it.

Authentic weathered door furniture

DOOR LATCHES AND HANDLES

When door handles, knobs, and latches were replaced in the past, they frequently found their way into the secondhand market. As a result, it is possible to buy matching sets of original door knobs from architectural-salvage companies, antique shops and dealers, and other antiques-trade outlets. And if you can't obtain an item of door furniture from any of these sources, there is a vast range of excellent reproduction hardware to choose from.

LATCHES

One of the earliest methods of keeping a door closed was with a short horizontal beam, pivoted at one end, that dropped onto a hook fixed to the doorframe. The beam, which in its crudest form was made from timber, would have been lifted by means of a length of string or leather thong that passed through a hole in the door to the outside.

More sophisticated latches based on the same principle were made in wrought iron by blacksmiths. The more successful versions were eventually mass-produced and are still to be found in manufacturers' catalogs. Handmade wrought iron latches that are perfect replicas of ones made by early blacksmiths can be obtained from specialist suppliers.

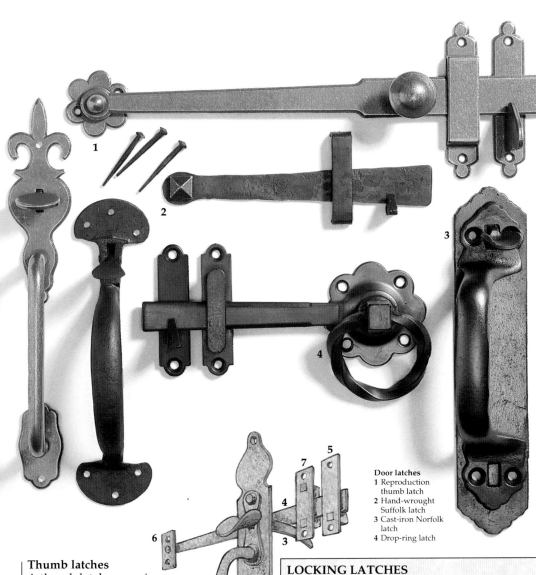

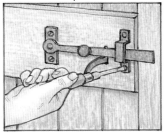

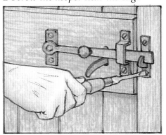

Door latches
1 Reproduction thumb latch
2 Hand-wrought Suffolk latch
3 Cast-iron Norfolk latch
4 Drop-ring latch

1 Screw the backplate to the door

2 Screw the keeper near the edge

3 Attach the stop to the post

Thumb latches

A thumb latch comprises a large, strong handle (1), sometimes fixed to a backplate (2). The handle incorporates a thumb-operated lever known as the sneck (3) that lifts the beam (4) off the hooked stop (5) on the other side of the door.

The beam is fixed to the door by means of a screwed plate (6) and a keeper (7).

The latch is operated from the inside by lifting either the end of the sneck or the beam itself.

Drop-ring latches

Latches that are operated by turning an iron drop ring were inspired by the Victorian Gothic-revival movement. Medieval-style drop-ring latches are still mass-produced.

Components of a thumb latch
1 Handle
2 Backplate
3 Sneck
4 Beam
5 Stop
6 Screwed plate
7 Keeper

LOCKING LATCHES

A device that prevents the beam being lifted from the outside effectively locks the door. This might be as simple as a small locking lever attached to the keeper (1), although some latches incorporate locks that can be operated by a key from either side of the door (2).

1 Latch fitted with locking lever

2 Latch with key

Fitting a thumb latch

If possible, fix a thumb latch near one end of the middle ledge of a batten door. The beam must always be on the side to which the door swings when it is opened.

Gauge the position of the handle and cut a small slot through the door for the sneck to pass through. Screw the handle or its backplate to the door (1) and check that the sneck is operating smoothly.

On the other side of the door, rest the beam on the sneck and slide it sideways until its tip overlaps onto the doorpost. Screw the beam's plate to the door, then slide the keeper in place and screw it near to the edge of the door (2). Close the door and screw the stop to the post (3).

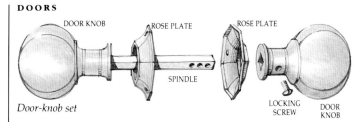

DOOR KNOB · ROSE PLATE · ROSE PLATE · SPINDLE · LOCKING SCREW · DOOR KNOB

Door-knob set

DOOR KNOBS

With the invention of rim locks and mortise locks, the latch was incorporated into the lock's mechanism in the form of a sliding latch bolt. A latch bolt is retracted by turning one of a pair of handles attached to each end of a square metal bar or spindle that passes through the lock.

From the Georgian period onward, these handles usually took the form of door knobs that were roughly circular or oval in shape. A wide variety of materials was used in their manufacture, including brass, ceramic, glass, wood, and even plastic, which was first used for door furniture in the early twentieth century. The principal rooms of a house, particularly throughout the Victorian period, were frequently furnished with impressive pairs of door knobs that were enhanced with cast or printed decoration.

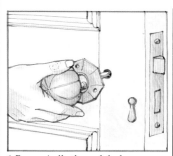

1 Pass spindle through lock

2 Locate second knob with screw

3 Some spindles are slotted

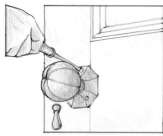

4 Fix roseplates with woodscrews

Fitting a door knob

Door knobs are normally sold in pairs, complete with either one or two rose plates (depending on whether they are intended for a door fitted with a rim lock or a mortise lock). A square spindle links the pair, and one of the knobs is usually fixed to the spindle. Slide this knob's rose plate up to it, then pass the spindle through the lock (1).

Slide the second knob and rose plate onto the other end of the spindle. In most cases the knob is secured by inserting a small machine screw through the neck of the knob into one of a series of threaded holes in the spindle (2).

Instead of screw holes, some spindles have a row of machined slots into which a pivoting "key" on the knob locates (3).

Screw the rose plates to the door (4). Some knobs are made with integral rotating rose plates and fit onto each end of a plain spindle. Screwing both plates to the door is sufficient to hold the knobs onto the spindle. Since the fixing screws are very small, use a bradawl to make pilot holes in the wood so that it is easier to insert them without damaging the screw slots.

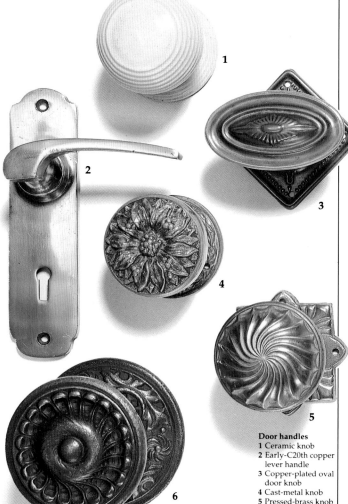

Door handles
1 Ceramic knob
2 Early-C20th copper lever handle
3 Copper-plated oval door knob
4 Cast-metal knob
5 Pressed-brass knob
6 Victorian door pull

DOOR PULLS

Door pulls for external doors are substantial iron or brass handles used to pull the door closed. Georgian and Victorian front doors were sometimes furnished with a single round or faceted knob or with a bar fixed to a backplate.

Fitting a door pull

Door pulls are invariably positioned centrally at about waist height and are fixed to the door with bolts. Round door pulls are often made with cast lugs on the back that are designed to bite into the wood and prevent the handle from spinning and unscrewing. You will need to drill shallow holes in a hardwood door in order to accommodate the lugs.

LEVER HANDLES

Lever handles were not common in Georgian or Victorian homes except on double doors in the grander houses. However, chromed or bronzed lever handles became fashionable in the 1920s and 1930s, when they were fitted to flush and paneled doors of the period. Like door knobs, lever handles are attached to square spindles that operate sliding latch bolts.

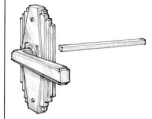

Art Deco lever handle with spindle

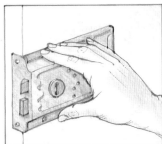

Victorian rim locks

PUSH PLATES

To keep the paintwork fresh and free from fingerprints, the Victorians used to screw metal, ceramic or glass plates to the closing stiles of internal doors.

Bedrooms normally had simple push plates. Much more elaborate plates were available for drawing rooms and parlors.

Push plates were sometimes sold in pairs, the larger one being positioned above the door handle and the smaller one (presumably for children) below the handle. Push plates were also made that combined the function of door-knob backplate and keyhole escutcheon.

Late-Victorian push plates

Art Nouveau door set, including push plate, knob and escutcheon

LOCKS AND BOLTS

In the earliest American houses, the only means of security were wooden or iron bolts that were attached to the inside of the door. However, since it is impossible to bolt a door from the outside, unattended houses remained insecure until the invention of a lock that could be operated from either side of the door with a removable key.

RIM LOCKS

Early locks were built into boxes screwed to the face of the door. The majority of these rim locks were purely utilitarian, being encased in iron, but by the eighteenth century the better-quality houses were being furnished with beautifully made brass-cased locks with sliding latch bolts retracted by turning a drop-ring handle or a small knob on the lock.

Rim locks, most of them manufactured from folded or pressed steel, were to be found in practically every home throughout the whole of the nineteenth century and the earlier part of the twentieth century. Wealthier householders fitted discreet mortise locks on some of their more important doors, but rim locks were used for the bedrooms and servants' quarters of Victorian homes.

A typical rim lock has what is known as a deadbolt, which is thrown by turning a key and locates in a cast-metal keeper screwed to the door jamb. When the deadbolt is withdrawn, the door is prevented from swinging open by a sliding latch bolt. The latch bolt is not only operated by turning a handle but, because the end is beveled, it is retracted automatically by being pressed against the keeper as the door is closed.

Normally, a small brass or ceramic knob was fixed to the lock itself. Another knob, sometimes of a grander design, was screwed to the other side of the door and connected to the lock by means of a metal spindle.

Fitting a rim lock

Place the lock on the middle rail, with its endplate hooked over the edge of the door **(1)**. If you are fitting a heavy Victorian lock, cut a recess in the edge of the door to accommodate the endplate. Early-twentieth-century locks were made from thinner sheet metal so the endplate would fit easily between the edge of the door and the jamb without being let into the wood.

Mark the position of the keyhole and handle on the door, then cut holes through the stile for them, using a drill. Replace the lock and insert the key and spindle from the other side of the door so that you can position the fitting accurately.

Drill through the holes in the lock to bore pilot holes for round-head fixing screws **(2)**. Screw the lock to the door and, if necessary, fix the endplate to the edge of the door with small countersunk screws.

Screw the keeper to the jamb opposite the lock **(3)**. If necessary, chop a recess in the architrave molding to accommodate the keeper. Screw or pin an escutcheon to the other side.

Pass the spindle of the door knob through the lock and fit a handle to the other side (see opposite page).

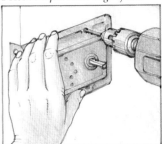

1 Hook endplate over edge of door

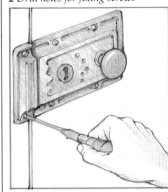

2 Drill holes for fixing screws

3 Screw the keeper to the jamb

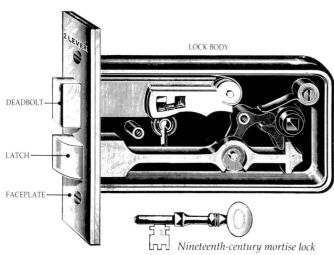

LOCK BODY

DEADBOLT

LATCH

FACEPLATE

Nineteenth-century mortise lock

MORTISE LOCKS

It is impossible to fit anything but a surface-mounted lock to a batten door (except for the framed variety). But the greater thickness of the paneled door made it feasible to install a lock in a mortise cut within the edge of the closing stile. The mechanism is contained in the body of the lock. Only the faceplate is visible when the lock is in place. The deadbolt and latch engage a striker plate let into the jamb or doorpost.

Fitting a mortise lock

Draw a line centrally on the edge of the stile and mark the top and bottom of the lock body on the door (1) to denote the extent of the mortise. Use a drill that matches the thickness of the lock body to bore out most of the waste (2), then square up the edges of the mortise with a chisel (3). Insert the lock and mark the perimeter of the faceplate (4). Chop a series of shallow cuts across the recess and pare out the waste till the plate fits flush with the edge of the door.

Holding the lock against the face of the stile, mark the center of the keyhole and the hole for the spindle (5). Drill and cut both holes, then install the lock and fix escutcheons to both sides of the door.

Extend the deadbolt and use it to mark the edge of the jamb or doorpost (6), then transfer these marks to the face so you can gauge the position of the striker plate. Cut a mortise and recess for the striker plate, then screw it in place.

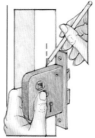

1 Mark center line on door

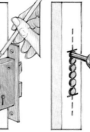

2 Bore out the waste wood

3 Trim mortise with a chisel

4 Mark the edge of the faceplate

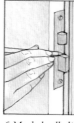

5 Mark keyhole and spindle

6 Mark deadbolt on doorpost

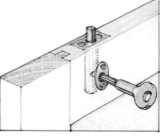

1 Unobtrusive key-operated rack bolt

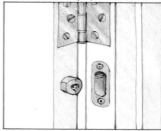

2 Fixed hinge bolts strengthen a stile

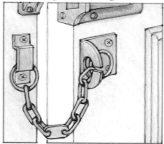

3 A security chain is essential

4 A viewer helps to identify callers

MODERN SECURITY RECOMMENDATIONS

When installing antique or period-style door furniture, don't ignore modern home-security recommendations. Surface-mounted locks, for example, are only as strong as the screw fixings in the wood, whereas mortise locks, being buried in the wood, are considerably stronger. An entrance door with an antique rim lock should be fitted with a mortise lock or modern security bolts as well.

Key-operated rack bolts (1) sunk into the edge of a door are extremely efficient. They are also unobtrusive, since a small escutcheon is all that is visible when the door is closed.

Inserting fixed hinge bolts (2) in the edge of the hanging stile prevents the hinged edge of a door from being levered open from outside.

A security chain (3) that prevents an intruder from pushing open a door when you unlatch it and a small telescopic viewer (4) that allows you to identify callers before opening the door are also discreet and worthwhile precautions.

ESCUTCHEONS

An escutcheon is used to cover the keyhole slot cut through a door. In its simplest form an escutcheon is a flat metal plate, but many escutcheons are made with a pivoting cover to prevent drafts. Stamped or cast-metal escutcheons are highly decorative and are much sought after by people restoring period houses.

A selection of period escutcheons

Original brass bell pull

KNOCKERS AND BELL PULLS

It has been customary at least since Georgian times for tradesmen and other callers to announce their presence by rapping on the front door with a metal knocker or by ringing a bell.

Door knockers

Old brass door knockers are usually very handsome. But, although good-quality replicas are made, modern reproductions sometimes look garish compared to mellow antique brass – and black-painted cast-iron knockers are better suited to many old houses.

Door knockers look best mounted centrally on a muntin at about head height. They are normally fixed to the door by bolts that pass through the wood, from the inside, into threaded bosses or nuts cast on the reverse of the knocker.

Bell pulls

In some early American homes a bell inside the house was attached to a cable that ran to the front door via a conduit buried in the wall plaster. The bell was rung by pulling on a knob mounted on the doorcase or surround. It was a system that was easily converted to electricity during the nineteenth century.

Devotees of the Arts and Crafts movement delighted in fitting twisted wrought-iron bell pulls, which were mounted vertically beside the front door.

Door knockers and letter plates
1 Cast-iron letter plate
2 Medieval-style door knocker
3 Reproduction iron knocker
4 Victorian-pattern brass knocker
5 Combined letter plate and knocker

LETTER PLATES

After the introduction of prepaid postage stamps in the 1830s, it was no longer necessary for a messenger to collect a fee from the recipient. Consequently, the letter plate became a desirable addition to the door furniture of a house, so mail could be delivered without disturbing the household. It is unusual to see an urban front door that has not had a letter plate added to it, although there was no genuine equivalent in the early houses.

A fitting alternative to a letter plate

TYPES OF LETTER PLATE

The earliest letter plates were probably of simple design cut from thick sheet brass, but the Victorians were never slow to embellish any item of door furniture. A homeowner was able to choose from a variety of fretted, stamped, pressed, and cast-metal versions. Knockers or door pulls were often combined with letter plates to make attractive and convenient single fittings.

Original letter plates are invariably too small for much of the mail that is delivered nowadays. A slot measuring 10 x 1½in (250 x 40mm) is a practical size.

Fitting a letter plate

A letter plate can be mounted vertically in the center of a door muntin or horizontally on the lock rail, whichever is more convenient and aesthetically pleasing. It should never be fixed to a door panel.

Mark out the position of the plate on the door and measure the size of the slot to be cut through the rail or muntin. You need to make the slot slightly larger than the flap of the letter plate.

Drill a small insertion hole in each corner of the marked rectangle, then insert the blade of a power jigsaw and cut out the slot. Clean up the inside of the slot with a file. Mark the center of the letter-plate bolts or screws on each side of the slot and bore through the wood. Attach the plate by passing the bolts through the holes from the inside of the house.

You can reduce drafts and also enhance the appearance of the letter plate by screwing a simple cover flap over the slot on the inside.

NUMERALS

As communities grew larger, especially with the building of rows of houses, it became desirable to be able to identify individual houses at a glance. Householders therefore began applying numerals to the front door, doorcase, or door surround.

Sometimes a signwriter was employed to paint the number on the woodwork or masonry; or a small ena-melled or engraved plate was fixed to the front door or to the wall of the house. Black wax was rubbed into engraved designs to make the numerals stand out. More often, individual cast or pressed-metal numerals were screwed centrally to the door muntin, while transom lights provided an ideal location for numerals etched or painted in reverse on the glass.

Early-C20th carved keystone

HINGES

Unlike most other items of door furniture, hinges are not usually chosen for aesthetic reasons, since they are primarily functional pieces of hardware. The hinge that works best in a given situation is therefore likely to look right, since our predecessors, too, were mainly influenced by functional considerations when selecting hinges.

FACE-MOUNTED HINGES

All early hinges were face-mounted, being visible on the door and frame when the door was closed. They were invariably rather crudely made in wrought iron and were usually nailed in place.

Strap hinges

Long tapering strap hinges were used for hanging batten doors. With a T-hinge, the strap is fixed to one of the ledges and joined by a knuckle joint to a relatively wide leaf attached to the doorframe.

The knuckle joints of this kind of handmade hinge were rather slack compared to those of modern machine-made hinges, but as soon as two or three hinges were fitted to a door all slackness was eliminated.

Other types of strap hinges were made by curling the end of the strap to form an eye that dropped over the vertical pin of a pintle – an L-shaped fitting with a spike **(1)** that was driven like a nail into a doorpost. Some pintles were made to screw into the wood **(2)**. Pintle hinges are difficult to fit accurately.

Strap hinges have been made continuously for centuries and they are still mass-produced, primarily for use on sheds and other outbuildings. However, accurate reproductions of old hinges are made for house-restorers who want an authentic-looking hinge.

Ideally, the length of a strap hinge should be about two-thirds the width of the door – although shorter hinges can be fitted near the bottom, where less strain is imposed by the weight of the door.

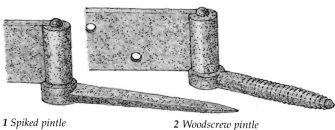

1 Spiked pintle   *2 Woodscrew pintle*

H and HL hinges

These face-mounted hinges were sometimes used in place of strap hinges to hang batten doors. They are also found on early paneled doors. An H-hinge has a pair of identical leaves joined by a knuckle joint. Fancier versions were made for wealthy clients. An HL or "Holy Lord" hinge has an extended leaf that lends greater support to a door.

Both H and HL hinges were fixed with handmade nails or screws. Replicas can be obtained from specialist suppliers. Choose 6 to 8in (150 to 200mm) hinges for an average door.

Fitting face-mounted hinges

Authentic-looking nails are sold by the suppliers of handmade wrought hinges for those who want to nail face-mounted hinges to a door in the traditional manner. The old joiners would "deaden" a nail by holding a metal block, such as a hammer head, against the reverse of the door so that the point of a long nail would be bent back into the wood, thus improving the grip and preventing the wood from splitting.

Two hinges are usually sufficient to support even a heavy door, but a third is often fitted to help prevent warping.

Fix a strap hinge centrally on one of the battens, with just the knuckle overhanging the edge of the door (1). H and HL hinges are fixed near the top and bottom of a door. The extended leaf of an HL-hinge aligns with the center of the top or bottom rail (2).

Fix face-mounted hinges to the door first. Then, with the door wedged securely in its opening, nail or screw the flaps to the doorpost.

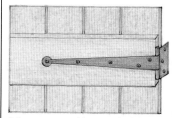

1 Screw a strap hinge to the ledge

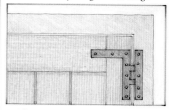

2 Align an HL-hinge with the rail

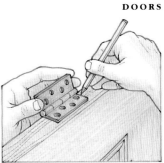

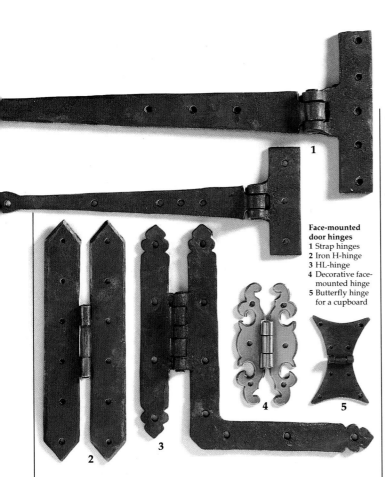

Face-mounted door hinges
1 Strap hinges
2 Iron H-hinge
3 HL-hinge
4 Decorative face-mounted hinge
5 Butterfly hinge for a cupboard

BUTT HINGES

The cast-metal butt hinge **(1)** was patented in 1775. This revolutionary hinge was designed to fit between a door stile and jamb so that only the knuckle was visible when the door was closed. Not surprisingly its discreetness appealed to architects and builders of the time, and by 1800 it was commonplace.

Early butt hinges were made of cast iron and were painted along with the door, but brass was used for more handsome hinges for show-wood doors. By the middle of the nineteenth century, cheaper hinges were being made by stamping them from sheet metal. Decorative brass butt hinges **(2)** became popular later in the century.

Improvements in manufacturing led to the lift-off hinge that allowed the door to be removed without unscrewing the hinges **(3)**.

The rising butt hinge **(4)** was a further development. The spiraling shoulders of this type of hinge cause the door to rise as it is opened, so it clears carpets and rugs. All butt hinges are screwed to the door and frame.

Fitting butt hinges

You will find two 4in (100mm) butt hinges are strong enough to hang the average paneled door. Add a third if the door is particularly heavy. Lightweight flush doors can be hung with two 3in (75mm) hinges.

First, wedge the door in its opening and mark the position of the hinges on the door stile and the jamb. The top hinge should be about 7in (175mm) from the top of the door and the bottom hinge about 10in (250mm) from the bottom edge. The recesses cut into the stile and jamb for each hinge must be an equal depth.

Support the door on edge and lay each hinge on the stile. With the knuckle overhanging, mark the position of the hinge by drawing around it **(1)**. Mark the depth of each hinge recess on the side of the stile, using a marking gauge **(2)**.

Make a series of shallow cuts with a chisel **(3)**, then pare out the waste **(4)** to leave a shallow recess for each hinge leaf. Neaten the edges and corners of the recess with a bevel-edge chisel, then insert the hinge to check the fit.

Screw the hinges to the door, then wedge it in an open position with the hinges aligned with the marks on the jamb. Draw around the hinges **(5)**. Mark the depth of the recesses and chop out the waste wood, as before.

Hang the door with one screw only in each leaf to check that the door swings and closes properly, then make any adjustments that are needed (see INSURING A DOOR CLOSES PROPERLY). Once the door swings and latches to your satisfaction, insert the remaining screws.

1 *Butt hinge*   2 *Decorative hinge*   3 *Lift-off hinge*   4 *Rising butt hinge*

1 *Mark the position of the hinge*

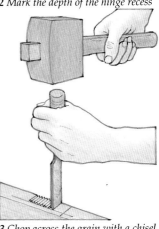

2 *Mark the depth of the hinge recess*

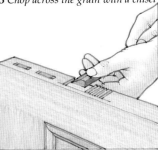

3 *Chop across the grain with a chisel*

4 *Pare out the waste wood*

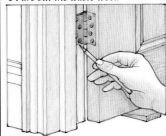

5 *Mark the hinge on the jamb*

CLEANING & FINISHING DOOR FURNITURE

WHETHER DOOR FURNITURE *should be cleaned and polished is a matter of controversy. There is no question that metalware that is seriously corroded or disfigured by layers of paint needs to be restored, but some people argue that cleaning old brass is ill-advised since the metal loses the mellow patina built up over the years. However, there are no hard and fast rules and, provided that you follow the maxim that in restoration one should never do anything that cannot be undone in the future, there is no reason why you should not follow your own inclination.*

STRIPPING PAINTED HARDWARE

Even if you intend to strip a door, it is best to remove the hardware so that the door and its furniture can be treated more effectively.

Arrange the hardware in one or more metal-foil dishes and pour chemical paint stripper into them. Stipple the stripper onto each piece of door furniture with an old paintbrush to insure that the chemicals penetrate all the crevices. Leave the stripper to do its work for 10 to 15 minutes, then check that the paint has begun to soften.

Wearing protective gloves, remove the softened paint from each item with fine steel wool. If there is still paint adhering to the fitting, return it to the dish and apply fresh stripper. Wash the stripped metal in hot water and dry it thoroughly with thick kitchen towels. If the fitting is hollow, stand it on a wad of newspaper to allow any water trapped inside to drain away.

STRIPPING METALWARE SAFELY

Follow the manufacturer's safety recommendations whenever you use chemical paint strippers.

Stipple stripper onto the fittings

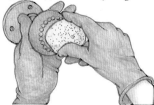
Soften corrosion with a salted lemon

CLEANING TARNISHED BRASS

Brass (which is an alloy of copper and zinc) develops a brown patina when left unprotected. It is a patina that does not lead to further corrosion, and many people find it attractive. Polishing brass door furniture that has been exposed to the elements for some time can be hard work, especially if it has begun to develop traces of green verdigris as a result of a higher-than-average copper content.

One traditional method for cleaning tarnished brass is to sprinkle some salt onto the cut surface of half a lemon and rub the metal vigorously with the fruit until the corrosion softens.

Another method is to make a cleaning solution of one level tablespoon of salt plus a tablespoon of vinegar in a cup of hot water. Dip a pad of fine steel wool in the solution and use it to swab the corroded brass.

Before polishing, rinse the brass in clean water and dry it thoroughly.

POLISHING DOOR FURNITURE

Metal polishes are mildly abrasive cleaning agents that remove small amounts of metal along with the dirt and corrosion. They should therefore be used sparingly on plated door furniture, since frequent polishing will eventually wear through to the base metal. It is safer to clean items such as copper-plated finger plates by washing off greasy marks with lighter fluid, then buff them with a clean soft cloth.

Burnish brass door furniture with a "long-term" brass polish that leaves an invisible chemical barrier on the metal and inhibits corrosion so the metal needs polishing less frequently.

Clean grimy chromium-plated door furniture with lighter fluid, or wash it in warm soapy water containing a few drops of household ammonia. Then burnish the metal with a mild cream chrome polish.

Protecting the paintwork

Clearly, it would be too much of a chore to remove door furniture every time you wanted to polish it. To protect the surrounding paintwork from abrasive cleaners, cut a template from thin cardboard to slip over each item of door furniture or stick low-adhesive masking tape over the paintwork.

If you don't want to remove door furniture with raised edges, such as a letter plate or the number of the house, you can leave the fittings *in situ* when you repaint a door. Allow the paint to coat the edges, but wipe it from the surface of the fitting with a cloth dampened with mineral spirits.

Once the paint is dry, you can polish the exposed metal without spoiling the newly painted woodwork.

CLEANING RUSTY IRON

Remove rusty wrought-iron or cast-iron fittings from the door and spray them with a penetrant oil for several hours, then clean them with fine steel wool. Dry the metal and treat it immediately with a chemical rust inhibitor before priming and painting.

FINISHING DOOR FURNITURE

You can protect polished brass with clear acrylic lacquer. Paint it on fairly quickly with a soft artist's brush. If you can't avoid leaving brush marks in the lacquer, stand the door furniture on a warm radiator before the lacquer sets really hard. The heat will soften the lacquer sufficiently for the brush marks to flow out naturally. If lacquer becomes discolored or is chipped, remove it with acetone then repolish the metal and apply fresh lacquer.

Iron door furniture is usually protected by applying a calcium-plumbate or zinc-phosphate primer followed by one or two coats of semi-matte black paint. However, some restorers prefer to keep wrought-iron hinges free from rust by wiping them occasionally with an oily rag.

CHAPTER NINE

WINDOWS

B Y THE EIGHTEENTH CENTURY *there were two designs for domestic windows in common use. The side-hung casement, which swung open like a door, was of medieval origin, and at the beginning of the century it was the chosen style for humble cottage and grand house alike. However, the last quarter of the seventeenth century saw the introduction of the sliding-sash window, which revolutionized building design and remained the most popular type of window, in Britain and America at least, for the next two hundred years.*

Probably of British origin, although some maintain that the Dutch were the inventors, the sliding-sash window consists of two overlapping glazed frames or "sashes" that slide vertically. The earliest versions had a single sliding sash, which was held open with wedges or by inserting pegs in holes drilled in the wooden frame that lined the window opening. However, the double-hung sash window, which has two movable sashes, was to become the standard model by the mid-nineteenth century. Save for a few minor variations, it has remained unchanged ever since.

A double-hung sash window is a sophisticated piece of design, the sliding sashes being suspended from pulleys on weighted cords or chains so that they will remain in any position required. Leaving the window open at top and bottom provides an ideal means of promoting efficient circulation of air within the room.

Keep in mind that many houses of all ages have had their original windows replaced. If you suspect that the windows in your home are not original, you might investigate other houses of its vintage to determine what the windows were like. The detailing of multi-light sash windows adds character to a house, both inside and out.

Turret window in mansard roof

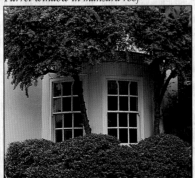
Bowed sashes needed skilled glazing

Early C20th metal casements resemble earlier window styles

Shutters are useful and decorative

Nicely proportioned fixed lights

GEORGIAN SASH WINDOWS

EARLY SASH WINDOWS *were divided by thick wooden glazing bars, or muntins, into anything from 16 to 24 almost-square panes; but by the second quarter of the nineteenth century, the classic "six-over-six" sash window had become a universally accepted norm.*

The classic six-over-six sliding-sash window

PROPORTIONS

The shapes of eighteenth-century window openings were based on geometric proportions that appealed to architects, builders, and clients alike. The width and status of a particular window often determined the height of the opening. A window on the main floor, or *piano nobile*, which was normally located on the second floor of grander houses, was usually a double square, being twice as high as it was wide. The height of a window on the "chamber" or bedroom floor might be 1¼ times its width, while windows at attic level, where the majority of the servants' rooms were situated, tended to be square. These proportions are responsible for the elegant appearance of many Georgian town houses.

Attic level
Servants' quarters and nursery

Third floor
Family bedrooms

Second floor
Formal reception rooms

First floor
Dining room and parlour

Cellar
Kitchen and scullery

Window proportions

The elevation of an English late-Georgian house demonstrates the principles of geometry used to arrive at the proportions of the windows. These principles were not adhered to rigidly but served as useful rules of thumb. Wide windows were divided by extra vertical glazing bars to keep the size of the panes constant.

Tall windows need additional panes

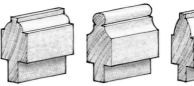

1 *Ovolo* **2** *Astragal & hollow* **3** *Sash ovolo* **4** *Lamb's tongue*

1 *Basic straight-head sash window*

2 *English segmental-head window*

GLAZING BARS

The glazing bars, or muntins, that divide each sash are rebated on the exterior to support a pane of glass on each side. The putty that holds the glass in place is shaped to form simple bevels. Muntins are molded on the inside and are perhaps the most decorative elements of the design. Although there were innumerable local variations, certain styles of glazing-bar molding can be identified as typical for different stages in sash-window development.

Early Georgian windows were made with thick square-ovolo moldings **(1)**. The number of glazing bars decreased when larger panes of glass became fashionable. At the same time, they became thinner and thinner, with more refined moldings. By the beginning of the Greek revival in the second quarter of the nineteenth century, the curve of the muntins had assumed an elliptical shape and had thinned to an almost delicate profile.

Although the majority of windows were made with a straightforward grid of glazing bars, some decorative windows were enhanced by rearranging the muntins to create narrow marginal lights, and semicircular-head and elliptical-head windows afforded the opportunity for decorative radial and curved patterns of glazing bars.

3 *Late-Georgian semicircular head*

4 *Elliptical-head sash window*

WINDOW SHAPES

The basic rectangular straight-head window **(1)** is common-place in Georgian houses, but in the eighteenth century windows with segmental heads were fashionable too **(2)**. Some high-style houses were built with semi-circular-head **(3)** or elliptical-head windows **(4)**.

VARIATIONS ON THE SASH WINDOW

Although one thinks of a typical Georgian or Federal house as having a more or less symmetrical façade with regularly placed individual windows, architects also sometimes grouped sash windows, usually in combinations of three.

The Venetian or Palladian window is the most obvious example. A semicircular-head sash window is flanked by narrow, slightly lower, sashes that are sometimes fixed. In order to keep the mullions between the windows as narrow as possible, the counterweight cords for the moving sashes in the middle often ran over the top of the flanking windows so that the weights could hang on each side of the group.

Bow and bay windows were frequently a combination of three separate windows, and in many cases all three of them were working sash windows.

BLIND WINDOWS

Fake sashes or simply plain recesses in the masonry are often found in Federal houses where, from the outside, one would expect to see a genuine window. In wood-framed houses of the Victorian era, window frames were sometimes installed without a sash. No opening was visible on the inside, but from the outside blinds or shutters gave the impression of a windowed opening. Blind windows were usually inserted so as not to disturb the rhythm of a façade when a real window would have broken some internal feature. Although a blind window is often no more than a simple recess in the wall, sometimes part of the masonry is set back slightly to cast a shadow that resembles a lower sash. More elaborate examples are constructed with glazed but non-working sashes in the recess and may include a painted facsimile of a window blind to complete the illusion.

Early-eighteenth-century Palladian window

VICTORIAN & EDWARDIAN SASH WINDOWS

W INDOW STYLES *did not, of course, suddenly change when Victoria assumed the British throne. However, the prevailing feature that distinguished Victorian windows from earlier ones was the larger panes of cheap mass-produced glass, supported by fewer and fewer muntin bars. Four-over-four, two-over-two, and eventually one-over-one are all typical Victorian windowpane arrangements. Again, earlier windows were often "modernized" by removing the original glazing bars to install larger sheets of glass, which is why horned windows are found in some earlier Georgian buildings.*

 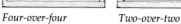 

Four-over-four   Two-over-two   One-over-one

Ornate surrounds for simple sashes

Gothic-revival lancet window

Composite sashes admit more light

THE INTRODUCTION OF HORNED SASHES

The elimination of glazing bars put additional strain on the relatively slim meeting rail of the upper sash, especially on the joint at each end of the rail. From about 1840 this joint was sometimes modified to include a wedged through tenon, which necessitated extending the vertical stile to reinforce the joint. This extension, known as the "horn," was either beveled or molded.

Horns strengthen the meeting rail

VICTORIAN WINDOW SHAPES

The Victorians continued to employ semicircular and segmental-head windows, and the Gothic-revival movement was responsible for the widespread use of the pointed-head or lancet window. However, since rectangular window openings were easier to build, these shapes were frequently incorporated within a rectangular sash, creating "triangular" lights in the top corners of the window.

COMPOSITE SASH WINDOWS

The desire for larger areas of glass, which would admit more light, is reflected in the Queen Anne and Georgian revival style by the combination of sash windows in pairs and groups of three. In the majority of cases, all the sashes slide and the counterweights are housed in the dividing mullions. Palladian windows feature in more grandiose and ornate houses throughout the later Victorian period.

BAY WINDOWS

Curved bow and square or canted bay windows, often running the full height of the house to the eaves, are so widespread that they are practically synonymous with nineteenth-century housing. Bay windows enrich the seemingly endless streets of row houses built during the era. They also have the practical advantage of greatly increasing the field of view from inside.

Oriel windows, cantilevered from the upper stories, are charming variations of the traditional bay. Square and canted oriels with windows on three sides were used to light major bedrooms. Small triangular oriels illuminate small bedrooms and staircases. Oriel windows recur from time to time in later revival styles, particularly in the neo-Tudor housing of the 1920s and 1930s.

Canted bay window   *Stone-built oriel window*

Restricting glazing bars to the upper sash was a common Victorian practice

Colored-glass marginal lights frame these Victorian sash windows

GLAZING-BAR ARRANGEMENTS

With their characteristic enthusiasm for anything decorative, the Victorians employed a much greater variety of glazing-bar arrangements than their predecessors and delighted in marginal lights incorporating colored glass. Often, however, decorative arrangements of muntins were restricted to the upper sash, with a single undivided pane of glass in the sash below. The Queen Anne revival during the last quarter of the nineteenth century saw the reintroduction of the early-Georgian-style multi-pane sash with thick glazing bars.

Elegant glazing-bar arrangement   *Imaginative use of glazing bars*

HOW SASH WINDOWS WERE MADE

DOUBLE-HUNG SASH WINDOWS *vary in the details of their construction, but the basic principles described here are common to all windows of this type. A sash window is a complicated piece of joinery, yet is designed in such a way that it can be dismantled easily when it is necessary to carry out maintenance and repairs. Most windows are made from softwood, although oak and mahogany have been used for better-quality windows.*

CONSTRUCTION OF THE SLIDING SASHES

Each sash comprises two vertical stiles (1), a top rail (2) or bottom rail (3), and a meeting rail (4). The meeting rails oppose each other when the sashes are closed, and their adjoining faces are beveled (5) so that they close together tightly in order to keep drafts and rattles to a minimum. They are sometimes bevel-rebated to prevent a knife blade or similar implement being slipped between the rails to open the window fastener from outside. Sash rails are rebated on the outside (the lower-sash meeting rail is grooved) to accept the glass, and they are molded on the inside. The glass is retained with sprigs (small nails) or glazing points (flat triangular metal fixings) and linseed-oil putty.

The top rail of the upper sash and the bottom rail of the lower sash are joined to the stiles with through mortise-and-tenon joints (6). Joints are glued and usually reinforced with wedges from the outside or with locking dowels through the sides of the joints.

Meeting rails are wider than stiles in order to close the gap between sliding sashes. They are joined to the stiles with a form of dovetailed bridle joint (7). Often a stronger mortise-and-tenon joint is used for the upper sash, and the stile extended to form a "horn" that strengthens the bottom of the mortise.

Glazing bars

Narrow wooden glazing bars (8) are used to hold relatively small panes of glass within the sashes. These are rebated for the glass and molded on the inside. Vertical glazing bars are usually continuous, and are jointed into the rails (9) with mortise and tenons. The shorter horizontal bars are made with similar joints. Alternatively, all the glazing bars may be continuous, in which case they are joined with halving joints (10) where they cross. A single vertical glazing bar may be joined to the meeting rail of the upper sash with a wedged through tenon.

CONSTRUCTION OF THE WINDOW FRAME

The frame within which the sashes slide comprises two vertical jambs (one on each side), a head across the top and a sill across the bottom. Because a jamb needs to be hollow to house the sash weights, it is made in three parts: the inner lining (11), the outer lining (12) and the pulley lining (13), together forming a three-sided box. With better-quality work, a rough-sawn back lining (14), nailed to the inner and outer linings, strengthens the jamb and prevents the sash weights from getting caught on any projections from the wall behind. The weights are separated from each other by a narrow strip of wood, called a parting slip (15), which is housed in a slot in the head and suspended from a nail or peg. The parting slip stops about 4in (100mm) short of the sill.

The head is constructed in a similar way to a jamb, with inner and outer linings plus a soffit lining (16). Since there is no top lining, glued triangular blocks (17) are used to strengthen the head. The sill (18) is cut from a single piece of solid wood and is shaped so that water flows away from the sashes to the outside. A recess is formed for the upper sash by the projecting lips of the outer linings together with the two parting beads (19) that are nailed into grooves cut in the pulley stiles and a similar bead running across the soffit lining. Stop beads (20) nailed all around the frame hold the lower sash in place.

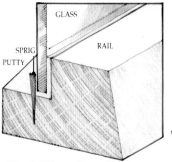

Glass held by sprigs and putty

Joint between bottom rail and stile

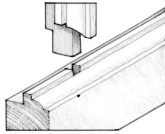

Halving joint for glazing bars

Joint between glazing bar and rail

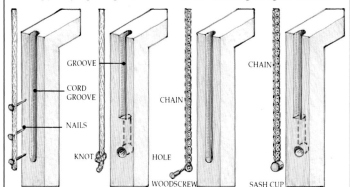

Attaching cord to sashes

Attaching chain to sashes

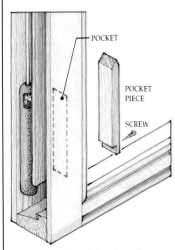

Access to sash weight via pocket

WEIGHTS AND PULLEYS

A pair of counterweights (21) is attached to each sash with waxed cords (22) or chains that pass over pulley wheels (23) screwed to the jambs or tape balances. Each cord is nailed into a groove cut in the sash stile or, alternatively, the knotted end of the cord may be located in a hole drilled into the stile. Chains are attached with woodscrews or by means of a metal lining (sash cup) for the hole in the stile.

Access to sash weights is by means of openings known as "pockets" (24) cut through the pulley stiles. Each pocket is closed by a strip of wood, or pocket piece, which may be fixed by a single screw at the bottom – although often pocket pieces are simply held in place by the beads and lower sliding sash.

EARLY WINDOW FRAMES

Original windows that remain in eighteenth- or early-nineteenth-century houses will most likely have solid timber frames. Made of softwoods, generally about 100mm (several inches) in width and thickness, these frames are joined at the corners with pinned mortise-and tenon joints. The runways in which the lower sash moves are recesses cut into the solid frame.

Broken glass
■ Try to find matching glass to replace broken windowpanes (page 106).

Damaged weatherseal
Mortar used to seal around the frame shrinks and falls out.
● Seal the joints as soon as possible (page 109).

Seized pulley wheel
Paint can jam a pulley, making a sash difficult to open and close.
● Lubricate or strip pulley (page 104).

Broken cords
■ It is worth replacing all the sash cords when one breaks (page 103).

Loose joints
Sash joints shrink and work loose.
■ Repair them before water penetrates and rots the wood (page 104).

Loose putty
Loose putty is a security risk and encourages wood rot.
● Replace it with fresh putty (page 107).

Dry rot
Dry rot can develop inside the jamb.
▲ Have it inspected and treated by an expert (page 108).

Sticking sashes
Swollen sashes or a build-up of paint can cause a wooden window to jam.
● Ease sash (page 104).

Rotted rails and glazing bars
Condensation and rainwater run down the glass and seep behind loose putty. Decay develops.
● Patch and preserve (page 108).
■ Replace the rotted wooden components (page 109).

Rotted sill
Being the lowest horizontal member, the sill often rots.
■ Dig out and patch the rotten wood (page 108).
▲ Have the old sill replaced with a new hardwood sill.

Components of a sash window
1 Vertical stile
2 Top rail
3 Bottom rail
4 Meeting rail
5 Beveled face
6 Through mortise and tenon
7 Dovetailed bridle joint
8 Glazing bar
9 Mortise and tenon
10 Halving joint
11 Inner lining
12 Outer lining
13 Pulley lining
14 Back lining
15 Parting slip
16 Soffit lining
17 Triangular block
18 Sill
19 Parting bead
20 Stop bead
21 Counterweight
22 Sash cord
23 Pulley wheel
24 Pocket

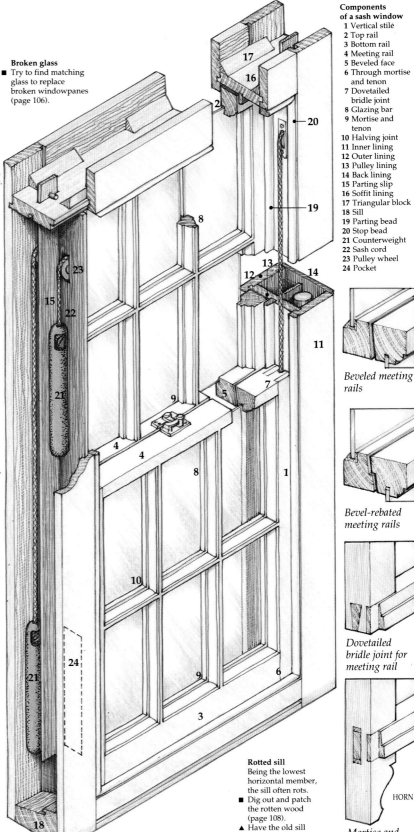

Beveled meeting rails

Bevel-rebated meeting rails

Dovetailed bridle joint for meeting rail

Mortise and tenon with horn

An unusual sash in a wooden wall

SASH WINDOWS IN TIMBER-FRAME WALLS

When a sash window was fitted in a timber-frame wall, it was centered in the opening with wooden shims, then the soffit lining was nailed to a header or lintel and the sill nailed to a subsill. The inner and outer linings form a casing that hides the joint between the window frame and the wall.

SASH WINDOWS IN MASONRY WALLS

From the last quarter of the eighteenth century, wooden window frames were made to be a close fit in the window opening, and the jambs and head were recessed behind the brickwork on each side and behind a stone lintel or brick arch above. Sometimes wedges were inserted around the frame to center it in the opening. The wooden sill sits on top of a stone subsill built into the wall. A metal strip forms a weatherproof joint between both sills. The head might be nailed to a wooden lintel that supports the masonry behind the stone lintel or brick arch. Once the internal wall is plastered and the architraves (casings) have been fitted, the window frame is firmly fixed in place.

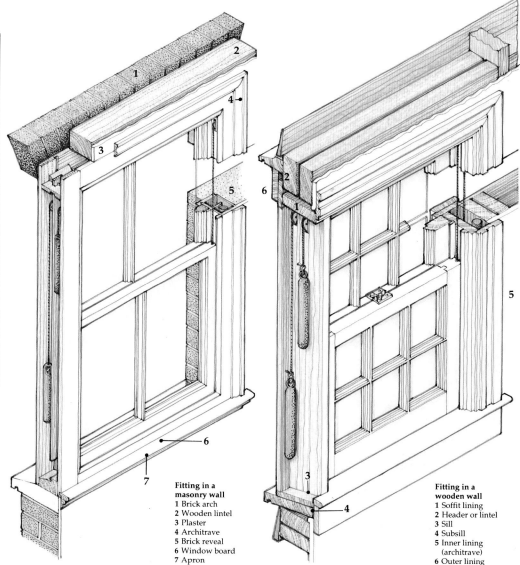

Fitting in a masonry wall
1 Brick arch
2 Wooden lintel
3 Plaster
4 Architrave
5 Brick reveal
6 Window board
7 Apron

Fitting in a wooden wall
1 Soffit lining
2 Header or lintel
3 Sill
4 Subsill
5 Inner lining (architrave)
6 Outer lining

BUILDING LAW OF YORE

Often in studying building technology, we discover that only the laws of an era can explain peculiarities in a structure. For example, in London, thanks to the Building Act of 1709, window frames were required to be set back by 4in (100mm) to reduce the risk of fire spreading (2). Prior to that date, the window frames had been set practically flush with the façades of houses (1). The act was strengthened in 1774, and from then on frames had to be recessed behind the brickwork (3).

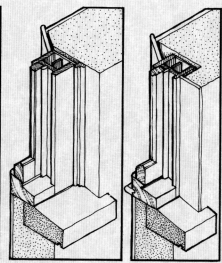

1 Before 1709
Flush with brickwork

2 From 1709 to 1774
Set back 4in (100mm)

3 After 1774
Set back and recessed

REPAIRING SASH WINDOWS

CONTRARY TO THE PROPAGANDA *put out by some manufacturers and installers of replacement windows, it is nearly always possible to repair wooden-sash windows. It is also very satisfying to preserve what are important features of a period house, especially when it proves to be much cheaper than replacing them. Some aspects of the work are quite time-consuming, but most of it is well within the capabilities of a reasonably competent woodworker.*

CORDS AND CHAINS

When replacing sash cords, try to match the old cord with replacement cord of the same size and weight. If special sash cord is not available, clothesline is usually to be found at hardware stores and may be a suitable substitute. Beware of cords that are too light (they may break) or too small (they may catch in the pulleys).

Very heavy windows may be hung from chains. The cheaper chains are made with folded metal links. Better-quality ones are made with riveted links.

Try not to smear paint onto cords or chains when redecorating. Paint clogs chain links and weakens cotton cord.

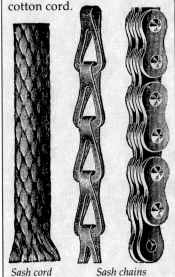

Sash cord   Sash chains

Broken sash cords

When one or both sash cords break, a sash window becomes difficult to open. A sash with weight on one side only may be out of balance; and if both cords are broken, the sash may be too heavy to lift. If you have to dismantle a sash window, it is worth taking the opportunity to replace both the cords before reinstalling it.

Drive a wide paint scraper between the stop bead and the jamb on one side of the window (1). Starting halfway up the window, use the same tool to begin prying the bead away from the frame. Once a few nails lose their grip, bend the bead by hand until you can free the miter joint at each end. This will allow you to swing the lower sash out of the frame. Disconnect intact cords or chains and lower the sash weights to the bottom of the jambs.

To remove the upper sash, pry out the parting beads (2) and disconnect cords or chains as before.

Retrieve the weights by opening the pocket in the pulley stile on each side of the window (3). Pull the parting slips aside to reach the outer weights.

Using an old cord as a guide, mark off its length on the new replacement cord, but don't cut it to length at this stage. Tie a bent nail or a similar small weight to a length of string and pass it over the pulley into the hollow jamb (4). Lower the weight until it appears at the pocket, then tape the other end of the string to the new cord. Pull on the string while feeding the cord over the pulley until you can retrieve it from the pocket.

Tie the cord to the ring on the end of the sash weight (5), or make a figure-of-eight knot to locate in the recess cast in some weights (6).

Pull the weight up to the pulley on the inside of the jamb, then lower it by about 4in (100mm). With the sash resting on the sill, nail the premarked cord into the groove in the sash stile, using three large blued tacks. Fix the lower 6in (150mm) only (7), then cut off excess cord with a sharp knife. Alternatively, fit a knotted cord in the sash stile – or screw a sash chain to the stile.

Attach other weights and cords, then replace the sashes, checking that they run smoothly before nailing the parting beads and stop beads to the jamb.

1 Break paint seal with a scraper

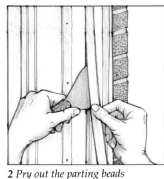

2 Pry out the parting beads

3 Take out the pocket piece

4 Pass weight over pulley wheel

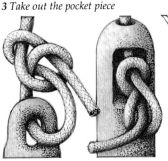

5 Tie cord to the sash weight   *6 Or tie a figure-of-eight knot*

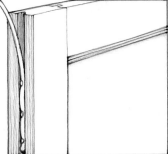

7 Nail the sash cord in the groove

EASING A STICKING SASH

One of the most common and frustrating properties of sliding-sash windows is their refusal to budge or to open and close smoothly. Not only is a sticking sash window annoying to live with, but the strain imposed by forcing it to move puts additional load on joints that may be weak already. There are several reasons why a sash can stick, so it pays to try the simpler solutions first.

Overpainting

Unless a freshly painted sash is moved regularly while the paint is drying, there is every possibility that the wet paint will act as an adhesive. When this happens, if the next painter does not bother to free the sash and simply paints it *in situ*, that makes matters even worse.

Take a sharp utility knife and carefully score around the sash, then work the blade of a wide paint scraper (or, better still, a flexible filling knife) between the sash and the surrounding beads. You may loosen the sash from the outside in the same way.

Grasp the meeting rail and try shaking the sash from side to side in order to break the paint seal.

Misplaced beads

A sash may be difficult to move because a misplaced stop bead is virtually clamping it against the parting beads. Pry suspect beads from the frame and reposition them.

Seized pulley

If a pulley is not running freely, the friction will impede the movement of the sash cord. A drop of penetrating oil may be all that's needed to free the pulley – but you are more likely to find that it has been overpainted at some time, causing it to seize up. If so, disconnect the sash cord and remove the pulley, which is normally fixed to the stile with two woodscrews. Use paint stripper to dislodge the paint, then lightly oil the pulley before reassembly.

Swollen or distorted sash

During humid or damp weather, a wooden window can expand considerably, especially if it has been neglected and the paintwork is in poor condition. If a sliding sash sticks intermittently, wait for dry weather then prepare and paint it to seal the wood.

A twisted or bowed sash probably sticks most of the time, and it will usually exhibit signs of wear or scuffing in areas that are rubbing against the frame. Take the distorted sash out of its frame (see BROKEN SASH CORDS) and shave the worn areas with a sharp block plane. Before you reinstall it, lubricate the sash by rubbing a candle along its running surfaces.

Trim a twisted sash with a plane

Loose sash joints

South-facing windows are particularly susceptible to the effects of weathering. With the alternate swelling and shrinking of the wood, glued joints begin to work loose, exhibiting wide gaps along their shoulders. An expanding sash may jam in its frame, but more serious problems can arise when rainwater and condensation penetrate the joint and rot the wood.

As a temporary measure, rake out loose material from the gap along each shoulder and close up the joint as best you can. Screw an L-shaped metal plate onto the outside of the sash to clamp the joint and prevent it from deteriorating further. To make a more permanent repair, dismantle the sash and reglue the joints. Remove the sash and lay it flat on a convenient surface so that you can remove the glass without breaking it. Lay the glass aside, then clamp the frame to a bench.

Inspect the joints to see if there are any wedges or locking dowels that would prevent them from coming apart. If necessary, chop wedges out with a small chisel. However, you may find they are loose or missing. Locking dowels can be drilled out.

Try tapping the joints apart with a hammer, using a softwood block to protect the sash (1). Work alternately, first at one end of the stile then the other, to avoid breaking a joint. If any of the joints is stuck fast, play steam from a kettle along the shoulder line to soften the glue – then tap again.

Using a chisel, scrape old glue from the joints. Before reassembling the sash, consider stripping the paint

Mend a sash temporarily with a plate

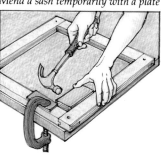

1 Tap joints apart with a hammer

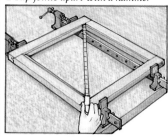

2 Check that the sash is square

and applying a liquid preservative to all surfaces, including the joints.

Use a waterproof synthetic-resin adhesive to glue the sash and use long sash clamps to pull the joints together. Measure from corner to corner (2) to check that the sash is square. Both diagonals should be identical. Replace wedges or dowels. When the glue has set, replace the glass and reinstall the sash.

CURING RATTLING SASHES

Our forebears used to stop sash windows rattling by driving small rubber wedges between the sashes and the beads. Another solution is to fit a fastener that has a cam action, which will pull the two meeting rails together.

REPLACING GLASS

IT IS DIFFICULT TO APPRECIATE *the quality old glass gives to a building until you see a façade with all its original glazing, each pane catching the light at a different angle and distorting reflections. It pays to preserve any antique glass you find intact and to replace it with a similar form of glazing when broken. The various types of glass described below were used for glazing domestic windows from the eighteenth century onward.*

Making cylinder glass in the traditional manner

CROWN GLASS

Until about 1830 windows were glazed with handmade crown glass. This was produced by blowing a bubble of molten glass, which was then attached to a metal rod, called a pontil, directly opposite the glass-blower's pipe. Once the blowpipe was cut from the bubble, the glass was heated again and spun on the pontil until it formed a disk about 4 to 5ft (1.5m) in diameter. The disc was then cut into square, rectangular or diamond-shape panes for glazing windows. The center of the disk, which had a scar left by the pontil, was either thrown back into the furnace or sold as cheap glazing for poorer houses or agricultural buildings. The popular belief that bull's-eye panes were fitted for decorative reasons is a modern idea. Crown glass is thin and brittle, and the spinning process left curved ridges or striations in the glass that distort the view through a window. It is these subtle flaws and imperfections, coupled with its highly fire-polished surface and variations in color, that endow crown glass with its special character.

Spinning crown glass

CYLINDER GLASS

Cylinder, or "broad glass," was the only real alternative to crown glass for windows until the middle of the nineteenth century. Although not of the same quality as crown glass, larger panes could be made from cylinder glass. A large sausage-shape bubble of glass some 4 to 5ft (1.5m) long and 10 to 12in (250 to 300mm) in diameter was blown over a pit, which provided room for the extending cylinder. The two ends of the cylinder were removed, then it was split lengthwise before being reheated and opened out to make a flat sheet about 3ft (900mm) wide. The top surface of the sheet was relatively flat, but the underside inevitably puckered as the cylinder was unrolled, creating a slightly wavy surface that breaks up reflections in a most attractive manner when cylinder glass is installed in a window.

Genuine crown or cylinder glass enlivens a façade

PLATE GLASS

As a result of mechanization, manufacturers were able to make larger and larger cylinders of glass. But there was clearly a need for a process that could produce large flat sheets.

Plate glass was invented as early as the seventeenth century, but its production was so labor-intensive that it was almost exclusively used for making mirrors for the wealthy.

Molten glass was poured onto a metal casting table. Then, after cooling, it was painstakingly ground and polished to make a sheet that was optically almost perfect.

During the second half of the nineteenth century improvements were made whereby the glass was rolled flat, but the texture left on both sides of the sheet by the rolling process still had to be laboriously ground out before polishing.

DRAWN-SHEET GLASS

Although rolled-plate glass was popular for store windows it was too expensive to be widely used for houses. However, the development of drawn-sheet glass early in the twentieth century made it possible to manufacture large flat sheets much more economically.

A ribbon of molten glass was drawn vertically from the melting pot and allowed to cool. Since the thickness of the glass was determined by the speed at which it was drawn from the pot, it was impossible to guarantee a uniform thickness.

As a result, although early drawn-sheet glass lacked many of the imperfections of handmade glass, it still tended to distort reflections and so produce a distorted view through a window.

Early-Victorian plate-glass rolling mill

FLOAT GLASS

Float glass is a relatively modern development, having been pioneered in the 1950s. This optically superb glass has a highly polished surface, made by floating it on molten metal. Float glass tends to look a little too perfect when installed in an old house, especially if it can be compared with old glass in other windows.

CURVED GLASS

If you have to replace curved glass – in a bow window, for example – you will need to employ a specialist glazier. The making of curved glass demands considerable skill as it cannot be cut to size once it has been shaped and must therefore be measured accurately beforehand. A flat sheet of glass is heated in a furnace and allowed to sag onto a curved metal mold. Making a new mold is costly, but an experienced glazier may be able to adapt existing stock. Measure the window sash carefully and make an accurate cardboard template of the required curve. Alternatively, take the sash itself to the glazier.

FINDING REPLACEMENT GLASS

You can buy genuine old glass from an architectural-salvage company, but it is expensive and you will find that it's quite difficult to cut antique glass without breaking it. If you use crown glass, it looks best with the convex side outward.

Cylinder glass is made for restoration purposes, in the traditional manner, in sheets 1/8in (3mm) thick measuring up to 2 x 3ft (600 x 900mm). Although it is far more expensive than modern float glass, cylinder glass will integrate perfectly with original glazing and is often used for restoring colored leaded lights. This restoration glass is, for the most part, imported from Germany.

Another possible source of glass is a demolition or window-replacement job in your neighborhood. If the glass being removed has the waves and imperfections of older glass, ask the contractors if you can buy it.

1 Remove the broken glass

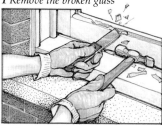
2 Chop out the remaining putty

REPLACING A BROKEN PANE

Wearing goggles and thick work gloves to protect your eyes and hands, remove the broken glass piece by piece, rocking it gently backward and forward to loosen the putty (1). Chop out what remains of the putty from the rebates with a glazier's hacking knife (2) or an old chisel. Using pliers, remove the sprigs or glazing points that hold the glass in place, then clean out the rebates with a stiff bristle brush. (Glass is held in rolled-steel windows with small spring clips.)

Apply primer to the rebates, to prevent oil being soaked out of the new putty; or use linseed oil diluted 50 per cent with turpentine.

Measure the height and width of the opening. If you don't want to cut the glass yourself (see opposite), you will need to order replacement glass 1/8in (3mm) smaller from top to bottom and from side to side.

Knead a fist-size ball of glazing compound until it has an even consistency. Remove some of the oil from

3 Secure the glass with sprigs

4 Smooth the putty with a knife

sticky fresh compound by rolling it in newspaper. Conversely, soften stiff compound with a drop of linseed oil.

Shape the compound into a thin "rope" and press it firmly into the rebates all around the opening. Set the new pane of glass into this bedding putty, pressing around the edges only, to squeeze excess compound from the rebates. Secure the glass every 8in (200mm) or so with sprigs or glazing points, tapping them into the wood with the edge of a firmer chisel (3). Cut excess compound from the inside with a putty knife.

Press more compound into the rebate to cover the points, smoothing it to form an even bevel with the point of a putty knife (4). Dip the knife in water from time to time to prevent it from sticking to the compound. Clean smears from the glass with mineral spirits.

Leave the compound for a week or so to harden, then paint it within a month. To seal the edge, let the paint overlap very slightly onto the glass.

RENEWING OLD PUTTY

Old putty is often so loose you can pick it out with your fingers. Not only does loose putty admit water to rot the woodwork, it is also a security risk since it enables a pane of glass to be removed silently. Old putty is extremely hard; and if sections are still firmly attached to the sash, trying to chop it out in the conventional manner may crack the glass. Soften hard putty with a coat of chemical paint stripper. A paste stripper is best because it can be covered with strips of plastic sheeting to keep it moist and active for up to 48 hours, until the putty is soft enough to scrape from the rebates. Prime the rebate, then apply new putty (see left).

Glaziers at work

CUTTING GLASS

If you have never cut glass before, practice on some spare glass before you start a job in earnest.

Lay a sheet of glass on a flat worktable covered with a blanket, then thoroughly clean the area to be cut with mineral spirits to remove traces of grease, which can cause a glass cutter to skid. An ordinary glass cutter has a steel wheel that scores the glass, but better-quality diamond-tipped cutters are also available. Use a wooden straightedge (preferably a T-square) to guide the cutter.

Lubricate the tip of a wheeled glass cutter by dipping it in light oil. Then, holding the tool between

your index and middle fingers (1), draw it toward you with one continuous movement that scores the glass from edge to edge. A harsh grating sound means you are pressing too hard, sending shock waves through the glass that could cause the cut to wander; a light irregular sound may mean you are not scoring a continuous line.

Slide the glass toward you until it overhangs the edge of the worktable, then tap the glass directly under the scored line (2) to start the cut. Place a gloved hand on each side of the line (3) and snap the glass with a twist of the wrists.

Cutting shapes

To cut a shaped piece of glass, make a thick cardboard template that fits the window opening but is 1/16in (1.5mm) smaller all around (not forgetting to allow for the thickness of the glass cutter).

Hold the template on the glass with double-sided cellophane tape and score a cut line along each edge (4). Run each cut out to the edge of the glass (5) and cut the waste alongside a curved edge into segments.

Snap the glass, holding it as previously described, or use ordinary pliers padded with masking tape to grip awkward pieces (6).

1 Hold a cutter between your fingers

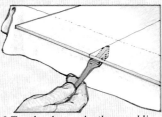

2 Tap the glass under the scored line

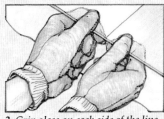

3 Grip glass on each side of the line

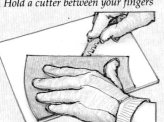

4 Score alongside a template

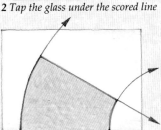

5 Run each cut out to an edge

6 Snap a strip with padded pliers

DEALING WITH ROTTED WINDOWS

RY ROT IS *a misnomer: no wood ever deteriorated simply because it was dry. Decay occurs in the presence of moisture; more decay results when the damp conditions alternate with dry ones, producing so-called dry rot. Dry rot is actually a fungus disease that attacks both softwoods and hardwoods. Wooden windows often suffer from the effects of such decay – given their exposure to the elements, it's hardly surprising. Decay most often occurs at points where moisture is able to penetrate* the end grain of timber, such as the ends of the sill, the bottom of both jambs and the joints.

Neglected paintwork is one of the most common causes of decay, as are the breakdown of the mortar seal around the frame, bad pointing, loose putty, and rising damp – in fact, anything that is responsible for the wood becoming saturated regularly.

Before attempting to treat the symptoms of decay, always locate and eradicate the source of the dampness that has caused the fungus to develop.

Checking for decay
Peeling paint, where the wood has expanded beneath, is often the first sign of dry rot. Wood suffering from decay is spongy when wet, but becomes dry and crumbly as it dries out in warm weather. It is always relatively soft, and areas of rot can be pinpointed by probing with the point of a screwdriver.

If you become aware of a strong musty smell when you are changing a sash cord or making some other repair to a wooden window, open the pocket and inspect the inside of the jamb with a flashlight and a small mirror. If you notice a dusting of red spores or any of the other signs of dry rot, have the window inspected and treated by a professional as soon as possible. Don't delay – dry rot can be progressive, and the earlier the repair is made, the less complicated and costly it will be.

Neglected paintwork and missing putty lead to rot

TREATING AREAS OF DECAY
Gouge out decayed wood until you reach relatively sound material, then apply preservative and consolidate the affected area by painting on a liquid wood hardener. One coat is enough to reinforce weakened fibers and seal the wood against future penetration.

After six hours, fill holes, cracks, and crevices with a flexible exterior wood filler.

Patching a deep hole
Having gouged out soft decayed wood to investigate the extent of the damage, chisel out a cavity that is slightly larger than the damaged area and, if possible, undercut the edges to lock the new patch in place (1).

Cut a patch from similar timber with the grain running in the same direction as that of the component. Shape the patch to match any undercuts, and leave it very slightly oversize in thickness and in width for planing down after fitting (2). Paint the prepared area and the new timber with a chemical preservative before gluing the patch in place with a waterproof synthetic-resin adhesive.

When the glue has set, plane the patch flush then coat it with preservative again before filling any gaps with a flexible wood filler.

1 Chisel out a cavity with undercuts   *2 Plane the patch repair to fit*

REPLACING ROTTED TIMBER
If the extent of the decay has structurally weakened a component of a wooden window, cut out the damaged wood and repair it by inserting a new section or replace the entire component.

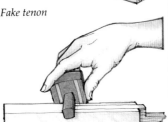

Repairing a broken sash-rail tenon

The tenon of a sash rail can become severely weakened by decay. Once you have dismantled the sash, you could replace the entire component, but that would involve having a matching molding cut into the rail. However, provided serious damage goes no further than the tenon itself, the joint can be repaired relatively simply by installing a fake tenon. The same repair is also appropriate for the tongue of a meeting-rail bridle joint.

Set a mortise gauge to the width of the tenon and mark an angled housing for the fake tenon on the outer edge of the rail (1). Cut off the remnants of the tenon flush with the shoulder of the joint, then mark the housing on the end grain (2).

Saw down each side of the housing with a tenon saw (3), then pare out the waste with a mortise chisel. Use similar wood to make a fake tenon that fits the housing but is slightly wider than the sash rail (4).

Treat both components with preservative, then glue the tenon into the housing. When the glue has set, plane and shape the tenon.

Last of all, insert a glued locking dowel to reinforce the joint (5).

Making replacement components

An entire rail, stile or glazing bar can be copied from the original. Whether you do the work yourself or employ a professional joiner, it is important to reproduce the moldings exactly. Some joiners use antique molding planes for this type of work, but it is probably easier to have an electric-router cutter ground to match the profile.

Fake tenon

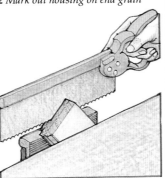

1 Mark out the housing

2 Mark out housing on end grain

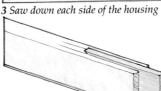

3 Saw down each side of the housing

4 Make the tenon slightly oversize

5 Shape tenon and fit a dowel

PREVENTATIVE TREATMENT

Considering the expense and time involved in curing the effects of rot in wooden windows, it pays to take preventative measures whenever possible.

Chemical preservatives

Having stripped a window for repainting, you should always take the opportunity to treat the bare timber with a chemical preservative. Two or three applications are ideal. You will need to leave it for between two and five days before painting, depending on drying conditions.

For new work, it is also necessary to paint on preservative yourself.

Repairing a damaged weatherseal

If a window has a decayed weatherseal, rake out loose mortar to expose the joint between the window frame and the masonry surround. The traditional way to fill large gaps was to stuff them with wet newspaper before reinstating the mortar seal, but it's probably simpler and more efficient to inject an expanding polyurethane foam, provided there is no possibility of it impeding the movement of sash weights.

Finally, seal the joint with a gun-applied caulk (1) or press-in-place strip sealant (2). To preserve the original appearance, you can cover the seal with mortar.

SAFETY WITH PRESERVATIVES

- Follow the preservative maker's instructions very carefully.
- Wear protective gloves to handle preservatives, and goggles when applying them. Use a face mask if you are working indoors.
- Make sure that there is adequate ventilation while preservatives are drying.

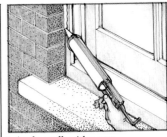

1 Apply caulk with a gun

2 Or use a press-in-place strip

REPLACING AN ENTIRE WINDOW

It is rarely necessary to replace an entire window, but dry rot can damage a window so extensively that replacement is your only option. However, it isn't necessary or even desirable to install inappropriate modern-style windows in a period house. Any competent joiner is capable of reproducing a sliding-sash or casement window, and there are companies that specialize in making exact replicas of individual windows in treated softwoods or hardwoods. The same companies will also supply double-glazed units, instead of conventional glass. The windows are fully draftproofed, and you can either install them yourself or get the millwork company to fit them for you.

CASEMENT WINDOWS

DESPITE THE POPULARITY OF *the double-hung sash window, hinged casements have never really been out of fashion. They have remained in use in one form or another since medieval times, with a notable revival around the turn of the century. They are likely to comprise simple wooden frames divided by one or two glazing bars, constructed as individual windows or in pairs that close together with rebated stiles down the center. Alternatively, there might be a single casement that opens within a group of fixed sashes. French doors are perhaps the most extreme example of twin casements, being in effect pairs of tall windows opening onto a terrace, patio or balcony.*

Edwardian bay with leaded-light casement windows

THE REVIVAL OF THE CASEMENT WINDOW

The earliest casements had wrought-iron or wooden frames surrounding a tracery of cames (grooved lead strips) that held small diamond-shape or square glass panes. Similar forms of casement reappeared in Victorian times with the revival of Gothic and Queen Anne styles.

The same nostalgic sentiments were expressed in the fenestration of late-Victorian houses, some craftsman-style houses, and neo-Tudor interwar housing. Elegant mass-produced rolled-steel casement windows represented an opposing taste during the interwar decades, their uncluttered and severely practical lines being ideally suited to the avant-garde Art Deco architecture of the 1930s.

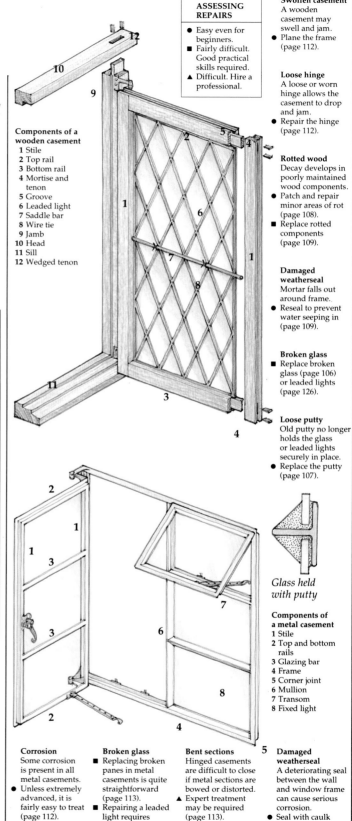

ASSESSING REPAIRS

- ● Easy even for beginners.
- ■ Fairly difficult. Good practical skills required.
- ▲ Difficult. Hire a professional.

Components of a wooden casement
1 Stile
2 Top rail
3 Bottom rail
4 Mortise and tenon
5 Groove
6 Leaded light
7 Saddle bar
8 Wire tie
9 Jamb
10 Head
11 Sill
12 Wedged tenon

Swollen casement
A wooden casement may swell and jam.
- ● Plane the frame (page 112).

Loose hinge
A loose or worn hinge allows the casement to drop and jam.
- ● Repair the hinge (page 112).

Rotted wood
Decay develops in poorly maintained wood components.
- ● Patch and repair minor areas of rot (page 108).
- ■ Replace rotted components (page 109).

Damaged weatherseal
Mortar falls out around frame.
- ● Reseal to prevent water seeping in (page 109).

Broken glass
- ■ Replace broken glass (page 106) or leaded lights (page 126).

Loose putty
Old putty no longer holds the glass or leaded lights securely in place.
- ● Replace the putty (page 107).

Glass held with putty

Components of a metal casement
1 Stile
2 Top and bottom rails
3 Glazing bar
4 Frame
5 Corner joint
6 Mullion
7 Transom
8 Fixed light

Corrosion
Some corrosion is present in all metal casements.
- ● Unless extremely advanced, it is fairly easy to treat (page 112).

Broken glass
- ■ Replacing broken panes in metal casements is quite straightforward (page 113).
- ■ Repairing a leaded light requires different skills (page 126).

Bent sections
Hinged casements are difficult to close if metal sections are bowed or distorted.
- ▲ Expert treatment may be required (page 113).

Damaged weatherseal
A deteriorating seal between the wall and window frame can cause serious corrosion.
- ● Seal with caulk (page 113).

HOW CASEMENTS WERE MADE

ALTHOUGH RELATIVELY SIMPLE *in construction, a wooden-casement window is similar to a sliding-sash window in that the various components are jointed together and, when necessary, can be dismantled for repair or replacement.*

A rolled-steel casement window, on the other hand, is made in complete sub-assemblies at the factory. The hinged casement itself can be removed, but it is impossible to replace individual components except by cutting and rewelding sections.

WOODEN-CASEMENT CONSTRUCTION

A hinged wooden casement comprises two vertical stiles (1) and horizontal top (2) and bottom rails (3) jointed at the corners with wedged through mortise and tenons (4). The outer faces of the stiles and rails are rebated to accept the glazing and are usually molded decoratively on the inside. A groove (5) around the outer edge stops water seeping in.

Although they may be divided by wooden glazing bars, casement windows are often glazed with leaded lights (6). These consist of a lattice of lead "cames" (grooved strips) holding square or diamond-shape panes of glass. To support this relatively weak lattice against wind pressure, 1/4in (6mm) steel or iron saddle bars (7) are placed at strategic intervals. Each end of a saddle bar is located in a hole in the stile, and lengths of copper wire soldered to the lead cames (8) are twisted around the bar to tie the glazed panel securely in place.

Most casements are side-hung, like a door, being attached by hinges to a vertical stile. You sometimes find small wooden casements placed above larger ones, such as door-height French windows. They are usually hinged at the bottom and open inward. When open, they are supported by metal stays or chains.

METAL-CASEMENT CONSTRUCTION

Early metal-casement windows were handmade from wrought iron, but late-nineteenth-century technology made it possible to mass-produce window casements and frames from rolled-steel sections. The stiles (1) and top and bottom rails (2) are made from identical Z-section pieces of metal. T-section glazing bars (3) divide the casement and support the glass panes, which are held in place with spring clips and a special putty formulated for use with metal.

Construction of the frame

The surrounding frame (4) is constructed from the same metal section used for the casement. The corner joints (5) are welded. Frames may be divided by T-section mullions (6) and transoms (7), and often include fixed lights (8) as well as the hinged casement.

Wooden casement windows

Construction of the frame

A simple casement is hinged from a surrounding wooden frame comprising two vertical jambs (9), a top rail or head (10), and a sill (11) across the bottom. If the frame was to hold two or more casements, it was divided vertically by a mullion and, if need be, horizontally by a transom. A tenon on each end of the jamb passes right through the head and sill, and is secured with glue and wedges (12). These joints are sometimes pinned with dowels in the manner of a sliding-sash mortise and tenon. The frame is rebated externally to receive the casement.

Metal casement windows

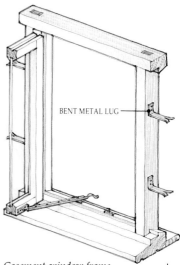
BENT METAL LUG
Casement-window frame

HOW WOODEN WINDOWS WERE FITTED

Wooden window frames were nailed directly to a timber-frame wall or to preservative-treated pallets (wooden strips), which were built into the mortar joints at 2ft (600mm) intervals as a masonry wall was being constructed. Another method was to nail into wooden plugs driven into holes cut in a finished masonry wall. Alternatively, bent metal lugs screwed to the frame at strategic points were bedded in mortar joints during the building of the opening. As well as being bedded in mortar, frames may also have been sealed with caulking.

HOW METAL WINDOWS WERE FITTED

Rolled-steel windows were fitted by screwing them to a wooden surround or to plugged masonry; alternatively, bent metal lugs bolted to the metal frame were built into the mortar joints.

The window frames were bedded in caulk.

Fixing lug bolted to a metal frame

RESTORING CASEMENT WINDOWS

WOODEN-CASEMENT WINDOWS *generally suffer from problems very similar to those associated with sliding-sash windows, although leaded lights need special care and you may have to hire an expert to deal with extensive deterioration to the leadwork and the glass itself.*

REPAIRING WOODEN CASEMENTS
As with sash windows, rotted wood may have to be consolidated and either filled, patched, or replaced, joints may need to be dismantled and reglued, loose putty replaced, and new panes of glass inserted. Joints around a frame can be resealed with caulk.

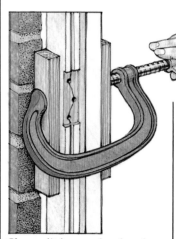

Glue a split frame and apply a clamp

CORRECTING A LOOSE HINGE
You may find that a hinged casement is binding against its frame because a loose hinge is allowing it to drop.

First of all, inspect the upper hinge for missing or loose screws; then lift the casement *in situ* to see if the hinge knuckles are worn and have become slack. Swapping the top and bottom hinges may be enough to even out the wear and correct the fault.

Alternatively, the screws may have lost their grip as a result of the wooden frame splitting. The best solution in this case is to remove the casement, then work some waterproof glue into the split with a knife blade.

Close the split with a clamp until the glue sets. If the split will no longer close because the wood has expanded, fill it flush using an exterior wood filler that is tough enough to accept a woodscrew.

EASING A SWOLLEN CASEMENT
If a casement sticks or is difficult to open, inspect its edges for signs of abrasion where it is rubbing against the frame. Skim those areas with a finely set block plane until the window opens and closes smoothly. Take care not to remove too much wood, especially if the swelling could be due to humid conditions.

REPLACING A WOODEN CASEMENT
If a window has deteriorated beyond repair, have a joiner make an exact replica. Avoid the temptation to buy a cheaper, ready-made casement window from a window supplier. The chances of its being a suitable style for an old house are very remote .

Rolled-steel casements are often sadly neglected and needlessly replaced, largely due to a widely held view that metal windows are not worthy of conservation. But a rolled-steel window may be no less important to the integrity of a building than a Georgian sash window in a different context.

REPAIRING METAL CASEMENTS
Many people are under the impression that metal-casement windows are more difficult to restore than wooden ones, but with basic metalwork skills and equipment it is possible to do a great deal of repair work and restoration before it is necessary to replace a window.

DEALING WITH CORROSION
Corrosion, or rust, begins whenever moisture is able to penetrate the protective paint that coats a rolled-steel window. Neglected decoration is perhaps the most obvious cause of corrosion, but defective putty can lead to even worse symptoms, allowing corrosion to eat away at the metal section beneath. A faulty weatherseal around the perimeter of a metal frame is equally damaging, allowing rust to develop unnoticed until it eventually breaks through the paintwork.

Flaking or blistered paintwork is often the first sign of corrosion. Probing the affected area with a pointed tool will detect the degree and extent of the rust, which in turn determines the required treatment.

Light rust
If the metal is firm and the flaking paint is due simply to a light accumulation of rust on the surface, rub it down with silicon-carbide paper dipped in mineral spirits to remove the rust, feathering the edges of sound paintwork surrounding it. Wipe away the dust with a cloth dampened in mineral spirits,

then paint the bare metal immediately with a rust-inhibiting primer. Repaint the window with two coats of paint that is compatible with the primer.

Medium rust
If the metal flakes when probed, wire-brush all corroded surfaces until you reach sound metal. For extensive corrosion, use a wire-brush attachment in an electric drill. Wear goggles and a face mask, and protect adjacent masonry and glass. First neutralize the rust by applying a rust-converter treatment (available at many hardware and auto parts stores). Fill pitted metal with an epoxy-based car-body filler. Prime and paint the window.

Heavy corrosion
If corrosion is ignored for a long time, it can weaken metal-window components to such an extent that your only recourse is to cut out damaged sections and weld new ones in their place. The casement or even the frame itself may have to be transferred to a workshop to be repaired by an expert. Replacing a rolled section of metal can be difficult unless you have an identical scrap window from which to salvage parts.

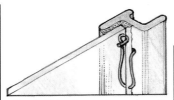

Glass held in place with a spring clip

REPLACING BROKEN GLASS

To reglaze a rolled-steel casement, follow the instructions for removing broken glass and installing new panes in a wooden window. However, the glass is held in place by spring clips, which you should remove and put aside for reuse. Use a special metal-window putty, available from a glazier or hardware store.

STRAIGHTENING BENT COMPONENTS

Bent components can make it impossible to close a metal casement properly, perhaps leaving gaps that cannot be draftproofed successfully. A badly distorted window will have to be repaired professionally, but you may be able to straighten a slightly bent component *in situ* yourself. After removing the glass, apply pressure to the bent component, using a stout wooden batten to spread the load and prevent the metal from kinking.

REPLACING A DECAYED WEATHERSEAL

Rake out any loose material from around the metal window frame, then seal the gap between the frame and the surrounding masonry with a gun-applied caulk.

REPLACING STEEL WINDOWS

Some manufacturers have continued to produce rolled-steel windows unchanged since their introduction in the 1920s and 1930s that can be used as replacements for earlier versions. They are also available with superior galvanized or stoved finishes and can be ordered with draftproofing and double glazing.

SHUTTERS

WINDOW SHUTTERS *seem to come in and out of fashion, and sadly many have been rendered inoperable or have been ripped out. Yet it is hard to imagine why this should be so, considering that shutters are extremely practical, screening out harsh sunlight and noise, preventing drafts, and providing additional security.*

Folding shutters
1 Folding leaves
2 Shutter box
3 Splayed reveal
4 Paneled wall
5 Staple
6 Rebated edge

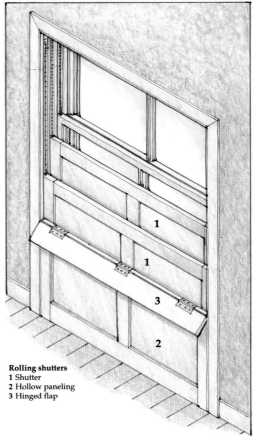

Rolling shutters
1 Shutter
2 Hollow paneling
3 Hinged flap

INTERNAL SHUTTERS

Folding or rolling shutters were a feature of many early American and Victorian interiors. Yet they were so ingeniously designed to be unobtrusive that sometimes householders are completely unaware of their presence.

Folding shutters

Paneled shutters, which generally comprise a pair of leaves on each side of the window **(1)**, fold back into deep shutter boxes **(2)** in the reveals. The reveals may be square to the window, but often they are splayed **(3)** to admit more daylight. The wall below the shutter boxes **(4)** and the window is usually paneled to match the shutters themselves. Once folded out flat against the window, the shutters may be fastened by latches or metal bars that engage strong staples **(5)**. Leaf stiles are rebated **(6)** to make lightproof joints.

Rolling shutters

Rolling shutters are comparatively rare and are even more unobtrusive. They work on the same principle as a sliding-sash window, being counterbalanced by cords and weights.

The shutters **(1)** are housed behind paneling **(2)** constructed between the window and the floor, and are accessible by means of a hinged flap **(3)** that forms the internal window board.

REINSTATING INTERNAL SHUTTERS

If you have wood-paneled reveals or unusually deep window boards, it might be worth stripping a small section to see if there are shutters hidden beneath layers and layers of paint. There's every chance that the shutters themselves are in perfect condition, perhaps requiring a drop of oil on the hinges or a new set of cords.

If you decide to strip all the paint from paneled shutters, either do it yourself or make sure a professional stripper uses a cold-chemical dip – since a hot-caustic stripping solution can split the relatively thin paneling used for shutters.

EXTERNAL SHUTTERS

With outward-opening casements it is difficult, if not impossible, to reach exterior shutters from the upper floors of a house. This problem has been overcome in some houses by the use of an ingenious worm gear that controls the position of each shutter by cranking a handle on the inside.

Small houses and cottages are most likely to be fitted with shutters of frame-and-panel construction or simple ledged-and-braced boarded shutters, with strap hinges that are either screwed to the wooden window frame or hung from hooked pins driven into the wall.

Routine maintenance is all that's required with these types of shutters, and even complete replacement is no problem to a reasonably competent joiner. Unless they are traditional in the area where you live, avoid having shutters made with cutouts – which so often make an attractive cottage look cutesified.

Paneled shutters fold out of deep shutter boxes

Adjustable louvered shutters control the light

LOUVERED SHUTTERS

Louvered shutters or blinds are found most often on Colonial-style and early-Victorian homes. Especially valuable are the ones with pivoting slats that are operated simultaneously by a vertical wooden rod attached to the edge of each slat with staples.

Banks of small louvered shutters are sometimes mounted one above the other to provide a greater degree of flexibility when in use. The bottom half of a window, for example, can be screened for privacy while the top half is left partly open for light and ventilation.

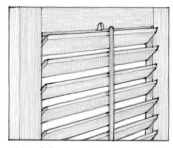

A stapled rod operates pivoting slats

Attractive external louvered shutters

Sturdy framed shutters with raised-and-fielded panels

FANLIGHTS

T HE TERM FANLIGHT *was coined in the eighteenth century to describe a semicircular fixed light or window with a radiating pattern of glazing bars. It was installed above a doorway to admit light to the hallway or passage beyond. In time, "fanlight" became a general term for similar fixed lights of any pattern, including elliptical and rectangular ones.*

FANLIGHT PATTERNS

A simple fan of wooden glazing bars was probably the earliest fanlight pattern. It was developed sometime during the first quarter of the eighteenth century. The techniques required to make this type of fanlight would have been familiar to a joiner used to constructing semi-circular-head or segmental-head sash windows.

Fanlights of similar design were made by fretting the pattern of glazing bars from a single piece of solid wood. However, fretted fanlights that break with tradition are often extremely decorative. Wooden fanlights were often embellished with "compo" (a mixture of whiting and glue) and hand carving.

The introduction of metal fanlights in England in the 1770s made it possible to produce the beautiful traceries that are a feature of Georgian design. There were countless variations on the original fan, and patterns such as the umbrella and the batswing and its derivative the teardrop were extremely popular too.

Traditional patterns were frequently adapted to suit rectangular fanlights; and abstract patterns such as intersecting circles or Gothic arches were devised to make the most of the increasingly fashionable rectangular fanlight shape.

A relatively early fretted and carved fanlight

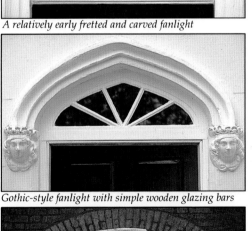

Gothic-style fanlight with simple wooden glazing bars

Variation on the fan motif in a wooden doorcase

Classic metal fanlight above a Georgian door

Typical metal teardrop fanlight

Delicate umbrella-pattern fanlight

Simple rectangular fanlight

Batswing with hinged ventilator

METHODS
OF CONSTRUCTION

A wooden fanlight has a substantial outer frame (1) enclosing glazing bars (2) that accommodate the glass in the usual way. But, unlike most wooden windows, the molded side of a fanlight faces the street.

A metal fanlight has brass or tinned wrought-iron ribs (3) fixed inside a wooden sash. Decorative lead-alloy strips (4) soldered to the leading edges of the ribs form the glazing rebates. Very often they incorporate rosettes or scrolls, or various other ornamental motifs, that do not support the glass in any way. (In the same way, wooden fan sashes may feature applied decoration.) The metal framework is attached to the sash by means of thin strips of tin (5) which are nailed to the wood.

REPLACING FANLIGHTS

There are relatively few professionals with the skill and knowledge required to repair, let alone reconstruct, authentic metal fanlights. As a result, the space above many a Georgian door is now filled with a blank sheet of glass or a cheap imitation of a period fanlight.

Look for a craftsperson who will remake corroded ribs, attach new tin fixing strips, and resolder cast-lead ornamentation. A first-class workshop will even cast new sections from existing fragments to reproduce missing ornamentation. A craftsperson with this type of experience will probably be able to make a copy of a neighbor's fanlight if your own has been discarded at some time in the past.

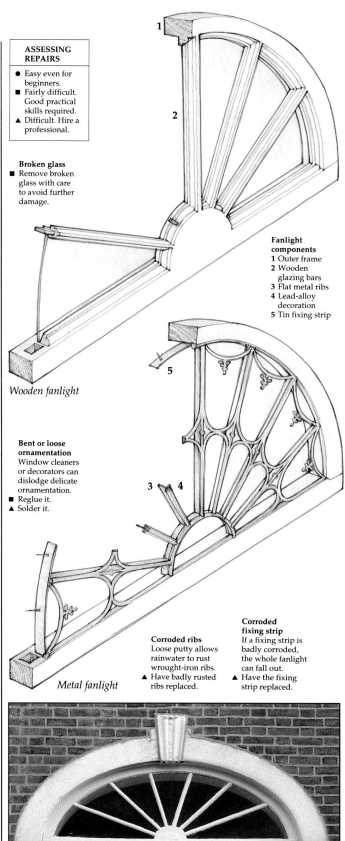

ASSESSING REPAIRS

● Easy even for beginners.
■ Fairly difficult. Good practical skills required.
▲ Difficult. Hire a professional.

Broken glass
■ Remove broken glass with care to avoid further damage.

Fanlight components
1 Outer frame
2 Wooden glazing bars
3 Flat metal ribs
4 Lead-alloy decoration
5 Tin fixing strip

Wooden fanlight

Bent or loose ornamentation
Window cleaners or decorators can dislodge delicate ornamentation.
■ Reglue it.
▲ Solder it.

Corroded ribs
Loose putty allows rainwater to rust wrought-iron ribs.
▲ Have badly rusted ribs replaced.

Corroded fixing strip
If a fixing strip is badly corroded, the whole fanlight can fall out.
▲ Have the fixing strip replaced.

Metal fanlight

Elliptical-head fanlight designed to fit above a wide doorcase

Some fanlights incorporate lanterns

REPAIRING FANLIGHTS

Restoring a wooden fanlight is no more difficult than working on any other similar window, except that if you need to remove the whole sash you will probably have to hack away some interior plasterwork. Look for signs of filler covering the sash-fixing nails, and drive them right through the outer frame with a punch.

Metal fanlights, especially ones that have reached an advanced stage of corrosion, can be extremely fragile; and clumsy attempts to repair them can make matters even worse. Inspect a fanlight closely before you start work to ascertain whether you need expert help or advice.

Avoiding damage to the glass

Old fanlights sometimes contain the original crown glass, which should be preserved if at all possible. When you are removing glass, especially from a metal fanlight, soften the putty with paint stripper to avoid distorting the frame and cracking other panes.

Replacing loose cast-metal ornamentation

You frequently find cast-lead strips and ornamentation that are bent or peeling away from the metal glazing ribs behind them. Straighten the components, and refit them with an epoxy glue or get an expert to resolder them.

WINDOW FURNITURE

THE APPROPRIATE HARDWARE *or "furniture" is important to the security and smooth operation of both casement and sliding-sash windows. It is preferable to restore antique hardware, but if you need to replace a broken or missing fitting you can buy reproductions that are almost indistinguishable from original pieces. Whenever possible, it is best to remove fittings for cleaning, lubricating, or stripping. So you can refit the fittings in their original positions, don't fill fixing holes when decorating. Brass screws should be used for attaching brass fittings.*

SASH FASTENERS

Antique fasteners made to secure double-hung sash windows provide minimal security and prevent sashes from rattling in the wind. Some fasteners were designed so that they could not be opened by a blade slipped between the meeting rails, but by themselves they do not conform to modern standards of home security. It is therefore recommended that you fit a lock or security bolt with a removable key to any accessible window, in addition to a traditional sash fastener.

Cam fastener

Cam fasteners have been fitted to sash windows since the eighteenth century. A lever on one half of the fitting engages a cam-shape lug on the other, pulling the meeting rails together. Cam fasteners, originally made in bronze or brass, are often very decorative, with brass or ceramic knobs fitted to the lever.

Screw the fitting to the tops of the meeting rails as close to the center of the window as possible. Fit the lever first (on the upper sash) and use it to position the lug, making allowance for the cam action.

Fitch fastener

A Fitch or crescent fastener is even better for windows with loose sashes. The rim of a helical metal cam engages a hook on the other half of the fitting. Turning the cam forces the sashes apart vertically while pulling the meeting rails together.

Screw the hook to the upper sash first, then use it to position the cam on the other meeting rail.

Always remember to turn the cam back completely before opening the window, or the fastener may gouge wood out of glazing bars in the upper sash.

Screw fastener

Like other sash fasteners, a screw fastener pulls the meeting rails together – this time by means of a knurled nut on the end of a pivoting lever. Unless the lever is raised properly when the window is opened, it will get caught under the meeting rail of the lower sash when you close the window.

Victorian sash screw

Sash screw

A sash screw passes right through one meeting rail into the other so that neither sash can be opened. Period brass sash screws are most attractive – however, unlike modern ones that can only be extracted with a key, security is compromised if a pane of glass is broken.

SASH LIFTS

Sash lifts are screwed to the bottom rails of heavy lower sashes to make them easier to open. They are fitted approximately 6in (150mm) from each end of the rail.

Hook lift

Simple brass lifts are still manufactured today, but antique hook lifts with cast decoration are even more attractive. On some lifts the hook forms a complete ring, but they offer little practical advantage over the simple hooked variety.

Flush lift

Flush lifts provide a more positive grip, but because a recess has to be cut in the wood in order to set them into the rail they are more difficult to fit.

SASH HANDLES

Upper sashes without horizontal glazing bars that form finger grips are difficult to open. One solution is to screw a pair of D-shaped handles to the underside of the meeting rail close to the stiles. Sash handles can only be reached by raising the lower sash.

Sash furniture
1 Cam fasteners
2 Fitch fastener
3 Screw fastener
4 Sash handle
5 Flush lift
6 Hook lifts

CASEMENT FASTENERS

A hinged casement is held closed by a one-piece pivoting handle sometimes known as a cockspur fastener. The window is held open in a number of positions by means of a metal bar or stay.

Casement fastener

A casement fastener comprises a metal handle with a projecting spur that engages a slotted striker plate screwed to the frame or, alternatively, a hook screwed to the face of an adjacent fixed casement.

The traditional iron rat-tail fastener with its coiled handle looks good on a casement of any period up to the end of the nineteenth century. Twentieth-century casements are generally fitted with cast-metal fasteners, made from either iron, bronze, or aluminum alloy. Similar fasteners for rolled-steel casement windows are frequently of "two point" or "three point" type with slotted spurs. The slots locate on the edge of the window muntin or stile, holding the casement ajar to provide ventilation.

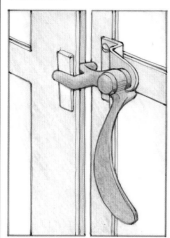

A two-point cockspur locates on the muntin to hold the window ajar

Casement stay

A casement or peg stay is a flat, rigid metal bar pivoting on a metal plate screwed to the bottom rail of a hinged casement. A short peg screwed to the sill engages one of a series of holes running the length of the bar, holding the window open. When the window is closed, a second peg holds the bar parallel to the bottom rail. You can buy stays made to match the various styles of fasteners.

Sliding stays that are fixed permanently to rolled-steel casements are secured in an open or closed position by a thumbscrew or lever.

Sliding casement-window stay

CASEMENT HINGES

Standard butt hinges are fitted to many wooden-casement windows. However, special extension hinges are sometimes used to facilitate cleaning both sides of the glass, especially on windows situated on the upper floors of a house.

Extension hinge

When a window is open, extension hinges provide a clearance of about 4 to 5in (100 to 125mm) between the hinge stile and the frame, giving sufficient room to be able to clean the outside of the window from inside the room. Rolled-steel windows are invariably fitted with extension hinges.

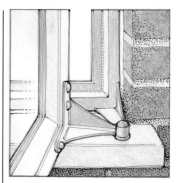

Metal-window extension hinge

ESPAGNOLETTE BOLTS

Victorian and Colonial Revival French doors are frequently fitted with espagnolette bolts. Turning a centrally fitted door handle simultaneously closes two substantial bolts running parallel with the closing stile of the window. One bolt shoots into the window head, the other into the sill.

Casement furniture
1 Rat-tail casement fastener
2 Rat-tail stay
3 Iron peg stay
4 Simple casement fastener
5 Brass two-point fastener

Espagnolette bolt secures door-height French doors

CHAPTER TEN

ORNAMENTAL GLASS

WHETHER IT IS THE FEELING OF OPTIMISM *engendered by early-morning sunshine streaming through a colorful landing window or the welcoming sight of a backlit stained-glass door on a winter's evening, ornamental glass can influence our emotional attachment to a house in a most direct and effective manner.*

In fact, decorative glass is such a valuable asset, financially as well as aesthetically, that any homeowner would be well advised to preserve even the most modest items and to replace any that have been removed.

For a period of a hundred years or so, from the mid-nineteenth century onward, grand and humble houses alike were enriched with all manner of decorative glass. But the beginnings of handcrafted glass are very much earlier. Stained glass, for example, has a pedigree stretching back to before medieval times. Nevertheless, crucial aspects of the technology had to be rediscovered by the Victorians before the craft could be exploited with a fresh momentum that would carry it beyond the ecclesiastical tradition into the wider domestic context.*

The technical innovations of the Industrial Revolution introduced more and more possibilities for using glass cheaply as well as decoratively in practically every Victorian home. In particular, with the increased density of urban housing, various forms of acid-etched, sandblasted, and machine-rolled glass were used instead of clear glazing to preserve Victorian sensitivities.

A spectacular Art Deco door panel

The welcoming sight of stained glass is most appealing

Detailed Victorian landing light

Late-C19th hand-painted glass panel

PATTERNED GLASS

S O-CALLED PATTERNED GLASS *was made by pass-ing it in a molten state between water-cooled rollers, one of which was embossed in order to press a texture on one side of the sheet. A notable feature of patterned glass is that it's impossible to see anything through it except for vague distorted images. Sometimes known as obscured glass, from Victorian times onward it has been used in bathrooms and elsewhere to afford privacy.*

But it was not only its practical applications that appealed to the Victorians. They were also quick to recognize the aesthetic qualities of patterned glass. It was used extensively in door panels and sidelights; and in windows it was often employed in the form of marginal lights or as small decorative panes across the top of a sliding sash, thus providing a contrast to large panes of clear glass.

Even in the early twentieth century its popularity was such that literally hundreds of patterns were offered for sale. However, very few are stocked today, even by specialist glaziers, and the number of patterns available varies according to the whims of the market. The ones listed below are modern copies of original patterns that can be used as substitutes for old glass no longer produced.

Muffled and waterglass
Muffled glass, which closely resembles rippled water, was widely used in Victorian and turn-of-the-century leaded lights. Fortunately, there is still a fair range of colors to choose from.

Waterglass is a modern glass similar to some old versions of muffled glass that are no longer manufactured. Several colors are available.

Cathedral
Cathedral, also known as "German cathedral," is a subtly textured glass used for decorative leaded lights. "Rolled cathedral" is a version that includes flecks and air bubbles.

You can buy a wide range of single-color and "streaky" (two-color) cathedrals from specialist glass suppliers.

Muranese
A handsome but hard-to-find type of glass, Muranese has a pattern resembling a crystalline structure. The modern version generally has a finer texture than its Victorian equivalent. It may be found in several colors as well as clear.

Reeded
Victorian and Colonial Revival glaziers employed the unremarkable texture of reeded glass to spectacular effect in leaded lights by arranging quarries (small panes of glass) in such a way that the flutes made a variety of linear patterns. However, it may be difficult to match using modern glass, which is generally made with comparatively wide flutes. It is only produced as clear glass.

English patterned-glass window

Rich combination of patterned glass

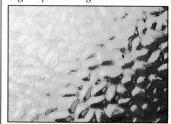
Muffled glass

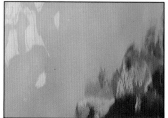
Waterglass

Cathedral glass

Muranese glass

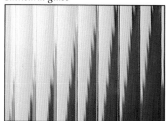
Reeded glass

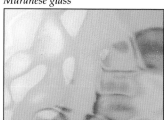
Flemish glass

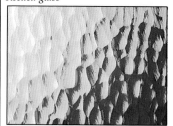
Hammered glass

Ice-crystal or sparkle light glass

LEADED LIGHTS

Detail from a 1930s door panel

Flemish
Another clear "commercial" glass that can still be found today. Our forebears could choose between "big" and "little" Flemish, but you will probably be offered only one size.

Hammered
This Victorian textured glass is still available in some places. Its closely dimpled texture makes it look as if the glass has been struck repeatedly with a ball-peen hammer. Hammered glass is usually clear, but you may come across colored versions.

Sparkle light
Clear glass with a texture resembling crushed ice has been manufactured under various names including sparkle light and ice crystal. The texture in the glass made today tends to be finer than in earlier examples.

CUTTING AND FITTING PATTERNED GLASS
When cutting patterned glass, score the flat side (not the textured side).

For ease of cleaning, fit the glass with the textured surface facing the inside of the house.

T HE TERM STAINED GLASS *is commonly used for any colored window – but unless the window includes painted glass, strictly speaking it is a leaded light. This does not imply that leaded lights are inferior. The "palette" of glass available to Victorian artisans was such that many a house is enriched with colored windows and door panels that do not contain a single pane of painted glass.*

Leaded lights were all constructed in a similar way, the only real difference being the way the lead was incorporated. The leadwork for clear-glass windows is constructed from straight cames only. But colored glass arrests the eye and focuses attention on the dark lines created by the leadwork – so artists and craftsmen often formed the lead into sinuous shapes, almost as if they were drawing with it.

Clear-glass leaded lights

A beautiful example of free-flowing linework and colored glass

GLASS FOR LEADED LIGHTS

If you look closely at a decorative leaded light, you may be surprised to see just how many different types of glass have been used in a single window. Victorian stained-glass artists in particular had a vast range of both handmade and mass-produced glass to choose from. Although today the selection is much more limited, many of the original types of glass are still manufactured, so you stand a good chance of finding a similar pattern, color, or texture, if not an exact replica of the original glass.

Antique glass

Leaded lights were once commonly fashioned from handmade glass, either spun into a disk (crown glass) or formed into a large tube that was split lengthwise then opened to make a flat sheet (cylinder glass). Today, clear and colored handmade "antique" glass is still being produced, using precisely the same methods employed by our forebears. These traditional processes imbue the colored varieties in particular with interesting characteristics not found in mass-produced glass.

Even clear glass can be bought as "plain" (free from blemishes and of uniform thickness), "reamy" (rippled due to variations in density), or "seedy" (containing trapped air bubbles).

Colored types (1) include "pot colors" (strong even color throughout), "tints" (pale tones), and "streaky" (two or more colors mixed in one sheet). Some colors, such as deep red or blue, are too dense to use as pot colors. Instead, they are applied as a thin layer over a sheet of clear or colored glass. These are known as "flashed" colors (2). Glass is flashed with pure gold to create dramatic pink or ruby hues. "Opal" glass is made by flashing opaque white on clear glass. "Opalescent" is opal glass mixed with at least one other color to create a marbled appearance.

Rolled glass

As if the range of handmade glass was not sufficient, leaded-light artists availed themselves of the variety of patterns and textures created commercially in the form of machine-rolled glass.

Roundels

A roundel (3), or "bull's eye," is a disk of spun crown glass that includes the scar left at its center by the glass blower's pontil. Roundels were, and still are, made specially for leaded lights.

Jewels

Jewels (4) are faceted square and circular pieces of glass that were set among flat quarries to catch and break up the light. You can buy modern "jewels" – but some professionals consider them to be inferior to nineteenth-century examples, which are sold at a premium whenever an old window is broken up for scrap.

A bold yet simple art-glass design   *Formalized fruit-bowl motif*

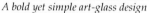

Art Nouveau transom light incorporating a floral wreath and swags

Jewels and roundels

CAMES

Each piece of glass in a leaded window is surrounded by H-section strips of lead known as cames (5). These are made either with a convex surface (round lead) or with a flat one (flat lead). Flat lead is the earlier type.

Because lead is a very soft metal, the cames are practically unmanageable until they have been stretched. This both straightens and work-hardens the came. It is done by holding one end in a vice and pulling the other end sharply with pliers.

Toward the end of the nineteenth century a new technique for joining glass quarries was developed in America by Louis Tiffany. A strip of copper foil was wrapped around the edges of each. With the foiled quarries butted together, a bead of solder was run along both sides of the window to make a neat continuous joint. It is an ideal method for joining small pieces of glass. However, the cost of restoring or remaking a copper-foiled window is likely to be higher than for a conventional leaded light.

Round lead   *Flat lead*   *Copper foil*

5
3
4
2
7
6
8
1

Components of a leaded light
1 Colored glass
2 Flashed glass
3 Roundel
4 Jewel
5 Cames
6 Soldered joint
7 Cement seal
8 Saddle bar

ASSESSING REPAIRS
● Easy even for beginners.
■ Fairly difficult. Good practical skills required.
▲ Difficult. Hire a professional.

Loose wire ties
The solder breaks from joints.
■ Replace the wire ties (page 125).

Cracked quarry
Slamming a door or window can crack the quarries.
■ Strap with lead (page 126).

Broken joint
Weak lead cracks near joint.
■ Resolder joint (page 126).
▲ Have lead replaced (page 127).

Corroded lead
Lead becomes brittle due to pollution.
▲ Have lead replaced (page 127).

Seriously damaged panel
Severe damage can be caused by a break-in.
▲ Have the panel professionally repaired (page 127).

Missing panel
Panel discarded or sold by a previous owner.
▲ Have replacement made (page 127).

Dirty glass and lead
Airborne pollution leaves deposits on leadwork and dirties the glass.
● Clean and polish (page 127).

Loose quarries
Brittle old cement falls out. Quarries rattle if you tap the window with your fingertips.
● Seal with fresh cement (page 125).

Broken quarry
A quarry may get broken as a result of an accident or vandalism.
■ Replace the quarry (page 126).

Buckled panel
A buckled window or door panel can be caused by slamming or wind pressure.
■ Straighten panel (page 125).
■ Install saddle bar (page 125).

SOLDER
The joints between lengths of came are secured with solder (6) made from 60 per cent lead and 40 per cent tin. Professionals tend to use gas soldering irons to melt the solder, but you may find a thermostatically controlled electric iron more convenient. Tallow, cast in stick form, is the flux preferred by professional stained-glass artists and restorers.

CEMENT
To create a weatherproof seal, a mixture of whiting (powdered chalk), linseed oil, and turpentine known in the trade as "cement" is packed into the gaps between the glass and lead (7). Stove polish or black is often included to color the mixture. You can buy ready-made cement, in the form of a special quick-setting putty, but for a single repair it is cheaper to use ordinary glazier's putty mixed with stove black.

SADDLE BARS
Vulnerable leaded lights are supported on the inside by steel or iron rods, $1/4$ to $3/8$in (6 to 9mm) in diameter, known as saddle bars (8). Copper-wire ties soldered to strategic joints in the lead are twisted around each bar to secure the window.

If straight saddle bars would spoil the appearance of a leaded light, they can be shaped to follow the line of the leading. Alternatively, steel inserts, known as lead strengtheners, can be run inside the cames.

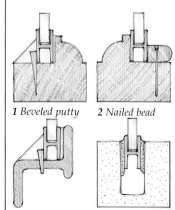

1 Beveled putty *2 Nailed bead*

3 Lead peg *4 Grooved stone*

HOW LEADED LIGHTS WERE FITTED

Leaded lights were installed in the same way as ordinary window glass. The panel was bedded in linseed-oil putty and secured in the rebates with sprigs or tacks, then more putty was added and shaped to form a bevel all around (1). When leaded lights were installed in sliding sashes, relatively large counterweights were required to counterbalance the weight of the lead.

Interior leaded lights were often secured with wooden beads screwed or nailed to the rebates (2).

Lead pegs driven into holes in the frame held leaded lights in metal casements, and putty was used to fill the rebates (3). If the leaded light has been repaired in the past, the pegs may have been cut off flush with the frame and the plugged lead used as fixing points for nails or tacks.

A leaded light fixed in a stone surround was located in grooves (or sometimes in rebates) cut in the masonry all around the opening (4). Deep grooves allowed the panel to be slid into place then centralized. If the grooves were shallow, the lead flanges around the panel were bent back for fitting then straightened out into the grooves. Pointing with mortar made the joints surrounding the window waterproof.

REPAIRING LEADED LIGHTS

ALTHOUGH MINOR REPAIRS *to leaded lights can often be undertaken by a reasonably competent amateur, full-scale restoration requires the skills of a professional. Don't expect your local glass shop to be able to restore stained glass. It is a craft that takes years of training and experience to perfect.*

Consequently, stained-glass artists are a relatively rare breed. When looking for a professional to work for you, it is therefore worth investigating local artisans who might be contracted to do your restoration work. Don't hesitate to ask whether the craftsperson has done similar work before – and to check references for satisfied customers. Most professionals will have a portfolio of their work to show you. You should also ask to see an actual job in progress in order to ascertain the quality of the detailing.

PLYWOOD SUPPORT   LEADED PANEL

1 Support a leaded panel on a piece of padded plywood

REMOVING A LEADED LIGHT

Try to disturb an old leaded light as little as possible. Careless repair work or clumsy handling may cause further damage, requiring expensive restoration.

Though some jobs can be done with the leaded light *in situ*, many repairs can only be tackled efficiently with the window laid flat on a bench.

If possible, take the whole casement or door off its hinges and lay it on a workbench with the leaded panel supported from below by a piece of plywood cut to fit the opening (1). If necessary, use newspaper to raise the support slightly.

If the leaded light is in a fixed frame or surround, or has to be dismantled to facilitate a repair, you have no alternative but to remove it from the opening. Cut wire ties with pliers, then remove wooden beads or use an old chisel to chop out the putty holding the leaded

panel in place. If the putty is very hard, it is probably safer to soften it first with paint stripper (see RENEWING OLD PUTTY).

Remove any nail fixings, then run a blade all around the leaded panel to loosen it.

If necessary, use a sharpened paint scraper to gently lever out the panel, working from the other side of the window (2). Insert the blade of the scraper as close as possible to joints in the lead, and work alternately on opposite sides of the frame.

Carry a leaded light on edge, keeping it as vertical as possible. If you cannot lay the panel flat on the bench immediately, rest it in an upright position against a wall and place a weight on the ground to prevent the bottom sliding outward.

If a leaded light has to be removed for more than a day, as a security measure temporarily install ordinary glass in its place.

2 Gently lever out the panel

WORKING SAFELY WITH LEADED LIGHTS

- You have to work with lead for relatively long periods before the metal presents a serious threat to your health. Nevertheless, it pays to wear protective gloves and to wash your hands thoroughly after handling it. Do not eat or prepare food in the workshop, and always be careful to work in an environment which is well-ventilated.
- Be sure to wear protective gloves whenever you are handling glass, and protect your eyes with safety goggles whenever you are cutting it.
- Be careful not to exert too much pressure on a leaded light – if the lead suddenly buckles, you may find that you have inadvertently thrust your hand or arm right through the window.

RECEMENTING LOOSE QUARRIES

If glass quarries are loose because of damaged cames, you will need to have the window releaded. However, you are more likely to find that the quarries are rattling because expansion and contraction of the lead has caused brittle old cement to fall out.

There's no need to spend money on special cement for just one or two quarries. Instead, you can knead a ball of ordinary linseed-oil putty to a fairly stiff consistency (if need be, removing some of the oil by pressing it between newspaper) and mix in stove black until the putty is dark gray.

Use your thumbs to push the putty under the edges of the cames surrounding the loose quarries (1). You can do this with the window *in situ*, but don't forget to fill both sides.

Remove excess putty by running a pointed tool along the edges of the cames (2), then consolidate the putty by brushing in all directions with a bristle brush.

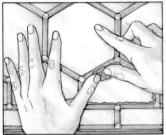

1 Push putty under the cames

2 Scrape off excess putty

FLATTENING A BUCKLED PANEL

The force generated by the repeated slamming of a door or window gradually bows the lead outward, and even strong winds have been known to distort a large leaded light. If there are no other obvious signs of damage, it may be possible to straighten out a bowed or distorted panel – but consider first whether this is really desirable.

Slight buckling of the lead creates interesting reflections that add to the character of a window. Furthermore, it is not always possible to flatten a leaded light satisfactorily. If the lead has been buckled for some time, it may have become inflexible and brittle and will resist any attempt to straighten it out. This is often exacerbated by the sharp edges of the glass cutting into the inside of the cames as you attempt to move them.

With great care, try to push the cames back into position with the window in place. Wear thick protective gloves, and press very gently and as evenly as possible. If the glass does not flex, do not force it – remove the light and leave it in the sun for a day with a weight, such as a book, carefully placed on the leadwork. If the panel flattens, renew the cement if necessary.

Before reinstalling the panel, consider whether adding a saddle bar might prevent a recurrence of the bulging in future.

If the window already has a saddle bar, renew the wire ties (see right) before you put the panel back *in situ*.

INSTALLING A SADDLE BAR

Most movable windows and doors, and any fixed light that is over 2ft (600mm) in height, are likely to benefit from the addition of a saddle bar. It is therefore worth installing one when leaded lights are removed for repair. You may need to fit several bars if the panel is very large.

Select a position for the bar (or bars) that will not detract from the design of the window. Saddle bars usually look best running alongside a continuous horizontal came or a row of soldered joints. Mark the chosen position on the inside of the window frame.

The length of the saddle bar should be the width of the frame plus 1/2in (12mm) at each end (1).

Drill holes for the bar (2) on both sides of the window. One hole should be 1/2in (12mm) deep; the other should be 1in (25mm). The deeper hole will allow you to slide the bar into place then adjust its position until it is located at both ends.

Cut 3in (75mm) lengths of copper wire to serve as ties, and solder their centers to conveniently placed joints that will align with the bar (3). Space the ties as regularly as possible.

Install the leaded light and saddle bar, then wrap each tie around the bar and twist the ends of the wire together with pliers (4).

Cut off excess wire and fold the twisted tail under the bar. Apply putty all around the window on the outside (see REPLACING A BROKEN PANE).

If beads are used on the inside to secure the panel, notch them so that they fit over the saddle bar.

EDGE OF FRAME

SADDLE BAR

1/2in (12mm)   1/2in (12mm)

1 Allow extra on length of bar

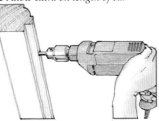

2 Drill holes in the frame

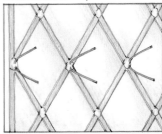

3 Solder wires to the joints

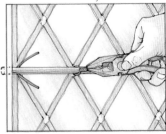

4 Twist wire ties with pliers

REPLACING A BROKEN QUARRY

If only one or two quarries are broken, provided the lead is in good condition you can replace them *in situ*.

Make a tracing of the broken quarry by drawing along the inner edge of the surrounding cames. This tracing will serve as a template for cutting the replacement glass.

Support the back of the window and, using a glass cutter, score what remains of the quarry with a series of crisscross lines **(1)**. Wearing protective gloves and safety goggles, tap the back of the glass in the middle of the quarry to break out most of the fragments **(2)**. Use a penknife to loosen small pieces of glass trapped in the cames, then scrape out the residue of old cement with a small screwdriver.

Cut the corner joints, on the inside only, with a stout utility knife **(3)**. Because you are cutting through solder, which is harder than lead, it is important to keep the knife blade at an angle that doesn't put sideways pressure on the leaded panel, making it buckle.

Use a small pair of needle-nose pliers, with the jaws padded with tape, to bend back the flanges all around **(4)**. Don't bend the flanges too far or they will crease, making it impossible to close them up neatly.

Select a piece of glass that matches the broken quarry and cut it to size (see CUTTING GLASS). The new piece should be 1/16in (2mm) larger all around than the tracing you made from the original quarry.

Insert the new glass and close up the cames, using a simple homemade tool known as a lathykin. Find a piece of plaster lath or another piece of wood about 1/4in (6mm) thick and 1 1/2in (40mm) wide. Round its end, and then use it to rub down the cames all around **(5)**. Make sure the corners are closed up neatly.

As this operation is performed on the inside of the window, it is not absolutely essential to resolder the joints. If you want to complete the job with solder, take the door or window off its hinges and lay it flat on the floor or workbench.

Seal the cames with cement (see RECEMENTING LOOSE QUARRIES). For at least the next week, close the door or window very gently.

STRAPPING A CRACKED QUARRY

Strapping entails soldering a flat piece of lead over cracked glass, in effect creating a false came. Although individual quarries can be replaced, it is sometimes desirable to strap cracked glass, especially if it is rare and expensive. Strapping a narrow strip of glass in a border, for example, is relatively simple and the repair is hardly noticeable.

Shorten the blade of an ordinary paint scraper and sharpen it to make a lead-cutting knife. Use this knife to make a strap by slicing off one flat side of a came **(1)**.

Clean a section of came next to each end of the crack in the glass by scraping the lead with a blade. Lay the strap over the crack and solder one end to the edge of the came **(2)**. Pull the strap taut and cut off the other end flush with the opposite came **(3)**. Solder it, then repeat the process on the other side of the window and darken the lead with stove black

1 Score broken quarry

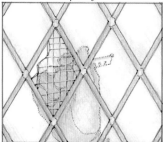

2 Tap the quarry to break the glass

3 Cut the joints with a knife

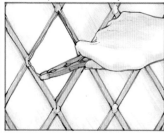

4 Bend back the lead flanges

5 Rub down the cames

1 Slice a flat strap from a lead came

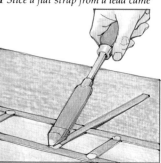

2 Solder one end of the strap

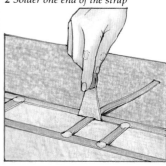

3 Cut strap flush with other came

REPAIRING A BROKEN LEAD JOINT

When a soldered joint in a leaded light cracks, it is not normally the joint itself that breaks but the piece of lead next to the solder.

You can repair the joint with solder; but if it breaks again, it's a sure sign that the lead is weak and you should consider having the window releaded.

REPLACING CORRODED CAMES

Decades of airborne pollution can seriously weaken leadwork. It becomes brittle, and pieces gradually break away until whole sections of glass are in danger of falling out. If you have a window in this state, get a professional to remove it and take it away for releading. He or she will make a rubbing of the window as an exact guide to the layout of the cames. A full-size drawing called a "cutline" is made from the rubbing, each line representing the position of the central web or "heart" of each piece of leading.

The leaded light is carefully dismantled and each piece of glass laid out in the correct pattern. The old cement is then scraped from around the edges of the glass with a lead-cutting knife. Any damaged quarries are replaced at this stage.

The full-size drawing is laid on the bench and two wooden battens are nailed through it, one aligning with the bottom of the drawing, the other with the left-hand side. Starting with the corner formed by the battens, new lead is cut and the old glass refitted, using the drawing as a guide. Specialty nails are used to clamp the loose cames in place as, piece by piece, the panel is rebuilt.

When it is complete, the joints are cleaned with a wire brush and tallow flux is wiped across each joint before soldering. Then the panel is turned over and the joints are soldered on the other side.

Using a small scrubbing brush, cement is brushed in all directions on both sides of the panel until the lead is sealed. Dry whiting is then sprinkled onto the panel to absorb excess oil.

About two hours later a pointed tool is used to remove cement from around the edges of the cames, then the panel is scrubbed again with a clean soft-bristle brush. After another two hours the lead is darkened with stove black.

Jewel about to fall from brittle lead

RE-CREATING A BADLY DAMAGED PANEL

A badly damaged leaded light, perhaps one that has been smashed by a burglar, can be re-created exactly by a professional stained-glass artist. He or she will take critical measurements, note the types of glass used, and make a rubbing of what's left of the leaded light.

If you happen to have another identical window, the artist can use that as a pattern for restoring badly damaged sections. Otherwise, he or she will have to deduce what the window looked like from the remaining fragments.

If the original window has been completely destroyed, then your only recourse is to find a restorer able to design a replacment (see below).

REPLACING A MISSING PANEL

You often come across clear-glass door panels and fanlights where a previous owner was not prepared to pay for the repair of leaded lights. If you want to have a new window made to the original style, you need to find a stained-glass artist with creative skills equal to his or her craftsmanship. Together, you can research the subject and may be able to track down an example in your neighborhood to serve as a model.

If you can't find a suitable authentic pattern or original to copy, you will need to discuss with the artist the style of design you want and the types of glass to be used. The artist will then prepare a colored drawing for your approval and will submit an estimate for making and fitting the window.

Make sure the artist gives you a date for starting the work and an estimate of how long the job will take. Also, any savings in cost or alterations to the design must be clearly agreed at this stage.

Each job is different, but normally you can expect to pay one third of the fee in advance.

ENLARGING OR REDUCING A PANEL

Salvaged leaded lights and stained-glass panels bought from a dealer are unlikely to fit your window opening without modification. However, a professional may be able to enlarge a panel by adding sympathetic borders.

Reducing the size tends to be more difficult – so if a panel is too large, it may be necessary to keep the best parts only and have the surround redesigned to fit.

PROTECTING FINISHED WINDOWS

Rare painted windows in churches and other public buildings are sometimes protected with a sheet of clear glass or plexiglass. If you choose to protect your glass in a similar way, consult a professional about the technical problems of sandwiching a sheet of plastic in the existing rebates. You may also want to check whether your window is valuable enough to warrant the extra expense.

CLEANING LEADED LIGHTS

Even if leaded lights are cleaned regularly, dirt tends to collect around the edges of each quarry. In addition, pollution affects the lead, which develops a white powdery deposit. Not only does this make the cames unsightly, but rainwater and condensation tend to wash it onto the glass, too.

Unless the glass is etched or sandblasted, clean the cames with a soap-filled pad or with a small brass-wire brush (such as a suede brush) dipped in moistened scouring powder. Wipe the lead with a rag, then wash the glass carefully with warm soapy water. Do a small area first and examine the result before proceeding.

Darken the cleaned lead with a touch of stove black on a shoe brush. Brush across the cames, not along them. If the glass is dirty, you may need to wipe the polish off, using a rag dampened with mineral spirits.

STAINED & PAINTED GLASS

GLASS PAINTING *is one of the foremost skills in a tradition of craftsmanship in glass that is centuries old – but in terms of its use in relatively ordinary houses, the Victorian era must surely rank as its heyday. In England an artisan's labor was then so cheap that even the aspiring middle classes could afford exquisitely painted windows and door panels; floral motifs and animals and birds were particularly fashionable themes, but a client could choose any subject from landscape to portraiture. While machine-made glass has always been the dominant material in this country, skilled glass workers practicing today can restore or reproduce a great variety of glasswork, domestic and imported.*

Birds and flowers have always been popular subjects

An exceptionally detailed autumnal scene

Bright luminous colors with the minimum of modeling

A landscape is the centerpiece of this circular door panel

REPRODUCING PAINTED GLASS

Developing the necessary skills for restoring stained glass is out of the question for the average amateur, especially if you only have to repair one or two pieces. Furthermore, the cost of the specialized brushes and vitreous paints needed (let alone a kiln in which to fire the glass) would almost certainly be higher than an expert's fee for restoring the glass. Nevertheless, it pays to familiarize yourself with glass-painting techniques so that you are able to discuss the various options with a professional.

A skilled glass painter can reproduce damaged portions of a window, using broken fragments or undamaged areas of glass as a guide. If you need to re-create an entire stained-glass window, the painter will either copy a suitable existing example or design a new window for you that is in character with your house.

Tracing

The glass painter's first task, known as tracing, is to paint outlines and other linework onto each piece of glass, using dark pigments (either brown, green, red or black) thinned with various media and mixed with a binder that makes the paint adhere to the glass.

After tracing, most artists fire the glass to fuse the paint to the surface of the

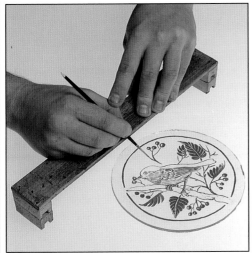

The linework is traced with a fine brush

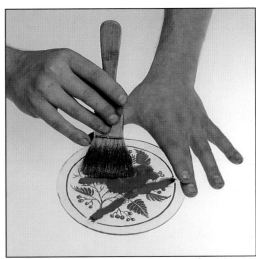

Matting is applied by stippling the glass with paint

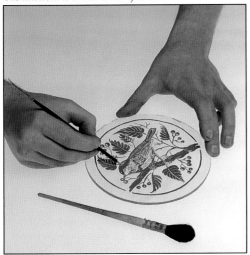

Scratching creates highlights and areas of light tone

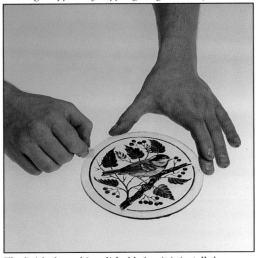

The finished panel is polished before it is installed

glass permanently. But some mix the pigments for subsequent layers of paint with a different medium that will not disturb the tracing, and delay firing till a later stage.

Matting
Areas of tone and modeling are applied to the painting using a process known as matting. An even layer of paint is brushed or stippled over the tracing. When it has dried, part of the paint is removed with a variety of brushes, pointed sticks, and pens, creating areas of lighter tone and highlights. After firing, a second matt, possibly in another color, can be applied over the first.

Coloring glass
Enamels are used to color areas of glass and for painting details. These paints are opaque when applied but become transparent when fired at a relatively low temperature. Considerable experience is required to determine the end result with any degree of certainty. Enamels are not as permanent as other vitreous paints.

Staining glass
A range of yellows, from pale lemon to a deep amber, can be achieved by staining glass with silver nitrate. Mixed with water, silver stain is milky in appearance when applied to the back of the glass. Firing causes the

stain to change color and permeate the glass. Inexplicably, this single process has been responsible for the term "stained glass" being used for the entire craft of making windows in colored glass, despite the multiplicity of techniques involved.

Etching
Hydrofluoric acid is used to modify the color of flashed glass. Depending on how long the glass is immersed in the acid, it is possible to grade tones or remove the colored surface entirely. Hard edges are created by masking areas of color, and acid can be painted on freehand in order to create a modeled effect.

AGEING THE APPEARANCE
Even though a stained-glass artist will attempt to match the glass, colors, and style of a window exactly, a restored window may still look too "new" when compared with an original. If the window is to be viewed from a distance, no one may ever notice the difference. But if it is to be fitted where it can be inspected closely (in a door, for example) then a stained-glass artist may decide to age its appearance artificially.

Metaling
Metaling is the term used by glass painters to describe the effect of overfiring silver stain, which acquires a darker, more opaque appearance as a result.

A painter normally strives to avoid metaling, but it may sometimes be the only way to match the color of old stained glass.

Heavy matting
A heavy application of paint during the matting process can reproduce the mellow colors typical of old painted glass.

Etching the glass
Careful use of hydrofluoric acid dulls the glass slightly to mimic etching caused by longterm pollution.

Distressing the lead
If you want to simulate the distressed look of old leadwork, tap new cames here and there with the blade of a knife or screwdriver before coloring them with stove black (see CLEANING LEADED LIGHTS).

ACID ETCHING & SANDBLASTING

ACID ETCHING *(also known as embossing)* *imparts a matte-white "frosted" texture to* *glass. By applying an acid-resistant mask to* selected areas, it is possible to create patterns with alternating clear and textured glass. Very beautiful, subtly toned etched images are made by repeating the process two or three times using different masks. Acid etching was developed toward the end of the eighteenth century or early in the nineteenth century. But, apart from the types of mask or "resist" used to protect the glass, the process remains virtually *unchanged, and modern production methods can reproduce old embossed glass exactly. Sandblasting, which was patented in 1870, is a newer industrial process. Bombarding the surface of the glass with fine aluminum-oxide grit (sharp sand was used originally) leaves a texture similar in appearance to acid etching. Although it is possible to vary the texture by the depth of cut, sand-blasting cannot reproduce the subtlety of two-tone or three-tone embossing. However, it is much cheaper, and only an expert eye can distinguish between sand-blasting and single-tone etching.*

Authentic Art Nouveau design

Overall patterns are still available

Triple-etched Victorian door panel

BUYING FROSTED GLASS FROM STOCK

Semi-obscured frosted glass was installed in Victorian and turn-of-the-century windows, landing skylights, and doors of almost every conceivable kind.

Glazing with an overall repeat pattern, similar to wallpaper, was cheap and could be cut to fit any size or shape of window. Certain patterns are still available as stock glass.

A frosted background provides maximum privacy, while a fine pattern etched on a clear background is the ideal form of glazing for conservatories and other areas where an unobscured view is required.

You can buy antique-style frosted-glass transom lights and door panels from most glass shops. Only a limited range is available, but if you are fortunate you may be able to find an item that is an exact fit. If that proves to be impossible, there are lights without borders designed to fit most locations.

INSTALLING FROSTED GLASS

Sandblasted and acid-etched textures attract dirt, which is why the textured face of a decorative window always faces inward.

Mask the outer edges of the textured face to prevent linseed oil from fresh putty spreading and staining the frosted area. Brush dish-washing detergent onto the outermost 2in (50mm) of the glass all around the panel (or rub a cake of soap onto it). When the liquid becomes sticky, fit the panel in the normal way, taking care not to touch the textured face with oily fingertips. Leave the putty to dry for a couple of weeks before washing off the protective soap.

CLEANING FROSTED GLASS

A new replacement pane installed next to old frosted glass often looks too white by comparison. Clean the old glass with a soft-bristle brush dipped in undiluted household bleach. Rub the bleach into the texture with small circular brush strokes. After half an hour, repeat the process and then wash the window. You can remove specks of paint from frosted glass with chemical paint stripper, but don't touch the surface with an abrasive or a metal blade.

BRILLIANT-CUT GLASS

FINDING PROFESSIONALS

It isn't practicable for an amateur to reproduce an antique embossed or sandblasted window – not least because both processes are subject to very strict health and safety regulations. Sandblasting can only be performed inside a specially built enclosure, and hydrofluoric acid (the medium used by professional etchers) is so corrosive that it's not generally available to the public. A weaker acid paste is available in kit form for etching small items of glassware, but it is not really suitable for reproducing the majority of antique embossed windows.

Inquire at your local glass shop as to where you might find reliable professionals for acid etching or sandblasting glass work. If they are unable to help you, you might try the Yellow Pages for the nearest large metropolitan area. Other possible sources are advertisements or reference services for tradesmen found in some specialist magazines.

REPLACING AN ACID-ETCHED WINDOW

If one of a pair of embossed door panels is broken, a professional acid etcher can make an exact reproduction of the surviving window. It may be possible to make a rubbing of the glass, but if the etching is too shallow a professional will have to trace the design instead. At the same time, he or she will make a note of the different textures involved and measure the opening.

Back at the workshop, the rubbing or tracing is converted into an accurate drawing before transferring the design to a sheet of glass. This is achieved by masking all areas that are to remain clear with a resist. Most professionals employ a form of screen printing to apply an acid-resistant coating, but simple shapes can be cut from self-adhesive film stuck to the glass. Areas to be etched are peeled off before the glass is immersed in acid.

To create a second tone, acid-resistant paint is brushed over selected areas before the glass is returned to the acid. The etched glass is then washed thoroughly to remove the resist.

REPLACING A SANDBLASTED WINDOW

Sandblasted glass can be copied using methods similar to those employed for acid etching. However, sandblasted designs are hardly ever deep enough to be picked up as a rubbing, so it is usually necessary to make a tracing.

Provided the design is relatively simple, such as a numbered transom light, you can cut your own mechanical mask from the type of self-adhesive film used to cover kitchen shelves.

Because the textured surface always faces the inside of the house, remember to reverse your design so that it will appear the right way around from the outside of the house.

Having stuck the film to the glass, draw your design on it; then cut the film and peel it from areas you want to be textured. Rub down all the edges of the mask before taking the glass to be sandblasted.

If the window you want to reproduce has a very fine or complicated pattern, ask a professional to print a resist onto the glass and sandblast it for you.

B RILLIANT CUTTING – *a craft that America introduced to Britain in the middle of the nineteenth century – consists of grinding a pattern or motif into glass with a stone then polishing the cut until it sparkles. It is a highly skilled process that demands near-perfect hand and eye coordination, with little room for error. The effect is luxuriant, especially when deeply cut polished decoration is set off by matte-white acid etching.*

Brilliant cutting is often found in commercial premises such as banks, department stores, and other public buildings. But, except for the ubiquitous "glory stars" that were set into the corners of thousands of doors and windows, it was seldom used in private homes except for those built on a relatively grand scale. In keeping with that type of house, brilliant cutting is frequently found in glazed doors leading from an entrance lobby into a hallway.

BEVELED GLASS

Examples of beveling (a poor relation of brilliant cutting) can be found in a good many private homes. Until comparatively recently mirrors were quite often made with beveled edges, the glass being ground to a shallow angle then polished, since it was felt that they gave a mirror a "finished" appearance. For the same reason, windows and leaded lights were frequently beveled as part of the brilliant-cutting process.

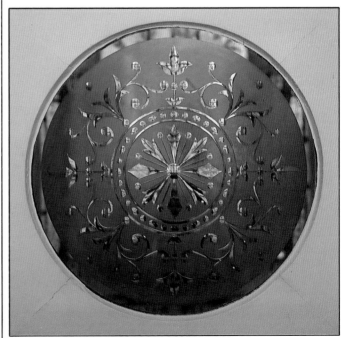

Brilliant-cut and etched panel from a Victorian door

Brilliant-cutting by hand in 1840

REPLACING BRILLIANT-CUT WINDOWS

Brilliant-cut glass is not as vulnerable as some other forms of ornamental glass. It is too tough to wear out and usually too thick to break easily; and if it's mounted indoors, it will not be affected by atmospheric pollution. However, if a brilliant-cut window does get broken, unless you can find a suitable reproduction, you have no choice but to find a professional able to make a replacement.

Brilliant cutting was always done by hand and, although modern computer-controlled machines can cut very intricate patterns, they can't reproduce hand-cut glass exactly. The furniture trade relies on cutters and bevelers to reproduce old mirrors and glazed doors for display cabinets, and a good antique-furniture dealer may be able to recommend a small firm who can copy hand-cut glass. A local glass shop may also have contacts, but the price is likely to be lower if you deal with a brilliant cutter direct.

1 Square edge cuts flowing curves

2 Round edge grinds hollows

3 Miter cuts V-shaped grooves

REPLACING GLORY STARS

Decorative marginal lights were often enhanced with corner panes of flashed ruby, blue or green glass featuring brilliant-cut star-shaped motifs. You can buy reasonably-priced reproductions from most decorative-glass suppliers to replace missing or damaged originals.

Copying the design
Take the broken glass to the cutter, who will tape the fragments together and make a rubbing of the decoration. This rubbing is laid under a sheet of plate glass, and the outline traced onto the glass with a felt-tip pen.

Cutting the glass
The sheet of glass is pressed against the edge of a vertically mounted sandstone wheel that revolves slowly. Straight lines and flowing curves are cut on the corner of a square-edged wheel **(1)**, while round-edged wheels are employed for grinding hollows **(2)** and "miter" wheels for incising V-shaped grooves **(3)**. The brilliant cutter may use any of these wheels in combination to follow the pen lines traced from the original window onto the new sheet of glass.

Polishing the cut
Grindstones leave a striated gray finish that has to be polished out of the glass in two stages. Traditionally the first stage of polishing was done on willow or elm wheels, but nowadays many cutters use a synthetic-rubber wheel, with pumice powder mixed with water as a polishing agent. The result is very attractive, though it is still matte and parts of the design may be left untouched after this first stage of polishing. But for the true brilliant-cut finish, a cork wheel is used with cerium-oxide powder to buff the cut until it's gleaming and the glass is clear.

BEVELING
Today straight edges, and even simple curves, are usually ground by machines with diamond-grit wheels and felt polishers. However, some bevelers in the antique-restoration trade still employ traditional methods when called for.

Hand beveling is similar in principle to brilliant cutting, but larger, horizontally mounted stone wheels are used and the glass is ground on the sides of the wheels, not on the edges. The glass is shaped initially on a silicon-carbide wheel lubricated with water, followed by a sandstone wheel that smooths the bevel. A thick wooden wheel coated with pumice is used for the first stage of polishing, then the job is completed on a hard-felt wheel dressed with rouge.

Modern reproduction glory stars

RESILVERING MIRRORS
Antique mirrors are often "fogged" by damp that has penetrated the silvered backing. Resilvering an antique mirror may reduce its value; but if you want to restore a mirror so that it's usable, you can have the damaged silvering stripped and replaced.

First, they strip off the old silver, using acid, and wash the glass thoroughly with distilled water. They then brush tinning solution onto the back of the mirror before spraying on silver nitrate. This is much faster than the traditional method, which involved pouring it from a jug onto a sheet of glass supported on wooden wedges. The wedges were then adjusted to control the flow of nitrate until it covered the back of the mirror.

The silver was once coated with varnish to protect it from damp, but nowadays it is sprayed with a copper solution then dried by being passed under a blower.

Last of all, paint is rolled onto the back of the mirror and any residue of silver that remains is washed from the face with acid.

CHAPTER ELEVEN

PLASTERWORK

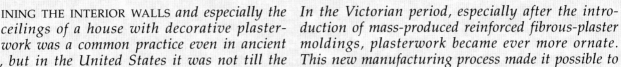

L INING THE INTERIOR WALLS *and especially the ceilings of a house with decorative plaster-work was a common practice even in ancient times, but in the United States it was not till the* eighteenth century that plastering developed as the highly skilled craft we recognize today.

The Georgian plasterwork of the eighteenth century was elegant, tasteful, and, very often, classically inspired. All the features familiar today were employed, including the ceiling centerpiece, the molded cornice masking the junction between wall and ceiling, the decorative frieze below the cornice, and strip moldings delineating wall and ceiling panels.

In the Victorian period, especially after the intro-duction of mass-produced reinforced fibrous-plaster moldings, plasterwork became ever more ornate. This new manufacturing process made it possible to prefabricate cornices, ceiling roses, overdoors headpieces for doorways, and other moldings that could be installed by general tradesmen, rather than calling for expensive specialist plasterers.

The First World War marked the end of decorative plasterwork in the average home. Fashionable taste dictated starker lines, the principal rooms of a house often being distinguished by nothing more than a simple cornice and, at most, a matching centerpiece.

Delicate mid-Victorian plaster centerpiece restored to perfect condition

Expertly painted and gilded ceiling with grapevine enrichments

Headpieces enhance a landing

Elaborate frieze upgrades a cornice

Cornice with modillions and rosettes

Highly ornate plaster corbels

THE STRUCTURE OF PLASTERWORK

THREE-COAT PLASTER *was troweled directly onto solid masonry walls or applied to laths (wooden slats) nailed across wall studs or ceiling joists. The first coat was squeezed through the spaces between the laths so that it spread out behind them to form keys that, when set, held the plaster in place.*

Prefabricated plasterboard became available toward the end of the First World War, but came to dominate in domestic construction only in the late 1940s.

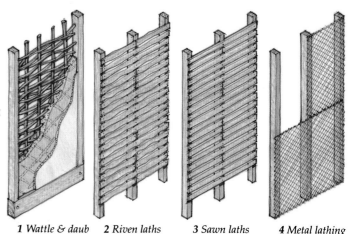

1 *Wattle & daub* **2** *Riven laths* **3** *Sawn laths* **4** *Metal lathing*

The structure of plaster

1 Scratch coat	7 Joists
2 Brown coat	8 Bracket
3 Finish coat	9 Cornice
4 Lath	10 Frieze
5 Plaster keys	11 Panel molding
6 Studs	12 Picture rail

ASSESSING REPAIRS

- ● Easy even for beginners.
- ■ Fairly difficult. Good practical skills required.
- ▲ Difficult. Hire a professional.

Overpainted moldings
Molded plaster-work may become clogged with paint.
- ● Wash off distemper (page 136).
- ■ Remove paint with chemical stripper (page 136).

Damaged or missing moldings
Moldings may be damaged or miss-ing due to neglect or modernization.
- ■ Run a new cornice (pages 140-2).
- ■ Cast and install new enrichments (page 142-3).
- ■ Fit new fibrous-plaster moldings (pages 141, 143-4).

Sagging ceiling
Ceilings sag when nail fixings decay or plaster keys are damaged.
- ■ Screw back the detached laths (page 137).
- ■ Secure ceiling from above (page 137).

Delaminated finish coat
The finish coat may flake due to damp or poor adhesion.
- ■ Seal and replaster (page 139).

Stains
Dampness and pollution stain plasterwork.
- ● Seal stains before you decorate (page 135).

Holes in plaster
Damp or vibration can make patches of plaster fall from walls and ceilings.
- ■ Fill holes with fresh plaster (page 138).

Cracked plaster
Shrinkage causes cracks, most of them harmless.
- ● Fill cracks before you decorate (page 137).

LATH-AND-PLASTER WALLS AND CEILINGS

Lath-and-plaster walls and ceilings are a development of wattle and daub **(1)**, the medieval-era practice of constructing timber-frame walls by smearing a mixture of lime, sand, straw, and dung onto a lattice of interwoven hazel twigs and upright oak or willow slats.

The earliest laths **(2)** were riven (split) by hand, which produced strips 1/8 to 1/4in (3 to 6mm) thick and 1 to 1 1/2in (25 to 35mm) wide. These were nailed to the structural timbers, leaving "keyway" slots approximately 3/8in (10mm) wide between the slats. In order to stop cracks developing as the plaster dried out, the laths were staggered and the butt joints between them positioned over the wall studs or the ceiling joists. From the 1820s machine-sawn laths **(3)** were introduced and increasingly became the norm. These had similar dimensions to hand-riven laths but were more regular.

Expanded metal lath was patented as early as 1797 in England. However, it was not widely employed as a plastering support **(4)** till the end of the nineteenth century – and even after that many plasterers continued using the tradi-tional wooden laths for at least another 30 or 40 years.

INGREDIENTS OF PLASTER

Up to the 1930s the normal practice was to apply plaster to walls and ceilings in three flat coats or layers.

First a "scratch" coat about 3/8in (8mm) thick was troweled on in order to grip the wall or ceiling securely, then the surface of the scratch coat was scored to create a key for the second layer.

The second or "brown" coat, which was about 1/4in (6mm) thick, provided an even surface for the final layer. Like the scratch coat, the floating coat was keyed in order to achieve more effective adhesion.

The last layer, known as the "finish" coat, was about 1/8in (3mm) thick and was troweled perfectly smooth to provide a suitable surface for decoration.

Traditional three-coat plaster was composed of lime and sand mixed with water. Animal hair was mixed into the first two coats in order to bind the material together. Quicklime (crushed limestone heated to a high temperature) was mixed with water on site and then left to slake (hydrate) for a minimum of three weeks. Thoroughly slaked lime, which had the consistency of soft butter, was known in the trade as lime putty. One part lime putty was mixed with three parts clean, sharp plasterer's sand to make "coarse stuff" for the scratch and brown coats.

Pure lime putty was sometimes used for the finish coat. Alternatively, three parts putty was mixed with two parts fine sand.

Lime plaster took about three weeks to dry between each coat. This considerably delayed the completion of any building. Consequently, toward the end of the nineteenth century the practice

Early-C20th representation of a tradesman mixing plaster

teenth century the practice of "gauging" lime plaster by adding gypsum or cement was introduced in order to speed up the setting time.

Patching plaster

When repairing plasterwork, purists strive to reproduce the properties of the original plaster by mixing traditional materials. If you decide to follow their example, you can buy commercially prepared hydrated lime. This is usable as soon as it is mixed with water; but if you leave the mixture for a further 24 hours or longer, it becomes an even better lime putty. Wear goggles, gloves, and a face mask when handling hydrated lime.

To make gauged plaster for the first two coats, mix one part perlited gypsum plaster with one part lime putty and six parts sand. For the finish coat, mix equal parts of gypsum and lime putty. It is not normally necessary to add hair to the mixture when patching plaster.

Especially for minor patch repairs, it is more convenient to use modern ready-mixed lightweight-aggregate plasters that are compatible with old lime plaster. In addition, modern plasters have the virtue of being formulated for specific purposes and different backgrounds (see PATCHING HOLES IN PLASTER).

BASIC REPAIRS & RESTORATION

HOUSE RESTORERS *are often, understandably, reluctant to tackle traditional plastering. However, cleaning and stripping or minor repairs to plasterwork do not require specialized skills and are well within the capability of most people.*

DEALING WITH SURFACE STAINS

Plaster can become stained for a variety of reasons. Dampness is a major cause of staining. As the moisture spreads it tends to draw impurities to the surface of the plaster, where they create permanent stains that are evident even when the plaster dries out. Damp conditions may also lead to black mold or efflorescence (white crystals), which spoil the appearance of plastered walls and ceilings. Nicotine and airborne dust both cause widespread staining, while wood preservative seeping from an attic leaves the most stubborn stains. Always seal stained plaster before redecorating, otherwise the stains are likely to bleed through the paint.

Damp and nicotine stains

Cure the source of damp and let the plaster dry out before applying an alcohol-based, pigmented shellac sealer to the affected area. Use the same sealer to prime a yellow nicotine-stained ceiling before redecorating it.

Preservative stains

When treating an attic for rot or insect attack, avoid flooding the ceiling with preservative. If it does soak through, wait till it is dry then paint the stain with an alcohol-based, pigmented shellac primer before redecorating.

Efflorescence

Efflorescence is the result of mineral salts from building materials being drawn to the surface by dampness, which must be eradicated before treating the condition. These same crystals can form on fresh plaster as it dries out.

Brush the crystals from the plaster with burlap or a stiff bristle brush. If you try to wash them off, the salts will be reabsorbed by the plaster and re-emerge when it dries. Keep removing efflorescence until crystals stop forming; then if you are planning to redecorate with an oil-based paint, seal the plaster with an alkali-resistant primer.

Mold

Black specks of mold can appear on damp plaster anywhere, but they often occur on ceilings below an inadequately insulated attic as a result of water vapor condensing on cold plasterwork. When this happens, since the mold tends to grow less vigorously on the comparatively warm and dry plaster directly below the joists, it may create pale stripes between the blackened areas.

The remedy is to brush a sterilizing solution of 1 part household bleach mixed with 16 parts water onto the ceiling (use a 1:10 solution if the mold growth is very heavy). It is advisable to wear goggles to protect your eyes. Four hours later scrape off the mold, then wash the ceiling again with sterilizing solution. Allow the plaster to dry naturally.

To stop mold recurring, install extra insulation in the attic and improve the ventilation in your home, which will reduce condensation.

STRIPPING PAINT FROM PLASTERWORK

Before modern emulsion paints were available, distemper was the preferred finish for plastered ceilings and to some extent for walls as well. Distemper, which is composed of powdered chalk or whiting mixed with glue size and water, dries to an attractive but powdery matte finish. The friable nature of distemper, combined with the fact that it is soluble in water, makes it a very poor base for redecorating with modern paints or wallcoverings. You can bind distemper to plasterwork by painting over it with a proprietary stabilizing solution. But if layer upon layer of distemper has been applied to decorative plasterwork by generations of decorators, the fine detail of the original may have been obscured or completely obliterated – in which case, it pays to strip the distemper down to the bare plaster.

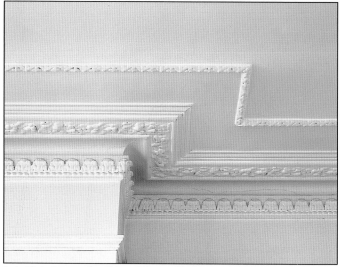

Late-Victorian cornice all but obliterated by layers of old paint

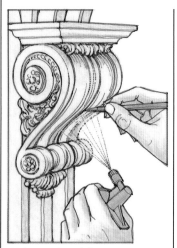

Pick out softened distemper

Removing distemper with water

You can sponge distemper from flat plasterwork with water containing a little proprietary wallpaper stripper. Cleaning decorative plaster takes greater care and effort.

Working on a small area at a time, moisten distempered plaster with water from a plant spray and, as the paint softens, scrape it from the moldings with an old toothbrush. You will have to pick thick distemper out of the deeper crevices with a sharpened stick. Finally, wash the plaster with clean water and apply a stabilizing solution to bind any traces of distemper.

Steam-cleaning plaster

Stripping a ceiling rose or an ornate cornice by hand with water is a laborious, backbreaking task. To save yourself several days of work on each room, you may be able to hire a specialist contractor to strip the distemper with steam. It is not easy to find professionals able to undertake this type of work safely and proficiently. Make sure they can protect the fabric of your house and collect the copious amounts of water generated by the process. A steam generator in unskilled or inexperienced hands can destroy irreplaceable plasterwork, so insist on references from recent customers.

Steam leaves plaster clean and crisp

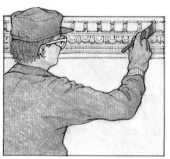

1 Stipple stripper onto plasterwork

2 Peel away fibrous-tissue covering

Using a chemical stripper

Special ready-mixed paste strippers will remove any combination of distemper, emulsion and oil-based paints. Sheets of laminated plastic and fibrous tissue, supplied with the stripper, are used to cover the paste while it softens and absorbs the paint. If you can't face the prospect of stripping a ceiling yourself, there are specialists who will do the work for you.

When buying this type of stripper, check the details on the container to make sure it is suitable for use on plaster. Follow the manufacturer's safety recommendations carefully when handling these chemicals. Wear long plastic gloves taped to your sleeves and protect your eyes, face, and hair from falling paint, dust, and stripper.

Stipple the paste into the nooks and crannies of molded plasterwork with an old paintbrush (**1**); then trowel it onto flat and convex surfaces, building up a layer of stripper 1/8 to 1/4in (3 to 6mm) thick. Straightaway, lay the sheets (plastic side outward) over the pasted plaster and press each sheet into the stripper, rubbing the plastic gently in order to expel air bubbles.

Leave the sheets in place for 24 to 48 hours, during which time the stripper will emulsify the paint and draw it away from the plaster. Lift the edge of one of the sheets from time to time and, when all the layers of paint appear to have been absorbed into the fibrous tissue, peel away the sheets (**2**) and dispose of them carefully.

Wash the stripped plaster with water using a scrubbing brush or sponge, then leave it to dry out for a few days.

1 Drag filler across crack

2 Then smooth it lengthwise

FILLING CRACKS

Hairline cracks in plaster are usually the result of shrinkage and require nothing more than filling followed by redecoration. However, wide cracks should be investigated to make sure that they are not a sign of serious structural movement.

With a masonry wall, probe the crack with a screwdriver or pencil to see if the damage extends farther than the depth of the plaster. If in doubt, chop out a small section of plaster on each side of the crack to determine whether the wall behind is affected. If you discover cracked masonry, get a professional to inspect further.

It is more difficult to tell with cracked plaster on a wooden loadbearing wall. If there are extensive cracks more than 1/8in (3mm) wide, have it inspected by a contractor, unless the damage has an obvious cause such as a burst pipe.

REFIXING A SAGGING CEILING

When the lath fixings fail, a lath-and-plaster ceiling will sag under its own weight (1), although the laths themselves provide some measure of reinforcement. If the plaster keys become detached or are broken due to damp conditions or physical damage (2), the unsupported plaster hangs free and the ceiling is likely to be in imminent danger of collapse. Go into the attic or lift a few floorboards in the room above, as appropriate, in order to inspect the ceiling and ascertain the most suitable course of action.

Screwing back detached lath and plaster

So long as the strips of lath are sound, it should be possible to resecure part of a lath-and-plaster ceiling that has become detached by screwing it to the underside of the joists with brass woodscrews and washers.

Carefully vacuum accumulated dust and debris from beneath the joists, then shore up the ceiling with plywood panels and softwood props (3). Protect the plasterwork by sandwiching a piece of carpet underlay or plastic foam between the plywood panels and the ceiling.

Drill pilot holes through the lath and plaster into the joists, then twist a coin into the plaster to make shallow depressions to accommodate the heads of the woodscrews and the washers. Insert the screws (4); remove the props and cover the screw heads and washers with wood filler or patching plaster.

Filling hairline cracks

Widen fine cracks by raking out loose material with the corner of a scraper. Moisten them with a paintbrush, then press joint compound or wood filler into the cracks. Drag the blade of a plasterer's knife across the cracks (1), then smooth the filler by drawing the blade along them (2). When it has set, use dry wall sanding paper to sand the filler flush with the plaster.

Filling wider cracks

Use a bolster chisel to undercut the edges of a wide crack and brush out loose debris. Thoroughly wet the crack with a brush, then fill it with a proprietary wall filler, building it up gradually in layers until it is raised very slightly. Let the filler set hard, then sand it flush. Fill deep cracks almost completely with plaster of Paris, which sets quickly, then finish the repair with a sandable filler.

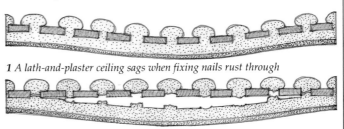

1 A lath-and-plaster ceiling sags when fixing nails rust through

2 Broken plaster keys leave a ceiling completely unsupported

Securing unsupported plaster

Clear debris from between the joists and support the ceiling on props, as when screwing back detached lath and plaster. Paint the upper surface of the lath and plaster with diluted plaster bonding agent. Spread a 1/2in (12mm) deep layer of retarded plaster of Paris (see RUNNING A PLAIN CORNICE) between each pair of joists above the damaged area.

Without delay, bed strips of expanded-metal lath or screening into the wet plaster to reinforce it (the strips need to be wide enough to span the space between the joists and turn up the sides). Trap the reinforcement with battens screwed to the joists (5), then add a second layer of plaster before the first has set. Don't remove the props until the plaster is hard.

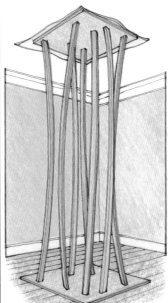

3 Support sagging ceiling with props

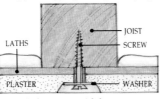

LATHS
JOIST
SCREW
PLASTER
WASHER

4 Fix lath to joist with brass screws

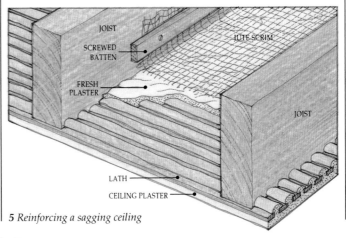

JOIST
SCREWED BATTEN
JUTE SCRIM
FRESH PLASTER
JOIST
LATH
CEILING PLASTER

5 Reinforcing a sagging ceiling

PATCHING HOLES IN PLASTER

To PLASTER A LARGE EXPANSE *of wall or ceiling successfully requires a skill that can only be developed with a great deal of experience. However, patching damaged plaster is not difficult and satisfactory results are practically guaranteed with a modicum of practice.*

Before embarking on a repair, tap the wall or ceiling in the vicinity of the hole to check that the area of loose plaster does not extend too far. If it sounds "hollow" over quite a wide area, get advice from a professional plasterer before you dislodge any more plaster.

The only specialized tools you need are a plasterer's steel trowel and a hawk – a small square sheet of wood or metal with a handle mounted beneath it, which is used for carrying the plaster to the wall or ceiling.

PATCHING HOLES OVER MASONRY

If plaster has broken away down to a masonry background, chop the loose plaster from the perimeter of the hole with a bolster chisel until you reach sound material.

Exterior walls

When patching plaster on the inside of exterior brick or stone walls, especially if there has been a history of dampness in that part of the house, it pays to use a modern renovating plaster – but make sure that the damp has been eradicated first. Paint the exposed masonry and the plaster at the edge of the hole with a cement bonding agent to insure that suction is consistent.

Following the maker's instructions, mix some liquid waterproofer (EVA) with the plaster for the scratch coat as a precaution against moisture still trapped in the wall. Pick up some plaster on your hawk, then tip the hawk toward you slightly so you can scoop plaster onto your trowel (1). Holding the trowel at a slight angle to the wall, spread the plaster on the masonry with a sweeping upward action (2). Cover the masonry to an even depth of about 3/8in (8mm) and, as the plaster begins to get firm, score it

with shallow scratches (3) to form a key for the next coat.

Let the scratch coat set for about two hours, then apply the brown coat in the same way – but this time there is no need to add a waterproofer to the plaster. Build the coat almost flush with the surrounding plaster, then scrape it level with a length of wooden architrave or some similar straightedge (4). You will find a zigzag action works best. Fill in any hollows with fresh plaster, then scrape again. Once the brown coat begins to get firm, use the trowel to scrape the outermost 6in (150mm) or so of the new plaster so that it is about 1/8in (3mm) lower than the edge of the old plaster around it (5).

Hammer some finishing nails through a piece of softwood till their points just protrude. Use this improvised tool to key the plaster with circular strokes (6).

About two hours later trowel on a finish coat of plaster. It will be easier to achieve an even thickness if

MIXING PLASTER

As a rough guide, you need to mix approximately equal proportions of clean water and dry powdered plaster.

Almost half-fill a plastic bucket with clean water and sprinkle plaster into it until the bucket is nearly full. Leave the plaster for a few minutes to absorb the water, then stir vigorously until it has a uniform creamy consistency. If you overstir the plaster, that will accelerate its setting time.

Plasterer's trowel   Hawk

you make two applications of plaster. Spread the first quite firmly (almost like buttering toast) to fill any hollows, then immediately apply more plaster, leaving it as smooth as possible and flush with the old plasterwork. When this coat is firm but has not yet set hard, dampen the trowel and use it to "polish" the plaster. Holding the face of the tool at a very shallow angle, sweep the trowel in all directions across the patch (7).

Interior walls

You can patch dry interior walls in the same way. But use a perlited gypsum undercoat plaster for the scratch and brown coats, and a similar general-purpose finish plaster or a universal one-coat plaster for the final coat. There's no need to add a waterproofer to the plaster, but a primer coat of paint will be required.

1 Scoop plaster onto a trowel

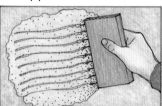

2 Sweep plaster onto the wall

3 Key the scratch coat by scoring it

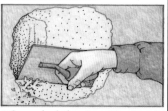

4 Level the brown coat

5 Scrape back the edge with a trowel

6 Lightly key the brown coat

7 Polish with circular strokes

CORNICE PATTERNS

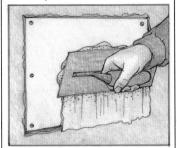

1 Screw plasterboard to studs

2 Finish with joint compound

PATCHING HOLES IN LATH AND PLASTER

Chop away the plaster at the edge of the hole to reveal the nearest studs or joists at each side. Cut a plasterboard panel to fit the hole and fix it over the laths using plasterboard screws driven into the studs or joists (**1**). Paint the edge of the surrounding plaster with diluted bonding agent, then trowel on joint compound to form a smooth flush surface (**2**).

REPAIRING DELAMINATED PLASTER

Areas of the finish coat can break away from a wall or ceiling even when the underlying plaster is perfectly sound. This may result from poor adhesion or from badly mixed plaster.

Provided that the plaster behind is sound and dry, scrape off any loose finish-coat plaster, then make sure the suction is consistent and stabilize the brown coat by painting on two coats of a plaster bonding agent.

While the second coat of bonding agent is still tacky, apply a fresh finish coat (see opposite page), using either a perlited gypsum finishing plaster or joint compound.

FROM THE EIGHTEENTH CENTURY *until the First World War no principal room would have been considered complete without a decorative wooden or plaster cornice at the wall-ceiling joint. As a result, cornices are among the most common plaster features that house restorers have to contend with.*

Plaster cornices can be categorized into two main groups – plain run and enriched moldings. Plain run cornices rely on a combination of concave flutes, convex beads, and square corners for their visual appeal. They were fashioned by plasterers who either ran metal templates through plaster in situ or created cornices on a bench then later fixed them in place.

Basically, enriched cornices were run moldings that incorporated flat areas to which separately cast decoration was applied in the form of continuous strips or individual brackets, rosettes, and other motifs. With the invention of fibrous plasterwork, it became possible to design an elaborate ornamental cornice that was cast as one long piece.

Plain-run turn-of-century cornice

Mid-C19th enriched cornice

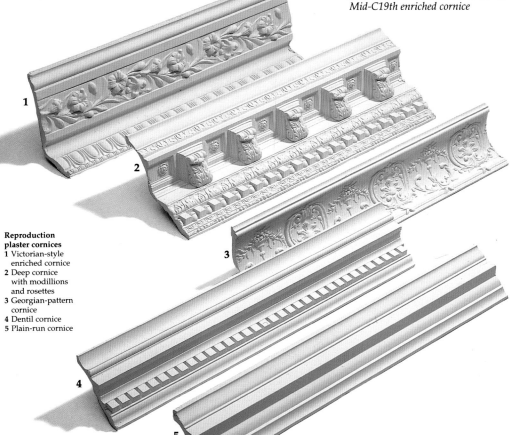

Reproduction plaster cornices
1 Victorian-style enriched cornice
2 Deep cornice with modillions and rosettes
3 Georgian-pattern cornice
4 Dentil cornice
5 Plain-run cornice

Anthemion motifs

Leaf and dart

Greek-key design

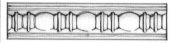

Bead and reel

Swags or festoons

Acanthus leaves

Egg and dart

Fluting

DECORATIVE MOTIFS

It is impossible to assign a specific date to motifs employed in decorative plasterwork, since many of them have been used in one form or another for centuries.

However, Georgian enriched cornices were invariably based on classical orders. The Ionic dentil cornice, with its row of small square "teeth," is a typical example; so are the decorative brackets known as modillions (often interspersed with paterae or rosettes) found on Corinthian cornices. Pictorial motifs such as the anthemion (stylized honeysuckle flower), elegant vases, human figures, and festoons (better known as swags) were also favorite Georgian and Federal motifs. All these motifs are also found on Victorian cornices, along with deeply modeled fruit, flowers, and foliage – but Victorian cornices are generally larger and more elaborate than the earlier versions.

Other motifs commonly incorporated into cornices are egg and dart, leaf and dart, bead and reel, Greek key, fluting, and acanthus leaves.

FRIEZES

Deep decorative panels or friezes were added on the wall below a cornice to make it more impressive. Similarly, narrow moldings were often run or stuck on the ceiling to increase the visual width of a cornice.

Deeply modeled plaster frieze with Art Nouveau influences

RUNNING A PLAIN CORNICE

IF YOUR ORIGINAL CORNICE HAS BEEN REMOVED *and discarded it is perhaps easiest to buy a suitable fibrous-plaster replacement. However, if you have a badly damaged plain run cornice, or one with fairly simple enrichments, you can copy an intact fragment and make a reproduction of the original cornice.*

Only a skilled plasterer can run a cornice in situ, but an amateur who is prepared to accept a certain amount of trial and error before achieving satisfactory results should be capable of running a cornice on a bench for fixing in place once the plaster has set.

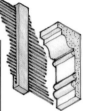

1 Profile gauge   2 Card template   3 Draw around a plaster template

DUPLICATING THE PROFILE

To match a cornice accurately it is necessary to copy its profile and reproduce the shape in the form of a metal template. Professional plasterers sometimes refer to the process of copying the profile as "taking a squeeze." You may be able to use a profile gauge, pressing its retractable steel pins against the molding (1) – but you are unlikely to find one that is large enough to accommodate the majority of cornices.

If you can saw a shallow slot in the cornice, insert a piece of cardboard and trace around the molding with a pencil (2). Alternatively, coat a small section of cornice with a film of cooking oil, to act as a release agent, then coat it with plaster of Paris 2in (50mm) thick. When the plaster has set, ease it off the cornice and saw through it to produce a section that can be used for tracing the outline onto the template (3).

MAKING A RUNNING MOLD

Cut the template from galvanized sheetmetal with snips and shape it with files. Burnish the cut edge to remove any burrs, which would create striations in the plaster. Cut a thick plywood backing board roughly to the shape of the template and cut back the edge to about 45 degrees (1). Pin or screw the template to the board, then screw a baseboard onto the backing board and secure it with a triangular brace (2).

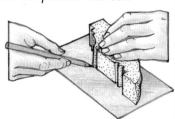

1 Plywood backing board

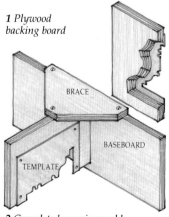

BRACE

BASEBOARD

TEMPLATE

2 Completed running mold

LINING THE BENCH

Make the running surface for your mold from a smooth board fixed to a workbench. The running surface must be kept flat, so a thick kitchen worktop is ideal. The base-board needs to project sufficiently to run against the edge of your running surface (1). In order to reduce the weight of a wide cornice, build a backing board on the your add a triangular wooden fillet (2). Add to the mold a second triangular brace running along the top of the backing board. You may wish to coat the sliding surfaces with a film of cooking oil.

RUNNING THE CORNICE

Sections of cornice approximately 10ft (3m) long are a convenient size to mold and install. You will find that plaster of Paris is the best material to use for running a cornice. Plain plaster is suitable for a smallish cornice, but since it sets in only a few minutes you may prefer to retard it slightly if you are molding a cornice that is large or complex. One pinch of cream of tartar in half a bucket of plaster should give you plenty of time (though some plasterers prefer to add wallpaper sizing). After a little experimenting, you will discover how much retardant suits your particular speed of operation. Mix the plaster of Paris to the consistency of pourable cream.

It is best to have an assistant mix and pour the plaster, so that you can concentrate your attention on running the cornice and washing the template between passes.

To reinforce the cornice, place one or two laths on the running surface along the line of the molding. Temporarily nail the laths at each end. Lay a strip of burlap or screening dipped in plaster on top and rub it down so that it sticks to the laths.

Pour the first coat of plaster onto the running surface and make the first pass with the mold, keeping it firmly pressed against the front edge of the running surface (1). Immediately, wash the remaining plaster from your mold in a bucket of water while your assistant pours another layer of plaster over the first. Then make another pass with the mold.

As the plaster begins to set, the shape of the casting starts to form rapidly. Continue adding more plaster to the hollows between passes until the cornice appears to be complete.

Once the plaster is firm, splash water along the cornice and make a pass without adding fresh plaster. This will skim the cornice as the plaster swells during the setting process. Repeat the process as often as necessary until the plaster is stable.

Remove minor blemishes from the set cornice with a scraper or chisel dipped in water. Fill any tiny holes or irregularities. After about 20 minutes, scrape off excess plaster left on the running surface on each side of the molding (2) and remove the finished cornice.

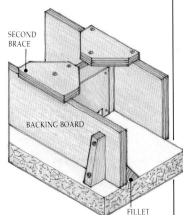

1 Make a pass with running mold

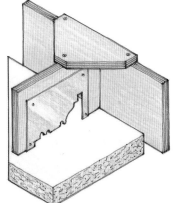
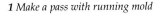

2 Scrape off excess plaster

1 Trace along edges of cornice

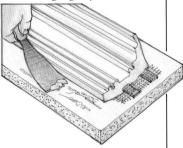

2 Transfer guideline to cornice

INSTALLING THE CORNICE

When installing lengths of plain run cornice to match an existing molding that is still *in situ*, strip and clean what remains of the original and cut the ends square so you can butt the new cornice against them. (The procedure described here is also used when installing ready-made fibrous-plaster moldings.) Before commencing work, you will need to erect a sturdy platform for you and an assistant to stand on.

Paint some bonding agent, diluted following the manufacturer's instructions, along the junction between walls and ceiling to insure that the suction is consistent. While it is drying, cut off a short section of cornice to use as a template for marking out guidelines.

Starting with the longest run of wall that is visible as you enter the room, hold the template in the corner so it fits snugly against the wall and the ceiling. Trace along the top and bottom of the cornice with a pencil (1), then repeat the procedure at the other end of the wall and join the marks by snapping a chalkline against the plaster. Continue in the same way around the room until you have marked every run, including the sides of any chimney breast or alcoves.

Using a backsaw or a fine-tooth tenon saw, cut the first length of cornice to fit between the two walls. With the help of your assistant, lift the molding into position and transfer the ceiling guideline onto the front edge of the cornice at each end (2).

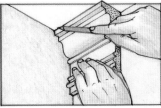

1 Baseboard runs against front edge

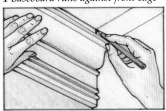

2 Running surface for wide cornice

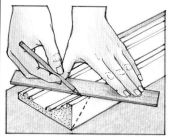

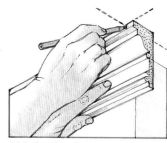

3 Mark compound miter at each end

4 Mark ceiling line at a corner

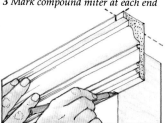

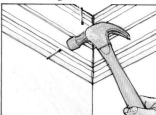

5 Then mark the corner itself

6 Support cornice on nails

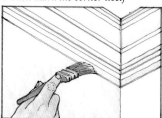

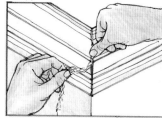

7 Clean off excess filler with a brush

8 Fill wide gaps with cheesecloth

Lay the cornice on its back and, using a straightedge, draw a line from the mark to the bottom corner **(3)**. After doing this at both ends, cut along these lines to form a miter joint. Irregularities can be filled after the cornice is installed. Repeat the whole procedure for the lengths of cornice on adjacent walls.

For external corners, cut the cornice a bit longer than required and mark on it the ceiling line **(4)** and corner of the wall **(5)**. Join these marks across the face of the cornice and cut along this line.

On a very long wall, you will need to butt two lengths of cornice end to end.

Use a bonding agent to seal the back of each section and joint compound to glue it in place. Spread the compound on the back of the first length of cornice, then press it against the wall and ceiling, squeezing out excess compound. The suction created will help to hold the cornice in place. Nevertheless, to keep it secure while the compound is setting, it is

best to drive galvanized nails or masonry pins through it at strategic points, carefully punching the nailheads below the surface of the plaster.

Alternatively, to avoid damaging delicate moldings, drive nails into the wall and ceiling so that they support the top and bottom edges of the cornice, then remove them once the compound has set **(6)**. Very heavy cornices should be fixed with brass wood-screws driven into joists or wall studs.

Before the compound sets, use a damp brush to clean off any that has squeezed out around the edges **(7)**; brushing the edges also helps fill any gaps between the cornice and the wall.

After fitting each length of cornice, fill any gaps and disguise all nailheads with joint compound. Fill wide gaps at corner joints with rolls of cheesecloth dipped in compound **(8)**. Use your finger to fill the joints flush, then smooth the compound with a damp cloth or brush.

CASTING ENRICHMENTS

MUCH OF THE ORNAMENTATION *that is found on cornices consists of individual castings glued in place with plaster. Even what appears to be continuous molded decoration is often made from short sections of cast plaster butted end to end. The same can be said of elaborate early ceiling roses, which were in fact constructed from dozens of individual castings glued together on the ceiling. Damaged or missing enrichments of this sort can be replaced by taking castings from specimens that are still intact.*

REMOVING AN ENRICHMENT
It is essential to strip paint from an enrichment in order to obtain a clean casting, so that the newly made replicas will resemble the original enrichments still *in situ*.

Once all the paint has been removed, you should be able to insert the tip of a screwdriver or old chisel behind the selected enrichment and pry it carefully away from the plaster so that you can make a mold on a bench.

MAKING A MOLD
Any number of individual enrichments can be cast from a custom-made flexible mold. Cold-cure silicone rubber is perhaps the easiest to use. Furthermore, if it is impossible to take down an enrichment without damaging it, you can buy an additive that enables you to brush the silicone rubber onto the ceiling or wall.

Hot-melt mold-making compounds are cheaper, but they require careful handling and you need a special melting pot to use them.

Construct a softwood box to surround the enrichment, leaving a generous margin all around so that the mold will have strong walls. Moisten the bottom of the box with coking oil. Stick the original to the base of the box with plaster and fill any

Cornice with applied enrichments

gaps to prevent molding compound flowing beneath the casting. Spray the original with the sealer/release agent supplied as part of the molding kit. Mix the cold-cure silicone rubber with its catalyst, following the manufacturer's instructions, then pour it slowly and steadily into the bottom of the box until the enrichment is covered completely. Leave the rubber to set overnight, then dismantle the box and peel off the flexible mold.

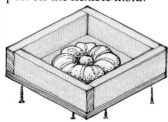

Make a softwood box with a base

FIBROUS PLASTER

1 *Level the plaster with a spatula*

2 *Score the plaster when it has set*

I T IS NOT DIFFICULT TO IMAGINE THE ENTHUSIASM *with which fibrous plaster was greeted when it was patented in 1856. For the first time it became possible to mass-produce a large, complex and detailed molding as a comparatively lightweight single piece that could be fitted on site without special skills.*

Fibrous plaster was also relatively cheap to produce and the range of standard castings was extensive. As a result, it was not long before decorative plasterwork was common even in fairly humble homes.

MAKING A CASTING

Lay the mold on a level bench and fill it to the brim with plaster of Paris. Tap the sides in order to encourage air bubbles to rise to the surface. Draw a spatula across the mold to level up the plaster **(1)**. As soon as the plaster begins to get firm, score the surface to form a key **(2)**. After 10 minutes or so peel off the mold, which can be used immediately to cast further identical copies.

INSTALLING AN ENRICHMENT

Use a pencil to mark the positions of the individual enrichments on the plaster, then key the spots where they are to be installed by scoring them with a pointed tool. Paint the scored plaster and the backs of the enrichments with bonding agent. Spread joint compound onto the back of each enrichment and press it into position, sliding it back and forth slightly to squeeze out excess compound. The suction thus created will grip the enrichment – nevertheless, it's best to hold it in place while you remove excess compound with a scraper and clean up with a damp paintbrush.

Fibrous-plaster reproductions
1 Oval centerpiece
2 Corbels
3 Wall plaque
4 Overdoor
5 Fluted pilaster with Ionic capital

143

FIBROUS-PLASTER MOLDINGS

Fibrous-plaster moldings, made from ordinary plaster but reinforced with scrim and strips of wood, are still manufactured in the traditional way and are sometimes cast from original molds. If plasterwork in your home has been removed or damaged, take comfort from the fact that there is an enormous variety of authentic-looking fibrous-plaster moldings available – ranging from the simplest coves to richly embellished combinations that include deep friezes and decorative ceiling plates.

Ceiling roses from which to hang pendant light fittings or chandeliers, range from elaborate centerpieces 4ft 6in (1350mm) in diameter to plain disks a mere 8in (200mm) across. Most are circular, but it's possible to buy roses that are octagonal or elliptical. Unlike earlier ceiling roses, which were often made by plastering individual enrichments together on the ceiling, fibrous-plaster roses are manufactured in one piece and so are very much easier to install.

Strips of delicate plasterwork that can be combined with cast plaques and fancy corner moldings are available for constructing wall or ceiling panels – which were considered vital for dividing up plain plaster surfaces into acceptable proportions.

There are more unusual items such as archway sections and ornate supporting brackets or corbels, and there is a huge selection of columns, pilasters, capitals, wall niches, door headpiece moldings, fire surrounds, and urns and statues.

FITTING A CEILING ROSE

A central ceiling "rose" made from plaster was a feature of practically every Victorian drawing room and parlor, from large country houses to modest cottages. The earliest ones were intended for use with gas lighting, and some of them provided a means of extracting unpleasant fumes: small holes that formed part of the molded pattern led, via pipes, to an airbrick in an outside wall. However, the prime function of the ceiling rose was to act as a focal point or to enrich what would otherwise have been a plain ceiling. The procedure for fitting a ceiling rose involves the same methods as fitting any simple fibrous-plaster molding.

Originally roses were often built up on the ceiling from separate enrichments

Accommodating an electrical fitting

Reproduction plaster centerpieces are often designed to house a light fitting. Sometimes there is just a circular recess at the center of the rose that accommodates a standard plastic backplate and a screw-on cover. However, the more elaborate ceiling roses are made with decorative plaster bosses mounted on the plastic cover, concealing the whole fitting except for the wire, which hangs from a hole in the center of the boss.

Always make sure that an electrical fitting is screwed securely to a ceiling joist – not just into the plaster rose. Unless you have the knowledge and experience to fit it yourself, get an electrician to install and wire the light fitting. The electricity supply must be switched off at the main panel while you are fitting the ceiling rose itself.

Preparing the ceiling

If necessary, strip paper and paint from the area where the rose is to be fitted. Hold the rose against the ceiling in the required position and draw a circle around it with a pencil (1). Score the plaster within the circle and seal it with a bonding agent. Treat the back of the rose in the same way.

Probe the plaster with a pointed tool to locate at least one joist within the circle. Mark the position of the joist with a pencil (2).

Fixing the rose

Orient the rose so you can bore two holes through it to align with the center of the joist, preferably within an area of pattern that disguises their presence. The holes are for brass woodscrews, which need to be long enough to reach through the rose, ceiling plaster, and lath into the joist itself.

Spread joint compound or ceramic-tile adhesive on the back of the rose. Press the rose against the ceiling, moving it slightly from side to side to squeeze out excess adhesive and to align the screw-fixing holes with the joist. Insert the screws (3) and clean off the excess adhesive with a damp sponge or paintbrush, then cover the screw heads with filler.

1 Draw around the ceiling rose

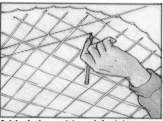

2 Mark the position of the joist

3 Screw through rose into joist

CHAPTER TWELVE

PAVING & WALL TILES

IN EUROPE, MOST EARLY FLOORS – *which were no more than rammed earth, frequently compounded with ashes and ox blood – have long been covered over with riven-flagstone paving, square quarry tiles, or brick-shaped paviors.*

In the United States, too, examples are to be found complete with the patina of color and texture produced by generations of foot-steps. The majority of them are utilitarian floors found in kitchens, workshops, and cellars – but, with increased affluence, ostentatious or aesthetically minded house owners chose to have entrance halls, vestibules, and passageways laid with

patterned floors constructed from colored stone or marble slabs.

Ceramic tiles were used initially for flooring, and at a later date for wallcoverings. Glazed wall tiles (both plain and decorative) were particularly popular with the hygiene-conscious Victorians, and they have remained the most practical surface finish for bathrooms ever since.

In the recent past, tiled surfaces were not infrequently carpeted over or obliterated with paint. Being hard-wearing and durable, many of them will have survived relatively undamaged, only waiting for someone to rediscover and restore them.

Colorful tiling is an asset that should be preserved at all costs

Well-preserved turn-of-the-century wall tiling and mosaic floor

PAVED FLOORING

ORIGINALLY, PAVED FLOORING *was a luxury only the wealthy could afford. But from the late seventeenth or early eighteenth century, with increased affluence and the availability of cheaper materials, it was adopted by all strata of society.*

Stone paving, one of the costliest forms of flooring to lay today, was more often used in humble dwellings or in the service areas of prosperous households.

Man-made tiles were equally practical, and with improved industrial processes quite ordinary home owners found they were able to afford elaborate floors composed of decorative ceramic tiles.

Attractive unfinished random-flagstone floor

Slate floors are found in period kitchens

Quarry-tile floor in an English farmhouse

STONE PAVING

Sedimentary rocks that split easily along the planes of natural bedding or cleavage were ideal for making flagstones, which could be anything from 1 to 4in (25 to 100mm) thick. Before the days of damp-proof courses, flagstones were laid over an earth floor on a bed of ash or coarse sand. As a result, porous limestone or sandstone floors were invariably subject to rising damp in all but the driest conditions.

Slate, on the other hand, being impervious to water, was ideally suited to paving, and houses with slate floors were always comparatively dry. Originally it was only used for domestic paving in areas where there were slate quarries within easy reach. But in the nineteenth century, thanks to vastly improved transportation, slate became readily available to Victorian builders in all parts of the country. As a result, many of them used it for paving basements and cellars in larger houses, where it is still to be found in perfect condition.

Marble, whether imported or one of the native varieties, was used for effect in the more public areas of a house.

Marble slabs were laid with tight-fitting joints and set out with precision. Often they ran diagonally across a room or hallway, with contrasting colors employed to make a checkerboard pattern.

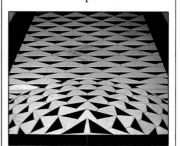
Early C20th mixed-marble hallway

QUARRY TILES

Where stone was not a local commodity, our forebears tended to use quarry tiles when a hard-wearing floor was required. Traditionally made from yellow or brick-red kiln-fired clay, quarry tiles were normally unglazed and laid to a grid pattern.

Old quarry tiles were not as standardized as modern mass-produced ones. They were mostly larger, being up to 1ft (300mm) square and some $1^{1}/_{2}$in (38mm) thick, but smaller square, octagonal, and hexagonal tiles, which tended to be thinner, were also produced.

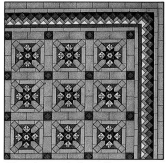

Manufacturer's floor-tile pattern

Medieval-style encaustic tile of 1845

Fully glazed Victorian encaustic tile

Interlocking patent mosaic tile

ENCAUSTIC TILES

The medieval practice of making inlaid clay floor tiles was lost with the dissolution of monasteries in sixteenth-century Britain. Hundreds of years later it was revived by Victorian tile makers inspired by the Gothic-revival movement, who developed mechanical methods for reproducing the designs that Cistercian monks had once made by hand.

A tile body, usually of soft red clay, was pressed into a mold that left an indented pattern. Once fired, the indentations were filled flush with slip (liquid clay) of different colors, then the tile was fired a second time.

Initially these unglazed tiles were manufactured for Victorian churches built in the fashionable neo-Gothic style and for paving other large-scale public buildings. But they were so striking and attractive in appearance that encaustic tiling was enthusiastically adopted around the turn of the century for domestic use. As a result, a great many houses still have encaustic paving in the entrance hall and corridors, frequently extending to conservatories and exterior pathways and patios. True encaustic tiles were sometimes mixed with simpler plain-colored tiles of different sizes and shapes known as "geometrics." Laid with consummate skill and patience, these paved areas are one of the most delightful legacies from the late Victorian era.

This encaustic-tile floor has retained its fresh colors since it was laid in 1869

An intricate late-Victorian pattern of geometrics and small encaustic tiles

MOSAICS

Mosaics composed of tiny colored ceramic tesserae are also to be found on the floors of Victorian buildings, but are much less common in domestic interiors. They were painstakingly pieced together in factories where female workers pasted the tesserae one at a time onto a full-size drawing to build up the required design. When complete, the mosaic was cut into convenient pieces and transported to the house, or other building, for laying.

Typical of Victorian ingenuity were the "patent mosaic tiles." These were relatively large colored floor tiles manufactured with deeply incised grooves. Once a complete area of tiling had been laid, the grooves were filled with cement to create the impression of genuine mosaic paving.

Patent mosaics pass for real tesserae

PRESERVING FLAGSTONE FLOORS

FLAGSTONES *are fairly large random-sized slabs of stone used to provide a hard-wearing floor. Most old stone floors have a mellow, rustic quality well worth preserving. They are an important period feature – and minor problems, such as an irregular surface or a somewhat cold feel, are a small price to pay for preserving such an attractive form of flooring.*

DEALING WITH WORN FLAGSTONES

Worn flags are an intrinsic feature of an old stone floor and, unless they are dangerous, should be accepted as part of the character of a house. If a stone has sunk unevenly, it may be sensible to lift and re-lay it. Similarly, a badly worn slab can be lifted, turned over, and reset in mortar. When lifting out a slab, take care not to damage it or the surrounding stones with the prying tools.

CLEANING STONE FLOORS

Stone floors generally need nothing more than regular sweeping to keep them in good order. However, some stones are more porous than others and, particularly in work areas, may become heavily soiled.

Wash a lightly soiled stone floor with a bucket of water containing two tablespoons of baking soda. For a dirty waxed floor, use a cupful of soda and detergent to a bucket of water. Coat the whole floor first, then work back over it with a scrubbing brush before rinsing.

Use a stronger household cleaner to remove deep grease stains and heavy soiling. Rinse the floor thoroughly after scrubbing the surface. Be sure to protect your eyes and skin.

Treat organic growths such as mildew with dilute household bleach or a biocide.

For removing stains from marble, see FIREPLACES.

FINISHING STONE FLOORS

In most cases it is unnecessary to apply a surface finish or sealant to flagstones. In fact, it is often regarded as inadvisable, on the grounds that it can create a dangerously slippery surface on impervious stones, and trap moisture in more porous ones, leading to structural breakdown.

However, polishes and sealants are available for finishing stone. These need to be applied to a dry, dust-free surface. Generally two even coats of sealant are recommended, applied with a paint roller. Always follow the manufacturer's instructions carefully. To maintain the slight sheen produced by a sealant you can apply wax polish from time to time. All finishes will darken and enrich the natural color.

To bring out the color of slate, apply a 1:4 mixture of linseed oil and mineral spirits, then wipe dry.

New flagstones can coexist with old weathered paving

DEALING WITH DAMP

Although stone is a relatively impervious material, damp can be a problem. It can, for example, permeate through porous stone or seep through mortar joints. In a kitchen or laundry area dampness may result from condensation, in which case better ventilation and heating may cure the problem. Surface sealants will not be a lasting solution if the moisture is rising through the floor. The best remedy is to lay a vapor barrier under the old floor.

Lifting and re-laying an old stone floor with a new sub-floor incorporating a vapor barrier is not something to tackle yourself unless you have relevant building experience. And even with experience, there is danger of damaging the stone. However, the risk of damage is preferable to covering the old floor with a cement screed to be finished with another material.

Before you lift the slabs, number each one with chalk and make a note of their layout and the width of the joints between them on a plan drawing of the floor.

Remove any baseboards. Chisel out the jointing mortar between one or two slabs, then pry up the flagstones from this point. Carefully stack the lifted slabs on edge away from the work area.

148

Improving the sub-floor

If the existing dirt sub-floor is weak it should be excavated to allow the addition of a concrete base laid on a bed of hardcore. A vapor barrier with the edges turned up the wall should be incorporated (see below). However, the vapor barrier won't inhibit rising damp in the walls, which will require their own damp-proof barrier. Get a builder to confirm the presence or condition of the walls' vapor barrier.

If the original sub-floor is really firm and stable, it may be sufficient to lay a vapor barrier and cover it with a leveled cement-mortar screed 2in (50mm) thick. In this case, you will only need to excavate to a depth of about 2¹/₂in (62mm).

Re-laying the flags

Mix a relatively stiff bedding mortar of 1 part cement to 3 parts sand. Spread it evenly between wooden battens to form a band that is wide enough to accommodate a row of slabs. The depth of the mortar should be about ³/₄in (18mm) – deep enough to accept the uneven back of the stone and bring the face of the slabs up to the desired floor level.

Lay the first row of stones, tapping them firmly in place (1) and checking that they are level. With split or well-worn stone, you can do no more than approximate the level – but try to avoid protruding edges. Set the slabs about ³/₈in (10mm) apart, or lay them as noted on your drawing of the floor layout.

Work over the whole floor in this way and leave it to set for one or two days.

Finishing the joints

Use a fairly dry 1:3 mortar mix for pointing the joints. The color should be similar in tone to the stone. If need be, you can add a pigment to the mortar (see REPOINTING BRICKWORK). To make sure that the final color is right, make up samples of different mixes in advance and see how they look when dry.

Fill the joints, and tamp in the mortar firmly with the edge of a trowel (2). Lightly brush the surface of the mortar to leave it just below the face of the stone. Try to keep the faces of the flagstones free of mortar, if need be using masking tape.

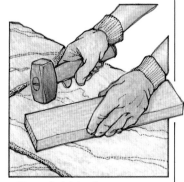

1 Tap each slab in place

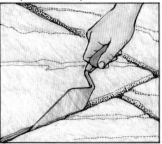

2 Tamp in the mortar

LAYING A CONCRETE SUB-FLOOR

A typical solid sub-floor comprises a slab of concrete laid on a bed of well-compacted rubble or gravel covered or "blinded" with a leveled layer of tamped or rolled sand.

Spread a vapor barrier of polyethylene sheeting over the surface of the sand and turn the edges up the wall to create a waterproof tray. The sheet must lap the wall's vapor barrier or tie into it. If more than one sheet is needed to cover the area, overlap the sheets by about 8in (200mm) and seal with adhesive tape.

Laying the base

Lay a relatively stiff mix of medium-strength concrete to a depth of not less than 4in (100mm). Tamp it down and level the surface, using a straightedge and spirit level (1). Leave the concrete to cure slowly for at least three days under polyethylene to prevent shrinkage cracking due to rapid drying.

Once the concrete has set, apply a screed up to 2in (50mm) thick in 24in (600mm) bands between leveled battens (2). For the screed, use 1 part cement to 3 parts sand. First dampen the concrete and brush a cement slurry, mixed with equal measures of water and bonding agent, onto it. Leave the screed to cure for about a week before laying the flagstones. The sub-floor will not normally be dry for about one month for every 25mm (1in) of thickness.

1 Tamp and level the concrete

2 Lay screed between battens

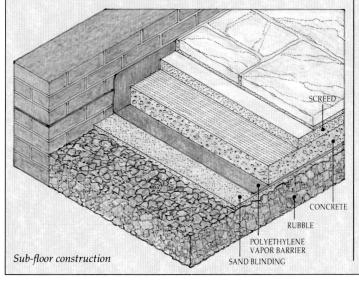

SCREED

CONCRETE

RUBBLE

POLYETHYLENE VAPOR BARRIER

SAND BLINDING

Sub-floor construction

Dining room paved with acceptable reproduction concrete flagstones

CERAMIC FLOOR TILES

QUARRY TILES *became a popular form of ceramic flooring for sculleries, kitchens and lavatories in Victorian houses. They had a pleasing unglazed finish and, despite their primarily functional status, were produced in a range of attractive natural colors.*

Quarries are made of thick, hard-wearing vitrified clay and will last for generations. Unfortunately, thanks to modern conversions and plumbing installations, many old tiled floors have been taken up or covered over. However, repairs to a damaged floor or the reinstatement of the entire floor can be done with new or reclaimed tiles.

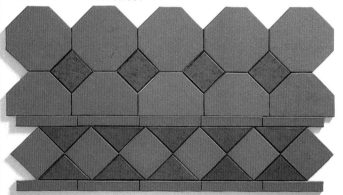

Victorian-style floors can be re-created with modern quarry tiles

STONE SUBSTITUTES

Nowadays old stone is quite rare, and replacing an entire stone floor is an expensive undertaking. If you have a run-down stone floor, it is more cost-effective to restore it to an acceptable state by replacing badly damaged or missing flags with reclaimed stone from an architectural-salvage company.

If an original stone floor has been stripped out, you might want to use a stone-substitute material, which is less costly. Simulated-stone slabs made from concrete are produced for garden use, but their color, regularity, and molded surface and edges are rarely suitable for interior paving. However, it is possible to find good replica flagstones that can be used. These are made in a range of rectangular sizes for random laying and have a constant thickness, which makes it easier to achieve an even floor surface. They can be laid on a screeded floor, using either a mortar bedding or a 1/4in (6mm) layer of floor-tile adhesive.

QUARRY-TILE SIZES

Since quarry tiles are usually laid in a regular grid pattern, any replacement has to be an exact fit.

The size and shape of old quarry tiles was far from regular. Indeed, old large-format tiles can be as much as 1 1/2in (38mm) thick, while the smaller ones may be as thin as 1/2in (12mm). Modern quarry tiles, on the other hand, are generally 1/2in (12mm) thick. They are also made in a range of shapes and sizes, 6in (150mm) square being most common.

Should you need to make patch repairs to an old quarry-tile floor, you may find you have to pack out replacement tiles that are too thin with bedding mortar or even cut back the sub-floor to accommodate ones that are too thick.

CUTTING STONE

Traditionally stone was cut using a bolster chisel and club hammer. The chisel was used to cut a continuous line across the faces and edges of the slab, which would cause the stone to break along the line. (This technique does not work quite so well with concrete-based slabs.)

If you need to cut a lot of slabs accurately, it is worth hiring a circular saw fitted with a stone-cutting disk. With a circular saw, it is only necessary to cut a deep groove in the top face and edges. You can then split the slab with a chisel.

Hire a circular saw

Cutting quarry tiles

The thickness and hardness of quarry tiles makes them difficult to cut. You could score the surface and edges of a single tile with a tile cutter and give the back a sharp tap with a cross-peen hammer, but if you have to cut a number of tiles it is easier to hire a commercial heavy-duty tile-cutter.

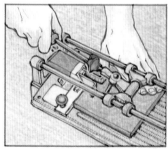

Use a tile-cutter

150

REPLACING A DAMAGED QUARRY TILE

If a cracked or worn quarry tile needs replacing, cut out the damaged tile or mortar filling carefully with a cold chisel and mallet **(1)**. Work from the center and avoid damaging the edges of surrounding tiles. If necessary, increase the depth of the recess by about 1/4in (6mm) to make room for a bed of cement-based tile adhesive.

Wet the recess and evenly cover the back of the tile with a thick coating of adhesive. Lay the tile in position and tap it down flush with the surface of the floor **(2)**. Center it to give an even gap all around. Once the adhesive has set, apply a grout that matches the color of the original grouting.

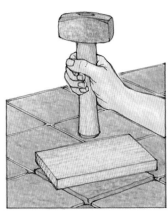

1 Chisel out old tile   *2 Tap down flush with floor*

SETTING OUT A TILED FLOOR

When setting out a tiled floor, if possible make the border symmetrical. Start by finding the center of two opposite walls and snap a chalk line between them. Dry-lay a row of tiles at right angles to the line **(1)**. If there is a gap of less than half a tile between the last tile in the row and the wall, move the line away from the wall by the width of half a tile.

Bisect the line, using an improvised compass made from a strip of wood, a nail, and pencil. Scribe arcs in the sequence shown in the illustration below, starting at the center of the line **(2)**. Use a straightedge to draw a bisecting line through the crossed arcs to give a line at right angles to the first **(3)**. Dry-lay a row of tiles from this line in order to assess the width that will have to be filled by the border tiles **(4)**, then if necessary reposition the line by half a tile.

Fix two guide battens at right angles to one another to run along two sides of the room. Set them in from the walls by the width of the proposed border tiles **(5)**. You can check the accuracy of the angle by measuring three units along one of the battens and four units along the other. Finally, measure the diagonal, which should be five units **(6)**.

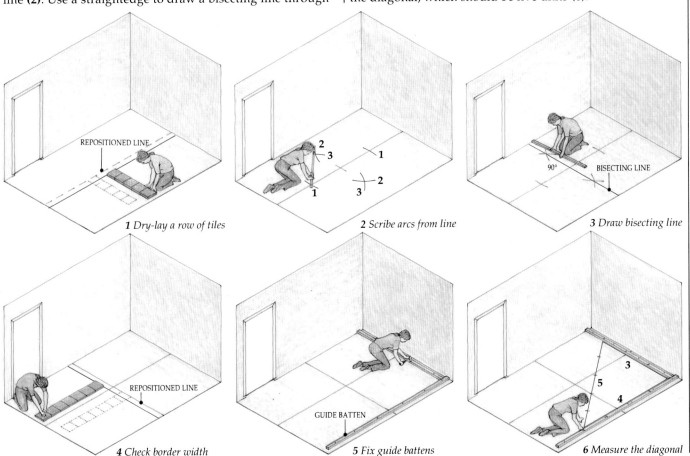

1 Dry-lay a row of tiles   *2 Scribe arcs from line*   *3 Draw bisecting line*

4 Check border width   *5 Fix guide battens*   *6 Measure the diagonal*

151

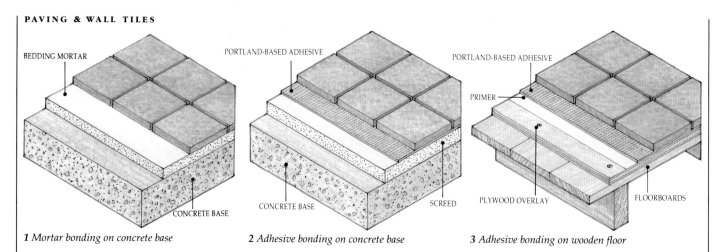

1 Mortar bonding on concrete base *2 Adhesive bonding on concrete base* *3 Adhesive bonding on wooden floor*

LAYING QUARRY TILES

Quarry tiles are best laid on a bed of cement mortar (1) or cement-based adhesive (2) over a solid sub-floor of concrete or mortar screed (see LAYING A CONCRETE BASE).

They can also be laid on a suspended wooden floor, provided that it is sufficiently rigid and strong enough to support the weight. For large areas, it may be necessary to remove the boards and fit bridging (short lengths of joist) at 12in (300mm) centers between the existing joists in order to stiffen the floor. A screw-fixed overlay of exterior-grade plywood not less than $^5/8$in (15mm) thick is used to make a firm base on which the tiles are laid with a Portland-based adhesive and primer (3). With wood constructions, provide good ventilation and allow for seasonal thermal movement.

When laying tiles on a bed of mortar make the thickness of the guide battens about twice that of the tiles. Level the battens, packing out any hollows. Dry-lay a square of 16 tiles into the angle, leaving a gap of approximately $^1/8$in (3mm) between them. Temporarily nail a third batten in place just touching the tiles and parallel with one of the fixed battens (4), then remove the tiles.

4 Nail batten in place

Bedding the tiles

Lay a bed of stiff mortar, mixed from 1 part cement to 3 parts builder's sand, between the battens to cover the area of the sixteen tiles. Level it with a straightedge notched to fit between the battens (1). Make the depth of the notch (2) the thickness of the tiles less $^1/8$in (3mm). Soak old porous tiles before laying (this is usually unnecessary with modern ones).

Just before laying the tiles, sprinkle some Portland cement onto the moist bedding and trowel it into the mortar. This will improve adhesion. Alternatively, mix and brush on a slurry of pure cement and water.

Place the tiles against the battens on three sides of the square, then add the center tiles. Space them evenly and tamp them down level with the guide battens, using the straightedge. Complete the first bay in this way, laying 16 tiles at a time (3).

Reposition and level the third batten to form a new bay, then fill with tiles as before. Complete the floor section by section, using this method. Leave to set for at least 12 hours, then remove the guide battens and fill in the border tiles.

Grout the joints with a proprietary Portland-based grouting. Some grouts are premixed and available in a choice of colors. Allow the grout to stiffen in the joints, and then wipe the tiled surface with a damp sponge.

TILE THICKNESS LESS $^1/8$in (3mm)

2 Depth of notch

1 Level mortar with notched straightedge

3 Lay 16 tiles at a time

MOVEMENT JOINTS

Modern heating systems cause building materials to expand and contract. To allow for this, provide an expansion joint around the perimeter of the flooring. Leave a $^3/8$in (10mm) gap at the junction with the walls, and fill with cork strips sealed with a polysulfide or silicone-rubber compound. The baseboard moldings will cover this.

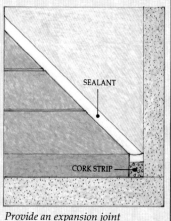

SEALANT

CORK STRIP

Provide an expansion joint

Reproduction encaustic tiles with a border of geometrics

Additional motifs are created when tiles are laid together

CLEANING TILES

Quarry tiles require practically no maintenance. To keep them clean, simply sweep them and wash them with warm water and household detergent. After washing, rinse the surface with clean water and a sponge mop.

For ingrained heavy soiling, apply a proprietary tile cleaner, using plastic scouring pads or a rented commercial scrubbing machine.

Cement stains resulting from laying procedures can be removed with a diluted solution of hydrochloric acid available as a proprietary product from specialist suppliers. Always follow the manufacturer's instructions and wear protective clothing when using these products.

Encaustic and geometric tiles have similar properties to unglazed quarry tiles, so can be maintained in the same way.

ENCAUSTIC & GEOMETRIC TILES

Encaustic tiles are still made by hand following the methods established by English ceramacist Herbert Minton in 1843. Each tile is based on a molded body, to which different colored clays are painstakingly added to build up a polychromatic decorative pattern. After firing for 24 hours, the tiles are measured for accuracy then cut on a diamond wheel to precise dimensions. The tiles are laid with their edges butting, with little or no allowance for grouting.

Encaustic and geometric tiles are made to special order for restoration work. The reinstatement of a traditional floor takes great skill and is a job for a flooring specialist.

Making repairs

Although very hard-wearing, both encaustic and geometric floors frequently suffer from loose tiles.

Fancy floors are particularly likely to have loose or missing tiles, since the small shaped tiles that make up the pattern do not bond so well. The close fit of the tiles helps keep them in place, but this should not be relied on since in time dirt and grit will build up under them. The edges exposed are then easily damaged, and small pieces may get dislodged and be lost.

Fixing the pieces

Carefully pry out the loose pieces from the floor, using either the blade of a knife or a narrow scraper. If the paving is indoors, providing the substrate is still sound, glue them back in place with a bonding agent.

For an exterior repair or if a large patch has become detached, make a reference drawing of the pattern prior to lifting all the loose pieces. Chisel away the old mortar to a depth of about 1/4in (10mm). Vacuum the surface and dampen it with water. Apply a bed of Portland-based flooring cement, then replace the pieces, tamping them down level with the surrounding surface. Once the cement has set, apply grouting if needed. A similar method can be employed for repairing a mosaic floor.

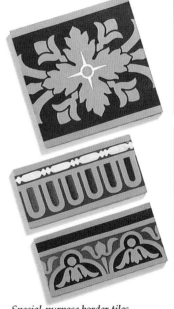

Special-purpose border tiles

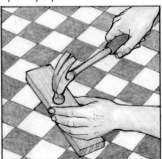

Tamp pieces level with surface

FINISHING FLOOR TILES

A traditional finish that is used to enhance the color of absorbent unglazed tiles is a mixture of 1 part boiled linseed oil to 3 parts mineral spirits. Pour into a saucer and apply a liberal coat with a cotton-cloth pad. Let it soak in, then wipe off the excess with a clean lint-free rag. A light coat of wax floor polish can be applied to maintain the finish.

A proprietary sealer can be used to finish a new quarry-tiled floor, or an old one that has been thoroughly cleaned and dried. This is applied in two coats with a brush or paint roller and maintained by regular washing. You can produce a gloss finish by polishing the sealed surface with dry buffing pads.

CERAMIC WALL TILES

D ECORATED CERAMIC TILES, *especially those made in Victorian times and earlier, are highly prized by collectors, and considerable sums change hands even for individual examples. If this is a measure of their value, one can appreciate how important it is to preserve areas of tiling that are still intact. Happily, unless damaged by acts of deliberate vandalism or as a result of woeful ignorance, ceramic wall tiles are practically indestructible, and they require very little maintenance.*

Hand-painted Victorian porch tiles

Dutch delftware overlaid with an English tile of 1750

Seventeenth-century Dutch polychrome delftware

DELFTWARE

Holland and Flanders had a thriving ceramic industry in the seventeenth century that exported tin-glazed earthenware, including handmade blue-and-white tiles, to all parts of Europe. At around that time, Dutch and Flemish potters set up workshops in England in order to manufacture these tiles, which became known as delftware after the most celebrated production center of the day. Before long, English potters began to compete with the immigrant tile makers, copying typical Dutch designs depicting figures, animals,

landscapes, and birds. By the middle of the eighteenth century, English tile makers had cultivated a substantial market – in England and America – for their wares and were designing tiles that were much less dependent on the Dutch themes.

Delftware tiles were made by cutting squares from clay that had been rolled flat like pastry. These blanks were fired in a kiln, then coated with a liquid glaze that dried leaving a powdery surface on the face of each tile. The design was painted freehand onto the absorbent surface,

then the tile was fired for a second time, which fused the color into what became a hard, opaque white glaze. Blue or sometimes purple was the color most often painted onto delftware, but yellow, green, or orange was also used occasionally.

In England the success of delftware was short-lived, as the increasing popularity of other types of ceramic began to force a decline in the manufacture of tin-glazed pottery and tiles. By the turn of the century, not one delftware manufacturer was still in business in the country.

VICTORIAN WALL TILES

In the first quarter of the nineteenth century, tile production in Britain was virtually nonexistent. Initially Victorian manufacturers built their businesses on the production of encaustic floor tiles, and it was not until the 1860s and 1870s that they started to make decorated glazed wall tiles in earnest. However, toward the end of the century the demand for tiles of every description was simply enormous, and the larger manufacturers exported their wares all over the world, including parts of Asia and America.

Glazed tiles were especially practical in kitchens and bathrooms, where washable surfaces were essential. Decorative tiles would often be used to form borders or to break up areas of cheaper white or plain-colored tiles. It was not regarded as necessary, particularly in a bathroom, to tile entire walls. Very often ceramic tiling was restricted to the lower part of a wall, forming a wainscot, or was simply used to create splashbacks behind the bathtub and basin.

Tiled wainscots were a fairly common feature in public buildings, and exterior porches were sometimes flanked with tiled panels that were decorated with painted landscapes or floral themes.

Sets of tiles that formed a design were also made for inserting in cast-iron fire grates (see TILED FIREPLACES) and were incorporated in washstands, coat racks, and other items of furniture.

New methods of production were required to meet the demand. Experiments in printing onto tiles had been fairly successful as early as 1756, when John Sadler

Transfer-printed tiles of c.1780

developed the process of transfer printing. An image incised into a wood block or engraved on a copper plate was transferred to the face of a tile by means of a soft-paper tissue. The printing on early tiles was vulnerable to wear, but the images on Victorian tiles were protected by a coat of transparent glaze. The basic design was normally printed in one color, usually black or dark brown, and areas of color were often added by hand.

An alternative method for mass-producing tiles was block printing, whereby simple areas of color were transferred from a metal plate on which the image had been created in relief. Each color used in a block-printed pattern required a separate plate.

Dust-pressing, invented in 1840, was yet another significant breakthrough in tile production. Slightly moist powdered clay was compressed between two metal dies, creating beautifully smooth, even tiles. It was a method ideally suited to the manufacture of embossed tiles, a shaped die being employed to create the same low-relief image on the face of each tile. Once fired, an embossed tile was either coated with a single glossy translucent glaze or parts of the image were picked out with different colors.

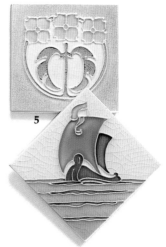

1 Block-printed tile made in 1880
2 Transfer-printed hand-colored tile
3 Multi-colored block-printed tile
4 Art Nouveau embossed tile
5 Glazed wall tiles manufactured between 1930 and 1935

TWENTIETH-CENTURY WALL TILES

From the turn of the century, tile production continued unabated until the First World War. During that time the Art Nouveau movement had a notable effect on the tile-making industry, and many of the tiles, especially embossed ones, exhibit Art Nouveau influences.

In the 1920s and 1930s taste changed dramatically. Tiling became more austere, often comprising nothing more than a field of plain white tiles with a border of slim red, blue, or black tiles. Some fireplaces were still tiled, but gone were the ornamental side panels – instead, the whole surround was usually faced with mottled tiles in subdued colors. The last spark of the decorative tradition was kept alive by devotees of the Art Deco movement who designed colorful tiles, some embossed, that incorporated bold geometric shapes.

Fully tiled bathroom originating from the late 1930s

PRESERVING CERAMIC WALL TILES

WALL TILES, *like ceramic floor tiles, are very hard-wearing and need little maintenance. Although generally the same standard size as most floor tiles, they can be recognized by their thinner body and glazed finish. Tile glazes vary in thickness, and cleaning methods should take the thickness of the glaze into account. If the surface is crazed or you are unsure how thick the glazing is, seek expert advice before cleaning with strong chemicals.*

Victorian embossed tiles languishing beneath a coat of red paint

CLEANING WALL TILES

The glasslike surface of glazed wall tiles not only enhances their decorative effect but also makes them easy to clean. However, the ceramic body of wall tiles is not as impervious as that of most floor tiles. Care must therefore be taken, particularly if the glaze is crazed, that dirt is not absorbed into the tile during the cleaning process. It is best not to bleach tiles *in situ*, in case the stains are absorbed. But if you have unfixed tiles that need cleaning, you can soak them in water (preferably distilled) then apply dilute household bleach – since presoaking the tiles will prevent dirt or stains from being drawn into the ceramic body.

Tiled walls need to be cleaned regularly in order to maintain their surface finish. All that's usually needed is to wipe the surface with a damp cloth or sponge. If dirt has been allowed to build up, wash it off with a household dishwashing liquid, or use a teaspoonful of baking soda in a bucket of warm water. Rinse the surface and wipe dry as you go.

For heavy soiling, use a proprietary tile cleaner and rinse the surface thoroughly. Tile cleaners are caustic and must be used with care, as they can cause some Victorian ruby luster glazes or gold finishes to fade. When working with them, wear rubber gloves and protect your eyes. Always try out cleaning agents on an inconspicuous area of tiling before you proceed with cleaning.

Use a fiber scouring pad to remove stubborn dirt. In some cases a pad of very fine steel wool can be used on thick-glazed tiles, but generally it is advisable not to use abrasive materials and cleaners at all on glazed ceramic tiles. If you use steel wool, all traces of metal particles must be removed so rust staining doesn't occur.

Cleaning grout

Grout is a cementitious material that is used to fill and seal the joints between tiles. The appearance of a field of light-colored tiles can be spoiled by dirty grout. To refresh sound grout, apply a tile cleaner or household cream cleaner with a stiff nylon toothbrush, working along the joint lines. Rinse down thoroughly as you go. Mold growth can be treated with a solution of household bleach and hot water.

If grout is in a poor state, remove it and regrout the joints. Use a dental pick or suitable pointed tool. Control the tool carefully, so as not to damage the surface. Leave any part of the grouting that is in good condition intact. Brush and vacuum out all loose material, then apply new matching grout (see GROUTING).

Gently scrape off paint with scalpel

Removing paint

You may find that ceramic wall tiles have been splashed with paint, or even painted over entirely in an attempt to alter the character or color scheme of the interior.

As a general rule, it's safer to use mechanical methods to remove paint rather than resort to chemical strippers. For example, it is possible to gently remove splashes of paint with a sharp scalpel.

However, if a sizable area of tiling has been painted over, you have little choice but to use a water-washable stripper. Apply it following the maker's instructions and remove the softened paint with a wooden or plastic scraper. Wash off the residue with water, working a bristle brush into crevices, and then wipe the surface dry.

DRILLING TILED WALLS

When appliances or fixtures need to be fixed to a wall, try to avoid drilling into the face of old tiles – especially ones that are decorative or rare. If you do have to drill the wall, position the hole or holes on a joint line or corner whenever possible.

To prevent a masonry drill bit skidding on the face of a tile, before drilling mark the center of the hole on the tile with a felt-tip pen and then stick a patch of cellophane tape over the mark. Run the drill at a slow speed and apply light pressure. Drill the hole to match the length of a suitably sized wall plug plus the thickness of the tile. Insert the plug into the hole fully, so when the screw is tightened the expansion of the plug will not fracture the glazed surface of the tile.

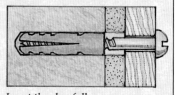

Insert the plug fully

REPLACING DAMAGED TILES

Having first removed the surrounding grout, carefully chisel out a cracked or broken tile with a narrow cold chisel and a mallet, working from the center. Chisel a recess into the background, then vacuum away all loose material.

Apply a wall-tile adhesive to the back of the replacement and press it into place. Allow the adhesive to set, then finish with matching grout.

FIXING TILES

Wall tiles can be applied to all commonly used building materials, including painted surfaces and other glazed tiles. The surface to be tiled must be flat, dry, sound, and free of contaminants, which can affect adhesion.

Tile adhesives are made to meet various specifications. Some are ready mixed, while others require mixing with water. Additives are also available to meet specific requirements. Your local tile supplier is likely to stock a range of adhesives suitable for most domestic situations.

Adhesives may be specified as "thin-bed" (for fixing wall tiles and mosaics in dry and low-moisture areas) or "thick-bed" (for heavy-duty wall or floor work and use in wet areas). Both are applied with notched trowels to give the appropriate coverage.

Spread the adhesive with the trowel held at an angle of 45 to 50 degrees to the wall, covering no more than 1 square yard (1 square meter) at a time. Fix the tiles within 20 minutes of applying the adhesive. If they have deeply recessed backs, fill them with adhesive just before placing the tiles on the wall.

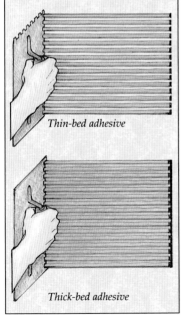

Thin-bed adhesive

Thick-bed adhesive

TILING WALLS

During the building boom that took place toward the end of the nineteenth century, speculative builders based their house designs on fashionable architectural styles but used their own judgment regarding the level of fitments and finishes appropriate to the proposed value of the property. As a result, houses of similar type would often differ so far as luxuries such as tiling were concerned.

If your house lacks attractive tiling due to penny-pinching by the builder, you might want to consider installing tiling in an appropriate style, using good reproduction materials. However, the introduction of tiling needs to be done with discretion, after the necessary research, and is normally only appropriate in areas such as kitchens and bathrooms.

Setting out

How you go about setting out the tiling will depend on the details of the wall and whether or not the whole wall area is to be covered. As a rule, the layout of the tiles should be planned to give a symmetrical arrangement.

On plain fully tiled walls, the cut tiles that form the border should be of uniform size and not less than half a tile wide. Use a feature such as a window or handbasin as a focal point and center the layout of the tiles on them. It looks best if you have whole tiles in the first row under a window or chair rail or above a basin, bathtub, worktop, or kitchen sink. Some judgment is required in balancing the overall layout. If there is to be a decorative paneled and border arrangement, work out the design on graph paper first.

Making a gauge stick

In order to help you set out the tiles, first make a gauge stick from a straight piece of 2 x 1/2in (50 x 12mm) wood cut to a convenient length. Using the selected tiles as a guide, mark their size and the space between them along one edge, spacing the tiles not more than 1/16in (2mm) apart **(1)**. Place pieces of cardboard between them to keep the gaps even.

Fixing guide battens

Hold the gauge stick vertically against the wall and plot the position of the horizontal tile joints. When fitting tiles from floor to ceiling if you find the top and bottom tiles are unequal in size, adjust the position of the stick. Mark the bottom edge of the lowest row of whole tiles **(2)**. Set a leveled batten on the mark and nail it to the wall **(3)** – but don't drive the nails in fully, so you can remove it later.

Place the gauge stick on the horizontal guide batten to set out the position of the vertical joints. Work from the center of the wall toward one end. If you find that the space for the border tiles is less than half a tile, move the center mark over by half a tile. Set a guide batten vertically on the last whole tile mark and nail it in place **(4)**.

Use a similar method if you are setting out tiles above a bath or basin, but set the first horizontal row of tiles the height of one tile above the top edge. If the rim of the bath or basin slopes, set the batten level from the lowest end; the bottom row will then have to be trimmed to fit. Around a window, you may have to cut the tiles to an "L" shape to avoid narrow strips above the opening (see next page).

1 Mark the edge of the stick

2 Mark bottom edge on wall

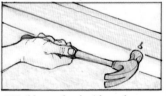

3 Nail batten level with mark

4 Nail vertical guide batten

5 Press the tile into place

7 Press grouting into joints

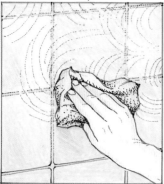

6 Wipe off excess adhesive

8 Compact grout with a stick

Bonding the tiles

Following the maker's instructions, apply an even layer of tile adhesive to the wall in the angle between the guide battens. Press the first tile into the adhesive **(5)**, then place two more on each side of it. If the tiles haven't got spacer lugs, insert cardboard or proprietary plastic spacers between them to form grout lines.

Build up the rows of tiles in this way, then apply a further square of adhesive and repeat the process until the whole field is covered. Wipe off excess adhesive from the joints with a damp sponge as you go **(6)**. Scrape off adhesive from the borders and let the tiling set before removing the guide battens. Finally, fix in place any cut tiles (see right) needed to complete the field of tiling.

Grouting

Grouts for filling the gaps between ceramic tiles are made in various types and colors. Some are specifically designed for exterior use. Choose one that meets your requirements. Ready-mixed grouts are suitable for most interior uses. Allow tile adhesive to set for at least 24 hours before grouting.

Apply the grout with a rubber-bladed squeegee or a damp sponge. Fill a small area at a time, pressing the grout well into the joints by working across the tiles in all directions **(7)**. Wipe off the excess from the surface with a damp sponge before it sets. Compact the grout in the joints with a piece of dowel or a blunt stick **(8)**. Clean the tiles with a damp cloth, and polish them with a soft cloth once the grout is dry.

CUTTING WALL TILES

In an old house walls and ceilings are very rarely true, so tiles have to be measured and marked individually where they meet a corner.

Hold the tile that is to be cut over the last tile in the row. Position another level with it, but with one edge held against the adjacent wall. Mark a line with a wax pencil on the tile that is to be cut, following the edge of the guide tile **(1)**.

Cut the tile following the line, allowing for the spacing between the tiles. Using a straightedge as a guide, score the glaze **(2)**. With thick tiles, you may need to also score the edges. Snap the tile over a wire strung across a board **(3)**, or over two matchsticks placed under the scored line. Alternatively, purchase a tile cutter complete with cutter arm and backboard to guide the cutter and snap the tile.

If you need to reduce the size of the tile by a small amount, nip the scored edge with pincers or special tile nippers **(4)**. The trimmed edge can be smoothed with a tile-sanding block.

Cutting an "L" shape

Where a tile needs to form an "L" shape (for example, where the tiling is to surround a window), cut out the waste using a tile saw. Score the corner marks first, then make a diagonal cut into the corner **(5)**. Snap out the triangular waste pieces.

Cutting around a pipe

Using the edges of the adjacent tiles as a position guide, draw lines from the top and side edges to give the center of the pipe. Where the lines cross, draw a circle slightly larger than the diameter of the pipe. Cut the tile in two, following one of the marked lines, then cut out the semicircular waste from each half, using a tile saw.

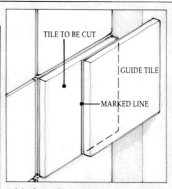

1 Mark cut line on tile

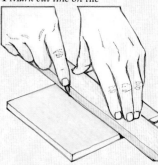

2 Score the glazed surface

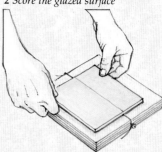

3 Snap the tile in two

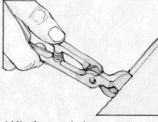

4 Nip the scored edge

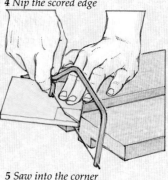

5 Saw into the corner

CHAPTER THIRTEEN

WALL PANELING

WOODEN WALL PANELING *was used for finishing the walls of the entrance hall and principal rooms in many Georgian-style eighteenth-century houses. It was classical in style, influenced by Renaissance architecture, and used sophisticated frame-and-panel joinery. The use of wood paneling as an attractive and practical wall lining was not new, having been employed for this purpose and as partitioning since the fifteenth century in England and later as simple wall sheathings in medieval-inspired Colonial dwellings.*

The early types of paneling were rather crude, with hand-wrought vertical planks either nailed in place or slotted into grooved studs or muntins and held by a sill and a head member. By the end of the fifteenth century a refinement in joinery techniques led to the development of Tudor frame-and-panel wainscoting. Although the style was not used in Colonial America, it saw a revival in the mid-Victorian period, when it was widely imitated.*

Tongue-and-groove wall-boarding, which was simpler to construct, was also used in the eighteenth century but was more refined than earlier boarding of this type. It usually featured a bead molding and was mostly found in provincial houses.

Elegant white-painted C18th wall paneling

Late-C19th Tudor-style oak paneling in an Arts and Crafts interior

TYPES OF PANELING

ENGLISH IMMIGRANTS TO THESE SHORES *brought with them a tradition of oak frame-and-panel wainscoting, employing a simple pegged mortise-and-tenon framework, often using pine. The frame consisted of a top rail and a bottom rail and a number of intermediate rails, all jointed into vertical stiles. Muntins (short vertical members) were jointed into the rails, usually spaced at equal intervals across the width of the frame. The inner edges of all the frame members were grooved to hold the panels without use of glue, to allow for expansion.*

Traditionally the edges of the frame that surrounded and held the panels were shaped with a simple stuck molding, which was cut by hand into the edge of the

wood using a scratch stock. Where the molding of the muntins met the edge of the rails, mitered corners had to be carved in the rails

In some early Colonial homes, the paneling consisted of vertical, mill-sawn boards that extended from floor to ceiling. They overlapped, often with molded edges, using tongue-and-groove or overlapping joints. Feather-edged sheathing ("feather-edge" meaning boards with one edge thinner than the other) and applied raised moldings to simulate paneling are also found in the first American period houses.

The popular (and often imitated) Georgian paneling came into vogue in the eighteenth century and featured full mortise-and-tenon joinery and panels.

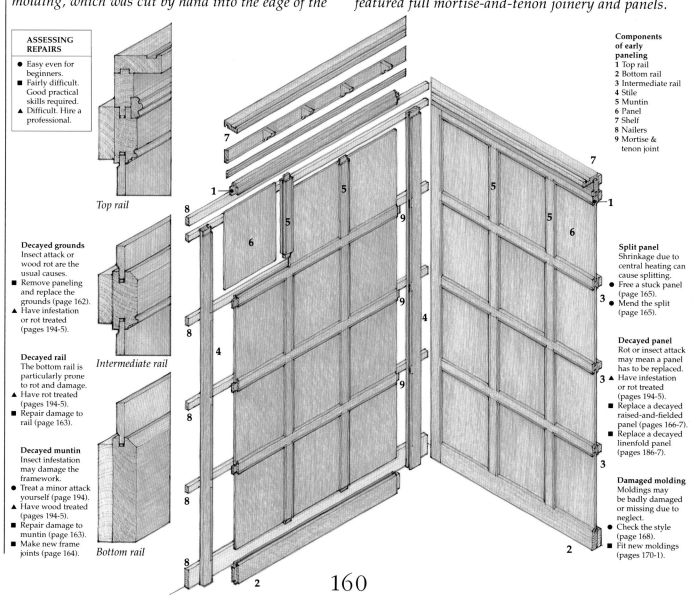

ASSESSING REPAIRS

- ● Easy even for beginners.
- ■ Fairly difficult. Good practical skills required.
- ▲ Difficult. Hire a professional.

Top rail

Decayed grounds
Insect attack or wood rot are the usual causes.
- ■ Remove paneling and replace the grounds (page 162).
- ▲ Have infestation or rot treated (pages 194-5).

Decayed rail
The bottom rail is particularly prone to rot and damage.
- ▲ Have rot treated (pages 194-5).
- ■ Repair damage to rail (page 163).

Intermediate rail

Decayed muntin
Insect infestation may damage the framework.
- ● Treat a minor attack yourself (page 194).
- ▲ Have wood treated (pages 194-5).
- ■ Repair damage to muntin (page 163).
- ■ Make new frame joints (page 164).

Bottom rail

Components of early paneling
1 Top rail
2 Bottom rail
3 Intermediate rail
4 Stile
5 Muntin
6 Panel
7 Shelf
8 Nailers
9 Mortise & tenon joint

Split panel
Shrinkage due to central heating can cause splitting.
- ● Free a stuck panel (page 165).
- ● Mend the split (page 165).

Decayed panel
Rot or insect attack may mean a panel has to be replaced.
- ▲ Have infestation or rot treated (pages 194-5).
- ■ Replace a decayed raised-and-fielded panel (pages 166-7).
- ■ Replace a decayed linenfold panel (pages 186-7).

Damaged molding
Moldings may be badly damaged or missing due to neglect.
- ● Check the style (page 168).
- ■ Fit new moldings (pages 170-1).

160

CLASSICAL INFLUENCES

By the late seventeenth century wider panels (known as wide-board paneling in America) had become fashionable, and their vertical dimensions reflected the proportions of the classical orders of architecture.

Solid oak was still in use, but increasingly pine was used for large and painted paneling. The panels were either plain or raised-and-fielded. The framing was worked with stuck molding, or the joins between the panels and the frame might be finished with an applied or a bolection molding.

Pilasters in the classical style were often used to add relief to a run of paneling or to serve as an architrave that hid the join between the stiles of meeting sets of panels.

This style of solid-wood paneling remained fashionable until the nineteenth century. However, only the owners of relatively grand houses could afford it, and painted plaster and wallpapers became more commonly used.

Classical orders influenced styles

THE PANELING REVIVAL

Wall paneling was revived by members of the Arts and Crafts movement, whose influence continued into the early twentieth century.

Started by William Morris in England, the ideas of the movement were taken up with enthusiasm by Gustav Stickley and the Greene brothers, among others, in America. The movement embraced artists, designers, and architects whose aim was to return to the simple, "honest" styles of earlier times as a reaction against the excesses of mass-produced ornamentation. Well-executed, functional designs employing tradition-al methods and materials were the principles on which they based their work.

Natural oak was widely used both for paneling and furniture. The designs were deliberately plain, with only restrained decoration to complement the natural features of the wood. Arts and Crafts wall paneling tended to stop around door or head height, often terminating with a shelf, the upper part of the wall being finished with painted plaster. This design was not adopted for purely aesthetic reasons. It also gave light to interiors that would other-wise have been gloomy in view of the dark wood and small windows preferred by architects working in the new style.

Although the aim of the Arts and Crafts movement was to keep the old craft skills alive, it did not halt the progress of mechanization. By the early twentieth cent-ury traditional paneling had become rare and machine-made plywood panels had taken over from solid wood.

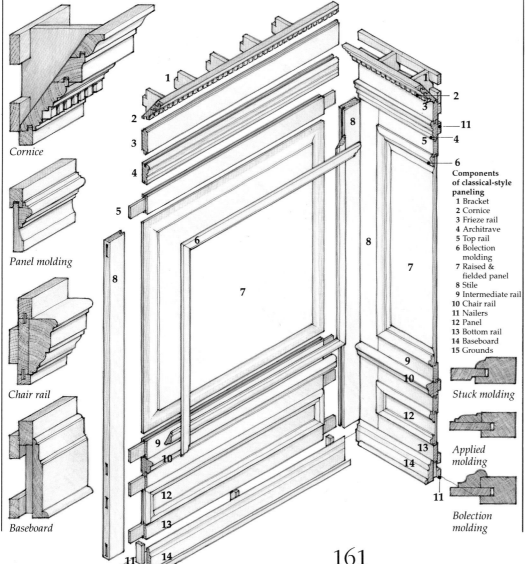

Cornice

Panel molding

Chair rail

Baseboard

Components of classical-style paneling
1 Bracket
2 Cornice
3 Frieze rail
4 Architrave
5 Top rail
6 Bolection molding
7 Raised & fielded panel
8 Stile
9 Intermediate rail
10 Chair rail
11 Nailers
12 Panel
13 Bottom rail
14 Baseboard
15 Grounds

Stuck molding

Applied molding

Bolection molding

WAINSCOTING

By Victorian times wainscoting generally only extended up to the chair-rail molding, forming a dado. The molding and dado protected the walls from being damaged by chair backs and general traffic. It also provided a visual division of the wall following classical principles. Dadoes were constructed using frame-and-panel methods or, in some cases, tongue-and-groove boarding.

By the mid nineteenth century the chair rail began to go out of fashion for main rooms, but it continued to be used as a finishing detail for embossed-paper dadoes in stairways and entrance halls. The last vestiges of the classical paneled wall were the picture rail and the baseboard. Picture rails were a common feature of 1930s interiors, and baseboards are still in use today.

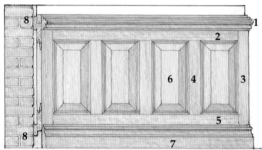

Components of a frame-and-panel wainscot
1 Chair rail
2 Top rail
3 Stile
4 Muntin
5 Bottom rail
6 Panel
7 Baseboard
8 Nailers

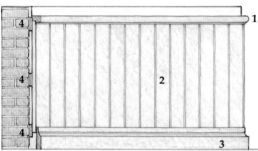

Components of a tongue-and-groove wainscot
1 Chair rail
2 Tongue & groove boarding
3 Baseboard
4 Nailers

Oak raised-and-fielded wainscot on a late-nineteenth-century staircase

HOW PANELING IS FIXED

Wooden battens or nailers are used for fixing paneling to brick or stone walls. The battens are leveled and nailed or screwed to plugs set in the wall. The fasteners used to hold the paneling to the grounds are either discreetly placed or hidden by wooden pellets cut to match the grain of the wood, or they may be disguised with a colored filler.

REMOVING PANELING

It's worth making strenuous efforts to preserve original paneling – but only remove it from the wall for repair when absolutely necessary.

The procedure for removing paneling should be the opposite of the way it was installed. Remove baseboards, chair rails, and cornice moldings first. These are usually nailed in place, but take care when dismanling them since some components may be fixed together with tongue-and-groove joints. Always try to make minor repairs *in situ* since removing panels can create further damage.

After removing the surrounding moldings, try to identify the means by which the paneling was attached to the walls. Most often, nails were used. Place a flat bar close to the nailing point, and exercise great care in prying the paneling free. You may find in the case of horizontal sheathing that the boards were attached by blind nailing. Again, work patiently, prying gently to loosen the fasteners.

Cut nails in nineteenth-century paneling will snap off when struck from side to side. Never tap nails back through the paneling, but pull through to the wall side.

PANELED CEILINGS

The earliest ceilings were little more than the underside of the roof covering or the floorboards of the rooms above. Plaster was sometimes used to finish the underside of the boards, leaving the beams exposed – a common feature of many cottages over the centuries. A lime-based whitewash was often used on both ceilings and walls.

By the late eighteenth century, the Georgian house featured plaster as the standard ceiling material. Then and into the early nineteenth century, American Dutch houses featured beams and undersides of floorboards that had been planed smooth. The beams often had chamfers or other molding shapes on their corners.

In some English-inspired revival houses (especially the Victorian Queen Anne and later neo-Tudor styles) frame and panel ceilings were fitted in a similar way to wall paneling. Timber paneling, too, saw a revival; in the Colonial revival of the early twentieth century, timber-boxed beams and false paneled ceilings (a grid of flat strips of wood) were used by designers of the Arts and Crafts movement.

Late interpretation of beamed ceiling

MAKING REPAIRS TO THE FRAME

S PLITS, CHIPPED EDGES AND GENERAL BRUISING *and discoloration are normally regarded as part of the character of old paneling. However, where wood rot or insect attack has seriously weakened the framework, you may have no option but to remove the paneling and replace the infected timber.*

Try to retain as much of the original paneling as possible. Before you begin work on repairs, take reference photographs of the paneling and make measured drawings of the components. Use a profile gauge to record the shape of the moldings, and transfer it to your drawing in the form of full-size sections. Cut out

the affected timber and make a new section to replace it. Make the new components from the same species of wood, with grain that closely matches the original.

The new wood will not, of course, be the correct color – but you can tone it down with wood stain or bleach it, as appropriate. This is less important when dealing with painted paneling. Some argue that new work should not be disguised in any way. However, if the color blends with the original, that helps maintain the harmony of the paneling as a whole, instead of drawing attention to the repair. Distressing the wood in order to age it is perhaps less justifiable.

Repairing a bottom rail

Support the paneling on a bench or trestles, depending on its size. Use lengths of wood spanning the trestles for extra support. The repair described here is for damage around the bottom rail, which is the most vulnerable area, but the method can be used for other parts of the paneling, too.

Carefully saw or router across the rail to remove the infected area back to sound wood (1). If there is a muntin tenoned into the part to be removed, carefully drive out or drill out any pegs holding the joint together. You can then knock the joint apart, using a hammer and a scrap of wood to take the blows. Should the joint be glued, soften the glue with steam from a kettle. A jet of steam from a flexible neoprene tube attached to the spout gives greater control. Wear protective gloves and take care not to scald yourself when working with steam.

Lap-joint the new wood into the old. First, cut the

shoulder of the lap in the ends of the old wood at 45 degrees to the face of the rail (2). Cut the shoulder lines not less than 2in (50mm) from the ends, and stop at the groove. Then pare off the waste to this level.

Cut the new wood to size. Plane a groove in the top edge to match the old one. Chamfer or cut a matching molding in the front edge. Shape the molding with a scratch stock, multi-plane, or power router, as appropriate. Cut away the back of the rail at each end to match the lap in the old material. Bevel the ends of the new lap to fit the angled shoulder already cut (3). If necessary, mark out and cut a mortise for a muntin tenon (4).

Try the new work for fit. If all is well, glue the lap joints and the mortise and tenon. Take care to keep the glue away from the panel, which must be free to move. If need be, remake or reuse the peg for the joint, drill a new hole for it, and glue it in place.

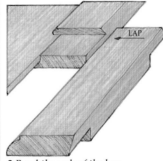

1 Cut out infected wood

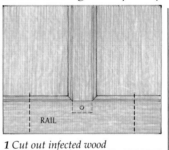

2 Cut shoulder to 45 degrees

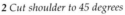

3 Bevel the ends of the laps

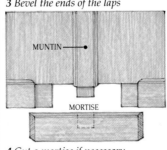

4 Cut a mortise if necessary

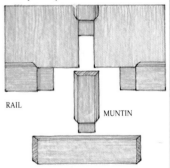

5 Repair muntin as for rail

Muntin repair

If the muntin members are damaged, proceed as for repairing the bottom rail (see left) then cut away the muntin and repair it with new wood lap-jointed into place (5).

Cut rail on outside of muntins

Panel repair

In order to take out a panel for repair, cut the bottom rail outside the muntins on each side then remove the rail and slide out the panel.

See MAKING A RAISED-AND-FIELDED PANEL and LINENFOLD CARVING for how to make a replacement for a damaged decorative panel.

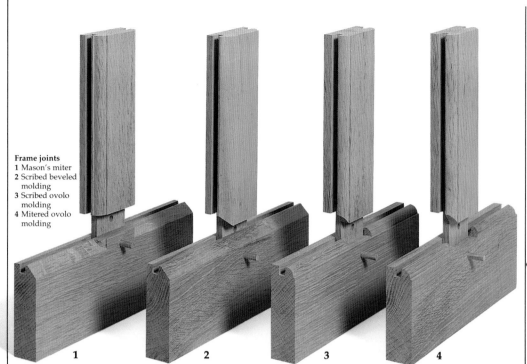

Frame joints
1 Mason's miter
2 Scribed beveled molding
3 Scribed ovolo molding
4 Mitered ovolo molding

1   2   3   4

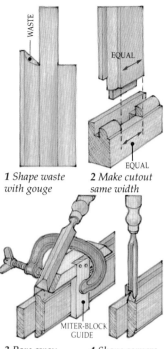

1 Shape waste with gouge   *2 Make cutout same width*

3 Pare away the corners   *4 Shape corners with gouge*

MITER-BLOCK GUIDE

FRAME JOINTS

Traditionally the framework for paneling was constructed with hand-cut mortise-and-tenon joints – the top, bottom and intermediate rails being tenoned into the stiles, while the muntins are tenoned into the rails.

Although the basic principles of making the joint apply to all periods, the techniques for dealing with the moldings vary. Early examples had the molding stopped or run out, or were given the appearance of a mitered corner by the use of a mason's miter.

Various methods for treating the molding are shown, using a muntin-to-rail joint as an example.

MASON'S MITER JOINT

This was a technique used by masons for carving a miter in stone blocks where two moldings met at an internal angle. Early joiners adopted the method, using a scratch stock and molding planes and chisels.

To make this type of joint, run the molding the length of the tenon member. On the mortise member you can't run the molding through, so work the molding with the scratch stock and stop close to the mortise. Using small chisels and carving gouges, carve the remaining "corner" in the form of a miter to meet the shape of the other member when the joint is assembled.

SCRIBED JOINTS

Joiners ran the molding plane through on the edges of both workpieces, then scribed the shoulder of the tenon member to the reverse contour of the mortise member. This method gave the appearance of a mitered joint when two matching molded edges, such as a bevel or an ovolo, met. It had the advantage over true mitered joints in that cross-grain shrinkage was less apparent.

The technique is still used today for molded joinery, since the edges of the parts and the end-grain shoulders of the tenons can quickly and accurately be shaped by machine.

Beveled molding

To make this joint by hand you have to cut a tenon member with one long and one short shoulder. The difference between the two shoulders is determined by the size of the molding. A simple beveled edge is shown above.

Plane the groove, cut the mortise, and form the bevel on the front edge of the mortise member. Groove the edges of the tenon member, then mark and cut the long-and-short shouldered tenon as required. Make the saw-cuts the same length **(1)**. Saw out the waste to match the bevel on the rail it joins **(2)**.

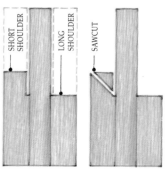

SHORT SHOULDER   LONG SHOULDER   SAWCUT

1 Tenon for beveled-edge joint   *2 Saw out waste on short shoulder*

Ovolo molding

This joint can be made in a similar fashion to a beveled molding, but you have to shape the beveled shoulder of the tenon further, using an in-cannel gouge **(1)**.

However, an alternative method for making a molding such as an ovolo is to cut away part of the molding from the mortise member.

Make the width of the cutout the same width as the face of the tenon member **(2)**. Now, instead of shaping the full width of the short tenon shoulder, it only remains to pare away the corners of the molding carefully.

To produce the required contour, first miter the end of the molding with the aid of a simple homemade miter-block guide. Clamp the guide block to the work level with the long shoulder. Pare away the corner with a chisel to form a miter **(3)**. Remove the guide block and, making vertical cuts with an in-cannel gouge, carefully pare away the wood in order to shape the corners, finishing on the line created by the miter cut **(4)**.

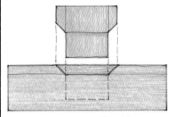

Miter muntin and rail molding

MITERED JOINTS

You can use mitered joints for moldings with any kind of profile – including under-cut moldings, for which a scribed joint cannot be used.

First, cut a long-and-short shouldered tenon. Then cut away the molding on the mortise member to the width of the face of the tenon piece. Using the miter block as a guide, pare away the corners of the molding on the tenon member. Clamp the guide to the mortise member, and miter the molding in the same way.

MITERING APPLIED MOLDINGS

When mitered corners are to be used, make sure applied moldings have a stable moisture content. If the wood should shrink after the miters are made, they will open up on the inside of the corner **(1)**; if it takes up moisture and expands, they open up on the outside **(2)**.

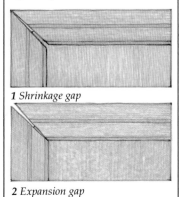

1 Shrinkage gap

2 Expansion gap

REPAIRING PANELING

OOD EXPANDS AND CONTRACTS *because of changing moisture conditions, the greatest movement taking place across the grain. The grain of the panels nearly always runs vertically; so, to allow for movement, more clearance is usually allowed in the side grooves of the frame than at the top and bottom. In order to keep the framework relatively light, it was necessary for the panels to be thin. This was not at all easy to achieve, since early panels were cut by hand and the edges had to be thinned down considerably to fit into the grooves in the framework. The thinning of the edges may be worked on the back, as with flat or sunken panels, or featured on the front to form a fielded panel.*

SPLIT PANELS

To allow for movement, solid-wood panels should never be fixed in their grooves. Nevertheless, distortion in the frame members or applied finishes can cause them to stick. Should a stuck panel shrink due to excessive drying out, it is likely to split. The decision then has to be made as to whether a split should be repaired or left as part of the panel's ageing character. Also, any repair must take account of the need for the wood to move. But, first of all, you need to try to free the panel in the groove.

Freeing a panel

Should a panel be held fast by a distorted frame, there is not much you can do to free it short of removing the entire assembly – a remedy that is hardly justified by the problem. Usually the situation only arises if the wood shrinks due to dry conditions, as may occur if a woodstove or other space heater is located nearby.

If the panel is stuck with paint or varnish, carefully tap around the edge to try to free it; don't strike the panel itself, but place a batten along the edge. Otherwise, try sliding a knife blade between the panel and frame.

Dealing with splits

Splits in naturally finished show-wood panels can look quite acceptable. The split is likely to follow a weakness in the wood that relates to the grain **(1)**. If the split runs

in from one edge and tapers off, it would be difficult to close up, anyway, and filling with a colored filler would not be acceptable.

In the case of a wide painted panel where a butt joint between two narrow boards has opened up, it may be visually desirable to close the "split." If the panel is free to move, clean the joint by scraping it with a narrow blade and work woodworking glue into the joint. Push the parts together with the palms of your hands **(2)**, wearing rubber gloves to increase friction. Tape the joint while it sets.

Alternatively, use two narrow chisels to lever one part up to the other **(3)**, protecting the frame with cardboard. Wipe away any excess glue and, when it has set, fill the indentations in the wood before repainting.

Flat or sunken paneling

Raised-and-fielded paneling

1 Split is likely to follow the grain

2 Push the parts together if free

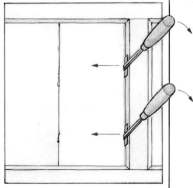

3 Carefully lever panel with chisels

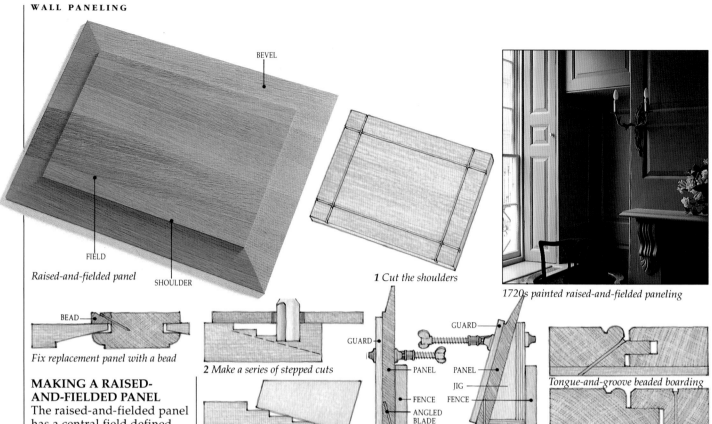

BEVEL

FIELD

SHOULDER

Raised-and-fielded panel

1 Cut the shoulders

1720s painted raised-and-fielded paneling

BEAD

Fix replacement panel with a bead

2 Make a series of stepped cuts

3 Use rebate plane to finish surface

GUARD

GUARD

PANEL

PANEL

JIG

FENCE

FENCE

ANGLED
BLADE

*4 Always guard
the saw blade*

*5 Use a jig on a
non-tilting saw*

Tongue-and-groove beaded boarding

Rebated beaded boarding

MAKING A RAISED-AND-FIELDED PANEL

The raised-and-fielded panel has a central field defined by a shallow raised shoulder combined with a beveled border. If you have a panel of this type that is beyond repair (due to insect attack, for example) make a replacement to match the original.

The paneling will need to be removed and the frame dismantled to make replacement possible. Alternatively, particularly in the case of a middle panel, free the damaged panel by routing out the back of the groove in the frame. You can then drop the new panel into the resulting rebate and pin a bead behind the panel to secure it.

Preparing the wood

If possible, use the old panel as a pattern; if not, take the dimensions from adjacent panels. Select new wood that closely matches the original (take the old panel or a piece of it with you to your lumberyard) and have it machined to thickness. If you are unable to find wood that is wide enough, you can butt-joint pieces together. Leave the panel to acclimatize for several weeks in the room where it is to be fitted. Use a moisture meter to check the moisture content of the new wood against that of the old paneling.

Cut the panel to width and length. Then use a marking gauge to mark the width of the fielded border on the face of the panel and to mark the depth of the bevel all around the edge.

Cutting the bevel

Originally raised-and-fielded panels were shaped with specially made panel-raising planes. These wooden planes had the sole shaped to the contour of the border, with the blade set at an angle so that they cut cleanly across the grain at the ends of the panel. Although some craftsmen still use these planes, it is possible to shape the edge with a rebate plane, power router, or table saw, or to use a combination of these.

First, cut the shoulders using a table saw or a power router (1). You can continue to remove much of the waste in this way by resetting the depth of cut and making a series of steps (2). Use a rebate plane to finish the stepped surface (3). In order to save all the resetting, use the rebate plane by itself to shape the bevel.

If you decide to cut the bevel on a table saw, use a stiff tungsten-carbide-tipped blade; if your table saw has a tilting facility, set it to the required angle and depth of cut. Clamp a piece of board to the face of the panel to act as a guard when cutting the bevel (4). If your saw table is non-tilting, make a jig to hold the work at the desired angle (5). Plane the sawn surface to finish it.

Finishing the panel

Sand all the faces with fine sandpaper, then apply the finish to both sides. This will help to keep the panel stable. When it is thoroughly dry, install the panel in the framework.

BEADED WAINSCOTING

Beaded wainscoting is a form of paneling that uses either tongue-and-groove or rebated boarding. The boards are nailed into place along one edge, the beaded side being held by the fixed edge of the adjacent board. Each board is thus free to move. The molded bead forms a definite visual break that also helps mask the variable gaps at the joints.

Replacing a damaged board

Beaded wainscoting is still a popular wall finish and is available from most lumberyards; however, most modern bead board is narrower and more regular than period wainscoting. If you need to replace a few boards, you can make them yourself.

Have new boards machined to the required size by your supplier. Use a power router or combination plane to tongue and groove the edges. Cut the bead molding with a router or plane.

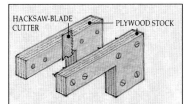

HACKSAW-BLADE CUTTER — PLYWOOD STOCK

HOW TO MAKE A SCRATCH STOCK

This is a simple homemade tool used for shaping small moldings or parts of larger moldings.

Make the stock of the tool from two L-shaped pieces of ³/₄in (18mm) plywood cut to 6 x 3in (150 x 75mm). Fix them together with 1¹/₄in (32mm) countersunk screws. Fashion the cutter from a piece of old hacksaw blade. This is made of very hard steel and can be snapped to length. File the reverse shape of the bead profile in the end of the cutter blade. Clamp the cutter between the stock pieces at the desired setting.

To shape the molding, hold the shoulder of the scratch stock firmly against the edge and push the tool away from you, working the tool with even strokes.

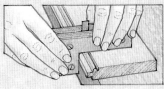

Work the tool with even strokes

MAINTAINING A WOODEN CEILING

Little maintenance is needed for sound wooden ceilings other than general cleaning, preservative treatment, and, if appropriate, repainting. Exposed beams should not be stained black, as there is no historical precedent for this. Painted woodwork that would originally have been a natural color should be chemically stripped (see STRIPPING DOORS) and either left unfinished or waxed.

FINISHING THE REPAIR

Unless you plan to strip the entire wall of its finish, you will need to use a compatible finish for your repair so as to preserve the original patina.

By the early nineteenth century shellac polishes were available, but by this time paint (which was both made in the home and manufactured using a wide variety of base materials) had become the fashion for wood paneling.

If you are fortunate enough to find paneling finished with early casein (milk-based) paint or with a grain-painted finish (consisting of a base coat and a second coat that has been applied in a grainlike pattern), it should be preserved.

Testing the finish

To determine which finish to use, test a small unobtrusive area of paneling. Clean dirt and wax polish from the surface, using a cotton cloth dampened with a solution of four parts mineral spirits to one part linseed oil. Next, wipe the surface with a cloth dampened with denatured alcohol, which is the solvent of shellac. If the finish softens and can be wiped off, then it is shellac. Oil-based varnishes and paints will not react to alcohol in this way – and mineral spirits, which is their solvent, won't redissolve them.

If you are aiming for total authenticity, have a slice of the finish analyzed by an expert to establish its type and date. A national or local conservation organization will tell you who to contact for this specialist service.

Preparing the new wood

To prepare the new wood for a natural finish, you will

Wax polish gives natural-wood paneling a subtle sheen

need to stain it to tone down its color.

Water-based stains are simple to apply and wipe off easily if the color proves to be too strong; however, they may raise the grain. Alcohol-based stains do not raise the grain, but they dry rapidly, so they are difficult to apply evenly. Oil-based stains are thinned with mineral spirits. They are easy to apply and will not affect the grain, but they may bleed into an oil-based varnish.

You can buy stains in a variety of common wood shades. To test the color of a stain, apply it to offcuts of the wood used for the repair. Dilute the stain if necessary, or for darker shades apply extra coats. Different colors can be obtained by mixing stains of the same type. When dry, apply a wax or varnish finish to evaluate the darkening effect it has on the color. Modify the stain accordingly.

When you have achieved a match with the original material, proceed to color and finish the repair. Make sure the stain is dry before applying the finish.

Wax finish

For a wax finish, prepare the newly stained wood with a coat of clear sanding sealer. This prevents the first coat of polish from sinking in excessively. A range of ready-prepared traditional wax polishes is available. Apply two or three coats of polish, using a pad of fine steel wool or a cloth. Allow each coat to dry, then buff with a soft cloth.

Varnish finish

Newly applied varnish can never match the worn patina of an old finish, nor will it have the subtle character of a wax finish. However, if you are trying to match an old varnish finish, use a compatible oil-based varnish (never a modern polyurethane one).

Apply an oil varnish with a brush, laying the finish on evenly in thin coats. Let each coat dry, and rub down with fine silicon-carbide paper between coats. After varnishing, apply a wax polish on a pad of fine steel wool.

Paint finish

Color matching is never easy, and matching old paint can be particularly difficult. If you think your interior finish is original, discuss the work with a specialist or an adviser from a historical society before embarking on any repairs.

ARCHITECTURAL MOLDINGS

OLDED BASEBOARDS, *chair rails, picture rails, and cornices play an important part in creating the attractive character of an old house, and deserve to be preserved or reinstated if they have been removed. Although their use may have been primarily functional, they were also employed to give balance and enrichment to the wall surface to which they were applied.*

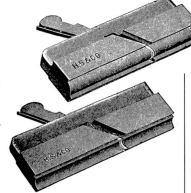

Traditional wooden molding planes

Moldings enrich the wall surface

Stuck molding

Applied molding

Wooden interior moldings
1 Victorian-style baseboard
2 Torus baseboard
3 Cornice moldings
4 Straight-run chair rail
5 Carved-type chair rails
6 Small straight-run chair rail
7 Small carved-type chair rail
8 Astragal panel molding
9 Picture rail

WOODEN INTERIOR MOLDINGS

Moldings are produced by making a series of shaped parallel cuts that combine to give a contoured form to the edge or face of a workpiece. There are two types: either the molding is worked directly into the component (in which case it is known as a stuck molding) or it can take the form of an applied molding (a molded length of wood that has to be fixed to the background).

Most wooden moldings are intended to be painted and are therefore made from an inexpensive softwood. Nevertheless, good-quality selected boards are used in order to avoid knots that are difficult to cut. Before the woodworking trade became mechanized, all moldings were laboriously fashioned by hand using molding planes. Each one needed an individual size or shape of plane, and some required the use of several special planes.

The earliest moldings were relatively simple and were worked in vernacular styles by local craftsmen. But from the early eighteenth century moldings began to be influenced by classical styles, and by late in the eighteenth century wooden moldings inspired by Roman and Greek architecture were the standard forms.

The Roman versions were rather heavier in style than the Greek ones – the former being based on segments of a circle, while the latter were based on elliptical curves.

Baseboards

Baseboards are used to line the base of interior walls. They help conceal the junction between the wall and floor and protect the wall from impact damage.

The size and complexity of the molding and the materials from which it is made are dependent on the quality of the house. Most old baseboards are made from single softwood boards up to 8in (200mm) in height and shaped with a simple classical molding. Some Victorian baseboards, however, can be up to 14in (350mm) in height and made from two or three elaborately molded softwood or hardwood sections. The shoulders of the tongue-and-groove edges fall on a line of the molding to disguise the joint.

Main rooms and hallways were fitted with impressive decorative baseboards, while bedrooms were mostly fitted with a simpler style. Attic and basement rooms were normally fitted with plain square-edged boards.

Standard moldings are available, but you may need to have matching baseboards made-to-order by a specialist millwork company. Give them a sample of the molding or a dimensioned sketch as a guide.

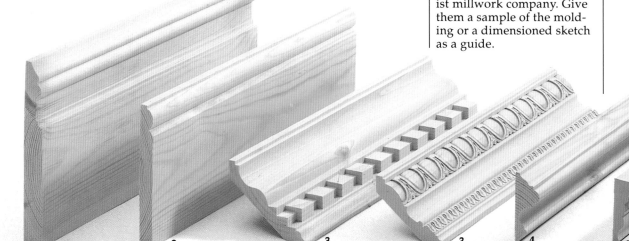

1   2   3   3   4   5

Chair rails

Chair rails, sometimes called dado rails, are a legacy from classical paneling and the wainscot or dado paneling of Victorian times. The cap molding of dado paneling served as a rubbing strip that protected the wall finish from wear and tear by chair backs. The chair rail, which was usually set about 3 to 4ft (1 to 1.2m) from the floor, continued this tradition after the use of wood paneling had declined. Chair rails have not been standard features in the twentieth century, but they were still widely used as a trim for the fashionable embossed wallcoverings that lined the dadoes of so many halls and stairways in late-Victorian times. Chair rails had ceased to be a common architectural feature by the mid 1920s.

Straight-run and carved moldings in hardwoods and softwoods are available from specialist sources.

Picture rails

Like the dado molding, the picture rail is an echo of the earlier paneled walls. The position of the rail varied according to the height of the room, but it was usually positioned 1 to 1ft 8in (300 to 500mm) below the ceiling cornice to form a frieze. For this reason, it is sometimes known as a frieze molding. The true picture rail had a quirk (narrow groove) in the top edge, into which picture hangers fitted.

The picture rail figured widely in Victorian interiors and is a common feature in many houses well beyond the 1930s. The later versions tend to be smaller and less fussy than the Victorian ones. Traditional moldings are available from specialist suppliers in softwoods and a limited range of hardwoods.

Cornice moldings

Wooden cornice moldings were used to finish the top of paneling that terminated below ceiling level. For full-height paneling, they were fitted up to the ceiling. The molding formed an integral part of the paneling.

In the nineteenth century, it became commonplace to use formed plaster cornices at the junctions between un-adorned plastered walls and ceiling. Wooden cornices are generally smaller than the plaster versions.

Suppliers who specialize in reproduction moldings stock a range of ornamental hardwood cornices.

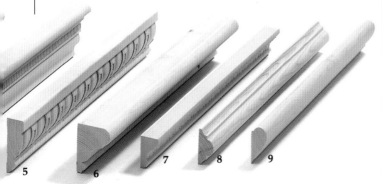

5   6   7   8   9

RESTORING MOLDINGS

I F MANY OF THE ORIGINAL DETAILS *of the interior of your house are gone, you will need to find references to serve as a guide for repair work. In an urban setting, the chances are that your house will be one of a number in your street built in the same style. Not all will have been altered in the same way, and with luck you may find an original example.*

Decorative moldings used to perfection in a late-Victorian sitting room

DETECTING MISSING MOLDINGS

Unless your walls have been replastered, you will be able to detect the use and original position of missing moldings when the wallpaper has been stripped. Parallel streaks of varnish or paint on the plaster of the wall will indicate the exact location of a chair or picture rail. You can also use the patches of plaster covering the original nail holes as a guide. If the walls have been painted over, you may find that you can detect the patches by shining a light obliquely across the surface to show up irregularities.

CHAIR AND PICTURE-RAIL FIXINGS

Picture rails and chair rails were fixed with cut nails, driven into the masonry or into wooden plugs set in the vertical joints of the plastered brickwork. Timber-frame walls had the rails nailed directly to the studs. The plugs are unlikely to have survived – so when fitting new rails to masonry, use cut nails or modern masonry nails, or drill and plug the walls for screw fixings. Match the original nails for timber-frame walls.

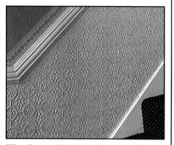

The chair rail defines the panel below

Fitting a new rail

Using a long straightedge and a spirit level, mark a horizontal line at the required height. If you have no original marks to go by, position a chair rail about 3 to 4ft (1 to 1.2m) from the floor. For a rail following the slope of a staircase, use a chalk line to snap a straight line onto the wall. Hold each end of the string at a point where vertical lines level with the end of the baseboard of the hall and landing meet the line of the horizontal dado at the top and bottom of the staircase.

The position of the picture rail depends on the period of the house. Houses at the turn of the century had high ceilings, and the rail was generally positioned about 1 to 1ft 8in (300 to 500mm) below the cornice molding.

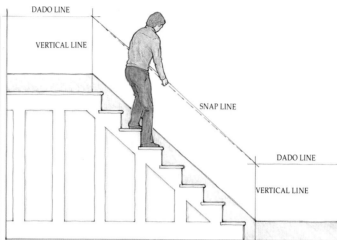

Setting out a chair rail on a stair

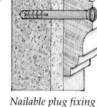 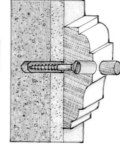

Plug and screw fixing   *Nailable plug fixing*   *Counterbored and plugged screw fixing*

Later interiors usually had lower ceilings, therefore the picture rail was fitted at door height.

Cut the rails to length as you work around the room, and miter or scribe the ends where they meet. With the aid of an assistant, hold the rail on the marked line and nail it in place. Sink the nail heads below the surface with a nail punch.

For screw fasteners, first drill countersunk clearance holes in the rail, at 2ft (600mm) intervals, for 2in (50mm) screws. Temporarily fix the rail in place by partly driving in a few nails. Mark the position of the holes on the wall and remove the rail. Drill the plug holes, then insert the wall plugs and screw the rail in place.

For a larger rail, you can use nailable plugs. Drill the wood and plug hole together and drive the plug through the face of the rail.

Fill the holes with a fine plaster filler and, when it is set, sand it smooth ready for painting. Alternatively, use a colored wood filler for a natural wood finish.

For a superior finish, you can countersink screws and make matching wooden plugs to fill the holes. Cut the plugs from offcuts of the wood, using a plug-cutting bit and an electric drill set up in a drill stand. Alternatively, turn the plugs on a lathe, with the grain running across the width of the plug. Glue the plugs into the holes, insuring that the grain aligns with that of the rail. When the glue has set, carefully pare off the waste.

Joining lengths of molding

Try to buy the moldings in lengths that will cut up economically – but always allow extra for waste, particularly if you are having the moldings specially made.

For a long wall, you will no doubt have to join lengths together. Cut the meeting ends to form a mitered butt joint, as this is neater and more effective than a plain butt joint. Mark the top back edges of both pieces of the moldings where they will join. Cut the angles accurately, with the molding held vertically in a miter box.

For wide moldings such as baseboards a miter box is impractical, so use a circular saw or power jigsaw with the blade set to 45 degrees. Mark the required length on the bottom edge of each piece. Mark the angle with a miter square, and square the line across the face. Use a hand square or pin a wooden strip to the surface to guide the sole plate of the saw. Set it the required distance from the cut line (1). Cut on the waste side of the line on each piece (2).

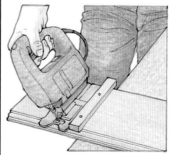

1 Pin guide strip to surface

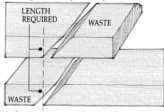

2 Cut on waste side of each piece

BASEBOARD REPAIRS

Whereas seemingly redundant chair and picture rails may have been stripped out by fashion-conscious home owners, the baseboard are likely to remain, as they still perform a necessary function. However, you may find that an attractive period baseboard has been ripped out and replaced by a plain modern version.

Most original baseboards suffer some form of damage, such as dents or overpainting. A certain amount of denting is acceptable; but if the baseboards are badly dented, repair them with a fine plaster or wood filler prior to repainting. When the filler has set, wrap

Baseboard fixings

The method used for fixing baseboards will usually depend on the quality of the building. Cut nails may be used to fix the boards directly to a plastered masonry wall or driven into wooden plugs set into the wall to receive them. In better-class houses softwood nailers are fixed to the wall and the plaster is worked up to them. The nailers consist of horizontal battens, one of them set close to the top of the baseboard, and vertical blocks known as "soldiers" set 2 to 3ft (600 to 900mm) apart. In Victorian houses that have elaborate built-up baseboards, stepped soldiers may be used.

If the nailers pull away from the wall when you are removing a baseboard, they can be refixed with masonry nails or screws and wall plugs. Make sure the nailers are level and true. Replace any that are rotten or badly infested with woodsworm. Treat the wood with an insecticide before fitting.

sandpaper around shaped blocks and sand the filler to the contour of the molding.

Blurring of the molding's detail due to overpainting or poorly applied paint (often incorporating dust from the floor) can be remedied by stripping the paint back to bare wood then repainting. Use a hot-air gun (but not on old lead paint) or a chemical stripper to soften the paint, then scrape it off carefully. Remove the paint from fine decorative molding with a pad of steel wool dipped in chemical stripper. Most strippers are hazardous, so protect your eyes and skin and ventilate the room when working with them.

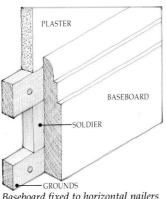

Baseboard fixed to horizontal nailers

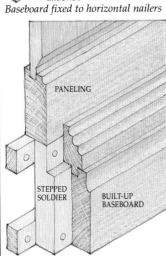

Built-up baseboard fixed to soldiers

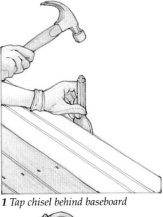

1 Tap chisel behind baseboard

2 Protect the plaster with plywood

Removing baseboards

You may be forced to remove more of the baseboard than you want to if the damaged section is trapped behind an adjacent scribed board.

Starting at an end or at an external corner, tap a bolster chisel between the top of the baseboard and the plaster (1). Lever the baseboard away from the wall, taking care not to split short lengths. Wedge it with a thin strip of wood, and work along the edge to the next nailing point. Use a crowbar if better leverage is required. Place a piece of 1/4in (6mm) plywood behind the crowbar to protect the plaster (2). Expect some bruising and scuffing of the plaster at the edge where it meets the baseboard, but try to minimize the damage. Continue in this way until the baseboard pulls free.

If you want to reuse the baseboard, pull the old nails out through the back. If you try to knock them out from behind, you risk splitting the face of the board.

Fitting baseboards

When replacing a damaged piece of baseboard, you can use the old piece as a template. This is particularly helpful if the end is scribed. It is best to check that the old baseboard was a good fit, as gaps may have opened up if the building structure has moved due to settlement. In any event, you will need to measure the length of wall.

Mark and cut the board to length. Scribe or miter the end, if required. Mark the position of soldiers, if fitted, on the face. Level the board, and nail it in place with appropriate nails. If you are replacing all the baseboards, follow the sequence shown below. Scribe internal corners and miter external ones.

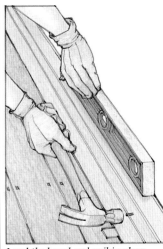

Level the board and nail in place

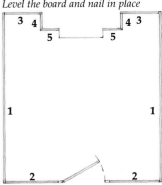

Sequence for replacing baseboard

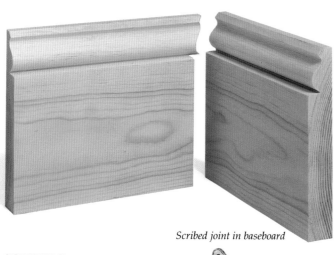

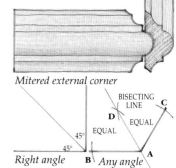

Mitered external corner

BISECTING
LINE
C
D
EQUAL
EQUAL
45°
45°
D
A
Right angle B *Any angle*

Bisecting an angle
Place compass point on A. Scribe arc at B and C. Place point on B and C, then scribe arcs at D. Draw bisecting line through D and A.

Scribed joint in baseboard

SCRIBING INTERNAL CORNERS

Where moldings meet at an internal angle (for example, at the corner of a room), use a scribed joint. This has one molding scribed to the reverse profile of another. For architectural moldings it is preferable to a mitered joint, as it gives a neater join when there are irregularities in the surface of the wall. Moldings that have an undercut profile cannot be scribed and need to be mitered.

To scribe small chair- or picture-rail moldings, first mark the lengths and miter the end that is to be scribed to 45 degrees, using a miter box and backsaw. Now cut the reverse contour of the molding by following the line formed by the face and the mitered end. Use a coping saw and make the cut perpendicular to the front face (1). The same method is used for cornice moldings.

Baseboard can be cut in a similar way, but the width makes mitering a little more difficult. Instead, mark the profile on the back face using a piece of scrap as a template held level with the squared end of the board (2). Saw off the waste with the teeth of the coping-saw blade facing the back of the board (3). This prevents breakout of the fibers on the front face.

1 Make perpendicular sawcut

2 Use an offcut as a template

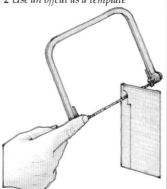

3 Saw off the waste

MITERED EXTERNAL CORNERS

When two moldings meet at an external corner (when a cornice or a baseboard runs around a chimney breast, for example), you will need to miter them. Most corners are right angles, so require each meeting part to be cut to 45 degrees. Miter squares and miter boxes are preset to this angle.

If an external corner is not a right angle, then you will have to calculate the angle of the miter. To do so, set a sliding bevel to the angle of the corner and transcribe it onto a piece of paper. Bisect the corner angle, using a pair of compasses, then reset the blade of the bevel on the bisecting line.

Use a miter box for cutting moldings to 45 degrees. For other angles, make a jig or modify the miter box. For wide baseboards, use a circular saw or power jigsaw with adjustable blade angle.

Cut mitered work in miter box

PACKING PIECE

Use packing to keep cornice molding steady in miter box

SCRIBING THE EDGE

Old floors are often bowed or out of level, causing uneven gaps under a level baseboard. You can pin lengths of quadrant molding to the baseboard to mask an existing gap. Otherwise, you will need to scribe the bottom edge of a new baseboard to fit. To do so, level and temporarily pin the board in position. Pack a pencil up to the level of the bottom edge of the board at the point where the gap is greatest. Drag the pencil and packing along the floor to trace the contour of the floor onto the face of the baseboard. Remove it from the wall and plane the edge to the marked line, then fit the board to the floor and nail it in place.

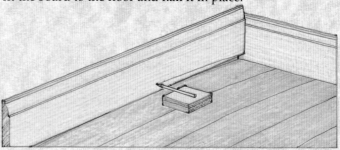

Trace contour of floor onto baseboard with pencil set on packing

CORNICE MOLDINGS

WOODEN CORNICES *are relatively large and intricate moldings, and so are difficult to make yourself. A range of classically styled moldings that reproduce the architectural patterns of the past is available from specialist suppliers. Made from fine-textured poplar for painting and oak for staining or polishing, they can often be purchased with scribed internal and mitered external corners.*

A simple straight-run cornice molding finishes the top of the paneling

Fitting a wooden cornice
You will find that it is easiest to apply a wood stain or the required finish before installing a cornice. Sawcuts and nail holes can be touched up after you have fitted it.

Mark parallel lines on the wall and ceiling, using a small piece of molding as a guide **(1)**. Starting at a left-hand corner, temporarily tack or tape a short piece of molding into the corner. Fix the first pre-scribed internal-corner piece to the wall and ceiling with fine nails and paneling adhesive, butting the shaped end up to the short molding in the corner **(2)**. Remove the short temporarily fixed piece. The resulting end gap will be filled by the final piece.

Cut the butting end of a long section of molding to match the repeat pattern of the corner piece **(3)**. If need be, cut it to length. Fix it in place with nails and adhesive. An alternative method for fixing the cornice is to nail or screw a triangular blocking into the angle and to tack or screw the molding to it **(4)**. If this piece does not reach the next corner, cut and fix another piece in the same way **(5)**. At the next internal corner, fix a prescribed corner piece butted up to the fixed molding **(6)**.

Continue in this way all around the room, finishing by inserting the last piece into the gap left at the start of the operation.

For an external corner, first fix one half of the premitered corner molding in place, then apply adhesive to the mitered ends and fit the other piece up to it **(7)**.

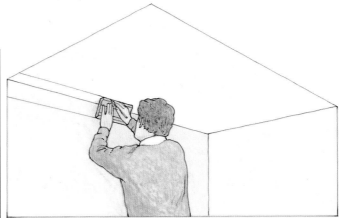

1 Mark guidelines on the walls and ceiling

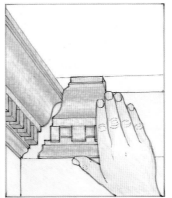

2 Fix pre-scribed corner piece

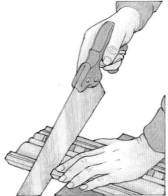

3 Cut butting end to match pattern

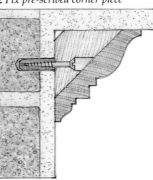

4 Alternative fixing using blocking

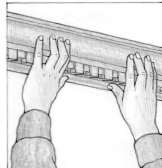

5 Cut and fix straight sections

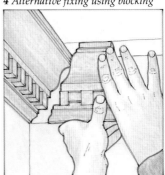

6 Fit pre-scribed corner piece

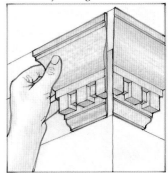

7 Fix the premitered corners

EMBOSSED WALLCOVERINGS

I N THE EIGHTEENTH CENTURY, *wallpaper began to be imported from England and France. It was hand-made, and immediately caught on as a fashionable wall finish in the grandest houses. In 1765 the first American wallpaper factory opened in New York.*

Wallpaper became more available in the early nineteenth century when paper-making and printing machines were developed that could mass produce wallpaper at an affordable price. The first wallpaper printing machine was imported into America in 1844.

Then in 1877 Frederick Walton invented Lincrusta, a high-relief wallcovering that quickly became popular because of its durability and washability (both selling points attractive to Victorian householders) as well as its decorative appeal. Some ten years later Anaglypta, a lighter-weight embossed paper, appeared. Both were intended for painting and were widely used for dadoes and friezes and as general wallcoverings.

Should you strip a wall, particularly in a hallway or beside a staircase, and discover a dado-height band of different plaster or numerous patches, you can be sure that an embossed wallcovering has been removed. In this case, using a Lincrusta or period Anaglypta wallcovering will restore the original decorative style.

LINCRUSTA

Frederick Walton had been involved with the manufacture of linoleum for some years, and Lincrusta was a dense and moderately stiff material based on a similar formula to linoleum. A mixture of oxidized linseed oil, resin, paraffin wax, fiber, and whiting was applied to a canvas backing (this was later changed to waterproof paper) then passed through rollers under high pressure. One roller was decoratively engraved, leaving a continuous impression in the soft compound. The material was left to dry in a heated environment for two weeks.

When, in 1883, Lincrusta was manufactured under license in America, it quickly established itself as a very popular wallcovering and a variety of new patterns were introduced specifically for the US market. Lincrusta went out of fashion in the second quarter of the twentieth century and ceased to be produced – until recently, when manufacturers reintroduced a limited range of panels, rolls, and borders featuring original patterns.

The late-Victorian patterns were inspired by classical decorative themes (one was called "Italian Renaissance"). Several of the later patterns had Art Nouveau motifs.

A Lincrustra frieze provides an attractive border to the upper part of a wall

Classically inspired embossed dado

Painted Anaglypta stairway dado

ANAGLYPTA

At the time when Lincrusta was finding a ready market in America, the launching of its rival, Anaglypta, was being proposed in Britain. It was Thomas Palmer, one of Walton's employees, who suggested making a cheaper, lighter, and more flexible embossed wallcovering from cotton and paper pulp. When Walton rejected the idea, Palmer patented the process, left the company (in 1886), and, together with the Storey brothers, developed the material, which became available for sale by 1888.

Like Lincrusta, Anaglypta was intended for painting and was washable; however, it was not so durable. Being relatively easy to hang, it was particularly suitable for friezes and ceilings. It very soon became widely used in place of Lincrusta and has continued to be available, in modern as well as traditional designs, to this day.

You can detect whether an old embossed wallcovering is Lincrusta or Anaglypta by pressing the raised surface. If it is compressible, then it is Anaglypta, which is hollow.

As with Lincrusta, the embossed patterns reflected current fashions, and Palmer employed leading artists and architects to devise fine Art Nouveau and floral designs.

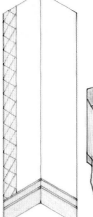

1 Wet the back of each piece

2 Trim off waste with utility knife

3 Measure the width

4 Bevel the cut edge

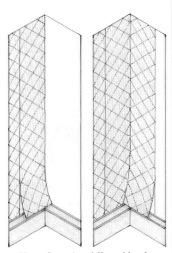

5 Hang first piece followed by the offcut set on a plumbed line

HANGING LINCRUSTA

Although it is relatively stiff and heavy and requires careful handling, Lincrusta is not a particularly difficult material to hang. As with other decorating techniques, thorough preparation of the surface and careful setting out are necessary.

Since it is a fairly expensive wallcovering, calculate your requirements accurately. Most patterns are a straight match, but some have offset or random designs – in which case, you will need to make allowance for waste.

Papered walls
Remove traces of old wallpaper and paste, and inspect the bare plaster surface for holes or loose patches. Smooth where necessary with plaster filler. When it is dry, apply a wallpaper size.

Painted walls
Scrape off powdery, flaking, or blistered emulsion paint, and bind the surface with a primer.

Wash off most of a water-based distemper-type finish from the wall before you apply a primer.

Roughen the surface of sound oil-based paintwork with abrasive paper; wash it down with sugar soap.

Lining the walls
If the wall plaster has been unevenly patched, lining paper will help to even out suction and create a smooth surface for the wallcovering.

First line the walls with a good-quality lining paper. Use a heavy-duty wallpaper paste containing a fungicide.

Applying the covering
Measure and cut individual lengths from a roll, taking note of any pattern matching required and allowing about 2in (50mm) for waste on each length. Trim the selvage from the rolled material with a straightedge and sharp utility knife. Hold the knife at a slight angle to undercut the edge of the material.

Using a chalk line, mark a plumb line on the wall. Hold the edge of the first piece of wallcovering on the line and check the fit of the top end against the ceiling, cornice molding, or picture rail. If need be, mark and cut the edge to fit any irregularities. Trim the other pieces to match, if required.

Sponge the back of each piece with warm water and leave it to soak for up to 30 minutes (1). This allows the material to soften and fully expand, so that it doesn't blister when you are hanging it. Wipe off any surplus water before applying the special Lincrusta glue. Stir the glue thoroughly and apply it evenly with a wide paintbrush or paint roller, depending on the length of the piece. Insure the edges are well covered with glue.

Apply the first piece to the wall level with the vertical line and butting the top edge. Press it into place with a cloth pad or rubber roller. Mark the line of the baseboard on each edge of the piece, then peel it back just far enough to place a piece of plywood under it on which to cut the end. Trim off the waste with the utility knife and straightedge (2), then press the edge down and clean off surplus glue with a damp sponge. Continue in this way, butting subsequent pieces together.

Dealing with corners
At the end of a run you will meet an internal or external corner. You can work the material around a curved corner without cutting it, but not around an angled one. The cut edges will need to be mitered, and an allowance made on the width for the thickness of the material.

If the wallcovering is to continue onto the adjacent surface of an angled corner, first measure the distance between the edge of the last piece and the corner. Take measurements from the top, middle and bottom (3). Mark the widths at corresponding heights on a length of the wallcovering (for an external corner, adding the thickness of the material). Cut it with a utility knife, holding a straightedge on the marks.

Control the knife carefully, as it will have a tendency to follow the pattern. Make the cut with a series of knife strokes. Bevel the edge with a sanding block (4). Hold the length flush with the edge of your worktable to provide good support. Hold the material face down when shaping an external-corner piece. (The thinner parts are brittle and likely to crumble, so handle with care.)

Hang the prepared piece of wallcovering in the usual way. The remaining offcut is now used to turn the corner. The pattern will then follow through, but there will be a slight mismatch because of the cut edges. The corner may not be quite vertical, so mark a plumbed line on the adjacent wall on which to set the straight edge of the offcut (5). Trim and level the cut edge as required.

After hanging this piece, continue to hang the covering as before. Fill the joints with plaster filler, and make good any broken edges.

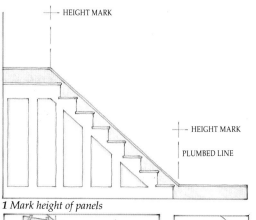
1 Mark height of panels

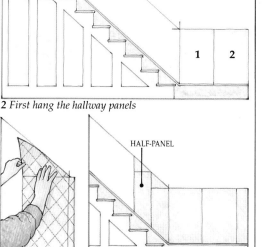
2 First hang the hallway panels

WAINSCOT PANELS

Lincrusta wainscot panels come ready trimmed to width and length (you can also buy a molded border). Applying them to a plain wall is therefore quite straightforward. However, if the wall has a chair rail, you may need to trim the height of the panels or even reposition the rail.

The panel designs form a complete pattern, so avoid reducing the height if you can. If you have to trim the panels, remove the surplus from the bottom edge only. Before hanging the panels, prepare the wall and line it.

To hang Lincrusta wainscot panels on a plain wall, mark a horizontal guideline at panel height **(1)** then set out and apply the covering as already described. If there is to be a border, after hanging the panels cut the border to length and glue it in place to finish the top edge **(2)**.

3 Crease the paper into the angle

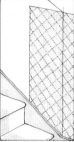
4 Hang the half-panel

5 Hang the corner piece

6 Cut and hang other half-panel

1 Mark horizontal guideline

2 Finish top edge with border strip

DEALING WITH STAIRWAYS

To set out wainscot panels for a stairway wall, mark a plumbed line at the foot and top of the stairs where the stringer meets the base-board. Mark the height of the panels on the vertical lines measured up from the baseboard **(1)**. On a long stair, set out intermediate marks in the same way, then join them up with a straight-edge – or use a chalk line.

Hanging the panels

Hang the panels in the hall first, working away from the vertical line at the foot of the stairs **(2)**. The panels that follow the slope of the stairs must be cut to the required angle before hanging. Cut the first panel vertically into equal halves. Make the cut dead straight, guiding the knife with a straightedge.

Cut a sheet of paper to the exact size of one of the half-panels in order to make a pattern (lining paper is handy for this). Temporarily tape the paper to the wall, with the long edge against the vertical line and level with the top of the chair rail at the foot of the staircase. Crease the paper into the angle of the stringer

(3). Remove the paper, and fold the end along the crease line. Trim off the triangular end along the line.

Lay the paper pattern over the half-panel, with the top and side edges flush. Mark the panel where the slope of the pattern meets its edge. Place a straightedge from the corner to the edge mark, and cut off the corner. Take care to make a clean cut and not to damage the triangular offcut, as it will be needed.

Prepare the panel and offcut for gluing, as already described. Hang the half-panel, with the angled cut edge butted up to the stringer **(4)**. Then add the triangular piece to the top of the half-panel level with the guideline and the long edge of the panel **(5)**. Cut and hang the other half-panel in the same way **(6)**. Follow this method up to the vertical line at the top of the staircase (you may have to make the last piece a narrower infill panel), then continue with full panels on the landing. You can finish the top edge with a border strip, mitering the ends of the strip at the top and bottom of the stair.

REPAINTING LINCRUSTA

Avoid stripping paint from Lincrusta unless absolutely necessary. Should you have to strip paint from the wall-covering, don't use a strong chemical stripper (which could dissolve the material). Before proceeding, test an inconspicuous corner of the wallcovering to make sure that the paint stripper is not too strong. Never remove old paint with a hot-air gun. Lincrusta is flammable and will soften with heat.

HANGING ANAGLYPTA

Anaglypta is hung on walls and ceilings in the same way as a conventional wallpaper.

After cutting the lengths to size, apply heavy-duty wallpaper paste and leave it to soak for about 10 minutes. Fold the paper on itself, then carry it to the wall or ceiling and apply it to the surface with a paperhanger's brush. Avoid using excessive pressure, so you don't flatten the embossing. Cut off the waste with scissors.

Let the paper dry out for a few days before finishing. Use an eggshell oil paint for walls, and an emulsion paint for a ceiling.

CHAPTER FOURTEEN

DECORATIVE WOODWORK

WOOD IS AN EXTREMELY VERSATILE MATERIAL that is relatively easy to work. These properties, coupled with the desire of craftsmen over the centuries to decorate their work, have resulted in all manner of shaped, fretted, or carved woodwork. Decoration was also regarded as a form of artistic expression, so both interior and exterior decorative elements are to be found that bespeak the gifted carpenter.

In Victorian times, speculative builders encouraged by the new wealth and manufacturing methods brought about by the Industrial Revolution indulged in widespread use of flamboyant decorative woodwork to embellish even fairly modest homes.

Most household millwork is made from cheaper softwoods, which suffer from weathering if not adequately maintained. In addition, later homeowners viewed Victorian styles as grotesquely old-fashioned. As a result, many fine examples of decorative woodwork have been reduced to a shadow of their original shape or ripped out and replaced by modern substitutes. However, for a fairly modest outlay it is possible to re-create period woodwork in the appropriate style, thus restoring a house to its former glory.

Pierced and fretted gable decoration

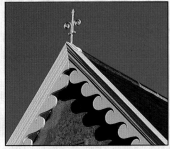

Attractive scroll-design bargeboard

Decorative fretted porch balustrade

Machine-made gable decorations on a "Carpenter Gothic" house

"Sunray" gable motif

Bold wooden brackets decorate soffits

"Gingerbread" decoration on fascia

DECORATIVE WOODEN DETAILS

THE EXTENT AND STYLE *of the decorative wooden detail will depend on the period and character of your house. In an early house it may simply* take the form of an elegantly carved doorcase, whereas in some Victorian homes exuberant fretted and carved details decorate almost every architectural feature.

Pierced and profiled shapes are generally two-dimensional and cast attractive shadows on the wall, while some modeled decorations have a three-dimensional effect similar to low-relief carving. Although the shapes are simple, used repetitively they create a lively form of decoration.

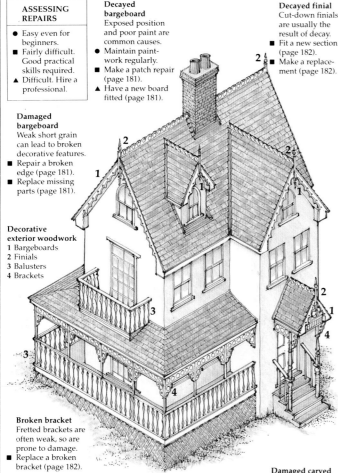

ASSESSING REPAIRS
- ● Easy even for beginners.
- ■ Fairly difficult. Good practical skills required.
- ▲ Difficult. Hire a professional.

Decayed bargeboard
Exposed position and poor paint are common causes.
- ■ Maintain paint-work regularly.
- ■ Make a patch repair (page 181).
- ▲ Have a new board fitted (page 181).

Decayed finial
Cut-down finials are usually the result of decay.
- ■ Fit a new section (page 182).
- ■ Make a replace-ment (page 182).

Damaged bargeboard
Weak short grain can lead to broken decorative features.
- ■ Repair a broken edge (page 181).
- ■ Replace missing parts (page 181).

Decorative exterior woodwork
1 Bargeboards
2 Finials
3 Balusters
4 Brackets

Broken bracket
Fretted brackets are often weak, so are prone to damage.
- ■ Replace a broken bracket (page 182).

Decayed console
Poor maintenance can cause decay.
- ● Strip old paint from decorative details and repaint (pages 183 and 75-6).
- ■ Replace a decayed console (page 183).

Missing carved woodwork
Damaged wood may have been stripped out.
- ■ Make a replica console (page 188).
- ■ Make a replica linenfold panel (pages 186-7).

Damaged baluster
Wood rot or insect attack may mean a baluster has to be replaced.
- ● Treat infestation or rot (pages 194-5).
- ● Make a new rail (page 184).

Damaged carved woodwork
Rot or insect attack can cause the wood to decay.
- ● Treat minor insect attack yourself (page 194).
- ▲ Have rot or major insect attack treated (pages 194-5).

SAWN WOOD "GINGERBREAD"

FRETTED WOODWORK, *known as "gingerbread" in this country, was a style of decoration featuring highly ornate sawn and turned detail. Although* the fashion originated in Britain under the influence of Victorian architects such as C. L. Eastlake, it blossomed most extravagantly in American Gothic-revival houses of the late nineteenth century. The "Carpenter Gothic" style was applied with abandon to houses with high-peaked roofs, regardless of size. This type of decoration was often painted in dark colors, contrasting with the lighter background colors of the house walls, and fine examples are greatly prized.

Late-Victorian house with a profusion of ornamental woodwork

Strong colors emphasize shapes

Porch with turned and fretted details

MAKING SHAPED CUTOUTS

Sawn edges and apertures and drilled holes make up much of the decorative detail of fretted woodwork. A hand-held curve-cutting saw with a narrow blade (such as a coping, bow, or keyhole saw or a power jigsaw) is needed for most of the work, although a panel or backsaw can be used for angular edge details. A band saw or a powered scroll saw is ideal for accurately cutting curved details in smaller work; some have a tilting table for angled cuts. Holes up to 1in (25mm) can be drilled with a brace and bit or an electric drill. For larger holes up to 3in (75mm), use an expansive bit in a brace or a hole saw in an electric drill.

Shaped holes add interest to porch

Cutting edge shapes

If you need to make several cutouts, use a power jigsaw. It will speed up the work – and the shoe or baseplate holds the blade square or at any set angle to the surface, allowing you to concentrate on following the line.

To make straight or easy-curved cutouts of a reasonable size, simply follow the direction of cut indicated **(1)**. For tight curves or where the waste would be large, make straight cuts in the waste up to the line **(2)**. The waste will then fall away in sections clear of the saw, thus avoiding the blade jamming in the cut or a large piece of wood breaking away at the end.

Lay the work on a folding workbench or across saw-horses. Depending on the size, either clamp it down or use your own body weight to steady it. Don't force the saw as you make the cuts.

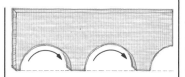
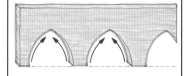

1 Follow the direction of cut arrows

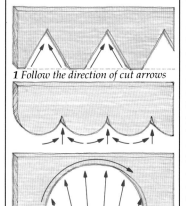

2 Make straight cuts in the waste

Drilling an aperture

Drilled holes are often used to enhance fretted woodwork. They also form the basis of the trefoil and quatrefoil motifs. To make these forms of decoration, set out center lines on a cardboard template and mark the centers of the chosen drill size. Place the cardboard in position, and mark the drill centers through the template with an awl. Set the center of the bit on the marks and drill the holes. The use of an electric drill held in a stand will help you make a clean steady cut, with less risk of wandering when cutting the last holes.

When drilling through a board, clamp a piece of scrap wood to the back to prevent the drill from splitting out. Alternatively, you can stop drilling when the center point breaks through, then drill from the other side.

Cutting an aperture

To cut a large round aperture through the face of a board, first drill a starter hole in the waste close to the guide line. Insert the saw blade and switch on. Cut out the center in one piece **(3)**.

In order to cut a straight-sided or pointed aperture such as a square, triangle, or lobe, drill a starter hole in one corner. Run the saw along one side and into the corner. Pull the saw back about 2in (50mm) before directing the blade toward and then along the next side. Use this method to cut into all the corners, then remove the remaining corner waste by sawing back the other way **(4)**. The method is also employed for cutting a castellated edge **(5)**; and a variation of this type of edging can be made using a large drilled hole and straight sawcuts **(6)**.

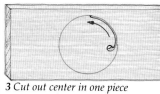

3 Cut out center in one piece

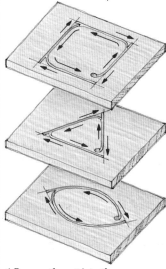

4 Reverse the cut into the corners

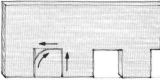

5 Cut a castellated edge similarly

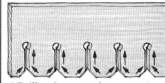

6 Drill and saw out the waste

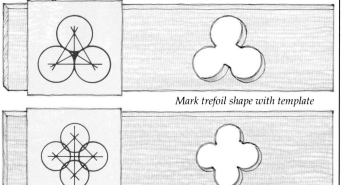

Mark trefoil shape with template

Mark quatrefoil shape with template

BARGEBOARDS

BARGEBOARDS (ALSO KNOWN AS VERGEBOARDS) *are used to finish and protect the verge of a gabled roof, porch, or dormer window. They provide a striking exterior feature and were first used to full effect in medieval Europe, where important houses had decoratively carved oak bargeboards.*

Simple modern versions are little more than wide plain boards, but elaborately fretted and carved bargeboards were fashionable during the Gothic revival of the nineteenth century. Indeed, the bargeboard's original function was sometimes almost forgotten in the enthusiasm for decorative extravagance.

A simple but striking design cut into the edge of a bargeboard

Carved-oak Tudor-style bargeboard   *Fretted shapes enliven a bargeboard*

TYPES OF BARGEBOARDS

Bargeboards can be fitted close to the wall, or may extend forward – in which case they are known as projecting gables. Usually, these are supported by shaped brackets and the underside is finished with a soffit board. Turned or shaped wooden finials or scrolled panels may be fitted at the apex to complete the decorative effect. Extensive use of cutouts produced highly ornate tracery designs. These were often structurally weak, so were sometimes applied to a backing board.

GABLE CONSTRUCTION

A simple gable roof consists of ordinary rafters notched over wooden wall plates, which are supported by the load-bearing side walls. The top ends of the rafters are nailed to a ridge board, while the bottom ends are tied together by the ceiling joist, forming a rigid triangular structure. A horizontal timber support, called a purlin, may be used to brace the rafters if they are likely to bend under the weight of the roof covering.

At a gable end of a brick-built house the ridge board and wall plates, and possibly the purlins as well, extend through the brickwork to provide fixing points for the bargeboard.

For an overhanging gable, rafters are usually fixed outside the wall on extended wall plates and ridge board.

Intermediate supports may be fitted between the inner and outer rafters, with a soffit board fitted to finish the underside **(1)**. The shaped bargeboard is nailed to the outside rafters to cover the ends of the battens or sub-roof used for fixing the shingles, and is set slightly proud of the top face of the battens to tilt the roof covering at the edge. This is to direct water away from the face of the board. A fascia molding is usually applied at the top of the board under the overhanging edge of the roof covering.

In wood-frame houses, the bargeboard may be nailed directly to the side wall in order to cover roof sheathing boards **(2)** or it may be cantilevered in a boxed-out structure **(3)**.

Components of a gable roof
1 Common rafter
2 Wall plate
3 Ridge board
4 Ceiling joist
5 Purlin
6 Bargeboard
7 Intermediate support
8 Fascia molding
9 Finial
10 Soffit

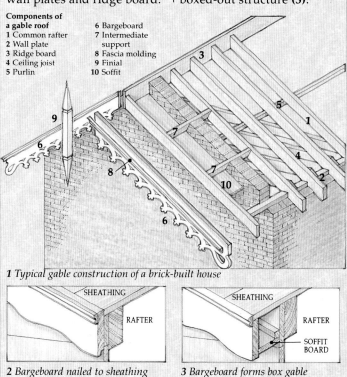

1 Typical gable construction of a brick-built house

SHEATHING

RAFTER

2 Bargeboard nailed to sheathing

SHEATHING

RAFTER

SOFFIT BOARD

3 Bargeboard forms box gable

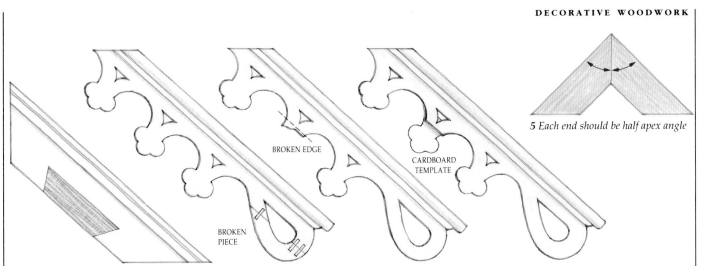

1 *Undercut the ends of the patch* 2 *Reinforce joint with dowels* 3 *Plane broken edge square* 4 *Mark planed edge on template*

5 *Each end should be half apex angle*

BROKEN EDGE

BROKEN PIECE

CARDBOARD TEMPLATE

REPAIRING A BARGEBOARD

Victorian and Edwardian bargeboards were made from soft-wood and finished with paint. Repainting the bargeboards is all too often omitted from general redecoration because of their height from the ground. Nevertheless, it's important to maintain the paintwork regularly, as the boards are in an exposed position and can weather badly.

If you have a decorative bargeboard that has decayed, it is worth making the effort to repair it in preference to fitting a cheaper, plain replacement. Try to make repairs *in situ* – but if the wood is beyond repair, remove it and make a new bargeboard to the old pattern.

Removing a bargeboard

Unless you have a single-story house, working on a bargeboard is a tricky oper-ation because of the height. Most bargeboards are large and awkward to handle, so it generally takes two people to remove them.

Always work from a safe platform, such as a staging tower, and make sure it is stable and well secured. If you are not confident when working at heights, call in a professional.

Nails are normally used to fix the joinery together, although screws may be used where short-grained wood is present.

Locate the nailing points. Then if the bargeboard is fitted with a fascia molding, remove it using a flat bar. Tap the bar between the molding and the board, and lever it off close to the fixings. Further nails may now be revealed, in which case you will need to pry the bargeboard free from the roof timbers.

Fitting a plain patch

If you find a minor patch of rot, rake out the infected wood and treat it with a preservative, a proprietary hardener, and a wood filler. Where the rot has occurred along a plain edge, cut it away back to sound wood. Undercut the ends to give improved holding. Make a patch of matching wood to fit your cutout (1). Fix it in place with an exterior woodworking glue. When it is set, treat the new wood with an exterior primer in readiness for painting.

Repairing a shaped edge

The projecting details of a decorative sawn edge some-times break away because of weak short grain. If that has happened, you may be able to make the repair *in situ*, assuming you still have the piece that has broken away.

Hold the piece in place and mark one or two lines at right angles across the break line. Square the lines across the broken edges of the two parts. Drill 3/8in (10mm) dowel holes at the marked lines or, if you own one, use a biscuit joiner to cut small mortises into the piece and the bargeboard. Then glue the broken piece in place, inserting dowels or biscuits to reinforce the joint (2).

Replacing missing parts

Bargeboards are often decor-ated with a repeat pattern. If part of the pattern has rotted or broken off and is lost, you can replace the missing part.

Take a rubbing of part of the decoration that is still intact, using a wax crayon and plain paper. Tape the paper onto the bargeboard for easier handling. Cut out a cardboard template, following the outline.

Plane the broken edge of the bargeboard square (3). Holding the template behind the bargeboard at the point where the section is missing, draw the position of the planed edge on it (4).

Mark the shape of the new section on a suitably sized board and cut it out with a power jigsaw or a coping saw. If the pattern includes pierced details, drill a hole in the waste so you can insert the saw blade (see MAKING SHAPED CUTOUTS). Smooth the sawn edges. Dowel and glue the new piece in position, and treat it with an exterior primer before priming and finishing with paint.

MAKING A REPLACEMENT

Neglected bargeboards in an exposed position can decay beyond reasonable repair, making replacement necess-ary. Remove the old one as carefully as possible, to keep it in one piece. If it looks too weak to survive removal intact, first record its size and shape with full-size drawings and photographs. Buy new boards of clear, straight-grained wood. The wood may need to be planed or ripped to the correct size.

Lay the original barge-boards or your drawing of them on the new boards and mark out the shape. Check the angle of the mitered ends with a sliding bevel. Each end should be half the angle of the apex (5).

Cut the board to shape with a power jigsaw or a coping saw, including cut-outs. If the boards are bev-eled and carved, use chisels and gouges to shape them (see CARVED WOODWORK).

Bring all the surfaces to a smooth finish, then treat them with an exterior primer, following the maker's instructions. When the sealer is dry, finish all the surfaces with a good paint system and nail the finished boards in place. Sink the nailheads, fill the recesses, and paint to match. Refit the original fascia molding or, if need be, replace it.

BRACKETS

FINIALS

The apex of a gabled roof is often fitted with a turned or square-sided wooden post called a finial that protrudes above the roof line. Sometimes the bottom end of the post extends downward and is detailed in a similar way (the part that projects downward is known as a pendant). The post may also be embellished with decorative wrought ironwork.

Reinstating a finial

Finials and pendants can be cut from flat board or from square-sectioned wood. They may be either nailed to the bargeboard or fixed to structural roof members with the bargeboards butted up to them.

If your roof has a not very interesting stub of wood at its apex, it is probably the remains of a finial that has been sawn off due to decay. If the remaining wood is sound, you can purchase a ready-made turned finial from a specialist supplier or have one made to order. Either dowel and glue the new component or use a screw dowel to fix it to the end of the old wood (1).

You can make square-sectioned finials with sawn decorative profiles yourself, using either a band saw or a powered scroll saw. Mark the profile, based on a suitable pattern, on two adjacent sides of the wood. Cut along the guide lines on one face. Tape the waste in place, then turn the wood over to present the other marked face and cut the second pair of sides (2). Fix the new finial in place, using the same type of fixing used for the original. Treat the finial with an exterior primer, and apply a good paint system.

Finial with pendant fitted at apex

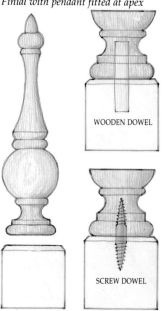

WOODEN DOWEL

SCREW DOWEL

1 Dowel and glue or use screw dowel

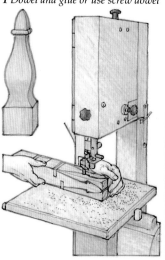
2 Tape waste and cut second sides

BRACKETS *are normally fitted to provide support between horizontal and vertical members, but fretted brackets are often used for decorative rather than functional purposes – to add richness and texture to gables, porches, or door openings.*

Shaped with a saw, quite elaborate brackets are relatively easy to make. Interior examples are generally made of thinner wood than exterior ones. You can have fancy brackets made to order or buy them ready-made from specialist suppliers. Choose a style that suits your house – don't be tempted by a design that is readily available but out of character.

MAKING A BRACKET

Make a pattern by tracing the shape of an existing bracket onto stiff paper. If you don't have a suitable bracket available, draw one to your own design, basing it on a pictorial reference from a library source or catalog. You may perhaps be able to determine the size of the missing original by looking at shadow or nailing marks left on the woodwork. If you need to produce a number of brackets, make a template. Transfer the shape of the pattern onto plywood, cut it to shape with a jigsaw or coping saw, and smooth the edge with sandpaper.

Prepare straight-grained, clear wood to the size and thickness required. If need be, glue several boards together to make up the thickness, using interior or exterior woodworking glue as appropriate. Mark out the shape of the bracket on the wood, positioning the pattern so that it follows the direction of the grain (1). This avoids short weak grain that can break easily (2).

Cut the bracket to shape, using a power jigsaw or a band saw. Finish the cut edges with a spokeshave, plane, or files, as appropriate. Use screws in preference to nails, which

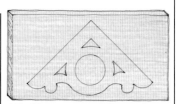
1 Position pattern to follow grain

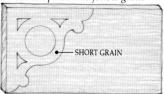
SHORT GRAIN

2 Short weak grain can break easily

may split the ends. Drill countersunk clearance holes for suitably sized screws.

Fitting a bracket

Hold the bracket in position, and mark the position of the screw holes with an awl. Drill appropriately sized pilot holes in the adjoining woodwork. If the holes are set at an angle, use the bracket as a guide for the drill. Apply caulk to the joining faces of the bracket, then fix it in place with galvanized screws. Fill the countersunk holes with glued wooden plugs. When set, trim the plugs to the contour of the bracket and apply a primer. Finish the new work with paint, making sure that the end grain is well covered.

Fretted and pieced brackets help support the porch roof

Decorative wooden brackets
1 Fretted porch bracket with spindles
2 Fretted porch brackets
3 Molded and pieced exterior consoles
4 Carved console

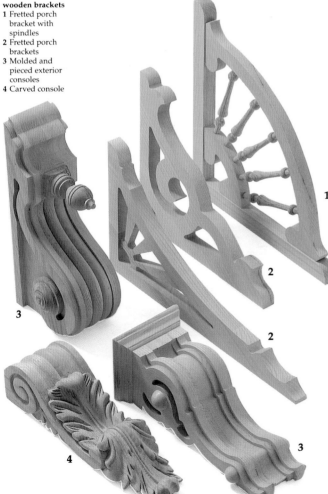

Wooden consoles decorate the soffit

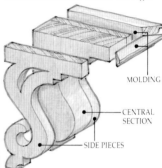

MOLDING

CENTRAL SECTION

SIDE PIECES

Console construction

CONSOLES

Consoles are pieced or carved solid-wood brackets. They were commonly used as an exterior feature under soffits in imitation of the stone corbels used in Italianate architecture. Italianate houses became popular in America during the second half of the nineteenth century, and are known as "American bracket style."

Wooden consoles are also used as interior features and may be found under mantel shelves, in door openings, or supporting beams. Many designs are available in softwoods and hardwoods from specialist suppliers.

Maintaining consoles

Both interior and exterior consoles are likely to suffer from overpainting, which obliterates the detail or crisp edges of the decoration. Where this has occurred, use a chemical stripper to soften and clean off the build-up of paint. When clean and dry, repaint the wood.

Making a pieced console

Exterior consoles exposed to the weather can develop serious decay. If the damage cannot be successfully treated with a preservative and repaired with wood filler, then you should make a new one.

Make a pattern for the profile, based on another console. Pieced consoles comprise a central section of thicker wood sandwiched between decorative scrolls or assembled side pieces made of thinner wood.

If the central section is to stand proud of the side pieces or the side pieces are to protrude beyond the central section, make a second pattern from the first, increasing or reducing the size as required.

Mark out the profiles on wood prepared to the correct thickness and cut them to shape. Smooth the edges. Pin and glue the side pieces to the center piece, with the back and top edges flush. Cut a suitable decorative molding to size with the meeting ends mitered. Pin and glue the molding around the front and side edges of the top part of the console.

Exterior wooden consoles are usually painted; interior ones may be either painted or stained and varnished. Apply a wood preservative and the finish to an exterior console before fitting it; an interior console can be finished after fitting. Fix the bracket with countersunk screws. Fill the holes with wooden plugs and trim to shape. If the console is already painted, finish the plugs to match.

BALUSTRADES

WOODEN PORCHES, VERANDAS AND BALCONIES *are delightful features that became nearly ubiquitous in the nineteenth century. Many Victorian and turn-of-the-century houses have porches in a variety of configurations. Designed to provide shade or shelter, or a vantage point for a pleasing view, they also serve as a link between house and yard. With their turned or slatted balusters, they add charm and character to a building.*

Fretted vase-shaped balusters produce attractive apertures

Ornate fretted softwood balusters

Balustrade with turned balusters

BALUSTERS

Slats and balusters – which simultaneously give a sense of security and allow air to flow – are often used decoratively, having shaped edges that in turn make shapes of the gaps between them. Sometimes cutouts within the width of the balusters add to the decorative effect.

Normally the top ends of the balusters are nailed to the underside of the handrail, which may be grooved to receive them, and are either fixed or jointed to a horizontal rail at the bottom.

If a flat baluster is broken or missing, it is usually a straightforward matter to make a replacement. Make a pattern from a sound identical baluster and cut a new one to match. Treat the new wood with a wood preservative, insuring that the porous end grain is well covered. Paint the surfaces with primer and, when it is dry, nail the new baluster in place. Fill the nail holes and apply a paint finish. For repairs to turned balusters, see WOODEN STAIR REPAIRS.

CARVED WOODWORK

CARVING *is a method for shaping and decorating wood using special chisels and gouges. The techniques are centuries old and have been applied to wooden artifacts and furniture as well as internal and external features of houses. Stylistically, woodcarving can range from abstract or naturalistic low-relief work to more sculpted high-relief or fully three-dimensional features.*

The techniques for carving low-relief decorative motifs are relatively easy to master, but carving in the round and high-relief work call for a keen eye and a well-developed sense of form. All early carved work was hand-cut, and repeat patterns often display subtle differences in shape. It is this human touch that makes early work more interesting and valuable than the machine-cut versions of recent times.

With practice you can undertake woodcarving yourself – but if the features are particularly ornate or important, it's best to have the work carried out by a professional. You may also be able to use ready-made carved woodwork available from specialist suppliers.

Decorative beam with relief-carved mythical beasts and painted motifs

A porch made of oak and decorated with low-relief carving

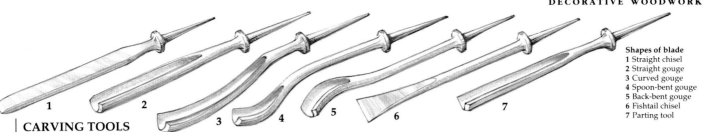

Shapes of blade
1 Straight chisel
2 Straight gouge
3 Curved gouge
4 Spoon-bent gouge
5 Back-bent gouge
6 Fishtail chisel
7 Parting tool

CARVING TOOLS

Woodcarving is so versatile that generations of craftsmen have developed hundreds of different tools to meet their needs. The blades are made in a variety of length shapes, cross-section profiles, and cutting-edge widths. There are five basic length shapes: straight, curved, spoon-bent (also known as front-bent), back-bent, and fishtail (or spade) tools. Eighteen cross-section profiles are available, most of them in a range of sizes from $^{1}/_{16}$in (2mm) to 2in (50mm).

The principal categories of carving tools are chisels, gouges, and parting tools.

Chisels are ground with a square or skewed cutting edge and are used for general shaping, cutting straight lines, detailing and finishing.

Gouges are the main tools for shaping. They constitute the largest group of carving tools, having a comprehensive range of shallow to deep sweeps (curved profiles). All the sweeps are true radius curves except for the veiner type, which has straighter sides. The larger gouges are used for taking the wood off quickly, the medium-size and smaller ones for general and fine shaping.

Parting tools are V-shaped in section and are made in three profiles. They are used for outlining, lettering, and detail work.

A basic set of carving tools might comprise a range of gouges, one or two straight chisels, a skew chisel, a parting tool, and possibly a veining tool for fine work. You will need a round-headed carver's mallet, which is heavier and more versatile than a carpenter's mallet. A selection of flat, round, and half-round rasps and files is desirable for shaping and finishing sculptural work. Rotary rasps held in a flexible drive or in the chuck of an electric drill are handy for shaping. Punches are used for adding texture to the surface and for refining detail, but are not essential for most work.

Carved and painted Phoenix motif

Using the tools

Carving tools can be driven by hand pressure or with a mallet. When using hand pressure for lighter work, grip the handle with one hand and steady the blade and the thrust of the tool with the other (1). Use the mallet for hard woods or larger cuts. Hold the carving tool low down the handle, with the mallet in your driving hand (2).

Carving tools have fine cutting edges and are prone to damage if driven into cross-grain hardwood. When a vertical cut on a line is required (known as setting in), use a small deep gouge or parting tool to carve a groove adjacent to the line. The remaining waste will then cut away cleanly with little effort (3).

The tools will readily cut across the grain. In fact, cross-grain cutting is generally preferred for roughing in the shape – since there is less chance of the grain tearing ahead of the tool or of the blade wandering off, which can easily happen when cutting with the grain.

Follow the grain for fine finishing cuts. When cutting at a tangent to the grain (if you are carving a groove around a circular motif, for example), work in the direction that will give a smooth cut on the motif side (4).

Use curved gouges to work the bottom of hollows where a straight tool would tend to dig into the wood (5). Spoon-bent tools are used for similar but more detailed work (6).

HOLDING THE WORK

Unless the wood is being cut *in situ* (when making a patch repair, for example), the work has to be held securely. Specialized vices, pivoting clamps, and a screw-in holding device known as a carver's screw are helpful. However, they are by no means essential as you can use most woodworking and metalworking vices and clamps quite effectively.

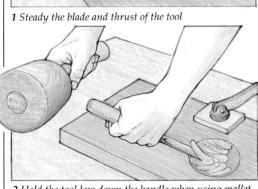

1 Steady the blade and thrust of the tool

2 Hold the tool low down the handle when using mallet

3 Cut waste

WASTE

WASTE

4 Cut in the right direction

5 Use a bent gouge for hollows   *6 Use a spoon-bent gouge for details*

LINENFOLD CARVING

LINENFOLD IS A TRADITIONAL PATTERN *for low-relief carving thought to have been introduced into England from the continent of Europe in the early fifteenth century. The design, which was inspired by the folds and creases of draped cloth, was probably ecclesiastical in origin. In England it became a popular decorative motif for frame-and-panel work in the Tudor era. Although the style is now almost synonymous with the oak wall paneling of the period, it was used for other frame-and-panel work, such as doors, beds and chests, too.*

At the time of early colonial settlements, the style was still a part of the woodcarver's repertoire, and with the Gothic revival of the Victorian era it became popular once again. Medieval examples were simple – yet, although following conventional forms, craftsmen produced a marvelous variety of designs. Later versions were bolder and more stylized, the Victorian examples being more regular and mechanical in feel. The early twentieth-century Tudor revival also saw the reappearance of some linenfold carving.

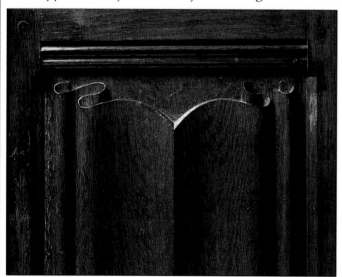

Detail of machine-made oak linenfold panel

CARVING LINENFOLD PANELS

If a carved linenfold panel is beyond repair, you can make a replacement yourself or have one made by a professional woodcarver. You will need a full-size drawing of the face, ends, and cross section of the panel. Use a profile gauge (an adjustable template with metal pins or plastic blades) to record the profile of the carving. The addition of shading will help you visualize the final three-dimensional shape. Note on the drawing the full thickness of the panel (including the folds) and the thickness of the edge.

Shaping the folds

Order a panel of straight-grained clear wood of the appropriate species, cut and planed to size. If you are a beginner and are planning to use a relatively expensive wood such as oak, practice the technique on cheaper wood first.

Set a marking gauge to the depth of the linenfold profile and mark the depth line on the edges all around. Reset the gauge and mark out the width of the border on the face **(1)**.

Using a power router or rebate plane, remove the waste from the border **(2)**. If the panel is beveled on the back to fit a groove, plane it down. Make a tracing-paper pattern of the end profile, and use it to mark the shape on each end of the raised part of the panel. Using a power router or a plough plane or multi-plane, make a series of parallel grooves in the center of the hollows. Adjust the depth of cut as required. Use the grooves to guide a round molding plane to shape the hollows **(3)**. If traditional wooden molding planes are not available, use a power router fitted with a core-box bit or a multi-plane fitted with a flute cutter. Reset either tool as required **(4)**. Use a block plane to round over the convex parts of the profile **(5)**. The inevitable faceted surface of the ridges and hollows can be smoothed with a sharp gouge of an appropriate sweep or a shaped scraper.

When smoothing the surfaces of the folds, it's best to avoid using sandpapers wrapped around shaped blocks – since you may lose the crisp shaping and dust can block the pores of open-grained woods such as oak.

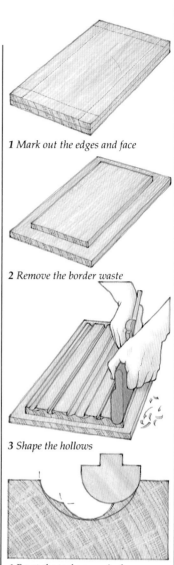

1 Mark out the edges and face

2 Remove the border waste

3 Shape the hollows

4 Reset the tool as required

5 Round over convex parts

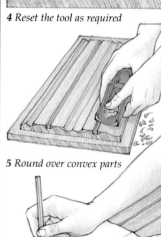

6 Mark around the pattern

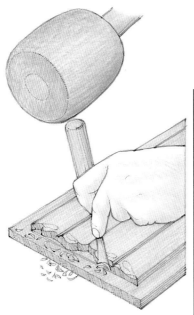

7 *Cut up to the end-shape line*

Marking the ends

Make a tracing paper pattern of the ends of the folds, taking it from the front-view drawing. Cut the pattern following the outside shape. Place it down flat, level with the ends, and mark around it (6). You will need to judge the shape by eye where the paper pattern does not touch the surface.

Draw in the other lines that complete the end shape freehand. In order to insure symmetry, work one half to a good shape and trace it onto a piece of tracing paper pressed into the contours of the folds. Use a soft lead pencil, so that when the tracing is reversed on the other half the graphite will be offset onto the wood as the line is traced over.

Shaping the ends

First, use a small gouge and chisel to set in the outside shape of the end. Cut up to the end-shape line – but stop the depth of the cut about $1/16$in (2mm) shy of the rabbited border (7). This is to avoid marring the surface with cut marks that could show when the ends are undercut at a later stage of carving.

8 *Cut a groove across the grain*

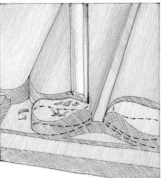

9 *Make vertical cuts on the line*

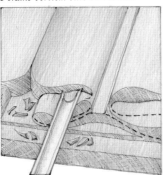

10 *Trim with horizontal cuts*

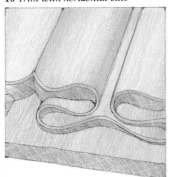

11 *Undercut the folds*

Cutting the folds

Using a deep narrow gouge or parting tool, cut a groove across the grain on the waste side of the uppermost fold line (8). The depth of the cut has to follow the contour of the lower fold, using the end guidelines as your reference. Set in the shape accurately with vertical cuts, using a shallow-sweep gouge (9). Trim out the waste carefully with horizontal cuts, working from the end (10).

Before shaping the lower folds, re-mark the guidelines that have been removed with the waste. As the surface is now stepped, you will need to draw them in freehand. To help visualize the shape, mark one cut end before cutting the next. Shape these folds in the same way.

Trim the background of the panel flush and undercut the folds in order to give the appearance of a thin edge (11). Finish the edge with a slight bevel trimmed with a small chisel or gouge, taking care to keep the thickness even. The toolwork should leave the surface smooth and crisp, so that sanding is not needed. Finish the panel in an appropriate way to blend with its surroundings.

Framed door with linenfold panels

CARVING IN THE ROUND

C ARVINGS IN THE ROUND *are fully three-dimensional pieces that are intended to be seen from all sides. They are not as common as relief carvings in most houses but may be used for finials, pendants, stair newel posts, brackets, or overmantel ornamentation. Some may be turned shapes that are then carved and decorated with floral motifs. The subject matter for sculptural carvings can be inspired by either naturalistic or fanciful forms.*

If original carved work has been stripped out in an attempt to modernize the interior, you may want to re-create the missing details. Take note of the style of ornamentation appropriate for the period, and seek out references on which to base your design from libraries and from houses of a similar type. You can then either commission a professional carver or, if the work is not too demanding, attempt it yourself.

Carved doorhood console

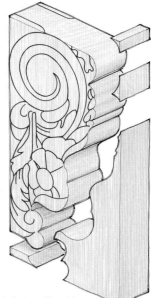

1 Cut profile with a saw

2 Rough in the shape　　*3 Shape the contours*　　*4 Refine the shape*

Choosing the wood

Virtually any wood can be carved, but some species are more difficult to carve than others. The best woods are those with a fine, even grain. Linden, a favorite of the master carver Grinling Gibbons, is a light-colored hardwood that carves and finishes extremely well. Softwoods such as ponderosa pine, yellow pine, and sitka spruce carve well, too.

If the work has to match an existing feature, then the choice is made for you. However, many tropical hardwoods are now classified as endangered species: so if a tropical hardwood such as mahogany was used for the original feature, make sure the new wood comes from a sustainable source.

If you cannot find a single piece of wood large enough for a particular carving, one solution is to glue sections of wood together. Gluing sections together also helps reduce the risk of shrinkage problems, such as splitting, which are often encountered with large or thick timbers of partially seasoned wood.

Though it's possible to carve "green" (unseasoned) wood, there's a much greater risk of splitting. Reducing the bulk of the timber and hollowing out the center helps to promote even drying out – but it is best to use seasoned wood whenever possible.

Setting out

A good eye for form and well-developed drawing and craft skills are required for carving in the round. It is essential to have a clear idea of the shape to be cut, and preparatory sketches and elevation drawings will help you to achieve satisfactory results. Some carvers also make a maquette (small model) so that they can see the shape and take scaled measurements from it.

Make full-scale drawings of the form, showing the front and side elevations and possibly the back and plan views too. You can either use printed graph paper or draw a grid with 1in (25mm) squares over your design. Use carbon paper to transfer the design to the faces of a prepared block of wood.

Basic shaping

Although you can use a gouge, it is usually quicker to do the rough shaping with a band saw or a powered scroll saw. Saw around the profiles marked on the faces of the block. With some shapes, only one profile may be cut in this way (1).

When two faces are cut, the waste from the first is likely to carry the profile for the other. Temporarily tape the waste offcuts back in position, then cut the second profile with the saw.

After sawing, remove the waste and draw in the outlines of the shapes that fall within the shaped block as a guide for carving.

Carving the shape

Begin to rough in the shape using a straight medium-sweep gouge and a mallet (2). As the work progresses, use suitably shaped smaller and flatter gouges to shape the contoured planes and hollows (3). Keep viewing the work from all sides. Refine the modeling and add textures and small details, using small gouges, chisels, parting tools, punches, and files (4). You may want to retain the tool marks to create an interesting texture. Otherwise, take the surface to a smooth finish with progressively finer sandpaper, folding the paper to finish fine inside details.

CHAPTER FIFTEEN

WOOD FLOORING

EARLY WOODEN FLOORS *used random-size hand-cut boards of oak, elm, pine, or fir. The boards were usually wide and of varying thickness. It is not uncommon to find thinner ones resting on packing over a joist, or the underside of thicker ones trimmed with an adze to make the floor level. In the eighteenth century the size of floorboards began to be more regular. Boards about 4in (100mm) wide were used in better-quality houses in order to avoid shrinkage and distortion problems, while simple houses continued to feature random-width boards. It was not until nearly the mid nineteenth century that the introduction of mechanized production methods made consistent floorboard sizes generally available.*

Elaborate early houses often had tongue-and-groove pine floorboards. They were usually left unfinished, but were sometimes painted, in some cases to resemble more expensive hardwoods. Other materials were imitated in some painted finishes, including marble, stone and slate set out in geometric patterns. Sometimes the boards were simply finished with a plain matte color. Floor coverings of carpet, painted cloth, or matting were also used. Painted canvas floor cloths in a wide variety of colors and patterns were in use from the mid eighteenth to the mid nineteenth century. As a cheaper alternative to carpeting, sometimes painted floors were decorated with attractive free-hand or stenciled designs.

Parquet, a flooring made from strips or blocks of wood laid in a geometrical pattern, appealed to the Victorians because of its decorative nature. Since it was fairly expensive to lay, initially its use was largely confined to better-quality houses. Nevertheless, parquet became increasingly popular and it retained its popularity into the twentieth century, and up to our time in new, prefabricated forms.

The pale-colored walls harmonize well with the unfinished pine boards

The dark stained and polished floorboards suit this period interior

TYPES OF FLOORINGS

A WOOD FLOOR, *like other features and materials in a period house, derives its character from the patina of age. Provided the material has been well maintained, the inevitable scrapes, wear, light stains, and all-over mellow tone combine to give an acceptable – indeed, often desirable – appearance that is worth preserving. Well-worn boards in high-traffic areas such as halls and doorways tell a story, and so long as they are not structurally weak they don't need to be replaced.*

Nevertheless, age and neglect can take their toll, and there are times when the introduction of "new" wood is unavoidable in order to preserve the floor.

MATCHING OLD WOOD
Always try to obtain the appropriate species of wood when making a patch repair or replacing part of an old floor. This may not always be easy, but flooring specialists stock many of the species used traditionally and often keep reclaimed wood for repairs of this kind. It is also worth trying lumberyards, who stock a wide range of woods from which boards can be cut.

New and even resawn old wood will not have the mellow color of the original, so you may find that the replacement has to be toned down with a wood stain, or needs bleaching if a lighter color is required.

TYPES OF WOOD
Floors are mostly constructed from softwoods, such as yellow-heart pine, Columbian pine, pitch pine, spruce, and fir. However, a number of hardwoods are used too, particularly for the parquet types that are laid on a sub-floor. Hardwood species used for flooring range from blond and dark-brown woods – including maple, ash, beech, elm, oak, walnut, and teak – to redder woods such as cherry, mahogany, utile, and jarrah.

Wood usually changes color as it ages, which can make identification difficult. If you are not sure of the species used for your floor, take a sample to a timber supplier, who should be able to identify it for you. If the underside of a board does not show the original color, plane off a shaving to reveal the true color beneath.

Handsome wide elm boards

Herringbone-pattern parquet floor

ASSESSING REPAIRS
- ● Easy even for beginners.
- ■ Fairly difficult. Good practical skills required.
- ▲ Difficult. Hire a professional.

WOOD FLOORING

Poor finish
An unsuitable or worn finish spoils the appearance of a wooden floor.
- ● Clean the surface (pages 197-8).
- ● Apply a suitable finish (pages 196-8).

Squeaking boards
Weak nailing can cause loose or warped boards.
- ● Fix with nails or screws (page 193).

Damaged flooring
Patched or rough wood may make repairs necessary.
- ● Sand the surface (page 196).
- ● Fill gaps (page 192).
- ● Repair splits (page 193).
- ● Treat minor insect infestation yourself (page 194).
- ▲ Have rot or serious infestation treated (pages 194-5).
- ■ Lift and replace boards (page 192).
- ■ Repair parquet floors (page 193).

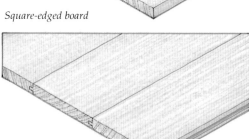
Square-edged board

Tongue-and-groove board

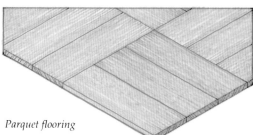
Tongue-and-groove strip flooring

Parquet flooring

TYPES OF BOARD
You can buy wood flooring in the form of boards, strips, and parquet. Boards come in long lengths and are planed to a finished thickness of about 3/4in (18mm) or more. Their width can vary from 4 to 12in (100 to 300mm), and the edges may either be planed square (plain-edged) or tongued and grooved.

Strip flooring is normally made from hardwoods in narrow tongue-and-groove widths of about 3in (75mm). Strips for laying directly onto joists have a nominal thickness of 1in (25mm). Thinner versions are made for laying on a sub-floor.

Parquet is made in various forms. The thicker versions are sometimes referred to as woodblock flooring. These have plain-edged or tongue-and-groove blocks approximately 3in (75mm) wide and 9 to 12in (225 to 300mm) long, with a nominal thickness of 3/4in (18mm). The thinner versions of parquet are made from strips about 1 to 2in (25 to 50mm) wide and 9 to 12in (225 to 300mm) long. You can also buy parquet panels, with short strips of wood bonded to a backing sheet. These are produced in various configurations and are laid like tiles.

FIXING METHODS

SELECTING BOARDS

Because it is a porous material, wood expands and contracts as it reacts to changes in its moisture content. The amount of "movement" also depends on the species of the wood and how the wood is cut from the log. The latter is a particularly important consideration for flooring.

Most logs, for reasons of economy, are flat-sawn (1). This produces wide boards with an attractive sweeping figure. However, they are prone to warping, splitting, and uneven wear. When boards are cut in this way, the annual growth rings run more or less across the width of the board or from edge to edge. Because wood shrinks more in the direction of the growth rings than across them, this leads to a greater reduction on the width of a board than on the thickness. Also, shrinkage is uneven, since the "longer" growth rings shrink more than those on the heart side (the side nearest to the center of the tree), which causes the board to distort or cup (2). The movement of the wood can cause nails to loosen; if the board is securely held, the movement may make it split.

Using boards that have been converted by the

Traditional log-cutting saw

quarter-sawn or rift-sawn method overcomes these problems. The log is cut more or less radially (3). This produces boards known as edge-grain timber with short even-length growth rings that appear as lines on the face sides. Since shrinkage is minimal across the growth rings, the effect on the width of the board is negligible.

Quarter-sawn boards are more expensive than flat-sawn ones, since the method of milling is more wasteful, but their greater stability and resistance to wear far outweigh the extra cost.

To check the cut of your old boards, look at the end grain (4). Always choose quarter-sawn boards for repairs, unless you are matching the figure of old flat-sawn floorboards.

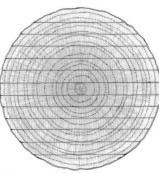

1 Flat-sawn boards

2 Shrinkage causes boards to cup

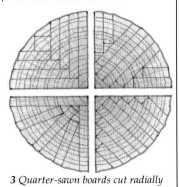

3 Quarter-sawn boards cut radially

4 Look at end grain to check cut

WOODEN FLOORING IS USUALLY FIXED *with nails or glue, or both. The method will depend on the type, quality, and profile of the flooring. The profile can be plain-edged, shiplapped (rebated), or tongued and grooved. Where nails are used as a feature, try to match their type and spacing when making repairs.*

PLAIN-EDGED AND REBATED BOARDS

The most common method for fixing plain-edged (plank) and rebated boards is to nail them through the face, using cut flooring nails. These are rectangular in section and are driven in with the wider face parallel to the grain. The square-cut tip is designed to sever the fibers as it punches through the wood – instead of parting the fibers, causing the wood to split, as can happen with pointed round wire nails.

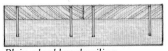

Plain-edged board nailing

Rebated board nailing

TONGUE-AND-GROOVE FLOORBOARDS

Tongue-and-groove boards are blind-nailed through the tongue. The grooved edge is held by the tongue of the previous board. Flooring nails are driven in at an angle of approximately 45 degrees. A nail punch must be used to sink the nails, as it is easy to mar the edges with a hammer. Professional floorlayers now use a powered nail gun, which drives the nails in quickly and neatly at a set angle.

Tongue-and-groove board nailing

PARQUET FLOORING

In England, the thicker type of parquet flooring was laid using hot bitumen. After the pieces of wood had been cut to shape, each piece was dipped in the hot adhesive and laid in place. Once the bitumen had set, the surface of the wood was planed and scraped level ready for finishing. In the United States, blind nailing was more common; today the usual method involves a cold adhesive spread over the sub-floor with a serrated-edge trowel. The wood blocks are then set in it.

Thinner parquet flooring is usually pinned or glued. If individual parquet strips need to be replaced, apply a flooring adhesive and fix with ³⁄₄in (20mm) dowel pins through the face. Sink the nailheads and fill them with a colored filler. To avoid splitting close-grained hardwoods, drill holes for the nails before fixing. The backing fabric of parquet panels provides a generous surface area for gluing, so they do not require pinning.

FLOATING FLOORS

Modern woodstrip "floating floors" are constructed from thin tongued-and-grooved hardwood boards. These are not secured to the sub-floor in any way, but are usually glued together edge to edge.

Although it isn't a traditional type of wood flooring, the style and quality of a floating floor can make it acceptable in a period house.

REPAIRING WOODEN FLOORS

WOODEN FLOORS *are subjected to considerable daily wear and tear, which may ultimately necessitate repairs. However, the patina of wood improves with age and a floor only looks old if it bears visible signs of its past. So, before undertaking repairs, consider whether there is a case for preserving the floor in its present state, especially if it contributes significantly to the character of the house.*

Gaps between boards, surface damage, splits, and insect infestation are the most frequently encountered problems that mar old floors. Not all of these will need attention if you are planning to cover the floor, but they can look unattractive if exposed.

DEALING WITH GAPS

As well as being unsightly, gaps between plain-edged floorboards admit drafts. Gaps are the result of shrinkage, usually caused by the introduction of a modern heating system. Provided that the wood has stabilized, they can be filled.

From the point of view of appearance, the most satisfactory solution is to lift all the boards and re-lay them so they fit snugly together, filling the space remaining at the end of the operation with an additional board or two. However, lifting and re-laying the boards demands considerable effort and can cause further damage to the floor – so it's best to have the work done by a tradesman unless you have some experience yourself, and only to have an old wood floor re-laid if absolutely necessary.

To fill wide gaps without lifting the boards, use strips of matching wood ripped to a slight taper **(1)** on a table saw. Not all the gaps will be the same size, and they may not all be parallel through-out the length of the floor. So you will need to make the strips slightly wider than the gaps and plane them down to fit.

Before cutting the strips, scrape the edges of the floorboards to clean them. You can make an ideal scraper tool with an angled end from a strip of steel. The angled end should be ground to a 1-in-20 taper **(2)**; the taper that you cut on the wooden strips needs to be the same.

Apply some woodworking glue to the angled face of the wooden strip and tap the strip into place. Wipe off the surplus glue and, when set, plane the top edge flush with the surface of the floor. If need be, apply wood stain.

For narrow gaps, use a flexible wood filler. Clean the gaps with an old saw blade and vacuum out loose material. Press the filler into place with a filling knife. To keep filler off the surface of the boards, lay strips of masking tape on each side of the gaps. When set, sand the filler to a smooth finish.

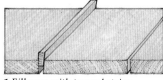

1 Fill gaps with tapered strips

2 Make a scraper tool from steel strip

1-in-20 TAPER

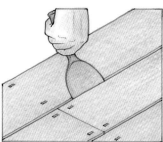

1 Lever up the end of the board

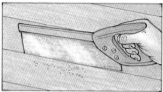

3 Saw at a shallow angle

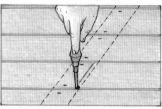

5 Cut board level with the joist

2 Cut the tongues to release board

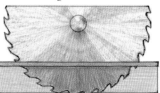

4 Set depth of cut to board thickness

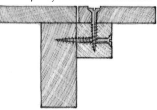

6 Screw wooden block to side of joist

LIFTING FLOORBOARDS

To lift plain-edged boards, insert a wide-bladed bolster chisel into the gap between the boards, close to the end. Start to lever up one edge of the board, trying to avoid crushing the edge of the one next to it **(1)**. Change sides, and repeat the operation to ease the end free. Move to the next nailing point along the board, and do the same again. Place a scrap of wood under the loose end to help the board pull free as you continue working along it.

To lift a damaged tongued and grooved board it is necessary to cut through the tongue on one or both sides of the board to be removed **(2)**. You can use a back saw or circular saw. If you use a back saw, the gap between the boards can serve as a guideline or you can tack a straight strip of scrap along the cut line to guide the saw. Make the cut at a shallow angle **(3)**. If using a circular saw, fit it with a carbide-tipped blade and fix a guide strip to the floor against which to run the baseplate. Position the strip so the

sawcut will be just clear of the adjacent board. Set the depth of cut to the thickness of the board **(4)**. Pry out the cut board with a wide chisel. If you need to lift the neighboring floorboards, they can now be levered up.

Before inserting the replacement, you will need to plane off the tongue to allow the board to drop into place. Fix the new board in position with finishing nails driven through the face.

When a section of board needs to be replaced, it is often simplest to remove the whole board and saw off the damaged part. However, if the board is continuous and is trapped at each end, you may have no alternative but to cut it to length *in situ*. To locate the joist nearest to the proposed cutting point, insert a knife blade between the boards. Drill a hole next to the side of the joist, insert a power jigsaw and cut the board level with the joist **(5)**. Screw a wooden block to the side of the joist in order to provide support for the new floorboard **(6)**.

DEALING WITH SPLITS

Splits occur where the fibers of the wood have parted, either at the end of a board or within the face, depending on the grain structure. They are usually caused by shrinkage but sometimes occur where nails have been driven in. Unless they are disfiguring or likely to cause splinters, they don't necessarily require attention.

If the boards do need to be repaired, glue the parts that have split (if need be, applying pressure by inserting wooden wedges between the boards); or use wood filler if the wood is stable and not liable to splinter.

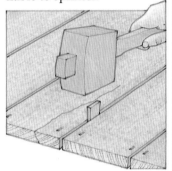

Use a wedge to apply pressure

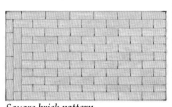

Square brick pattern

Diagonal brick pattern

Herringbone pattern

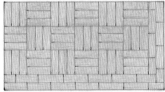

Square basket pattern

Diagonal basket pattern

PARQUET FLOORS

Parquet flooring is usually made from quality materials and, unless neglected, does not require major repairs. However, sections of a thick parquet floor laid on a concrete base can lift due to expansion of the wood. This may be caused by deterioration of the vapor barrier beneath the floor or by water that has been allowed to soak into the wood from leaking plumbing.

Eliminating the water leak and letting the wood dry out while pressed down flat with a weighted board may effect a satisfactory solution, but the area that has lifted may have to be refixed and will no doubt need to be refinished.

If the source of moisture is from below, you should consult a contractor. It is possible that the entire floor will have to be taken up and a new vapor barrier applied before the blocks can be re-laid. If you re-lay the floor yourself, number the blocks in sequence with chalk or a wax crayon before taking them up.

Patch repairs

If individual blocks get damaged, they can be replaced with blocks of matching wood cut to fit. First drill out most of the old wood, using a large drill bit, then trim out the remainder of the waste with a chisel. If the blocks are tongued and grooved, you will need to remove the tongues so the new blocks can be dropped into place. Spread flooring adhesive into the recesses, and tap the blocks down with a mallet and block of scrap wood.

A neglected thin parquet floor generally has a number of loose, warped, or missing strips. If it is laid on a wood sub-floor, refix loose strips with woodworking glue and fine nails, which must be set below the surface.

It may be possible to fix a slightly warped strip in the same way. If it is too badly distorted to respond to this treatment, pry the strip out and dampen it with water, then press it flat between two pieces of plywood held in a vice. Let the strip dry out completely before you fix it back in place.

Missing strips should be replaced with boards of the same species, bought from a flooring specialist or lumberyard. Unless you have machine tools for planing it, have the wood cut to size with the dimensions slightly larger all around than those of the finished piece. Leave the wood to acclimatize in the room for several weeks.

Make a paper pattern of the recess and transfer the dimensions to the wood. Trim it to size with a back saw and plane. Use a miter box for sawing the 45-degree angle needed on end pieces for parquet floors that have a diagonal pattern. Glue and nail the new strips in place. Then plane them flush with the surrounding wood, taking care not to mar the surface. Finish the new strips to match the rest of the floor.

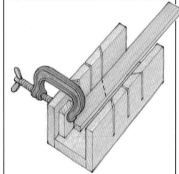

Use a miter box to cut the angle

CURING SQUEAKING BOARDS

Over a period of time, the flexing of the floor or expansion and contraction of the timber may loosen the floorboard nails. It is the resulting movement of the wood against the nails or against the neighboring boards that produces the typical irritating squeak.

The simplest cure for a face-nailed floor is to drive the floorboard nails in deeper with a nail punch, which allows the tapered edges of the nails to grip the wood more securely. However, this may not be a lasting solution. If the problem persists, use either larger or ring-shank nails. The latter are designed to give a better grip, but are not traditional and require clearance holes drilled through the boards. Fill any redundant holes with matching wood filler.

If the boards can't be renailed satisfactorily (for example, because of twisting or bowing), use countersunk stainless-steel woodscrews. Bury the heads of the screws deep enough to cover them with filler or with matching wooden plugs. Dampening the wood thoroughly before fixing will help it to "give" as the boards are screwed down.

INFESTATION

WOOD ROT, *which is associated with damp conditions, and woodboring-insect attack are the most common causes of damage to structural timbers and flooring, but the information given here applies to woodwork throughout the house. At the first sign of infestation, inspect the wood closely and take action to eradicate the problem before further damage is done.*

CHECKING FOR INSECT ATTACK

Just the mention of termites is enough to inspire fear in most owners of old houses. The damp, dark environments so characteristic of old house cellars with their porous fieldstone walls, low hanging beams, and aged timbers are the perfect medium for termites as well as other woodboring insects.

Ironically, termites and the equally destructive carpenter ants are social insects. They organize themselves into colonies, with a division of labor, complete with queens and workers and soldiers. The product of their labor, however, certainly doesn't qualify as sociable behavior, at least by human standards.

In the forest, termites tend to establish themselves in dead trees that have fallen to the ground. In the wild, they help maintain nature's balance, living on cellulose, the organic substance of which wood is composed. In so doing, they help clear away the old dead growth to make room for the new. In or near houses, they often establish their settlements in chunks of lumber or stumps in the ground, and from such outposts launch their assault on the structure of a house.

Dectecting the visitors

The first task in dealing with an infestation is to detect the presence of the insects. In the case of powder-post beetles, they offer evidence, little piles of sawdust most often seen on the cellar floor.

Carpenter ants are often seen wandering around the living spaces of a house. They are large, black ants with an hourglass shape.

Termites are not so easy to find. They avoid the rays of the sun, so are rarely seen. They bore their way along the grain at the heart of a piece of wood and, as a result, they are usually found only after they have spent years in the house timbers.

Danger signs

Any wood that is flush to the ground can provide termites or other insects easy access. Examine carefully wherever sills, wall cladding, trim, or other wooden exterior elements are near the ground.

The other likely area for infestation is in the cellar.

Probe such danger areas inside and outside the foundation with a screwdriver. If there is a heavy infestation, the tool may slide into the heart of the lumber when you stab it. Inside you may find channels eaten into the wood (called "galleries").

What to do

If the infestation is quite evidently localized, purchase an insecticide at a local houseware or garden center.

If the infestation is more widespread or you are unsure of its seriousness, consult a licensed exterminator.

WOODBORING INSECTS

Seasoned but untreated house timbers cut from hardwood or softwood (particularly the softer sapwood) and some plywoods are prone to attack by woodboring insects. Listed below are the insects that cause most concern.

TERMITES

Termites live in colonies of specialized groups. Although they resemble ants, termites have less well-defined divisions between head, thorax and abdomen; the abdomen is also longer than that of the ant's. The winged varieties of both types are dark in color and have four wings, but they can be distinguished by the difference in wing size. Those of the termite are all the same size, whereas one pair of the ant's wings is larger than the other.

WINGED ADULT

WORKER

SOLDIER

QUEEN

KING

There are three principal types of termites, the most common and damaging being the subterranean species. They measure about 1/4in (6mm) in length, and lives in moist conditions. When they infest wood above ground, they only feed on the interior material, making detection difficult. They also construct earth tunnels in order to reach wood not in contact with the ground, and penetrate weaknesses in masonry to infest house timbers.

Dry-wood termites look similar to the subterranean type but do not require damp underground conditions to survive. They will infest house timbers not in contact with the ground, including furniture and attic structures.

Internal damage due to termite infestation

CARPENTER ANTS

These ants are 1/2in (12mm) or more in length, with segmented bodies. They prefer moist wood. Look for them in the attic, especially if there is evidence that it has been damp.

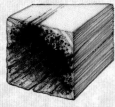

WINGED ADULT   WORKER

POWDER-POST BEETLES

Beetle attack can occur in structural timbers, joinery, and furniture. Adult beetles lay their eggs in crevices in the wood. The developing larvae then burrow through the wood, devouring the tissue and turning it into dust. Generations of larvae may be at work in the wood, which will ultimately collapse. The flight holes are the obvious signs of infestation.

There are three principal types of beetles (collectively known as powder-post beetles). The deathwatch beetle is one of the most common; it is about 1/8in (3mm) in length and usually attacks Douglas fir. The other common type is the true powder-post beetle; which feeds on hardwoods such as oak or ash. The third type, the lead-cable borer, is found only in the Southwest. It is about 1in (25mm) in length and gets its name from its proclivity for chewing lead-lined cables, but it will also attack hardwoods.

DEATH-WATCH BEETLE

TRUE POWDER-POST BEETLE

LEAD-CABLE BORER

WOOD ROT

Wood-rotting fungi need moisture to develop. Consequently, wood that's kept dry is not affected by rot. Rot promoted by damp conditions may force you to remove woodwork such as panelling, which you would normally avoid removing, in order to treat the source of the problem. Check the condition of any supporting structure, and replace it if necessary. Seek expert advice on the cause (poor exterior drainage, a leaking roof, or a plumbing problem) and have it rectified.

You cannot see the fungi themselves, as the parasites are microscopic. An abnormal color is an early sign of too much moisture in or on the wood – perhaps a brownish tone quite different from the rest of the wood, or a whitish, bleached, light gray. The wood has also usually lost its sheen. Decayed areas and healthy ones are seen on the same piece of timber.

Mold fungus under floor covering

Mature fruiting body of dry rot

Surface mold

Common mold can attack wood with a high moisture content. It frequently infects exposed and unprotected wood, such as window and door frames, and it can also break out where the plumbing is leaking or in damp cellars. Mold makes wood darken and become soft and spongy, with horizontal and cross-grain cracks forming.

The fungus on the surface of infected wood displays threadlike strands, which turn from yellow to black. As the fungus develops, a flat greenish-brown fruiting body is formed, from which spores are produced.

Depriving the fungus of moisture inhibits its further growth and stops continued deterioration of the wood. Treating the timber with fungicide should insure that the problem does not recur.

Dry rot

Dry rot, despite its name, is likely to attack wood that is alternately wet and dry. Outbreaks only occur in damp wood in dark unventilated conditions.

Once established, dry rot invades dry timber by conducting moisture through a network of fine tubular strands. These strands can spread very widely – even passing through weaknesses in building materials, including plaster, concrete, brick, and stone – to infect other wood.

It is for this reason that all trace of the fungus has to be eradicated and the surfaces must be treated with a fungicide over a wide area.

You may be able to detect an outbreak of dry rot by the pungent smell of the fungus. Painted wood may exhibit signs of buckling, and the surface may collapse due to

decomposition. The infected wood turns dark brown and, as it shrinks and splits, deep cracks form with and across the grain, breaking the wood up into cubelike pieces.

Dry rot appears as light gray strands with white padlike growths or as gray sheets with patches of yellow or violet covering the surface. A pancake-shaped brown-and-white fruiting body is produced by the mature fungus, from which spores are released to cover surrounding surfaces with a layer of fine rust-red dust.

The fungus can grow at a surprising rate – as much as 6in (150mm) in a month.

DEALING WITH MOLD

First eradicate the cause of the damp. If necessary, cut away structurally weakened wood and replace it with new preservative-treated timber (or treat the new sections of wood after you have installed them). Brush on three generous coats of fungicidal wood preservative. Cover all wood in any surrounding area where moisture may be a problem.

Pressure injection of timber

For the treatment of larger sections of timber *in situ*, such as structural timbers, it is possible to have the wood impregnated using a high-pressure injection system. This specialist treatment uses one-way-valve plastic injectors that are inserted into holes drilled in the vulnerable areas. A special gun is connected that injects the fluid until it fully permeates the cells of the wood.

After treatment each valve is driven into the wood and either capped or filled over. The wood should be left for 14 days before finishing.

DEALING WITH DRY ROT

As soon as you notice signs of dry rot, try to determine its extent. Rising damp and lack of ventilation are among the main causes of dry rot. Should you notice the fungus in ground-floor baseboards, the rot is likely to be more extensive than it actually appears, and a full inspection by a professional may be required.

This will involve removing as much of the surrounding material as necessary to establish the full extent of the rot and the cause of the damp. Treatment for dry-rot usually involves eliminating the source of the moisture; providing extra ventilation; stripping and destroying the infected wood and replacing it with treated timber; stripping plastered surfaces up to 3ft (1m) beyond the last sign of fungal attack; and applying an appropriate fungicidal solution to sterilize all woodwork, masonry, and associated materials in the infected area.

In special cases, it may be possible to have woodwork chemically treated *in situ*, although the work may not be fully guaranteed.

FINISHING FLOORS

I T IS POSSIBLE THAT ORIGINALLY *an exposed wooden floor in an old house, particularly if made of soft-wood, may not have been treated with a finish of any sort.* Over the years the bare boards would have acquired a patina produced by the effect of light on the color, absorption of dirt, burnishing from use, and the "natural" finish imparted by regular scrubbing.

Nevertheless, you are unlikely to find a wood floor that has remained untreated to the present day – since, with changes in fashion and ownership, virtually all uncarpeted floors have now been treated with a stain, oil, wax, varnish, or paint.

Which is the "right" finish to adopt now is debatable, so let the floor itself be your guide. If you have an old floor in good condition, use a traditional finish – but if the wood has been replaced or low maintenance is important, you may prefer to use a modern finish.

Reproduction of a decorative-boarded floor made for a Georgian house

SANDING FLOORS

Don't sand an old floor except as a last resort. Although wood changes color with age, it doesn't do so all the way through. So, unless the wood is very deeply stained, if you remove the surface the original color is revealed beneath.

It is possible to sand the floor of a small room with an orbital sander. But if you want to do the job quickly or have a large area to tackle, hire a commercial drum floor-sanding machine and also, for the edges, a rotary floor sander.

Preparing for work
Sanding is in effect part of the finishing process, so any repair work required should be completed first. Make sure all the boards are nailed securely. Work over the entire floor with a nail punch, sinking the heads of all the nails well below the surface of the boards. Then clear the room and seal all gaps around doors. Work with the windows open and wear a face mask, as sanding creates a lot of fine dust.

Operating a drum sander
Fit an appropriate sandpaper to the drum of the sanding machine, following the supplier's instructions. To operate the machine, tilt it backward and switch on.

Gently lower the drum until it comes into contact with the floor. There is no need to push the machine, which should be kept under control so that it moves forward at an even pace. Don't stop with the drum still in contact with the floor, or it will cut a hollow that is difficult to remove. Each "band" of sanding should overlap the previous one.

If the floorboards are particularly rough or uneven, first of all work across the room diagonally, using a coarse-grade sandpaper (1). Then sand the floor diagonally with a coarse paper for a second time, working across your first sanding (2).

Change the sandpaper and sand in the direction in which the boards are laid, using first a medium grade, then a fine grade to give the wood a smooth finish (3).

Vacuum the dust from the floor between each sanding.

Cleaning up
Using the rotary sander, sand the border areas missed by the drum sander. Finally, use a long-handled scraper to finish the corners and any other areas that are difficult to sand with a machine.

Sanded wood marks easily, particularly if it is a light color. So it is advisable to wear soft shoes throughout the sanding operation or, if the floor is not too rough, to work in stocking feet.

Once sanding is complete, vacuum the entire floor area thoroughly and wipe it with mineral spirits in readiness for finishing. If you are unable to proceed with finishing straightaway, cover the floor with clean paper. Rolls of wall-lining paper provide a handy way of protecting a large area.

1 Work diagonally across the room

2 Then sand the other way

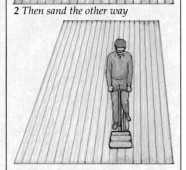

3 Follow the boards to finish

TYPES OF FINISHES

Floor finishes can be divided into two main groups: those that penetrate the wood and those that form a protective film on the surface.

Oil finishes such as linseed oil, tung oil, Danish oil, and teak oil are all penetrating finishes. Both traditional and modern lacquers and varnishes are surface finishes, as are paints – which are, in fact, pigmented varnishes. A wax finish can be either. It can be employed as a penetrating finish on bare wood, but it is more often used on surfaces that have already been sealed with one of the other types of finishes.

Oil finishes

Oil is a traditional finish for wood, especially for woods that are naturally oily, such as teak and afrormosia. Suitable both for hardwoods and softwoods, an oil finish gives wood a natural-looking and pleasingly mellow quality. It is ideal for most board and parquet floors.

Commercially prepared oil finishes such as Danish oil and teak oil are fairly quick-drying and simple to apply. Like all oil finishes, they are easy to maintain.

Varnishes and lacquers

Traditional varnishes were based on natural oils and resins, whereas modern ones are based on synthetic resins. Most varnishes use mineral spirits as a solvent – but they are not solvent-reversible and need a chemical stripper to remove them.

Polyurethane is a modern, hard-wearing, heat-resistant, and waterproof synthetic-resin finish available in gloss and matte versions. It is best suited to new dirt-free floors as careful preparation of the surface is required in order

Mellow early-C19th sealed and waxed pine board floor

to insure good adhesion. Its hard-wearing properties are useful in high-traffic areas such as hallways or kitchens.

Catalyzed lacquers give an extremely hard-wearing surface that is resistant to heat, solvents, and scratches. They are a modern invention and cure by chemical action. Pre-catalyzed lacquers include a hardener and set on exposure to air; two-part lacquers cure when a separate hardener is added.

All "clear" varnishes darken the wood to some degree, and some are pretinted. Oil-based ones mellow with age.

Paint

When painting a bare wood floor with a traditional paint system, a primer may be applied first, followed by an undercoat and top coat; on previously painted floors, the primer can be omitted. Some paints are now formulated in one-coat versions.

Old decoratively painted floors are now quite rare and should be preserved. If you have one that needs restoration, ask a specialist from a historical society for advice.

Wood stains

Stains are used to change the color of wood but do not act as a finish. You can buy ready-made water-based, spirit-based, and oil-based stains in a variety of shades.

Wax

Wax is a traditional finish for floors that protects and enhances the qualities of the wood. It can be used either on bare wood or as a finish for sealed floors.

Wax is available as a paste and in liquid form. Liquid waxes are less laborious to apply, so most people prefer them for polishing floors.

CLEANING FLOORS

Whichever finish you decide on, you will need to clean the surface thoroughly as a preparatory measure. In fact, you may find that cleaning is all that is required and the original finish is still in good condition.

Unfinished wood floors

Vacuum an unfinished floor to remove loose dust and grit, then wash it with warm water and detergent. To treat

light soiling, use a sponge and the minimum amount of water. To remove ingrained dirt, scrub the floor with a bristle brush, using a gentle scouring powder for bad patches. Rinse the surface as you go, then mop up the water quickly with a sponge and leave the floor to dry.

Waxed floors

Remove dust regularly with a soft brush, vacuum cleaner, or dry mop. When necessary, use a liquid cleaning wax to improve the appearance of a floor that is lightly scratched or soiled but otherwise in good condition. Apply the wax with a clean soft cloth, working a small area at a time. The cleaning wax contains solvents that soften the finish sufficiently for the dirt to be absorbed by the cloth and leaves a film of polish on the floor. Let the finish dry, then buff to a soft sheen. An application of floor wax can follow if required.

To remove a wax finish, use mineral spirits and steel wool, working with the grain. Wipe up any residue of wet wax with a clean cloth and mineral spirits.

Oiled floors

Remove dust with a vacuum cleaner or soft brush. Wipe the surface with a lightly oiled cloth to give the finish new life. If necessary, wash the floor with soap suds, using a well-wrung mop and working a small area at a time. Rinse with clean water, in the same way, then dry the floor with a clean cloth. Allow the surface to dry thoroughly before applying a fresh coat of oil.

Varnished floors

Varnished floors should not be washed unless absolutely necessary, as there is always a chance that the water will penetrate under the finish and cause staining. Instead, use a solvent cleaner made of 4 parts mineral spirits to 1 part linseed oil. Apply the cleaner with a cloth, or fine steel wool for stubborn dirt, then wipe the surface dry with a clean cloth. If a varnished floor has been heavily coated with a wax polish, clean it like a waxed floor (see previous page).

Painted floors
Wash painted floors with a solution of warm soapy water or with a commercial paint cleaner. Working only a small area at a time, apply the solution or paint cleaner sparingly with a cloth or sponge mop then wipe dry.

If a floor is to be repainted, rub the surface down, using fine sandpaper, and wipe clean with a tack rag before painting.

Clean decoratively painted floors with great care. After cleaning, apply a coating of wax floor polish to preserve the surface.

SAFETY
- Fumes from varnishes, paints and cleaners can be harmful when inhaled and should not be allowed to build up in a room. When using these materials, work with the windows open and wear a mask.
- Alcohol-based finishes and finishes with an oil or resin base are highly flammable. Extinguish all naked flames before working with them; and clean or destroy all used rags or cloths, especially ones that have been used to apply linseed oil, since they are liable to catch fire due to spontaneous combustion.

Pine floor decorated with attractive stenciled design in muted colors

APPLYING A FINISH
Before finishing a wood floor, all new work or repairs must be completed, the surface needs to be smoothed or cleaned, and color applied if not in the finish itself. When applying finishes, always follow the manufacturer's instructions.

Oil
When using a proprietary oil finish, apply a generous coat with a cloth or paintbrush. Allow it to soak in for a few minutes, then wipe off the excess. Let the wood dry for up to eight hours, depending on drying conditions, before applying a second and third coat in the same way. When dry, buff to a soft sheen.

Wax
On a bare wood floor, apply two coats of sealer, using either thinned varnish or a proprietary sanding sealer. Sand down the surface with very fine sandpaper. The sealer stops the wax from sinking in too deeply, which would draw dirt into the wood.

Brush on a liberal coat of liquid wax and leave it to soak in. About an hour later, work over the surface with an electric floor polisher. Apply further thin coats with a cloth pad charged with wax and buff each in turn. Leave the surface to harden, then burnish with the polisher next day.

Paste waxes need to be applied sparingly, using a cloth pad and building up the wax in layers until you have obtained a satisfactory finish. Never apply thick coats of paste in an attempt to achieve quick results. It will remain soft, hold the dirt and look dull. Between coats, burnish the wood with an electric floor polisher.

Varnish
New wood should first be sealed with a thinned coat of varnish, containing about 30 per cent solvent. Brush it in well, working with the grain. On a previously finished surface, use the varnish full strength for the first coat.

When it has set, apply two or three coats of unthinned varnish, allowing each to set before applying the next one. Work first across the grain, to spread the varnish evenly, then finish by brushing with the grain. Between each coat, rub down the surface with fine sandpaper.

If you can't complete the job in a single session, finish on a joint between boards. Don't work back over varnish that's partly set, as it will pick up brush marks.

Catalyzed lacquers
Mix a two-part catalyzed lacquer carefully, using the proportions recommended by the manufacturer. Apply an even coat of lacquer with a well-loaded brush, working with the grain. Do not brush the lacquer too much; allow it to flow freely from the brush so that it forms a smooth surface. Work quickly, to maintain a wet edge so that you can blend in each brushload without leaving brush marks. The coating should set in two hours.

Apply a second and third coat at two-hourly intervals. Rub down the surface with fine sandpaper before applying the last coat.

Paint and wood stains
Apply paint in even coats, using a brush 3in (75mm) wide and laying off with the grain. Allow the paint to set, and rub down between coats as required. Semimatte paints are best for floors, as their texture makes them easier to work. Always work toward a door if you are painting the whole floor, so you will have a means of exit without stepping on the newly painted surface. Let the paint dry thoroughly before walking on it.

To create a decorative pattern, prepare the floor then set out the design, painting it freehand or using stencils purchased from a specialist supplier. For the decorative elements, use a fast-drying acrylic paint to speed up the work, particularly if the pattern is multi-colored. Use a stippling technique for the smaller details; for the larger elements, brush away from the edges of the stencil.

You can apply wood stains with a stencil, too, using a cloth pad and the minimum amount of color so that the stain doesn't bleed into the wood and blur the pattern.

Protect newly painted floors with a polyurethane varnish. Stained floors can be varnished or waxed.

CHAPTER SIXTEEN

DECORATIVE METALWORK

IRON – which had previously been employed mainly for functional purposes – began to be used for decorative architectural work in America during the eighteenth century. Up to that time iron had been smelted in relatively limited quantities, its production relying on charcoal-fueled furnaces that required a ready supply of timber. This restricted the development of the material until in 1709 English founder Abraham Darby pioneered the use of coke for smelting iron ore.

In England, beautifully crafted wrought-iron gates and railings were produced by master craftsmen. The work of migrant blacksmiths such as Jean Tijou was to have a profound influence on English wrought iron during the first quarter of the eighteenth century, and by the end of the century the production of iron for both wrought and cast work was well established. Without it, the Industrial Revolution would have been impossible.

While less of the very elaborate ironwork was to be found adorning the American eighteenth-century house, wrought iron was nevertheless widely used for railings and balconies until well into the nineteenth century. Then cast iron superseded it for many uses as a more substantial-looking material offering better value. Iron founders were now able to produce ornate castings cheaply in any number of identical pieces. This meant that architects could choose decorative ironwork from pattern books, instead of relying on the relatively expensive work of blacksmiths. It also gave them the freedom to create their own designs.

A nineteenth-century decorative balcony with cast-iron balustrade

Beautifully preserved 1830s wrought-iron hollow-urn newel post

TYPES OF METALS

METALS USED FOR TRADITIONAL BUILDINGS *can be divided into two main groups: ferrous metals (metals that contain iron, including wrought iron, cast iron, and steel in its various forms) and non-ferrous metals (including copper, lead, and brass). Non-ferrous metals generally resist corrosion better than ferrous metals do.*

Wrought iron
Now rarely made, wrought iron is more often available as a recycled material. Its fibrous structure gives it good tensile strength and bending properties. A malleable iron, it is easily worked by forging and can be worked hot or cold. It can also be readily welded with modern welding methods.

Because wrought iron is a relatively corrosion-resistant metal, its traditional uses ranged from nails, locks, hinges and strapwork to fine examples of gates, railings, brackets, and balustrades.

Cast iron
A heavy and relatively corrosion-resistant metal, cast iron is strong in compression but does not have good tensile strength. Cast-iron components are not easily worked, but can be machined and welded to make a repair.

Cast iron has been used for a wide variety of household fitments, including weights and pulleys for sash windows, door fittings, fireplaces and stoves, staircases, decorative brackets, railings, gates, balustrades, porches, roof crestings, and rainwater pipes and gutters.

Steel
Steel is a refined form of iron. It is a hard, tough, and malleable metal. Although steel is very much a modern material, traditional "carbon steel" was produced in the eighteenth century.

The most common type of steel today is mild steel. A general-purpose steel that can be worked hot or cold, it bends readily when heated and is available in various sections as well as in sheet form. In addition to its many other uses, it is now used as a substitute for traditional wrought iron.

Mild steel machines well and can be welded, but it is more difficult to forge-weld than traditional wrought iron. It does not have good corrosion resistance.

Copper
Copper was one of the first metals used by Man. In fact, there is evidence that it was being annealed and worked as early as 4,000 B.C. A soft metal that can be welded, brazed, or soldered, it is both strong and malleable. Copper has excellent thermal and electrical conductivity and resistance to corrosion.

Brass
Brass is a yellow-colored alloy of copper and zinc. Available in strip, bar, rod, and sheet form, it is a common material for cast architectural fittings.

Lead
Lead is a heavy, malleable metal that is a bright-silver color when cut, but quickly oxidizes to a matt gray. It has excellent resistance to corrosion and is used for sheet roofing, flashings, pipes, and gutters, as well as for decorative cast work.

IDENTIFYING THE METAL

IT IS NOT NECESSARY TO UNDERSTAND *the technical properties of metals, but it is useful to be able to identify the type of material used so that you can maintain it in an appropriate manner. Most decorative metalwork such as railings, balconies, and brackets were made of iron. However, since they are usually thickly painted, it is not always easy to tell whether the metal is wrought iron or cast iron. Also, some of the decorative details may be made of other metals (for example, brass rosettes or finials cast in lead).*

Built-up construction and tapered scrolls are typical of wrought iron

Finely crafted wrought iron with delightful scrolls and repoussé work

Complex shapes and molded surfaces are readily reproduced in cast iron

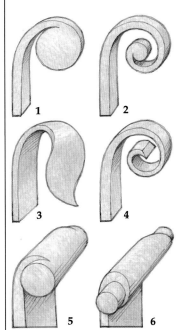

Wrought-iron scroll-work shapes
1 Halfpenny snub end
2 Solid snub end
3 Blow-over leaf
4 Ribbon end
5 Bolt end
6 Fishtail snub end

Ornate cast-iron window guard with molded scrolls

1930s Art Deco decorative wrought-iron panel

Wrought and cast iron

To distinguish wrought iron from cast iron, first look at the style of the metalwork and the proportions of the elements that make up the design. Wrought iron is mostly based on standard square and rectangular sections of iron bar that are worked into decorative scrolls, twists, and motifs. The ends of the bars are usually tapered or flattened and worked into snub ends or scrolls, each being individually shaped and subtly different from its neighbor. The overall appearance is crisp and elegant.

In contrast to wrought iron, each part of cast ironwork is precisely reproduced. Components tend to be thicker, incorporating a variety of sections and shapes, including turned forms. Look for "flash lines" (the seams that run down the sides of a casting at the join between the molds). The presence of flash lines provides conclusive evidence that a piece of ironwork is cast, not wrought, though on better-quality work these lines are filed away.

Typically the components of wrought ironwork are joined with rivets and collars, and incorporate joints familiar to woodworkers such as mortise-and-tenon and cross halving joints. Forge or fire welding is also used to blend one part into another. Cast iron is joined by lead-caulked sockets or nuts and bolts fixed through cast lugs.

The surface texture also differs. Wrought iron tends to be smooth, albeit with some roller or hammer marks, whereas cast iron has a more granular feel.

Cracked or broken ironwork indicates the use of cast iron. If you examine the break, you will see the brittle crystalline nature of the material. Wrought iron, on the other hand, is malleable, so impact damage takes the form of bent rather than broken components.

Mild steel

Mild steel, introduced in the latter part of the nineteenth century, is now commonly used for "wrought" ironwork. Sections tend to be slimmer than traditional wrought iron. Also, if gas or electric-arc welding has been used for the joints, then that indicates that the metal is mild steel.

Copper

Polished copper has a rich pinkish-red color, which oxidises to a matte brown and forms a green protective patina with long exposure to the atmosphere. Its main use in traditional buildings is as a sheet roof covering and for guttering, but it was also used for decorative details in Victorian interiors.

Weather vanes use various metals

Decoratively worked lead cladding

Brass

When stripped, the yellow color of brass clearly distinguishes it from iron and lead, which are gray. When decorative brass details are found, it can be assumed that they were intended as additional ornamentation to contrast with painted ironwork. These should be cleaned carefully and protected from the elements with a clear lacquer.

Lead

Cast lead details can cause problems when stripping paint from old metalwork, since the softness of lead means that they are easily damaged. You may be able to detect the presence of lead under the paint by testing the metal with a sharp spike, to find out whether it is hard or soft, or by scraping the surface of the metal to reveal the bright-silver color beneath.

In order to preserve lead components, when stripping them don't try to burn off the paint or use abrasive stripping methods. Soften the paint with a chemical stripper, then wash it off with a bristle brush. Protect your eyes and hands when using paint strippers.

DECORATIVE IRONWORK

W ELL-PRODUCED CHEAP CAST IRONWORK *was a boon to speculative builders, and during the eighteenth century townhouses boasted a display of prefabricated decorative ironwork.*

Handmade wrought ironwork was revived by Arts and Crafts designers who abhorred Victorian taste and machine-made products and valued traditional craftsmanship. The vogue only lasted until the 1920s, but their influence continues to this day.

ASSESSING REPAIRS

● Easy even for beginners.
■ Fairly difficult. Good practical skills required.
▲ Difficult. Hire a professional.

Damaged paintwork
Exposed ironwork is prone to corrosion.
■ Identify the metal (pages 200-1).
● Wire-brush loose rust (page 202).
▲ Have metal abrasive-cleaned (page 202) or flame-cleaned (page 203).
● Chemically strip paint (page 203).
● Apply fresh paint system (page 203).
● Fill pitted metal (page 207).

Exterior ironwork
1 Balcony balustrade
2 Fence railings
3 Gate
4 Window guards
5 Boot scraper

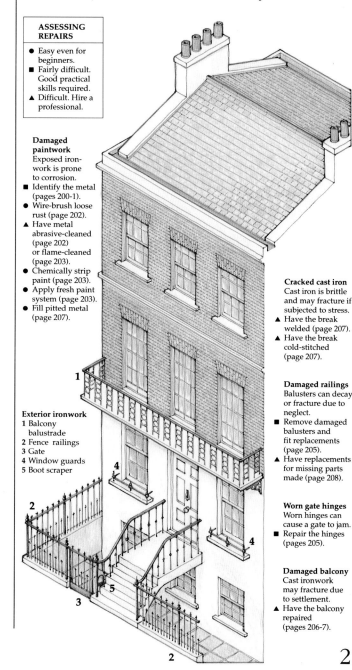

Cracked cast iron
Cast iron is brittle and may fracture if subjected to stress.
▲ Have the break welded (page 207).
▲ Have the break cold-stitched (page 207).

Damaged railings
Balusters can decay or fracture due to neglect.
■ Remove damaged balusters and fit replacements (page 205).
▲ Have replacements for missing parts made (page 208).

Worn gate hinges
Worn hinges can cause a gate to jam.
■ Repair the hinges (pages 205).

Damaged balcony
Cast ironwork may fracture due to settlement.
▲ Have the balcony repaired (pages 206-7).

PAINTING METAL

U NLIKE METALS *that form a protective oxide film, iron requires regular painting to protect it from corrosion. Good adhesion of the paint system is essential, and it is vital that the surface is thoroughly cleaned and prepared.*

A conventional paint system comprises a primer, undercoat, and top coat, although you can now buy some paints for metal that form a protective barrier in a single coat.

Preparing painted surfaces

The only preparation necessary for previously painted surfaces is to clean them before repainting. Wash the surfaces with a sugar-soap solution to remove all traces of dirt and grease. If there is a high-gloss finish, wash the paintwork then key it by rubbing down with fine wet-and-dry paper. Rinse and dry well before repainting.

Damaged paintwork

If the paintwork is damaged and localized corrosion has set in, causing blisters or flaking, remove the loose material with a scraper. Scrape away paint around the damaged area to expose all traces of rust. Clean the rusted areas to a bright finish, either by hand with a wire brush or using a brush attachment fitted into the chuck of an electric drill (1). Feather the edges of the old paint with sandpaper.

If the metal is pitted, it is very difficult to eradicate all traces of rust. To overcome the problem, apply a rust inhibitor (available from auto parts stores), which will convert it into an inert form of iron phosphate (2).

1 Wire-brush the rust

2 Apply a rust inhibitor

Abrasive cleaning

Dry abrasive cleaning (grit or shot blasting) offers an efficient and effective way to clean rusted metal. If you have a large area to clean, it could be worth employing a contractor.

The process creates a lot of dust, and if the work is being carried out *in situ* the contractor should provide some form of protective barrier around the work area. Old lead-based paints are poisonous and it is harmful to inhale the dust, so keep away from the area until the job is completed.

Thoroughly cleaned iron rerusts quickly, so the work should be prepared in stages and it is essential to apply a primer as soon as possible after cleaning.

Flame cleaning

Use a propane torch to help remove loose rust and scale from wrought iron and steel (but not cast iron, since it suffers from intense localized heating). Wire-brush the metal immediately after heating and remove fine dust prior to priming.

Thin metal sections may distort with this method, and fumes from burning lead-painted surfaces can be a health hazard.

Chemical stripping

Over a long period normal routine maintenance causes a considerable build-up of paint that can mask the fine detail of decorative pieces. Where this has occurred or the paint has been damaged or neglected, causing corrosion to set in, it may be better to strip the paintwork and repaint completely.

You can apply a paste or gel stripper to interior and exterior ironwork *in situ*, or if the item is portable send it to an industrial stripping company.

Apply strippers according to the maker's instructions. It's usually best to brush stripper onto fancy shaped work, so you can work the paste or gel into the crevices. Take care not to brush it on too thinly. Leave the stripper to soften the paint fully before scraping it off. You will find a stiff-bristle brush is best for cleaning paint from decorative details.

Most stripping agents are toxic. They therefore need to be handled with care during application, and materials contaminated by them must be disposed of according to local regulations. Wear eye protection, a face mask, vinyl gloves, and possibly rubber boots when working with these materials.

APPLYING PAINT

Brush-applied oil-based paints provide a good serviceable treatment for most interior and exterior decorative metalwork. Treat derusted iron and steel with a rust-neutralizing inhibitor (some inhibitors require rinsing after treatment, others are self-priming). Then apply one or two even coats of a metal primer. Always treat welded repairs with an additional coat. When set, brush or spray on two layers of undercoat followed by one or two top coats.

Choosing a color

Black has now become the standard color for painted ironwork. However, in the Victorian era, railings, balustrades, and decorative metalwork were often painted a color. Dark red, brown, blue, and dull green (a color inspired by the patina of antique bronze) have all been used in the past.

Changing the color of decorative metalwork in certain historic districts may require the consent of a local board or overseeing body.

Bear in mind that gloss paints give better weather protection than matte paints for exterior work.

Finishing non-ferrous metals

Brass and copper take on a mellow natural patina that can look attractive without treatment. However, where the atmosphere or degree of exposure is likely to cause corrosion, the metal should be protected with a clear varnish.

Clean the surface with a metal polish, then wash with a mild liquid detergent in warm water and rinse well. Dry the metal with a soft cloth, then apply a clear varnish or acrylic lacquer with a soft brush.

Lead develops an attractive coating of grey oxide that protects the metal, so does not need painting. However, new leadwork can discolor unevenly and stain adjacent materials, so a patination oil is used in order to provide a protective film while the natural patina is forming.

Although galvanization is a relatively modern process, you may find zinc-plated (galvanized) iron and steel have been introduced into an old building. When new the surface provides a poor surface for painting, though it will improve if allowed to weather for at least six months. However, if you apply a special primer, the surface can be painted in the normal way. Check at your paint store for the paints that are compatible with the primer.

Blue paint used as an alternative to the usual black finish

Late-nineteenth-century gilded wrought-iron railing

RAILINGS

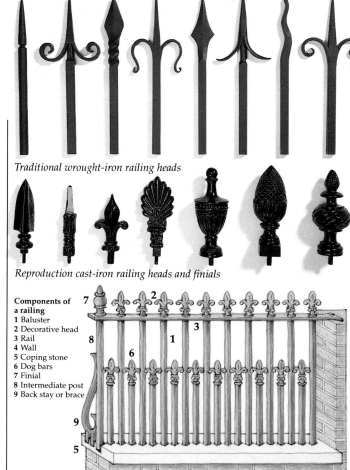

Traditional wrought-iron railing heads

Reproduction cast-iron railing heads and finials

Components of a railing
1 Baluster
2 Decorative head
3 Rail
4 Wall
5 Coping stone
6 Dog bars
7 Finial
8 Intermediate post
9 Back stay or brace

RAILINGS ARE THE MOST COMMON FORM *of traditional decorative wrought and cast ironwork in city and urban areas. If you walk down a street lined with Federal or Victorian houses that have basements, you are likely to find wrought-iron or cast-iron railings designed to prevent pedestrians falling into the basement "area." Iron railings were also used to flank gateways of town houses or country estates, to fence in small domestic yards and enclose communal gardens in city squares.*

Fairly plain cast-iron railings were relatively inexpensive and widely used after the mid-nineteenth century. Quite elaborate decoration was also used, with motifs that reflected prevailing tastes, from Colonial pineapples to classical volutes and the serpentine vegetation so characteristic of Art Nouveau.

Wrought-iron and cast-iron railings can be made to original patterns by blacksmiths or iron foundries that specialize in supplying traditional cast ironwork. A varied selection of ready-made cast-iron railings has once again become available, too. Nowadays some manufacturers use cast aluminum, which can be cheaper for small runs of elaborate designs.

Handsome nineteenth-century cast-iron paneled area railing

The elegant anthemion motif, used here for cast-iron railing heads

Construction

A typical iron railing has a run of uprights, or balusters, topped with decorative heads. The uprights are joined together, just below the heads, by a horizontal rail through which they pass. The tops of wrought-iron balusters were forged into decorative shapes, or cast-iron decorative heads were applied. The heads of cast-iron balusters were either cast as part of the baluster itself or made separately and screwed on.

The bottom end of the railing was usually supported by a low wall capped with a coping stone; often, a series of plinth stones was used instead of a wall. The method for joining the metal balusters to the stone was to set them in lead poured into drilled holes. The soft lead allows the metal a certain amount of thermal move-ment without damage to the stone and provides protection against corrosion. Lead was also run into the joints between the rail and balusters in some cases. The ends of the rail were fixed to metal posts or to brick or stone piers.

An elaborate railing may have short uprights (known as dog bars) between the main balusters, as well as additional rails and decorative details.

Railings that had balusters fixed into a supporting wall or plinth were assembled on site. However, railings were also often made as panels, with rails near the top and the bottom for fixing to a post. Where there was a long span between end posts or piers, a lighter intermediate post or a decorative panel fitted with a back stay was used to give extra support.

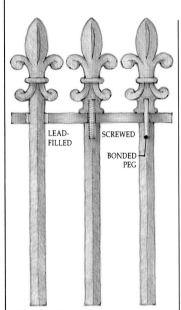

Fixing methods for railing heads

LEAD-FILLED · SCREWED · BONDED PEG

GATES

IN ADDITION TO PROVIDING SECURITY, *gates present the first impression of a property. Consequently, magnificent examples have been made in wrought* and cast iron for grand country houses. These were often very large and topped with a decorative arch spanning the gateway, known as an overthrow. But for most domestic architecture the gates were no more than waist or head height.

Traditional iron gates are usually hung on cast-iron posts or brick piers. They are normally fitted with a wrap-around hinge at the top and a ground pivot at the base. Because iron gates are heavy, the pivots tend to suffer from wear.

Grand pair of iron entrance gates

Replacing a baluster
Corrosion can set in where the base of a baluster is set into the stonework or around the joint with the top rail. If it is badly corroded, you may be able to find a matching replacement from an architectural-salvage company or reproduction manufacturer. Otherwise, you can have a new baluster made to order.

Chisel out the lead from the stonework socket. Use an old (but sharp) narrow wood chisel for this operation.

If there is a detachable head, detach it and remove the baluster. Some detachable heads unscrew; but if the head is fixed to a peg, you will have to cut the peg in order to free the baluster.

If the head is an integral part of the baluster, remove the lead from the top joint (either melt it, using a blow torch, or trim it out with a chisel) then pull the baluster through the rail.

Fit the new baluster into place, and either set it in lead or use a two-part epoxy adhesive. If there is a detachable head, screw it in; or if it fits onto a peg, drill out the remains of the old peg and bond the head to a new one with epoxy glue.

Bold cast-iron panels used in the railing make up this impressive pair of gates

Maintenance and repair
Keep the paintwork in good condition and grease the pivot points regularly in order to reduce wear and stop annoying squeaks.

Should the hinges be very worn they may need to be replaced. The "strap" of the top hinge, which wraps around a turned section of the gate-frame member, is usually bolted in place. Remove the bolts to check the condition of the parts. You may have to drill them out or cut them free with a hacksaw, in which case replace with a similar fitting.

Some assemblies include a bronze bushing. If the strap or bushing is badly worn and you are unable to do the work yourself, you can have a new one made by a blacksmith or foundry. Give the repairer the old part and, if possible, a dimensioned drawing of the assembly.

The bottom of the gate pivots in a metal collar or in a cup set in the ground, which should be kept free from dirt. If a cast-iron cup is broken, have a replacement cast by a specialist.

If an iron gate is missing, you can have a replacement made by a blacksmith or foundry. Some ready-made reproduction gates are available, too, but choose one that is in keeping with the character of the building.

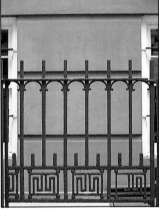

Area gate with Greek-key motif

Components of an iron gate
1 Strap hinge
2 Fixing bolt
3 Gate frame
4 Post
5 Pivot cup
6 Lock

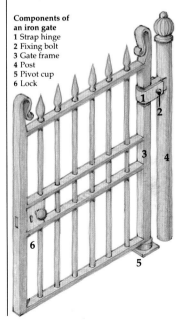

BALCONIES

Components of a balcony
1 Baluster
2 Handrail
3 Fishtail fixing
4 Cast-iron platform grid
5 Decorative bracket

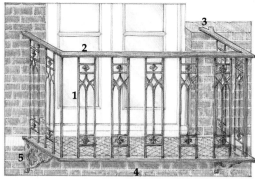

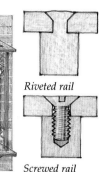

Riveted rail

Screwed rail

R ENAISSANCE ARCHITECTURE *was the inspiration for the balconies that became such a feature of numerous nineteenth-century townhouses. At second-floor level, they provided a projecting terrace that enabled the occupants to step outside to enjoy the open air or view the scene below. Some balconies ran the entire width of the building, forming a continuous design with those of neighboring houses, while others were only one window wide.*

Although stone was often used for the grander houses, most balconies were constructed of wrought iron or cast ironwork. These elegant and attractive structures were cantilevered from the façade, some having a projecting stone base surmounted by an iron balustrade while others were made entirely of iron. The latter type were usually constructed of panels of decorative cast iron. The heavier balconies were often supported by ornamental brackets, and sometimes by elegant cast-iron columns. Columns or traceried panel supports were also sometimes used when a balcony was surmounted by a roof or canopy.

Balcony construction
The stone bases of some balconies were built into the wall as the house was erected and formed an extension to the string course. The mass of the upper brickwork was used to counter the weight of the projecting stone, while brackets of stone or iron gave additional support. The supports for the iron balustrade panels were set into the slab and secured with lead. The ends of the handrail were fixed into a stone wall in the same way, but would be built into a brick wall. In the latter case, the ends were often split to form a "fishtail" fork in order to give better grip in the mortar.

Balconies constructed entirely of iron were usually supported by the string course or window sill and fixed by the handrail at the top and by embedded lugs at the base. Cantilevered arms built into the wall or decorative brackets held by lead-packed lugs or bolts provided extra support for heavier versions.

Elegant wrought and cast-iron balconettes complement the tall sash windows

BALCONETTES AND WINDOW GUARDS
The small bow or flat-fronted balconies, or balconettes, that grace a single window are often little more than window guards, their function being to provide a barrier for the tall second-floor sash windows that almost touched the floor.

Window guards are lighter in construction than balconies and normally are not supported by brackets. Some have a platform consisting of a metal grill or open bars. They may be little more than a flat panel across a window opening or a decorative rail fitted to a deep stone window sill.

A lead-covered canopy provides shelter for this simple attractive balcony

Anthemion cast-iron balconette

Lattice-pattern window guard

REPAIRING & REPLACING IRON

METAL IS A TOUGH AND DURABLE *material, but if neglected it decays. Regular maintenance is therefore needed to keep it in good order and avoid expensive repairs. Although it is not particularly easy to work, you can carry out certain repairs yourself – and fortunately there are experts who are able to deal with most problems and remake parts that are missing or beyond repair.*

Elegant cast-iron balconies, providing an ideal support for wisteria

Maintaining a balcony

A decorative iron balcony adds considerable character to a house. However, if it isn't maintained properly, its prominent position can make it a distinct liability. Chipped or worn paint may result in rusting, which can stain the walls of the house and, if untreated, lead to structural failure. Broken or missing rails create an aura of neglect, and weak fixings may cause structural problems that are costly to repair.

Renew the painted surfaces of balconies and railings at regular intervals. Use exterior paint that is appropriate for ironwork.

Be sure to treat all rust and deterioration before painting, and prime as well. Replace missing or seriously decayed parts.

From time to time, check the joints where a stone base meets the wall. The slab should slope away from the wall slightly in order to shed rainwater. If water is lying against the wall, it is likely to enter the wall of the structure, and in northern climes that can result in serious damage. The freezing-and-thawing cycle can produce a deterioration of the building's walling and structure. Have an engineer or contractor examine any such area for signs of problems that might require immediate correction.

Stresses caused by settlement can crack brittle cast iron. If balusters or decorative iron panels are cracked, have them welded *in situ*. Continuous balconies with large panels of ironwork need to expand and contract to some degree. It is therefore important that welding repairs should not restrict thermal movement, otherwise the ironwork may suffer from further fractures. Large platform grids in need of repair may require strapping with bolted stainless steel plates rather than welding.

Cold repairs to cast iron

Large hollow-sectioned porch or veranda columns, cast-iron newel posts, and heavy-gauge brackets (for example, in a conservatory) can crack when subjected to subsidence stresses or impact damage. In order to avoid having to heat a large mass of metal, cracks in cast iron that is not less than 1/4in (6mm) thick can be repaired by a specialist contractor using a technique known as cold stitching (1).

If a non-structural part such as a decorative detail has broken off a cast-iron component, you can repair it with a two-part epoxy adhesive. For small pieces, simply mix the adhesive according to the maker's instructions, apply it to the broken surfaces and fix in place. For larger pieces, drill holes in each part and fit pegs cut from stainless-steel rod to reinforce the joint.

Pitting in rusted cast iron can be filled with an epoxy car-body filler. Clean the metal thoroughly and apply a rust inhibitor. Mix the filler and apply it with a plastic spatula so it is just proud of the surface (2). When it has set, shape the filler with a file and rub it down with sandpaper to follow the contour of the metal, as required. Prime and paint the repair to match the finish of the work.

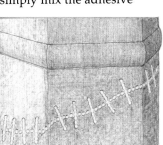

1 *Cold stitching on thick cast iron*

2 *Apply filler proud of surface*

Welding broken cast iron

Cast iron is brittle and may fracture when struck sharply or weakened by rust. If the break is simple, provided the metal is still in reasonable condition, you can normally have it arc-welded *in situ* by either a blacksmith or a welding service that undertakes cast-iron repairs.

In order to avoid setting up stresses in the metal, cast iron has to be heated as part of the welding process. The edges of the crack are ground into a "V," which is filled with weld metal. The weld should be continuous, without holes (which can encourage corrosion), ground flat, and thoroughly primed ready for painting.

IRONWORK MADE TO ORDER

If ironwork is missing or beyond repair, you can have a replacement made by a specialist. A number of blacksmiths and specialist foundries still exist, but sadly not as many as when ironwork was in its heyday.

Ordering wrought ironwork

Wrought ironwork is made by artist-blacksmiths using traditional craft skills. Now a rare breed, they fashion plain lengths of iron into beautiful forms by heating the metal and beating it on the anvil and on a variety of shaped stakes. This type of work has always been fairly expensive compared with mass-produced cast ironwork, but for one-off items it may be competitive. You can ask the blacksmith to reproduce an old pattern or to create a new design in a traditional style.

Ordering cast ironwork

Because cast iron is made in a mold, any number of identical pieces can be cast from the same pattern.

If you use an existing component as a pattern, you need to bear in mind that cast iron shrinks by about 1 per cent on cooling. For small items, the difference is insignificant. However, if a baluster or other item is 3ft (1m) long, the reproduction would be 3/8in (10mm) or so shorter than the original.

When a single baluster needs replacing, you may prefer to make up the difference with packing rather than spend money on having a special pattern made. On the other hand, if you have a number of balusters that need to be replaced you may consider it is worth getting the blacksmith or foundry to make a new pattern for you.

The patterns are normally machined and carved from wood, but clay and resins are used, too. To make the casting, a special type of sand is packed all around the pattern in a two-part mold. Various channels are formed in the sand and the pattern is removed, leaving a hollow into which the molten iron is poured.

When the iron has set, the sand is cleaned away leaving the casting and attached sprues (the iron solidified in the channels). These are cut away and the casting is fettled (filed) to remove the mold marks. Threads may then be "tapped" (cut) into the component, depending on the method of fixing.

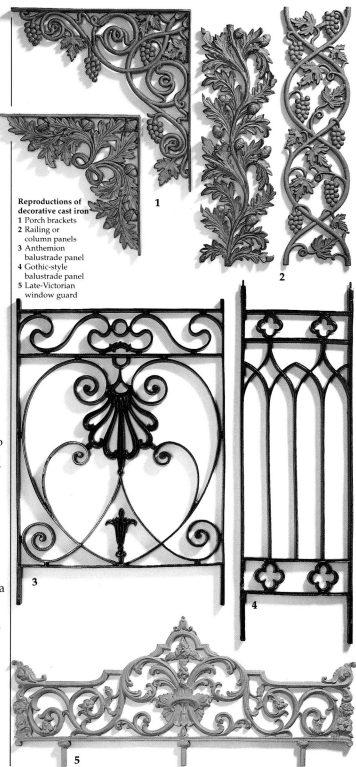

Reproductions of decorative cast iron
1 Porch brackets
2 Railing or column panels
3 Anthemion balustrade panel
4 Gothic-style balustrade panel
5 Late-Victorian window guard

CHAPTER SEVENTEEN

STAIRCASES

T HE EARLIEST AMERICAN HOUSES *rarely had stairs – ladders were generally used to reach upper levels such as attics. However, as* houses increased in size, and as the finishes became more sophisticated, staircases were introduced, frequently becoming important decorative elements.

From the start, wooden staircases were the rule in North America. Steep stairs were typical, and in northern climates they were often located at the front of the house immediately in front of the chimney stack. The stairs themselves often featured winders and turned decorative balusters. As houses increased in size, secondary staircases were frequently incorporated. They were typically simpler in design and were located at the rear of the house.

By the eighteenth century staircase building was highly developed, employing sophisticated building and joinery techniques. Main staircases continued to be mainly of wood, although stone stairs with iron balustrades were used in the grandest Georgian and Victorian houses. Since the foot of the main staircase was normally situated in the entrance hall, designers and makers took the opportunity to demonstrate their skills by constructing eye-catching straight or curving staircases. Some of these were relatively simple, while others became ever more ornate and finely carved.

Stairs leading to a basement were frequently made of wood or stone and metal, and some were entirely constructed from metal. These were usually plainer than the main stairs, but cast-iron types were invariably produced in decorative designs. Cellar stairs were of the simplest kind, mostly being open-tread straight flights made of thick sections of wood.

The staircase is an important feature of this C18th entrance hall

A fine early-C18th mahogany balustrade with molded handrail

TYPES OF STAIRS

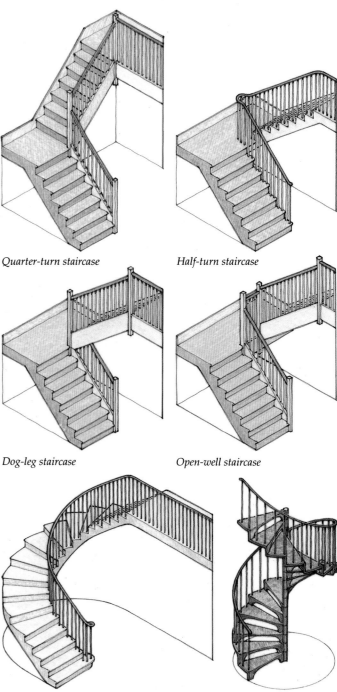

Quarter-turn staircase

Half-turn staircase

Dog-leg staircase

Open-well staircase

Winding geometrical staircase

Spiral staircase

THE SIMPLEST TYPE OF STAIRWAY *comprises a single straight flight of stairs. However, short flights linked by landings are quite common. This type of stairway may be known as a quarter-turn or half-turn stair, depending on whether the turn is made through 90 or 180 degrees. Some staircases have tapered steps, known as winders, instead of landings.*

Dog-leg and open-well stairs are types of half-turn stair. The former, which were used in small houses around the late seventeenth century, gets its name from its elevational shape. Used where the width of the stairway is restricted, it has the upper balustrade in the same plane as the lower one. The open-well stair has a space between the balustrades, thereby providing a more satisfactory arrangement for the layout of the handrail.

NEWEL STAIRS

The majority of staircases are constructed of wood, using a system of structural posts called newels.

Late-C19th newel staircase

These are positioned at the ends of each flight in order to transfer the weight of the stair to the floor and support the balustrades, which are jointed into the newel posts at each turn. An open-well stair therefore has two posts at landing level, whereas the simpler dog-leg type needs only one landing post.

BUILDING REGULATIONS

All stairs present a hazard to the user. To make them as safe as possible, building regulations include a number of rules governing their size and layout.

The rules relate to the shape, depth, height, level, and number of the steps, the pitch of the staircase, the clearance above it, and the width of landings. The provision of handrails and balustrades, as well as their related heights and the space between balusters, are also covered.

Building codes vary considerably from place to place, so you may need to consult your local building department.

The regulations apply to all new work, including installing stairs in a building when there is a change of use, such as a barn conversion, and may affect the reinstatement of a traditional-style staircase in an old house (but not repairs to an existing stair). This can make the re-creation of a staircase in an old building problematic, if not impossible, although you may be able to obtain a variance to the rules in special circumstances.

GEOMETRICAL STAIRS

Geometrical staircases are designed and constructed in such a way that supporting posts are unnecessary. The balustrade and inner string of this type of open-well stair form a continuous curving structure. In grandiose late-Georgian and Federal houses they were sometimes made of stone. Wide sweeping geometrical staircases with radiating tapered steps are known as winding stairs. Elliptical stairs are of similar construction.

Spiral stairs are simply a form of geometrical stair with radiating tapered steps. Most are metal and have a central supporting column. Spiral stairs that are made on the open-well principle are called helical stairs.

WOODEN STAIRS

T HE INTERIOR STAIRCASES *of the mid eighteenth century were mostly constructed of softwood, such as pine, though oak (which had been more usual back in England) continued to be used in the larger houses. Mahogany, at that time regarded as an exotic timber, began to be used for handrails and newel posts in better-quality houses, in combination with painted softwood balusters and framing.*

By the Victorian period mahogany had become much more commonplace. Most staircases were now fitted with mahogany, cherry, or walnut handrails, and sometimes the entire balustrade was made of the wood. Oak was popular too thanks to the Arts and Crafts movement, which used it to revive earlier styles.

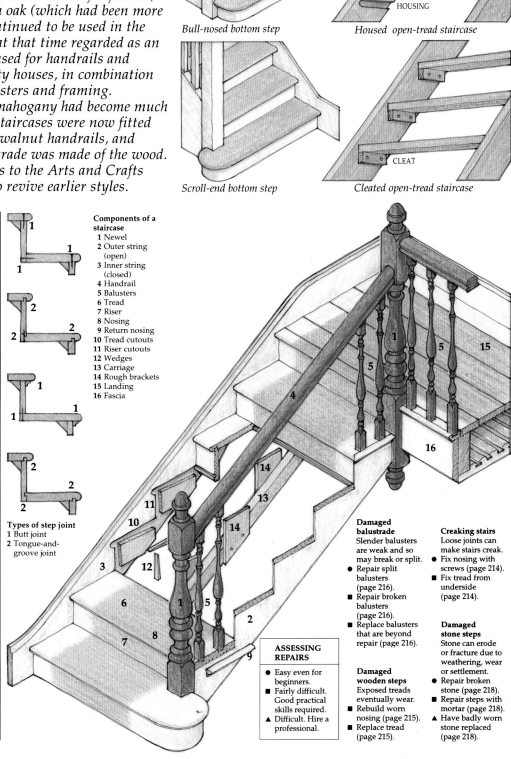

Bull-nosed bottom step

HOUSING

Housed open-tread staircase

Scroll-end bottom step

CLEAT

Cleated open-tread staircase

Steps

The steps of most wooden staircases are made in two parts, each step consisting of a horizontal tread board and a vertical riser. The risers are fitted between consecutive treads and are usually fixed to the treads with nail-fixed butt joints or with tongue-and-groove joints. Variations on these types of joints are also sometimes used for step assemblies.

The riser, which is about ³/₄in (18mm) in thickness, provides a closed back to the step. This allows the tread to be relatively lightweight, so the board is normally only 1¹/₈in (28mm) or so thick. The front edge of the tread, which is called the nosing, projects beyond the riser and is often rounded over.

The bottom step is usually made as a separate part that is added to the main flight. As it isn't fitted between the strings, it often has a shaped outer end. Bull-nosed and scroll-end steps are common examples.

The steps of a traditional open-tread staircase are of very simple construction, merely having a thick tread that is either housed or fixed with cleats to stringers on each side of the stair.

Components of a staircase
1 Newel
2 Outer string (open)
3 Inner string (closed)
4 Handrail
5 Balusters
6 Tread
7 Riser
8 Nosing
9 Return nosing
10 Tread cutouts
11 Riser cutouts
12 Wedges
13 Carriage
14 Rough brackets
15 Landing
16 Fascia

Types of step joint
1 Butt joint
2 Tongue-and-groove joint

Damaged balustrade
Slender balusters are weak and so may break or split.
● Repair split balusters (page 216).
■ Repair broken balusters (page 216).
■ Replace balusters that are beyond repair (page 216).

Damaged wooden steps
Exposed treads eventually wear.
■ Rebuild worn nosing (page 215).
■ Replace tread (page 215).

Creaking stairs
Loose joints can make stairs creak.
● Fix nosing with screws (page 214).
■ Fix tread from underside (page 214).

Damaged stone steps
Stone can erode or fracture due to weathering, wear or settlement.
● Repair broken stone (page 218).
■ Repair steps with mortar (page 218).
▲ Have badly worn stone replaced (page 218).

ASSESSING REPAIRS
● Easy even for beginners.
■ Fairly difficult. Good practical skills required.
▲ Difficult. Hire a professional.

Stringers

The ends of the treads and risers are jointed into thick inclined boards known as stringers (also as string-boards or strings). These are the structural members that run up each side of the steps. Two types are commonly used. The closed stringer has straight parallel edges with cutouts on the inner face to take the ends of the treads and risers. The open or "cut" stringer has a straight lower edge but is notched to the step shape along its upper edge to bear the treads and risers.

The stringer fitted to the wall is of the closed type and is usually referred to as the inner or wall stringer. The other, which carries the balusters, is usually called the outer stringer and may be either closed or open.

On some staircases an intermediate stringer, called a carriage, is fitted under the center to give support. This is necessary for a stair more than 3ft (1m) wide. The car-riage is usually a thick not-ched board, but may also be a bearer with rough brackets nailed to it. These brackets, which are short lengths of board, support the treads and are fixed to alternate sides of the carriage in order to distribute the load evenly.

On stairs that have a lath-and-plaster soffit, carriage bearers placed on one or both sides and at the center provide support for the lath, which is nailed across them. Sometimes the lath runs vertically, following the slope of the stair, and is nailed only to the underside edge of the steps.

Closed stringers have the treads and risers cut into them. The cutouts are some $1/2$in (12mm) deep, with a tapering bottom edge. Glued hardwood wedges are driven into the housings from the back to secure the treads and risers tightly. Triangular softwood "glue blocks," measuring about 4 x $1^1/2$in (100 x 38mm) are

glued into the angles between the tread boards and risers for extra support.

For open-stringer stairs, the joints between the outer string and the treads and risers are different to those of the closed wall stringer. The treads are simply glued and nailed to the horizontal edge of the stepped outer stringer. A "return" nosing

is nailed onto the end of the tread board to cover the end grain and the baluster joints. A carved or sawn bracket is sometimes fitted under the nosing for decorative purposes. To conceal the end grain of the riser, a mitered butt joint is made between the outer end of the riser and the vertical edge of the string.

Types of stringer joints
1 Closed stringer
2 Tread
3 Riser
4 Tread cutout
5 Tread wedge
6 Riser cutout
7 Riser wedge
8 Open stringer
9 Mitered butt joint
10 Return nosing
11 Baluster cutout

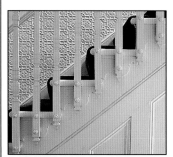

Late-C19th decorative stringer

C18th carved string brackets

C18th baluster-type newel made from mahogany

Mid-19th century staircase with solid newel post

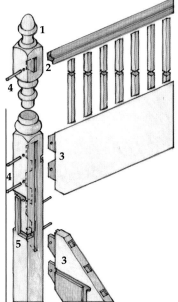

Construction details of a newel
1 Intermediate newel
2 Mortise-and-tenoned handrail
3 Mortise-and-tenoned strings
4 Dowels
5 Tread and riser cutouts

Newel posts

Newels were included in the construction of the earliest framed staircases. Placed at the foot and the head or turn of the stair, they support the staircase and balustrade. They are usually cut from solid wood, though paneled versions are also found.

The newel at the foot is a prominent feature of most newel staircases, by virtue of its material and its form or surface decoration as well as its size. However, instead of ending with a large post, eighteenth-century staircases frequently culminated in a cluster of balusters, which often included a fine newel.

Bulbous solid-hardwood newels, often turned and richly carved, were fashionable in the grand houses of the early nineteenth century. These inspired the vogue for turned newels, found even in modest houses until the beginning of the twentieth century. Eventually, simpler square-sectioned newels, in the manner of the earlier seventeenth-century style, were to supersede the turned forms. Some, however, were capped with a turned knob.

The newel at the bottom of the stair and usually the first intermediate post, too, are fixed to the floor. Often they are nailed to floorboards, but fixing to a joist gives greater rigidity. Hollow newels are sometimes fixed with a long threaded rod inside. The top newels of a dog-leg or open-well stair are fixed to the top floor and cut short, forming a decorative drop detail.

The newels are cutout to receive the steps and, if the post is paneled, the outer stringer as well. The string is tenoned into a solid newel and pegged for security. The handrail is cutout or tenoned into the post.

Typical patterns for round and square-turned balusters

Balustrades

The type of balustrade used for staircases from the seventeenth century until modern times consisted of a series of vertical balusters fixed to the top edge of the outer string or stair treads and to the underside of a handrail. On a newel stair the run of the balustrade is punctuated at every turn by the newel posts, while on a geometrical staircase the balustrade is uninterrupted.

The curving style of the geometrical stair became popular around the end of the eighteenth century and continued into the Victorian era. The handrails are molded or oval in section and relatively lightweight. At the foot of the stair, the rails often terminate with a volute supported by a group of balusters set on a scroll-endstep.

Early-nineteenth-century balustrades often have a handrail that terminates in a turned bun-shape cap attached to a slim newel post. Where the stairway changes direction or meets a landing, shaped handrail sections – turns, ramps, or swan necks – are used to cope with the change of level and direction. The various parts of the handrail are usually fixed together with dowel pegs or special bolts.

The balusters for newel and geometrical staircases may be decoratively turned (with a column-and-vase or twist pattern, for example) or they may simply be plain square sticks.

On well-constructed stairs the balusters are let into the underside of the handrail and into the top edge of the closed stringer. Otherwise, they are simply butt-jointed and nailed in place.

Open-stringer stairs may have either two or three balusters fitted to a tread. These are normally secured with tenons or dovetail joints, which are concealed by a return nosing fitted to the side of each step.

Painted mid-C18th Chinese Chippendale balustrade with mahogany handrail

C18th twist-pattern balustrade

WOODEN STAIR REPAIRS

MOST STAIRS ARE WELL CONSTRUCTED *and only require light repairs that can be carried out as part of your routine painting and decorating program. However, structural repairs may become necessary as a result of rough treatment or decades of use. Loose or weak parts should be repaired or replaced as soon as they are discovered.*

FIXING CREAKING STAIRS

Creaking stairs can be irritating and give the impression that a house is not properly maintained. The source is likely to be loose or flexing components rubbing together at their joints because of shrinkage or wear and tear. The most satisfactory repairs are achieved by working from the back of the step – however, if the stair has a plastered soffit it is much simpler to work from the front.

To identify the source of the creaking, remove any stair covering and walk up the stairs. Tread on and off each step, applying your weight to different parts to find out where the loose joints are situated.

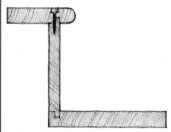

1 Screw the tread to the riser

Working from the front

One likely cause of creaking is a weak joint between the tread nosing and the riser. This is usually a tongue-and-groove joint, or a butt joint with a scotia molding set into the angle between the riser and the tread. In either case, the easiest solution is to drill and counterbore the tread to take two or three 1½in (38mm) screws set directly above the center line of the riser **(1)**. Inject woodworking adhesive into the holes and flex the board to help it penetrate the joint as far as possible. Insert the screws, which will pull the joint tightly together, and fit matching wooden plugs to cover the heads.

If the stair has featured hardwood treads, try not to use screws. Pry the joint apart a little and work glue into it with a brush. If this fails to get rid of the creaking, you will need to work from the underside.

Working from the back

If the underside of a staircase has a lath-and-plaster soffit, it will be necessary to cut into it to gain access to the problem area. To reduce the damage, locate the weak steps and note the position in relation to the underside. Chop away the plaster with a bolster chisel, then saw through or pull out the laths **(2)**. You will have to make good the plaster after completing the repair.

In some early houses the underside of the staircase leading up from the ground floor is enclosed with a partition between the outer stringer and the floor called a spandrel. This may be a lath-and-plaster stud wall or a wood-paneled frame. A door provides access to the cellar stairs or a cupboard space below the staircase. The underside of the stair is usually unfinished.

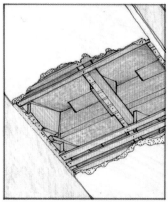

2 Clear away plaster and laths

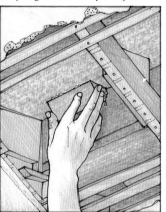

3 Inject glue into the opened joint

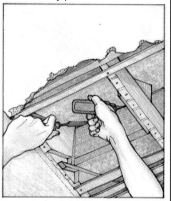

4 Rub-joint blocks into place

5 Glue and screw back joint

Fixing the tread

Glue blocks are normally fitted into the angle between the tread and the riser. If old glue has failed, knock the blocks off and clean the glue from the surfaces.

Use a chisel to pry apart the joint between the front of the tread board and the riser. Inject woodworking glue **(3)** and rub-joint the blocks in place **(4)**. To strengthen the joint, make and fit additional glue blocks.

Similarly, pry apart the joint between the back of the tread and the riser. Inject glue into the joint and insert screws to pull it tight **(5)**.

Do not use the stairs until the glue has set.

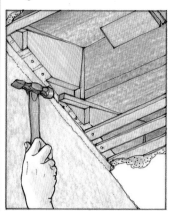

6 Fit new riser and tread wedges

Fixing worn cutouts

If the ends of the tread or riser are loose in their housings, pry out the wedges that help to hold the boards securely in position.

Use a narrow chisel to chip or pare out any hardened glue or splintered fragments of the old wedges that may remain in the housings.

Make new wedges of hardwood, apply woodworking glue, and drive them into place. Fit the vertical wedge for the riser and cut to length; fit the horizontal wedge for the tread **(6)**.

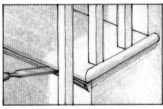

1 Guide the saw with a pinned batten

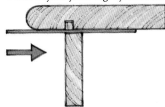

2 Saw in from front edge of the tread

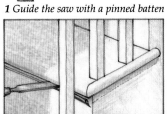

3 Pry off the nosing molding

4 Cut the riser tongue with a saw

REPAIRING DAMAGED STEPS

The treads of a wooden stair eventually wear at the nosing, especially if they are unprotected and made of softwood. Badly worn treads are dangerous and should be repaired or replaced without delay.

Treads are difficult to replace, since they may be held with tongue-and-groove joints across their width and the treads of closed-stringer stairs can only be removed from the back. Unless you have the necessary experience, it is therefore best to employ a builder or a carpenter – particularly if the staircase has carriage bearers, which can make replacement an even trickier operation.

Rebuilding the nosing

Mark cutting lines around the worn area. Hold a drill at 60 degrees to the surface, and at one end of the section that needs replacing drill four 1/8in (3mm) holes close together to form a slot. Set a power jigsaw to 60 degrees and make a sawcut along the line. To help make a straight cut, tack a guide batten to the tread (1).

At each end of the marked section, saw in from the front edge of the nosing to meet the first cut at right angles (2). You will need to reset the cutting angle of the saw for the second end. Tap the worn piece from below to free the waste. The end sawcuts will have cut into the riser, so these will need to be filled.

Cut a new section of wood to fit the cutout. If the riser board has a tongue, cut a groove into the underside of the new section to receive it. Shape the front edge of the nosing, then check the fit and glue the new section in place. When the glue has set, plane the surfaces flush.

Replacing a tread

Tread and riser assemblies may either be tongued and grooved or butt-jointed and nailed. In either case, the parts will probably need to be cut to free the tread.

Remove the glue blocks from under the tread and if there is a scotia molding under the nosing pry it free with a wide wood chisel (3). Also, remove any screws or nails. Try to pull out any nails – however, if the tread has a butt joint, you can cut through nails by sliding a hacksaw blade into the joint.

To free a tongue-and-groove joint, drill a continuous row of 1/8in (3mm) holes along the shoulder of the nosing joint to form a slot. Cut the tongue by hand. One method is to use a powered saber saw or jigsaw by inserting its blade into the slot (4). If it is an open-stringer stair, cut the rear tongue from the underside in a similar way.

How you remove the tread will depend on whether the staircase is a closed-stringer or open-stringer type (see below).

Closed-stringer stair

Remove the wedges from under each end of the tread. Using a hammer and a block of wood, give the tread a sharp tap from above to free the back joint and cutout joints (5). The tread should now be clear of the riser tongue at the rear, so you can drive it out of its housings from the front (6).

Make a new tread, but do not cut a groove on the underside. Build up the cut edge of the front riser with glued veneer or a thin strip of wood cut from a board with a machine saw. Apply glue, then insert the tread from the back and secure it with new hardwood wedges glued into place. Fit glue blocks inside the nosing. If needed, refit a scotia molding under the front edge.

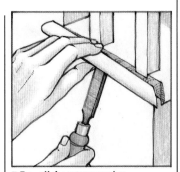

5 Strike the tread to free it

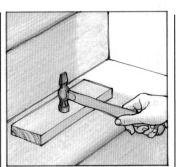

6 Drive out the tread from the front

Open-stringer stair

Pry off the return nosing carefully (7). Free and remove the balusters from the tread and handrail. Chisel out the wedge from under the tread housed in the wall string. Tap the open-string end of the tread from the rear to free it, then extract the board from the front (8).

Make a new tread of well-seasoned wood to match the shape of the old one and cut the joints for the balusters. Build up the cut edges of the risers with glued strips of wood. Glue and screw the tread to the risers and wedge the housing joint in the wall string. Fit the balusters, then fix the return nosing with a dab of glue and a nail at the mitered front end and a nail at the other.

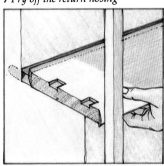

7 Pry off the return nosing

8 Pull the tread out from the front

215

REPAIRING BALUSTRADES

Much of the character of a staircase is provided by the balustrade. The repetition of the balusters, whether ornately turned or merely plain sticks, gives a pleasing decorative effect. If one or two balusters are damaged or missing, or have been replaced by non-matching ones, the symmetry is disturbed and the appearance spoiled.

Broken balusters are potentially dangerous, so should be repaired or replaced without delay. Try to preserve original turned ones. If they are beyond repair, either make replacements yourself or have new ones made to order.

Baluster fixings

On well-constructed stairs balusters are let into the underside of the handrail and the top edge of a closed stringer (1). However, you often come across staircases where the balusters are simply butt-jointed and nailed in place (2).

Open-stringer stairs may have two or three balusters to a tread. Usually, cutout or dovetail joints are used to secure them and the joints are covered with a return nosing (3).

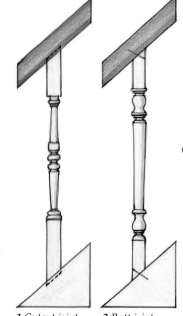

1 Cutout joint 2 Butt joint

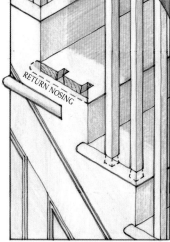

3 Dovetail-jointed balusters

Repairing a split baluster

Turned or slender wooden balusters tend to be fairly weak, and may break if they are struck from the side. A split baluster that has a long tapering break is simple to repair and there is normally no need to remove it from the balustrade.

Apply an even coating of woodworking glue to the surfaces of the break, then pull them together tightly with self-adhesive tape (4). Wipe off surplus glue with a damp cloth before binding up the repair. When the glue has set, peel off the tape. Clean up with a scraper and sandpaper, then finish to match the other balusters.

Repairing a broken baluster

If a break – at a narrow section of a turned baluster (5), for example – is short due to a weakness in the structure of the grain, gluing alone may not make a sufficiently strong repair. It is therefore better to remove the baluster and reinforce the repair with a wooden dowel.

To enable you to drill a stopped hole that will accurately align in both parts, first drill a $^3/_8$in (9mm) diameter hole about 2in (50mm) deep down the center of one of the parts (6). Make sure that the part you choose has beads and coves or similar details close to the end.

Saw off the broken end with a fine, thin-bladed saw. Make the cut on a shoulder line of the turned decoration (7), having made a pencil mark across the shoulder so you can align the parts when reassembling the baluster. Then glue the broken ends together carefully.

When the glue is set, drill down the other part of the baluster (8), using the glued-on piece as a guide – and again making the hole about 2in (50mm) deep. If need be, glue a piece of veneer to the end to make up the sawcut waste. Trim out the center to reopen the hole.

Cut a length of $^3/_8$in (9mm) dowel, then chamfer the ends and cut a groove along its length. Apply glue to the parts and assemble the doweled joint, using the pencil mark to help you realign the parts correctly (9). Wipe away surplus glue with a damp cloth.

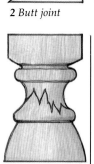

4 Bind break with tape   5 Weak section of baluster

6 Drill a hole down one part   7 Saw off end on a shoulder line

8 Drill the other part of baluster   9 Glue and dowel the parts

Replacing a baluster

If a baluster is beyond repair or missing, you will need to replace it. Select matching wood unless the baluster is to be painted. Plain square-sectioned sticks can easily be planed to size if they are not a standard timber section.

Making decorative turned balusters involves the use of a lathe. If you have access to one and have the necessary woodturning experience, make a cardboard template of the baluster's profile or take out a sound baluster to act as a guide. You can construct the template profile with drawing instruments, or use a profile gauge to take an impression of the shape.

If you lack the facilities to make a replacement yourself, take a sample baluster to a specialist woodturner and have a reproduction of it made. Some woodturning companies have copy lathes that reproduce the shape of an original automatically.

Whether you make a replacement yourself or have one made to order, the new baluster should be made overlength for cutting to size before fitting and finishing.

STONE STAIRS

STONE *is primarily an exterior building material and is not commonly employed indoors. However, it has been used to provide attractive interior features. Grand stone geometrical staircases are occasionally found in large late-eighteenth-century and nineteenth-century houses, as well as secondary stone stairs leading to the basement. Decorative wrought-iron or cast-iron balustrades were generally used to complement the solidity of stone staircases.*

Many houses of this period have a basement or semi-basement. To enable a large window and a doorway to be built at the front, an open "area" was created between the footpath and the front of the basement wall. Usually stone steps and a stone platform bridged the gap between path and front door, while a decorative iron or stone balustrade guarded the open area. The basement itself was reached by descending a stone or metal stairway that led down into the area.

1860s stone staircase with sweeping spandrel steps and cast-iron balustrade

STONE STAIR CONSTRUCTION

The design of stone steps can range from thick rectangular blocks (1) or thinner slabs forming treads and risers (2) to the more sophisticated carved wedge-shaped sections of spandrel steps (3).

Spandrel steps are used in the construction of interior open-well geometrical stairs. The inner ends of these steps are left square and built into the wall for support. Each step sits on the back edge of the one below and is located by a mortared splayed rebate cut in the lower front edge.

The shaping of the nosing usually follows the conventional rounded form used on wooden stairs, including the return nosing detail at the side and sometimes a scotia molding at the front.

Landings are made from slabs of stone built into the wall. To make installation easier they are constructed from pieces of a manageable size, which are locked together with special joints (a kind of stopped tongue-and-groove joint).

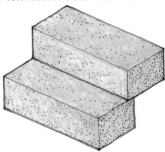

1 Rectangular-block stone steps

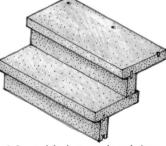

2 Stone slabs form treads and risers

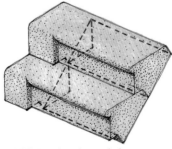

3 Wedge-shaped spandrel steps

Balustrades

Decorative iron balustrades are commonly used with stone stairs. The balusters were set in dovetail-shaped holes cut in the treads and secured by pouring molten lead into each hole. The solidified lead was then caulked and a stone-colored mortar used to fill and finish the recess (4).

Sometimes, where the stairs are narrow or simply for visual effect, the balusters are made to overhang the ends of the steps (5). These are fixed into the side face of the step with caulked lead in a similar way.

The handrail of an iron balustrade may be made of iron, in which case it is attached to the top ends of the balusters with countersunk machine screws (6). Alternatively, an interior stone staircase may have an elegantly molded handrail made of a hardwood such as mahogany. A wooden handrail is secured with woodscrews through an iron strip that is fixed to the balusters with machine screws (7).

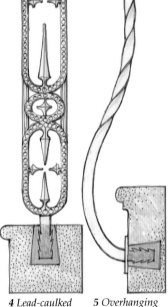

4 Lead-caulked metal baluster

5 Overhanging metal baluster

6 Metal handrail fixing

7 Wooden handrail fixing

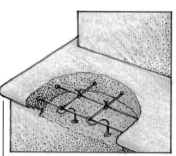

1 Reinforce repair with metal rod

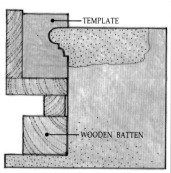

2 Make a running mold

REPAIRING STONE STAIRS

Even indoors stone eventually wears; and if settlement takes place in the supporting material, it may crack. Interior open-well stairs showing signs of distortion should be checked by an engineer. If it is not possible to cut out and reset or replace individual steps, a specialist builder may be able to build a framework of steel beams to reinforce the structure and box it in discreetly with a plaster soffit.

Worn exterior steps, especially when covered with ice, are dangerous and should be repaired or replaced. An outdoor metal balustrade needs regular maintenance if it is to remain a safe and attractive feature (see DECORATIVE METALWORK).

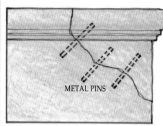

Reinforce the joint with metal pins

Repairing a damaged step

Working stone is a specialized skill and for any major repairs you need to employ an experienced craftsman, but it is possible to undertake simple repairs yourself.

To refix a small piece of broken stone, mix a two-part epoxy adhesive and apply a very thin coat to both faces. Press the broken piece into place and, if need be, secure it with adhesive tape until the glue has set. Many glues will only set at a specified temperature, so do the work on a warm, dry day.

If there is still a gap along the break line, mix some crushed-stone dust with a little adhesive to make a filler. Apply it with a putty knife, taking care not to spread it on the surface.

A larger broken piece can be replaced in a similar way, but needs reinforcing with non-ferrous metal pegs. Use a power drill fitted with a masonry bit to bore two or three 1/8in (3mm) stopped holes about 1/2in (12mm) deep in each part. Rock the

drill to open up the inside of the holes slightly. Drill the holes in the broken piece first. Position it and tap it to deposit some residual stone dust onto the other half. Remove the piece carefully and mark around the spot of dust then drill matching holes on the marked positions.

Cut short lengths of 1/8in (3mm) stainless-steel or brass rod for the pegs. Apply resin adhesive to the holes and to the broken faces of the stone. Insert the pegs and position the piece, then tape or clamp until the adhesive has set.

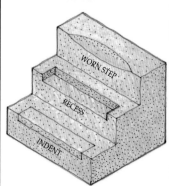

Indenting makes an effective repair

Fitting new stone

Indenting is an effective method for repairing steps that are badly worn. The damaged area is cut away to form a recess, then a stone "indent" is fitted and resin-bonded into it. This is a job for an experienced builder or a flooring specialist.

Mortar repair

Patching the stone with mortar (commonly known as a "plastic" repair) is a possible method for repairing worn or damaged steps. However, very careful preparation of the old surface is necessary. In addition, it is important that the mortar is capable of standing up to the physical demands put upon it, and it has to be compatible with the original stone.

Mixing a suitable mortar is the most difficult part of the operation, requiring a good deal of trial and error. Most mortars are mixes of lime, cement, and sand or stone dust (see REPAIRING DEFECTIVE STONE). A local stonemason should be able to supply small quantities of dust from common types of stone.

Mix small portions of the materials to test the strength, color, and texture. Make up a number of mixes, varying the ingredients slightly and keeping a careful note of each. Leave them to mature and weather for some weeks (the longer, the better). Test their hardness by scraping the surface; also, judge their appearance against the natural stone. The strength of the mortar should always be weaker than the material being filled. To match a rough surface, use a coarser aggregate. To give a more weathered appearance, dry brush the surface lightly before the mortar sets.

Using masonry chisels and a small sledge-hammer, cut back the worn area to sound stone to form a level recess. Undercut the edges to prov-

ide a key and a well-defined cutout, as mortar laid to finish with a feathered edge is likely to break away.

For recesses that are larger than 1 1/2in (38mm), metal reinforcement is necessary, particularly at the edges of steps. Use non-ferrous metal, such as brass rod and wire bent to shape, and set in epoxy-resin-filled holes (1). The reinforcement should be not less than 3/4in (18mm) from the finished surface.

To help form steps with a shaped nosing, make a template from thin steel plate. Take the shape from a sound section of the step, using a profile gauge. Transfer the outline onto the metal and cut it to shape. Mount the plate in a running mold (2) (see PLASTERWORK). Square-edged steps can be shaped with a trowel.

Apply the mortar in layers or "coats" to prevent shrinkage and cracking. Dampen the stone, then apply the first coat. Build up the full thickness with coats no more than 3/8in (9mm) thick. Key the surface of each and allow it to set hard. Dampen the previous coat before applying the next one.

Apply the last coat of a molded step so it stands just above the surface. Set up a straight wooden batten on which to run the mold. Shape the mortar to the finished profile. In order to stop the mortar drying out too rapidly, cover the repair with plastic sheeting or dampen it occasionally with a light spray of water.

CHAPTER EIGHTEEN

FIREPLACES

WITH THE INTRODUCTION of closed stoves and, later, central heating systems in the late nineteenth century, the open fire gradually ceased to be the focus of family activity. For centuries the solid-fuel fire had provided warmth, energy for cooking, and in some cases light. The earliest open-hearth fireplaces were literally at the center of the household, but as buildings and chimney systems developed the fireplace took up its now familiar place against the wall.

In most seventeenth-century houses, logs were burned on the hearth within large fireplace openings, but technological advances in design and, in the nineteenth century, the popularity of coal fires meant that the size of the opening was gradually reduced. Nevertheless, the architectural importance of the fireplace did not diminish. With the coming of the Industrial Revolution designers and manufacturers devised all kinds of patent grates and stoves, and these helped to insure that the fireplace remained the focus of attention in the room until its decline in recent times.

Some fireplaces are grandiose and ornate, others elegantly stylish or plainly functional. All have character and add a certain charm to the home. As a result, many period fireplaces, stripped out to make way for central heating or modernized décor, are now being reinstated to bring back the original character of the interior.

A restored late-C18th open fireplace with molded surround

Late-Victorian fireplace with classically styled mantelpiece

MANTELPIECES

Inigo Jones-style chimneypiece

T HE MANTELPIECE FORMS *a decorative "fireplace surround" – a term frequently used today – that frames the fireplace opening. Traditionally the surround was made from stone (including marble and slate) or from wood or cast iron.*

Early rural fireplaces were simply large functional openings without any surround. The inglenook type, with its massive timber lintel supported by exposed or plastered brickwork, provided a wide enclosure for heating and cooking and sometimes for seating, too. In more formal interiors, the fireplace was shaped in the current architectural style and had simple moldings carved into the stone that formed the opening.

MANTELPIECE STYLES

In England ornamental mantelpieces began with the Renaissance-style chimneypieces found in important houses of the late sixteenth century. The classical detailing served as an inspiration for architects such as Inigo Jones and Robert Adam in the following centuries and had a lasting influence on the style of the mantelpiece.

Inigo Jones established the fireplace as an architectural feature with his grandiose chimneypieces. The jambs were treated as columns, pilasters, or volutes supporting a lintel or frieze in the style of an entablature. This was surmounted by an overmantel that continued the decorative detail to form a pedimented frame, which was sometimes filled with a painting or later a mirror.

In less grand houses, the treatment was simpler but followed classical forms. Late-seventeenth-century and early-eighteenth-century fireplaces had simple wood or stone surrounds with bold bolection moldings. This type of mantelpiece did not always provide a shelf.

The eighteenth century

By the mid eighteenth century the use of decorative columns, pilasters, and consoles to support a mantelshelf had become common. Elaborate rococo decoration came into vogue for a short time. Mirror glass, which had formerly been a luxury that only the very rich could afford, was now available from France and was used in England and occasionally America to make richly decorative overmantels that reflected light into the room.

Mirrored overmantels and other mantelpieces inspired by Robert Adam were less ornate, being embellished with sophisticated low-relief classical decoration.

Victorian mantelpieces

The Victorian mantelpiece reflected a number of styles, including bolder interpretations of the classical forms. Marble surrounds were shaped to accommodate the cast-iron arched grate introduced around 1850. Mirrored overmantels also adopted an arched top. White and colored marble continued to be used widely and, to cater for the fashionable black color, slate was introduced too. This was sometimes artfully painted to simulate marbles, and gilding was often added to highlight incised moldings. Frequently, softwood mantels were painted to simulate marble or hardwoods.

Elaborate cast-iron mantelpieces also appeared. Some were made entirely of iron, while others had wooden shelves. Ornate overmantels that had mirrored panels and fancy display shelves became fashionable in the late-Victorian period.

The twentieth century

The influence of the Arts and Crafts movement was reflected in the designs of the early twentieth century. Natural materials such as oak, stone, and brick were now once again used for mantelpieces. The wooden mantels of the period were often ornamented with Art Nouveau fretted brackets and panels. Art Nouveau decoration was also applied to brass and copper hoods and to tiles used in cast-iron grates. But by the 1930s taste had changed, and marble, brick or plainly tiled mantelpieces had become the rage.

Impressive turn-of-the-century wood chimneypiece

Elegantly carved C18th stone mantelpiece

Grand stone mantelpiece with carved frieze and caryatid jambs

COMPONENTS OF A MANTELPIECE

The basic components of a mantelpiece are the jambs **(1)**, which support the frieze or lintel **(2)**, which in turn carries the mantelshelf **(3)**. The jambs may be in the form of columns, pilasters, carved caryatid figures, or simple architectural moldings. The frieze or lintel may be a matching architrave molding or a plain or decorated panel. The degree of ornamentation is dependent on the grandeur and style of the mantel. The shelf may be plain-edged or molded.

Most marble mantelpieces are supplied as separate elements for assembly on site. The jambs and frieze are usually constructed from marble panels or slips (narrow strips), which are held together with plaster of Paris and reinforced with plaster-bonded spacer blocks fitted inside. Wooden fireplace surrounds are made of boards glued and nailed together and assembled as a single piece. Cast-iron ones are made in one piece except for the shelf, which is a separate bolt-on fitting.

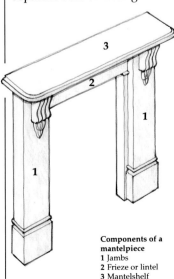

Components of a mantelpiece
1 Jambs
2 Frieze or lintel
3 Mantelshelf

HOW A MANTELPIECE IS FIXED

Marble mantelpieces are fixed to the wall with steel-wire ties or hooks fixed into the back edge of the parts. These are set in plaster or tied with wire to screws or nail hooks set in the wall.

Wooden ones are held in place with screws or nails fitted through metal plates attached to the jambs.

Cast-iron mantelpieces have cast lugs at the top and foot of the jambs for screws. If there is a shelf, it is bolted to the top of the casting before the mantelpiece is positioned against the wall.

With all types, plaster is applied around the mantelpiece to conceal the fixings and help hold it firm.

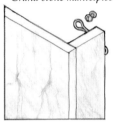  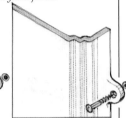

Marble attachment   *Wood attachment*   *Cast-iron attachment*

CLEANING MARBLE

Marble's variety of subtle colors and markings and ease of working have made it a favorite material for mantelpieces for centuries. However, it is a porous stone that can easily become dowdy or stained – which is why you sometimes come across marble mantelpieces that have been painted over. With care, marble can be stripped and cleaned to bring it back to its original finish.

General soiling

Use a soft brush and cloth to remove loose dust from the surface and crevices. Wash off surface dirt with warm, soapy distilled water, working up from the bottom to avoid leaving streaks. Use a bristle brush to clean moldings, and a toothbrush for fine detail. Rinse with clean water, then dry with a cloth.

For more persistent dirt, a commercial marble cleaner is often effective. Alternatively, use a solution of household ammonia, or try hydrogen peroxide in a solution of 1 part peroxide to 3 parts water (a few drops of ammonia can be added to it). Wear rubber gloves, a mask, and eye protection when working with any of these substances. Wet the surface before applying the solution to prevent dirt being drawn into the marble. Don't use household bleach, as it can etch the marble. Also, don't mix bleach with ammonia, as toxic fumes are produced.

Removing stains

To remove deep stains, you need to apply a poultice. Commercial poultices are available, or you can make your own. It consists of an absorbent substance (fuller's earth, powdered chalk or talc, or pulped white blotting paper or paper tissues) to which a stain solvent is added. Use baking powder mixed with distilled water as the solvent for soot stains; mineral spirits or acetone for oily stains; and ammonia or hydrogen peroxide for organic stains.

Mix the absorbent and solvent to make a paste and apply a layer, not less than $^1/4$in (6mm) thick, over the stain. Tape plastic film over the poultice to stop it drying too rapidly. Leave for a day or two before removing the plastic covering. The solvent will be absorbed into the marble to activate the stain, then as the poultice dries the stain substance is drawn out with the solvent. When the poultice is completely dry, scrape it off. You may have to repeat the process and change the solvent several times if more than one type of stain substance is present.

Finishing marble

Apply a thin film of marble polish or a fine white-wax polish and buff to a natural sheen. Maintain the surface by periodically washing with a mild soap solution then applying a little polish.

FIRE GRATES

THROUGHOUT THE EIGHTEENTH CENTURY *wood was the fuel most commonly used for open fires. Although wood will readily burn on the hearth, large logs were often supported on a pair of andirons or firedogs.*

With the advent of railroad transport, it became more economical to burn coal. Coal burns at a higher temperature than wood and needs a good flow of air. Wrought-iron fire baskets were therefore produced to contain the fuel and concentrate the heat. They also kept the coals clear of the floor, improving air flow and combustion while allowing ash to fall away. Although it is often possible to date a fireplace by the type of grate, this can be misleading since many old fireplaces have been modified over the years.

FIREBACKS

The early wood-burning open fires were simply laid in stone or brick-built fireplaces. In order to protect the masonry at the back of the fire, cast-iron firebacks were introduced. Produced in various sizes, with ornamental tops and decorated with allegorical subjects, they were very widely used. As a result, a great many eighteenth-century firebacks have survived to the present day. Excellent replicas are also readily available, taken from original patterns.

FROM A SMOKY LIFE
AND A SCOULDINGE WIFE
ALL MEN THAT DOE ME SE
TAKE PETIE AND DELIVER ME

Inscription on C17th fireback

DOG GRATES

Dog grates (also known as basket or stove grates) were introduced in the early part of the eighteenth century in England and were used to burn coal. A freestanding fire basket, which incorporated a fire-back and had iron or steel bars in front, was supported on legs similar in style to firedogs.

By the middle of the eighteenth century these grates had been transformed into refined examples of metalwork, with polished steel bars at the front and decorative steel or brass legs, which were joined by a handsome pierced-metal apron. Late-eighteenth-century designs intended for quality houses followed neo-classical styles and sometimes included Adam motifs. Today this type of grate can be found in period-style houses that have a large brick-built open fireplace, although the modern interpretation is likely to be a gas-fuelled coal-effect or log-effect fire.

FITTED GRATES

The decline in the use of wood as a domestic fuel, coupled with a better understanding of fireplace technology and the development of mass-produced cast iron, led to a proliferation of novel designs for more efficient fitted grates in the early nineteenth century.

Hob grates

During this period the hob grate, which was fitted into the lower half of the fireplace opening, became popular, especially in England. This type of grate featured wide decorative cast-iron front panels, fitted on each side of a high fire basket, and hob plates that provided a useful surface.

Register grates

The register grate was more common in America. This had a front frame or plate that fitted the opening. The early examples had cast-iron back and side panels, which lined the upper part of the fireplace. Above, a closure plate sealed off the chimney opening except for an aperture controlled by an

C18th hob-style register grate in an English house

Attractive reproduction cast-iron grate

Stylish 1930s marble-faced fireplace

adjustable plate known as a register. However, the name "register grate" eventually came to mean any grate with a front plate that fitted the fireplace opening, regardless of whether a register was fitted or not. Today this type is often referred to as an insert grate.

One configuration of register grates in polished steel had wide baskets with small side hobs, under which ran a pierced decorative apron.

Although the register plate offered some control of heat loss up the chimney and slowed the rate of burning by restricting the air flow, it didn't solve all the problems – especially since the basket was still set high.

Arched grates
Until the mid nineteenth century grates were generally square or rectangular and most were still made entirely of cast iron. The second half of the century

saw the introduction of the arched grate. This had a smaller fire basket which was set at a lower level and lined with fire bricks, while the register became a semi-circular flap or damper that was opened once the fire was alight. The style remained popular until the end of the century.

Splay-sided fireplaces
Around 1870 a new style emerged that had a narrow rectangular opening with splayed sides decorated with tiled panels. The fire basket was now set very low. It was most popular in England, as central heating systems were evolving in the United States.

This pattern continued, as, by the 1930s, cast-iron grates had been ousted by plainer one-piece units in England, combining fireplace and mantelpiece as a single entity. In twentieth-century America, such grates were relatively uncommon.

MAINTAINING A GRATE
When open fires were in constant use it was considered necessary that the grate was polished daily with black lead. Grate polish is still available, although modern heat-proof paints can now be used to reduce regular maintenance.

Blacking the grate
If you need to brighten up your grate, use a traditional-style graphite grate polish. This imparts an attractive silver-black finish that is ideal for highlighting decorative details. Apply it evenly with a brush, then polish with a soft cloth.

If a cast-iron grate shows signs of rusting, remove the rust with a wire brush – then either use grate polish or, for a stronger finish, apply stove black. The latter is specially designed to withstand high temperatures and produces a matte black finish.

Polishing metal
Dull or lightly rusted polished steel can be revived with fine steel wool dipped in thin oil. Wear rubber gloves to protect your hands. Rub the surface to a bright finish, always working in the same direction, then use a cloth to wipe it dry. Alternatively, apply an abrasive liquid cleaner with a cloth.

Polish dull brass or copper with a suitable metal polish, following the maker's directions. If need be, use a heat-resistant transparent lacquer in order to protect the newly polished surface.

SOLID-FUEL STOVES
Wood-burning stoves are efficient space heaters, popular as a means for heating homes in Europe and America since the eighteenth century. Made of cast iron or steel plate, and in some cases incorporating heat-retentive soapstone, they have been manufactured in a great variety of sizes and styles. Restored originals and reproductions of old designs are available from antique dealers and stove shops.

The basic stove
Solid-fuel stoves are mostly designed to be freestanding, although you do sometimes see one fitted into a fireplace opening. Essentially a stove is an enclosed chamber that is provided with a regulator for controlling the air flow. The fuel burns slowly and completely, the heat being absorbed by the casing then radiated out into the room. A stovepipe fitted into the top or rear carries away the smoke and also helps to radiate the heat. A hinged door, which may be glazed, or a removable top plate gives access for loading the fuel. Some stoves have a decorative top, while others provide a flat surface that can serve as a hotplate.

The general trend toward the use of cleaner fuels and central heating systems in the early twentieth century meant that old fireplaces and stoves became redundant in many homes. However, there is now a resurgence of interest in traditional heating methods and many disused fireplaces are being opened up or fitted with stoves.

Old stoves
It's easy to be tempted by an attractive antique stove – but make sure when buying one that it has been properly restored or is in genuinely good order. If you purchase an antique stove and intend to use it, establish that it is safe to use and that it meets

your heating requirements. Consult a stove specialist should you have any doubts.

A modern reproduction that can burn a variety of fuels may be a better option if you are planning to use a stove as your main source of heating, since most antique stoves are not airtight and are therefore much less efficient producers of heat.

Installation
In theory it is possible to fit a freestanding solid-fuel stove yourself. Nevertheless, it is advisable to consult a specialist, as the risk of fire is great in the event of the stove being improperly installed.

Most stove suppliers offer advice and an installation service designed to suit their customers' needs.

TILED FIREPLACES

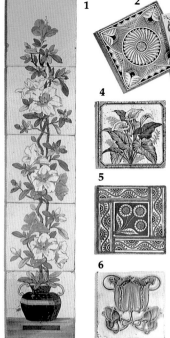

T HE IMPORTANCE *of fireplaces to interior design is evident from the degree of decoration that has been applied to them throughout history. Mantelpieces of stone, wood, and later cast iron, which relied as much on the color and texture of the material as on carved embellishment for their effect, provided an ornamental frame around plain, functional fire openings or somber cast-iron grates. However, this was to change during the nineteenth century as the use of colored glazed tiles for grates and mantelpieces became increasingly popular.*

Fireplace tiles

The production of tin-glazed tiles had been developed in Holland during the sixteenth century. Dutch designs and techniques inspired and influenced the English tile industry, which became established in the eighteenth century. The fire-resistant properties of clay tiles, as well as their tough easy-to-clean surface and decorative qualities, made them ideally suited for fireplace use.

As well as plain tiles and tiles in the Dutch "Delft blue" style, decoratively molded tiles were produced and a variety of fine tiles depicting domestic scenes, ancient and modern stories, animals, and plants. Tile-manufacturing techniques newly introduced as a result of the Industrial Revolution, combined with the mass production of cast-iron grates, meant that tiled grates could be produced fairly cheaply. During the Victorian era decorative tiles became quite commonplace in the parlors of even modest homes.

Tiled grates

The typical tiled Victorian grate had splayed side panels with five 6in (150mm) square picture tiles fitted one above the other, although sometimes these were separated by plain or patterned half-tiles or quarter-tiles. It was also possible to buy sets of decorative tiles that, when assembled, made up a complete panel. The tiles were fixed with plaster into a pair of metal backing frames.

REPAIRING TILES

In order to extract a cracked tile for repair, it is necessary to remove the entire fireplace. Consequently, unless the break is particularly unsightly (if, for example, the tile is smashed and the parts have become dislodged), you may be better advised to live with the crack.

If, on the other hand, you have bought a damaged grate from an architectural-salvage company or have to take out a fireplace temporarily for any reason, then it is clearly worth repairing any broken tiles.

Removing tiles

Remove any rust from the threaded fixing studs on the back of the grate with a wire brush. Apply penetrating oil to the threads to help free the nuts fitted on the studs. Remove the metal backing frame and pry out the tiles very carefully.

Cleaning tiles

Scrape off the old plaster from the backs of the tiles. These tiles are not grouted, so very little plaster will need to be cleaned from the edges. Wash them with a solution of detergent and distilled water. If tarry soot deposits have marked the surfaces, apply a coating of water-washable paint stripper. This will, of course, also remove paint if the tiles have been painted over.

Soak the tiles in distilled water before applying the stripper. This prevents the dirt from being absorbed into the ceramic body. Remove the residue of the stripper from smooth-surfaced tiles with a plastic or wooden scraper, or with a bristle brush from textured ones. Wash the tiles in clean water and leave them to dry.

The grate is enhanced by the tile-paneled overmantel

Floral tiles decorate the sides and hood of the grate

Gluing the break

Dry-assemble the fragments to check the fit. If the tile is broken into several pieces, it may only be possible to re-assemble it in a certain order.

Use a ceramic adhesive for bonding a clean break in thick earthenware, it will dry clear. Wet the broken edges, then apply the glue to them evenly. Wipe squeezed-out glue from the surface of the tile with a damp cloth. Hold the pieces together with strips of cellophane tape till the glue has set (1).

A two-part epoxy-resin adhesive mixed with a little titanium dioxide (available from pharmacists) will give a strong joint and is suitable for colored tiles with a white ceramic body. Heat the tubes on a radiator or in direct sunlight for a short time, to make the glue flow better, then mix the two components together and add the titanium-dioxide. Apply the glue and assemble the pieces on a flat worktop covered with polyethylene sheeting. Wipe any glue from the surface of the tile with a cloth dampened with denatured alcohol. Tape the join until the glue has set. If a white line remains, you can touch in the color with enamel paint from model shops (2).

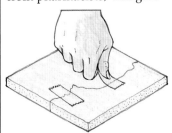

1 Hold parts together with tape

2 Touch in colors with paint

Patching chipped edges

If the colored glaze has been chipped at the edge as a result of the break, add some talcum powder to the epoxy adhesive to make a filler. Using a knife, apply the filler so it is raised just above the surface. When it has set, scrape it flush with a putty knife. Paint the patch with enamel to match the color of the tile.

Fitting the tiles

Set out the repaired tiles on the two backing frames and bolt them to the rear of the grate's side frames. Pack out the back of the tiles with small pieces of wood so that they butt snugly against the front (1). Apply plaster of Paris over the back of the tiles to fix them in place (2).

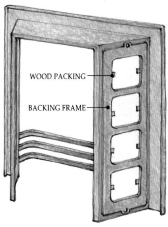

WOOD PACKING

BACKING FRAME

1 Pack out the back of the tiles

2 Fix the tiles with plaster

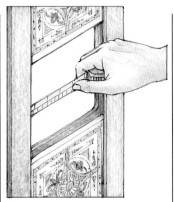

1 Measure the depth of the groove

Replacing tiles

When you need to replace a tile but removing the entire fireplace is impractical, it is sometimes possible to work from the front. The replacement has to be cut down in width slightly – so if the tile is a rare one this may not be an appropriate repair.

Protecting your eyes, chip out the broken tile with a cold chisel; then clean out the grooves in each side of the iron frame. Measure the depth of the grooves (you will need to measure the deepest one if they are different) to determine how much to cut from the new tile (1). Reduce the width of the tile by half the depth of the groove, taking the material off both side edges, so that the design remains symmetrical (2). Wearing a mask and eye protection, remove the waste with a power grinder or with coarse sandpaper.

Remove just enough to allow the tile to be fitted into the hole when one edge is pushed fully into the side groove. Apply a strip of self-adhesive tape to the face of the tile to form a tab, so you can hold the tile (3). Apply plaster of Paris to both side grooves and the back of the tile. Insert the tile fully into the side groove, then slide it back halfway into the other. Hold the tile until the plaster has set. Before it hardens, clean away the surplus from the face of the tile.

2 Insure design is symmetrical

3 Apply an adhesive-tape holding tab

HEARTH TILES

Cracked hearth tiles are common, as they tend to get broken by falling objects, such as fire irons. Loose ones also frequently occur, due to failure of the original cement adhesive. Old hearth tiles are not normally grouted. As a result, it is often possible to lift out loose tiles cleanly for replacement or repair.

Use a chisel and hammer to chip out some of the old cement to make sufficient room for fresh ceramic-tile adhesive, taking care not to damage the edges of the tiles still *in situ*.

Apply a thin bed of adhesive and press the new or repaired tiles into place. Use a straightedge to check that they are flush with the surrounding ones. If the old bedding cement is hard and difficult to remove, bond them in place by brushing on an adhesive.

ANATOMY OF A FIREPLACE

MANTELPIECE AND GRATE STYLES *have altered, but the basic structural elements of a fireplace have not radically changed over the centuries. The early combination of a large stone or brick opening with a chimney built over it evolved from the obvious fact that smoke rises, rather than from a scientific understanding of how a well-devised flue system functions.*

Open wood and, later, coal-burning fires were very inefficient and it was not until Benjamin Thompson, known as Count Rumford, produced his thesis on the principles of fireplace design in 1799 that smaller grates and improvements in the internal shape of the opening were introduced.

ELEMENTS OF A FIREPLACE

A brick or stone enclosure **(1)** forms the basis of the fireplace. Variously known as the firebox, fireplace opening, or recess, it may be set flush with the wall itself or built out into the room, forming a chimney breast **(2)**. A chimney breast rises through the height of the house, emerging through the roof to form a chimney stack. The throat **(3)** and flue **(4)** carry the smoke up the chimney. If the chimney is shared by several fireplaces on different floors, it may contain more than one flue.

The masonry over the fireplace opening is supported by a lintel or a brick arch **(5)**. Old inglenook fireplaces used massive oak beams, whereas a sturdy iron strap usually supports an early brick arch. Later fireplaces may have a straight arch supported by angle iron (an L-shaped iron bar), and early-twentieth-century ones often have a cast-concrete lintel. On no account should these structural beams and lintels be cut into or taken out without expert advice.

A hearth, constructed from non-combustible materials such as stone or tile-faced concrete, projects out into the room to protect the floor from falling embers **(6)**. In most old houses the hearth was set flush with the floor, although sometimes a super-imposed hearth was used to raise the level. The area within the fireplace opening, which is known as the back hearth **(7)**, is usually level with the hearth itself.

A dog grate for burning wood or coal **(8)** may be placed on the back hearth. However, by the mid nineteenth century the cast-iron register grate, which filled in the opening, had become the fashion (see FIRE GRATES).

To complete the assembly, a mantelpiece – or fireplace surround, as it is often called today – is fitted to frame the grate or firebox **(9)**. The mantelpiece itself may be constructed from stone, slate, marble, wood, or cast iron. The walls around it may be finished with wood paneling, or more commonly with plaster, and in some instances the mantelpiece extends upward to form an impressive chimneypiece. Mirrored overmantels were introduced in the late eighteenth century, and these became a common feature of Victorian sitting rooms.

Fireplaces

Poor design or lack of maintenance can cause smoke.
- ■ Modify the fire opening (page 227).

Mantelpieces

The mantelpiece may be missing or in poor condition.
- ● Clean a soiled or stained marble mantel (page 221).
- ● Strip a painted mantelpiece, if appropriate (page 228).
- ■ Glue a cracked cast-iron surround (page 229).
- ▲ Or have it welded. (pages 228, 229)
- ■ Replace a missing mantelpiece (page 230).

Grates

The grate may be damaged or missing.
- ● Maintain a grate regularly in order to preserve it (page 223).
- ■ Repair a damaged grate (page 228).
- ■ Replace missing or badly damaged decorative tiles (page 225).
- ■ Replace cracked or loose hearth tiles (pages 225, 229).
- ■ Choose and fit a replacement grate (pages 229, 230).

ASSESSING REPAIRS

- ● Easy even for beginners.
- ■ Fairly difficult. Good practical skills required.
- ▲ Difficult. Hire a professional.

Components of a fireplace

1 Firebox
2 Chimney breast
3 Throat
4 Flue
5 Brick arch
6 Hearth
7 Back hearth
8 Dog grate
9 Mantelpiece

Flues

Blocked or decayed flues are unable to function properly.
- ▲ Have the chimney swept (page 227).
- ● Check that the flue is clear (page 66).
- ▲ Have the flue lined (page 68).
- ▲ Have the chimney repaired or rebuilt (pages 66, 67)

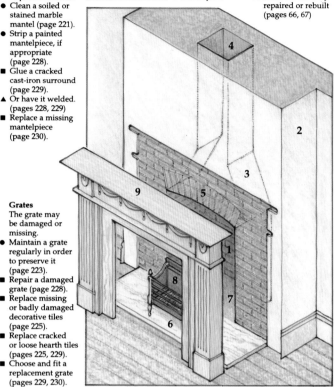

SOLID-FUEL OPEN FIRES

An open fire burning wood or coal is a cheerful sight, but if it is your only source of heat, as it was for centuries, the romantic image can soon fade – especially if the fire does not burn properly. Getting a fire started and keeping it alight then becomes a challenge, if not a chore.

How the system works

For wood and coal fires to burn well a good supply of air is needed under the grate **(1)**, as well as a means of escape for the hot gases and smoke **(2)**. The firebox **(3)** safely contains the fuel, which is laid on an iron grate **(4)**. The barred grate holds the fuel clear of the hearth and allows air to circulate through it. As the fuel is consumed, waste ash drops through the grate so the fire isn't stifled. If the chimney is inadequate or the flow of air restricted, the fire will not function effectively.

How the system works
1 Air supply
2 Hot gases
3 Firebox
4 Iron grate

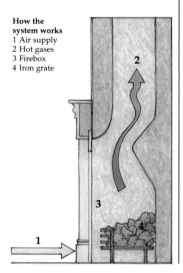

SMOKING FIREPLACES

The efficiency of an open fire depends not only on the supply of air but also on the size of the flue compared with the size of the fireplace opening. Count Rumford (see right) recommended that the cross-sectional area of the flue should be about a tenth of the size of the opening. However, fireplaces tended to be smaller after the mid nineteenth century. Modern flue-liner manufacturers favor a ratio of one to seven, and there are sizing charts published that give details of current standards.

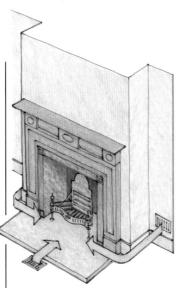
Alternative positions for air vents

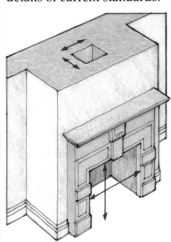
Check flue and fireplace opening dimensions (flue area/opening area ratio should be about 1:7 or 1:10).

Improving ventilation

If your fire smokes or won't burn properly, see if opening a window improves matters. If it does, you need better ventilation in the room.

One solution is to install a window vent, although this may cause an uncomfortable cross draft. A much more efficient form of ventilation is either a single ducted vent set into the floor in front of the fireplace or twin ducted vents set into the floor or external walls on each side of the chimney breast.

Improving air flow

When wood and coal are burned, flammable gases, tarry substances, acids, and dust are given off. However, because domestic fires are relatively inefficient not all of these substances are consumed. Instead, they rise up the chimney and some of them condense on the inside of the flue. Unburned carbon combines with these tars and acids, creating soot – which builds up over a period of time and effectively reduces the size of the flue.

Have chimneys that are regularly used swept at least twice a year – ideally before, during, and at the end of the heating season. A soot-laden flue is a fire hazard, since the unburned elements of the soot can ignite, causing a chimney fire which may reach high temperatures and damage the chimney.

Modifying the flue

If a flue is too large, it can be reduced by fitting a liner. A variety of methods and materials are used, including flue liners made of flexible stainless steel, ceramic, lightweight concrete sections, or concrete cast *in situ* (see CHIMNEY LINERS).

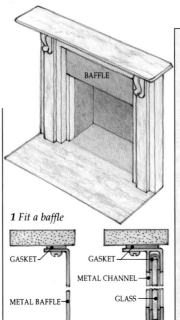
1 Fit a baffle

GASKET — METAL BAFFLE — GASKET — METAL CHANNEL — GLASS

2 Attach with discreetly placed screws

Modifying the fireplace opening

One way to reduce the size of the fireplace opening is to raise the hearth, though this may look out of character with the fireplace. In fact, it is probably both easier and more acceptable to install a baffle. This is fitted across the width of the opening (1) and can be made of steel, copper, or heatproof glass.

In order to establish the size of the baffle panel, with the fire alight temporarily tape a metal or thoroughly dampened plywood sheet across the top of the fireplace opening – then adjust it up and down to determine the most effective position.

Make or commission a panel of the required size in a style and material that will harmonize with the mantelpiece. Attach it with discreetly placed screws and fit a fiberglass tape around the joint to act as a gasket (2).

Fitting a hood or canopy

If a baffle is unsuitable or installing one is problematic, it may be worth asking a fireplace specialist whether fitting a metal smoke hood or canopy in the opening is the best solution.

RUMFORD'S REFORMS

Count Rumford in his essays on fireplaces proposed that the flue should be a specified proportion of the fireplace opening and that the area immediately above the fire should be narrowed down to form a throat. The throat causes the rising air to speed up as it passes through the constriction, thus improving the draft up the chimney.

To improve the efficiency of the fire further, he argued that the fireplace itself ought to be smaller and should be lined with firebrick. The sides, he suggested, should be splayed to reflect the heat into the room, and the fireback made one third the width of the opening. Also, the upper part of the fireback was to slope forward to reflect the heat. A smoke shelf formed at the throat by the sloping back helped prevent rainwater falling into the fire and was also thought to improve the air circulation within the flue.

Some large fireplaces in houses built before the late eighteenth century were modified in accordance with Rumford's principles. Some of these have splayed sides with marble or tiled panels around the fireplace opening where the original opening was reduced.

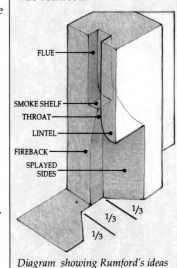
FLUE — SMOKE SHELF — THROAT — LINTEL — FIREBACK — SPLAYED SIDES — 1/3 — 1/3 — 1/3

Diagram showing Rumford's ideas

RESTORING FIREPLACES

ALTHOUGH FIREPLACES *contribute significantly to the character of a house, years of neglect can reduce a fine example to a poor state. Fortunately, however, the damage is often superficial.*

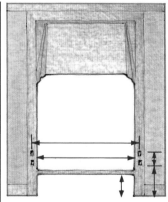

Chemical stripping, as shown on this partly stripped fireplace, will remove thick old paint to reveal the fine detail of the cast iron.

STRIPPING A MANTELPIECE

The efficiency of commercial chemical stripping processes and home-use strippers has created a fashion for stripping painted fireplaces and mantelpieces. However, stripping them is not always appropriate, as some mantelpieces were intended to be painted. Stripping paint from a marble mantelpiece would seem to be an obvious improvement – but beware, a marbled paint finish on wood or slate can look like the real thing. It was also a common practice to treat softwood mantelpieces with wood grain effects imitating the appearance of the more expensive hardwoods.

Always try to detect which materials have been used in the construction of a mantelpiece before you proceed to strip the paint. A wooden surround will feel warmer to the touch than stone or cast iron. Does it feel as warm as the baseboard nearby?

The decorative moldings applied to an Adam-style mantel were often made of plaster or gesso, and they can quite easily be damaged by stripping tools. If you discover a marbling paint finish that has been painted over, it is best either to seek the services of a specialist or to leave well alone.

Adam-style details made of gesso

Stripping methods

Cast-iron mantelpieces that have been removed can be efficiently stripped by an industrial stripping company, but it is better to strip all other materials by hand.

Modern chemical strippers can be used to remove paint from marble, wood, and cast-iron mantelpieces. Use a gel or paste stripper, applying it according to the manufacturer's instructions. Try it out on a small unob-trusive area first – and even if the test proves satisfactory, proceed carefully. Scrape off the softened paint (using a wooden or plastic spatula for marble) and clean out moldings and carved detail with a bristle brush.

Apply fresh stripper in order to remove any residual film of paint, particularly from open-grained timber such as oak, then wash the wood down and wipe dry.

REPAIRING A GRATE

Cast iron is brittle and prone to cracking if struck sharply. As a result, the lift-off bars of grates are frequently missing, having been damaged and then discarded. Fortunately, however, missing or broken parts can be repaired or remade.

Grate bars

Cast iron can be welded. So if you have a grate that has broken bars, a blacksmith or a garage repair shop or fireplace specialist may well be able to repair them for you.

If the bars are missing, measure the size of the grate and prepare a dimensioned drawing to enable a fireplace specialist to supply or reproduce a replacement.

Architectural-salvage companies may also be of help. They sometimes keep useful parts from old grates that are no longer serviceable.

Measure the width and height between the locating holes, and the height above the floor or grate.

Chipped edges

On a decoratively molded grate a chipped edge may not show sufficiently to be a problem, but on a plain grate the defect may be obvious.

Providing the chip is not likely to be exposed to high temperatures, fill it with an epoxy metal filler. Overfill the defect slightly and, when the filler has set, rub down flush with the surface. Apply stove black and grate polish to disguise the repair.

STRIPPING A GRATE

You sometimes come across grates no longer in use that have been painted to blend in with the décor. If you wish to restore the original finish, remove the paint with a chemical stripper. Hot-air stripper guns aren't suitable for this purpose as the mass of metal dissipates the heat.

Cover the area around the fireplace with polyethylene sheeting and apply a gel or paste stripper, following the manufacturer's instructions. Remove the softened paint from flat surfaces with a scraper, and from molded ones with a bristle brush. Wipe down and then apply grate polish or stove black.

A grate that has been removed can be taken away for dipping in a chemical stripping tank – or for a bright finish you can have it sandblasted and polished. Remove any decorative tiles from a grate before you send it for sandblasting – and if vulnerable, for stripping too.

FITTING A FIREPLACE

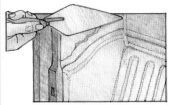

Fill the crack with fire cement

BROKEN FIREBRICKS

Firebricks can be repaired *in situ*, but seriously decayed bricks need to be replaced.

Rake out a crack with the tip of a pointing trowel after wire-brushing to remove soot. Dampen the brick with clean water and fill the crack with refractory cement or moldable firebrick compound specially designed for this purpose. Press the cement in well with the trowel, then smooth it flush with the surface. Do not use the fire for several days.

It is sometimes possible to repair a decayed brick in a similar way – but if it needs to be replaced, you will have to remove the grate in order to make the replacement. You may be able to purchase a matching firebrick from a masonry supply house or from a salvage company. If not, cast one yourself using fire cement.

REPAIRING CAST IRON

If you lever out a cast-iron fireplace surround without removing the fixings from the lugs cast in the vertical edge of the jambs, that may cause the metal to fracture.

Have cracks in cast iron welded – or if the damaged part will not be subjected to high temperatures, repair it with a two-part epoxy glue.

Before gluing them, clean the surfaces with denatured alcohol. Arrange the broken parts so gravity will hold them together or so they can be clamped properly.

Apply the adhesive to the broken edges and assemble the parts, making sure they are well seated. Cramp the parts or bind them with masking tape. Wipe off excess glue with denatured alcohol.

WITH THE DECLINE OF OPEN FIRES *in favor of more efficient or convenient methods, such as gas and electric appliances or central heating systems, many old fireplaces were removed and the fire opening filled in. Sometimes the fireplace was left in place and paneled over, making restoration a relatively straightforward job. Fortunately, there is a ready supply of original and reproduction grates and mantelpieces – so replacing a fireplace that has been taken out is not too difficult either, provided that the flue is in good order.*

REINSTATING AN OLD FIREPLACE

Before reinstating a fireplace it is advisable to check that the fireplace opening, hearth and chimney are all in good condition, and that proposed alterations will comply with building regulations.

These stipulate minimum requirements for the size and thickness of the hearth; the proximity to the chimney breast of combustible materials, such as joinery, joists, and floorboards; the thickness of the brickwork; height of chimney stacks, air supply and type of flue lining. A certain amount of flexibility may be allowed in special circumstances, so it is worth seeking professional advice.

Clearing the opening

It is safer to leave chimney repairs to a professional, but you can prepare the opening and fit a fireplace yourself.

Demolition work always creates a lot of dust, so cover the floor and any furniture that cannot be removed from the room. Chop away the plaster with a small sledgehammer and bolster chisel to expose the brickwork. Note the outline of the original opening where it contrasts with the brick or blockwork infill. Cut out the infill material, taking care not to chip the original brickwork, especially the lintel. Remove

all traces of old rubble, leaving a clear opening. If the opening has been sealed with plasterboard over a timber frame, strip it out with a crow bar.

Selecting a fireplace

When choosing a grate or mantelpiece, keep in mind the type and size of room as well as the date of the house. Original examples can be bought from architectural-salvage companies, either fully restored or in need of some work. The price will reflect their condition and rarity. Alternatively, you could buy one of the many excellent reproductions that are available.

A register grate will need to be the right size – that is slightly larger than the mantelpiece opening. If this proves difficult, you could fill the space with marble, slate, or narrow tiled panels plaster-bonded to the wall around the grate.

With luck, the overall size of the mantel can be determined by the outline left in the old plaster where the original was removed.

Preparing the wall

Chop away plaster around the fireplace opening back to the brickwork to leave a clearance of about 2in (50mm) all around the new mantelpiece when it is fitted.

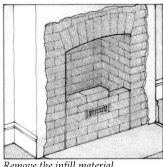

Remove the infill material

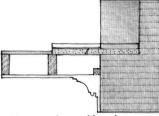

1 Fit a superimposed hearth

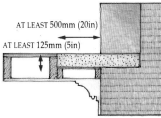

AT LEAST 500mm (20in)

AT LEAST 125mm (5in)

2 A new hearth must be correct size

Preparing the hearth

An inadequate hearth constitutes a fire risk. Cracked stone hearths should either be replaced or covered with a superimposed hearth **(1)**. To make one, have a slab of marble cut to size and set it level on a bed composed of 1 part cement, 1 part lime, and 6 parts sand. Build up the back hearth flush with the surface of the slab, using 1 part cement and 4 parts sand.

If you are using tiles for the hearth and plan to have an open recess with a dog grate, lay the front and back hearth together on a 1:4 mix.

If alterations to the fireplace constitute new work, the constructional hearth **(2)** must be made to project at least 20in (500mm) in front of the fireplace opening and 6in (150mm) on each side. It must be at least 5in (125mm) thick, or as stipulated in the building regulations.

FITTING
A REGISTER GRATE

Before installing a register grate, make sure that the size of the flue is appropriate for the grate opening and that there is a proper throated lintel to divert the smoke into the flue.

Position the grate on the hearth, placing it centrally in the firebox (or the chimney breast if they differ) and setting it against the wall. Check that it is plumb and square. If the opening is larger than the front plate, fill in the space at the sides with mortared brick. Should the top fall short, add a concrete lintel supported by the side brickwork **(1)**.

Temporarily position the mantelpiece to see whether it fits snugly against the grate. If need be, pull the grate forward to butt up to the back edge of the mantel opening. Remove the mantelpiece, and then seal and secure the front plate to the wall with refractory cement **(2)**.

FITTING A MANTELPIECE

The method for fitting the mantelpiece will depend on its construction. Wooden and cast-iron types are relatively straightforward. Hold the mantel up to the grate and centralize it. Check that it is plumb and level. Mark the position of the screw holes through the fixing plates or lugs fitted to the side jambs **(1)**. Remove the mantelpiece, then drill and plug the wall. Replace and fix the mantel with brass screws.

Backfill the area behind the grate with a lightweight concrete mixture of 6 parts perlite, leca, or vermiculite aggregate to 1 part cement. Fill the space through the damper aperture, and trowel the top surface so it slopes toward the opening **(2)**.

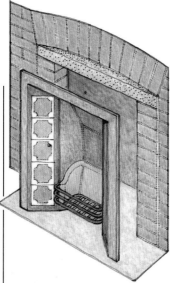
1 Reduce the opening if required

2 Seal the front plate with cement

1 Mark the fixing holes

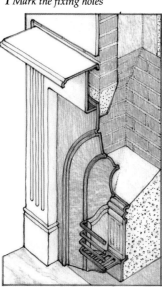
2 Fill the space through damper hole

Marble mantelpieces

Installing a marble mantelpiece requires a different technique, since the jambs, frieze, and mantelshelf are usually separate pieces. If corbels located on wooden dowels or metal pins are to be fitted, bond them in place with fine casting plaster. Fit the jambs first. These have to be set the right distance apart. Also, check that they are plumb, at the same level at the top and in the same plane across the front **(1)**.

Before fixing the mantelpiece in place, drill and plug the wall and fit fixing screws to fall inside the jambs close to the wire ties or hooks in the back edge. If no fixings are provided in the marble, use strips of expanded metal lath bonded with plaster.

First apply fine casting plaster on the hearth inside the base of each jamb. This sets quickly, so work fast. Bind the jambs with copper wire to the screws in the wall. Set them up accurately and apply a generous dab of plaster over the fixings. Apply generous amounts of the plaster adhesive inside the jambs, positioning them where you can reach to help hold them securely.

Spread a fairly thin bed of plaster on the top meeting surfaces and place the frieze member across the jambs **(2)**. Set the mantelshelf in place on a thin bed of plaster and bond it to the wall **(3)**. Prop the shelf, if necessary, and check that it is level before the plaster sets.

Clean away excess plaster from the joints before it sets hard, using a wooden tool or a damp cloth if the plaster is still wet. Finally, make good the plasterwork around the mantelpiece with gypsum plaster before proceeding to redecorate the wall.

1 Check jambs are set true

2 Place frieze member across jambs

3 Set mantelshelf in place

CHAPTER NINETEEN

LIGHTING

Today light is instantly available *at the flick of a switch. It can be made brighter or dimmed at will and is safe and clean, luxuries that were unknown before the turn of the century.*

In most homes, a naked flame – either from a smoky oil lamp, the hearth, or a candle – was the only source of illumination until the middle of the nineteenth century, when paraffin was discovered. And even then, many preferred candles to the new oil lamps. Lighting, in any case, was only for the comfortably off. The poor rose at dawn and went to bed when darkness fell.

The Argand lamp (see next page) and its successors the Astral lamp (which was patented in 1809) and the Solar lamp (which was introduced in the 1840s) all burned oil. In America this was most often

oil from the sperm whale. These sources of illumination made possible many activities in the evening, such as sewing, reading, and even card games.

However, since the lamps were expensive to run and to manufacture, their initial use was still largely the province of the wealthy homeowner. The introduction of gas (which occurred in urban areas during the 1820s) and the widespread use of kerosene (by the 1860s) meant that people of lesser means could stay up at night – and be safe on the streets, too.

Elaborate crystal chandeliers first appeared during the eighteenth century. However, these were so expensive to run, because of the large number of candles needed, that even in the most grandiose households chandeliers were lit only for special occasions.

An elegant combination of lighting for a period dining room

The opaline lamps form an integral part of this Art Deco interior

ARGAND'S OIL LAMPS

In the 1780s Aimé Argand's improved oil lamps arrived in England and America. However, these were fueled with rape-seed or colza oil, and oil lamps only became really popular with the introduction of whale oil and, eventually, kerosene in the l860s. A reasonable level of lighting was then available to all but the poorest via handsome brass, steel, or china lamps fitted with a wick, a tall glass chimney, and an engraved glass globe. Many of these early lamps have survived, and they make an attractive alternative to candles.

GAS AND ELECTRIC LIGHTING

Gas lighting first came to public notice in the early l800s, when street lights were installed along Pall Mall in London. But it was highly volatile stuff – explosions or asphyxiation from dangerous fumes were ever-present dangers – and gas lighting didn't become universally popular until the invention of the incandescent mantle in the 1890s. Fittings were based on oil-lamp designs featuring glass globes on elaborate brass brackets, and these remained in use in some rural areas well into the twentieth century.

Electricity had obvious advantages over gas – not least the fact that it did not smell or explode. Nevertheless, when Edison and Swan launched their light bulbs in the late 1870s they were not widely accepted; and Sir William Armstrong, whose house "Cragside" was one of the first to be lit by electricity, was regarded as eccentric, verging on mad. Initially fittings were adapted from those used for candles, oil, or gas, and it was only after the century's turn that designs were created specially for use with electricity.

Today, electrical fittings come in styles to suit every home, making it possible to integrate modern technology into a period interior and to provide flexible lighting suitable for a variety of family activities.

PLANNED LIGHTING

ALMOST NONE OF US WISH *to return to the shadowy, darkened rooms of the past. The sources of lighting that were to be found in our older homes would not serve our requirements today. Thus, many house restorers are willing to compromise their quest for historical authenticity.*

Even so, careful planning is essential, to serve both the spirit of the old house and personal needs.

Carefully positioned table and standard lamps in a formal drawing room

THE BASIC QUESTIONS

How will the room be used? And what kind of atmosphere or effect do you wish to create? In a working room, such as a kitchen, a strong level of lighting is needed – whereas in a bedroom or living room the general light should be softer, accented where necessary with table lamps or wall fittings.

Focal points

Which features of the room do you want to highlight? Focal points can include pictures or shelves, the fireplace, alcoves, or interesting architectural details such as coving. Think also about areas you would prefer to remain in shadow.

Working light

Will specific lighting be needed for food preparation, eating, reading and writing, sewing, or other activities?

Drawing up a plan

Having made decisions about these basic questions, draw a plan of the room. Mark in items to be highlighted, such as pictures, furniture, and plants, and any areas where working light is needed. This will help your electrician to work out the type and position of circuits and switches.

BACKGROUND LIGHTING

L IGHTING WALLS, FLOOR AND CEILING SEPARATELY *is a better idea than one central fixture, since the brightly lit surfaces will be reflected back into the room. And if you fit dimmer switches, that means the intensity with which they are lit can be controlled. There are various ways of introducing effective background lighting, and plenty of fittings discreet enough to blend with a period interior.*

DOWNLIGHTERS

Downlighters beam light down into the room from the ceiling. Modern recessed or flush fittings are unobtrusive and, if properly spaced, give a good level of light that can be controlled by dimmers. The most basic ones take reflector bulbs. More sophisticated fittings have an integral reflector that is designed to make the best use of the light emitted by the bulb. Choose silver for cool clear light, gold for a warmer effect. Gold works particularly well in a period interior, giving a mellow glow to old wood and brick.

Eyeball fittings

These descriptively named fittings are close relatives of the downlighter. They have a spherical base that can be swiveled to light a specific area, providing a mixture of accent and general light.

Low-voltage lighting

Low-voltage light fittings are a fairly recent development. Much smaller than fittings that take conventional bulbs, they require a transformer, usually concealed in a cupboard or in the ceiling space. Low-voltage bulbs cost more than conventional bulbs but last longer and are much more economical, producing about three times the output for the same wattage. They give out a clear white light, and are particularly good for illuminating paintings.

Fitting downlighters

Recessed downlighters are fitted into holes cut in the ceiling. They are suitable for all types of ceiling, including lath and plaster. The recess needs to be approximately 4in (100mm) deep for a low-voltage fitting, or 1ft (300 mm) for a conventional one.

Wall washers

Wall washers can be either ceiling-mounted or track-mounted. They are designed to cast light across and down the walls of the room and are available with conventional or low-voltage bulbs.

Wall washers are good for accentuating architectural features and interesting wall textures. They are also useful for highlighting bookshelves or a large display of pictures. Since washing a wall with light can create the effect of advancing it into the room, they are not recommended for limited spaces.

Positioning wall washers

Correct positioning is vital. If the washers are set too far back from the wall, people will be dazzled as they cross the beam. The best distance is 2ft 6in to 3ft (800mm to 1m) from the wall, with the space between one fitting and the next approximately twice that distance. Fewer fittings are needed if tungsten-halogen bulbs are used, as these light around twice the area covered by an ordinary reflector bulb.

Uplighters placed on top of cupboards, plus low-voltage specific lighting

Lighting used for display and to emphasize the textures of brick and wood

UPLIGHTERS

Fittings that beam light upward toward the ceiling include small floor-standing lights (which can be concealed behind plants or furniture), wall lights, tall lamp standards (which themselves provide a focal point), and slimline bulbs hidden behind ornamental cornicing.

Uplighters fitted with linear tungsten-halogen bulbs give a clean, clear, color-faithful light. They provide the perfect way to light an interesting ceiling or to make a low-ceilinged room seem higher. These bulbs are so efficient that just one 300W fitting will illuminate a ceiling 13ft (4m) square.

SPECIFIC LIGHTING

Once you have a good background scheme provided by any of the fittings described or a mixture of them, then you can add accent and task lights in order to give the interior atmosphere and to highlight specific areas.

Table lamps

Table lamps give a room a warm, homely feeling and are ideal for certain specific purposes, such as lighting a small collection on a table top or providing a warm pool of light in a corner or seating area.

The amount of illumination that a table lamp gives out can be controlled by the type of shade used. A shade made from pale fabric will reflect more light than one made from a dark, heavy material. If you want to light the whole of a table top, choose a shade that is wide at the bottom. Coolie shades cast the best general light. They have a narrow conical top and a wide bottom, and are made in a great variety of colors and patterns.

For safety's sake, install sockets close to table lamps. Floor sockets are well worth considering, as they allow lights to be used away from walls without the danger of trailing cord. Never run cord under a carpet – it can overheat and cause a fire.

Standard lamps

Tall standard lamps should be situated slightly behind and to the left or right of a chair to cast just the right amount of illumination for reading. Use a wide shade to give a good spread of light, and a floor socket to avoid trailing cord. Standard lamps are large and noticeable, so choose a design to suit the style of the room.

The shape and fabric of lampshades contribute to the character of a room

Lighting pictures

The traditional small brass picture light is probably the worst possible way to illuminate a painting or a piece of sculpture. A spotlight properly positioned on the ceiling and fitted with a true-color low-voltage bulb will light the whole object rather than just a section at the top.

To discover the best place to put a spotlight, wire it to a long lead and experiment till you find the ideal position for it. A large painting, print, or photograph may need two spotlights positioned so that the beams cross on the surface. Annoying reflections caused by spotlights are sometimes a problem, but you can avoid them by fitting non-reflective glass in the picture frame.

If you have a work of art you are particularly proud of, consider lighting it with a framing projector. The lenses and shutters of this type of low-voltage fitting allow the beam to be shaped to the exact size of the picture. As a result, it appears to be illuminated from the back.

Lighting a dining table

Rise-and-fall lights, which are fitted with a concealed pulley system, can be lowered to cast an intimate glow over a dining table. They are available in a variety of styles. A single fitting will light a table for four. Use two or three fittings for a larger circular surface, or a long fitting (rather like a billiard-room light) for a refectory table.

Rise-and-fall fittings are particularly effective if other lights in the room are dimmed. They should be fitted with a silvered-crown bulb to prevent diners being dazzled when the light is pulled down to eye level.

An alternative to a rise-and-fall fitting is an array of ceiling-mounted recessed lights above the table. Four lights will illuminate a table 5ft (1.5m) square.

COMBINING PERIOD & MODERN LIGHTING

If you have a handsome traditional fitting such as a crystal or metal chandelier that will not provide the appropriate level of light, you may want to combine it with more modern lighting.

Choose downlighters or wall washers to provide general lighting (angled for pictures where necessary), with the central fitting on a separate circuit so you can change the emphasis as and when desired. Add table and standard lamps for accent, and you will find that your scheme will work well without loss of important detail.

Modern lighting can also be successfully combined with sconces and with other period-style wall lights.

MODERNIZING OLD LIGHT FITTINGS

Antique light fittings add a touch of character to a room, but inspect them thoroughly before buying. Check metal components for rust, and electric fittings for signs of burning. Frayed cables or worn cord must be replaced. Never use an antique fitting until it has been checked by a qualified electrician.

Converting an old oil lamp to electricity detracts from its authenticity and reduces its value. Instead, insert a new wick, fill the lamp with oil, and use it as intended. The friendly golden glow provides a cozy atmosphere for dinner parties and is less of a fire risk than candles.

CHAPTER TWENTY

KITCHENS

COOKING, EATING, AND LIVING *in a single room remained an all too common way of life for the poor well into the twentieth century. However, the drawbacks of such an arrangement were obvious, and for the more affluent a separate kitchen soon became the norm. If possible, the kitchen was situated well away from the family's living quarters so that the smells, heat, and hubbub would not offend the sensibilities of the master and mistress. In a town house it was normally consigned to the basement, in a country house to an ell or a side wing.*

The evolution of the kitchen was dictated largely by advances in technology. For example, the open brick hearth and bake oven were

replaced, during the nineteenth century, by increasingly sophisticated iron stoves. The simple table and solo cupboard that had sufficed a few decades before were replaced by additional working surfaces and storage areas. The all-important advent of running water and the introduction of modern energy sources (gas and electricity) in the twentieth century both added to the assemblage of kitchen fixtures and considerably lightened the load of the cook. In countless older homes the pantry became a bathroom, a logical conversion of a convenient existing space. Indeed, very few kitchens as we know them today would be recognizable to our ancestors only a few generations ago.

Delicately colored cabinets and walls create a feeling of space

Open-plan kitchen with an atmosphere reminiscent of earlier days

KITCHEN DESIGN

Early American kitchen with cooking hearth and bake oven

ALONG WITH BATHROOMS, KITCHENS *are areas in many old houses where compromise has become the norm. On the other hand, kitchens are also the site of more than a little cutesey "old-time" invention that aims to replicate the spirit of the past – but succeeds more often in looking silly indeed. Your kitchen design should attempt to respect any original elements found in your kitchen, but avoid the pretense of aiming to be something it never was.*

In town houses, large noisy kitchens were often consigned to the basement

State-of-the-art gas range of the 1890s.

THE MODERN KITCHEN

Certain of the accouterments of modern life seem *de rigueur* today – refrigerators, microwaves, vast expanses of counter – and we see little need of forfeiting them for historical accuracy. Yet kitchen design has also come full circle, back to the days when the hearth was really the center of the house, used for cooking, eating, and entertaining.

A sympathetic approach

In most areas of the house the ideal is to restore everything to a condition or style that's close to the original, but modern living demands that at least some compromises are made when it comes to the kitchen.

However, considerations of convenience and hygiene don't mean your kitchen has to be out of sympathy with the remainder of your house. A suitable choice of period-style units or discriminating adaptation of original furniture, together with modern labor-saving appliances, can create a kitchen that is both efficient and aesthetically pleasing.

If you are thinking of relocating the kitchen, first of all look at it in context. You may come to the conclusion that it's in the wrong place and that it isn't large enough for your family's needs.

REORGANIZING SPACE

Georgian and Victorian town houses frequently have a basement kitchen with a ground-floor dining room above it. Such an arrangement is most inconvenient, as shopping and meals have to be carried up and down stairs. One possibility is to consider turning a ground-floor dining room and living room into a spacious eat-in kitchen, with the basement as a playroom or family living room and utility area.

In some houses, the basement has two or three small rooms. In this case, it may prove possible to remove dividing walls (or introduce arches or folding doors between rooms) and turn the whole space into a kitchen-dining-living room.

If the kitchen is too small and the house has a little-used dining room, you may find it more convenient to turn the larger room into an eat-in kitchen and the former kitchen into a utility room.

Adding an extension in sympathy with the style of the house or a conservatory that doubles as a dining room are other possibilities.

If you want to reorganize space or add an extension, it pays to consult an architect. Building and planning regulations are often complicated, and you could find that your proposed alterations require approval.

FURNISHING A KITCHEN

A functional kitchen with modern appliances means that cabinets of some kind are practically unavoidable. In any case, a run of cabinets in the area used for food preparation is more efficient and more hygienic than freestanding furniture, as your work space is uninterrupted and scraps can't fall down gaps between cupboards.

Kitchen layout

The ideal layout, if you have sufficient space, is a kitchen where one wall is occupied by the sink, the range and any appliances that need to be connected to drainage. Another wall can then be used for the freezer or refrigerator and storage units for pots and pans or non-perishable foodstuffs.

For the sake of convenience, the refrigerator must be within easy reach of cooking and food-preparation areas. Your freezer, which is used less frequently than the fridge, can be housed away from the main part of the kitchen. Consider turning a built-in cupboard or the area under the stairs into a niche where a freezer or laundry machines can share space with wine racks or shelves for non-perishable foods.

The cabinets, countertops, and finished surfaces needn't be antique; still, natural materials finished in a manner consistent with the time of construction of your house will look best.

An old-fashioned dresser is doubly useful – as display space for china, giving the kitchen a focal point, and as storage. A large central table can double as a working and dining surface.

Your kitchen does not, of course, have to be fitted and can be furnished with period furniture. However, when you want to move, a practical kitchen is a strong selling point, and a combination of freestanding appliances and furniture you want to take with you could deter buyers.

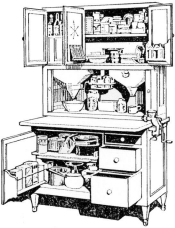

"Hoosier"-style kitchen storage unit

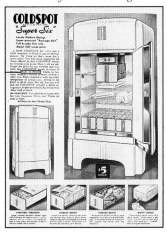

Early refrigerators were bulky

Kitchen-unit styles

For cabinets in a period house, solid wood or a combination of solid wood and veneer is more suitable than modern laminates. Popular woods and veneers include pickled, stained or antiqued oak; waxed or antiqued pine, and antiqued or stained chestnut, maple, cherry, and other woods as well. Antiqued kitchen units are given a patina by the manufacturer, and are often distressed by hitting the doors and any other visible surfaces with lengths of chain. Artificial wormholes and aged-metal hinges and escutcheon plates complete the period look.

Painted finishes such as sponging, rag rolling, dragging, or marbling also look attractive on kitchen units in a period house. .

Various forms of paneling are used for "period" units, including square, rectangular, or cathedral-arch styles, all of which help to create a kitchen that has considerable character.

An C18th open English cupboard, still in use after 200 years

A modern "period-style" fitted kitchen with paneled doors

COOKING APPLIANCES

FROM THE VANTAGE *of our century, the early American kitchen is almost incomprehensible. The fireplace was lit all year long (which is why in the South a "summer kitchen" was often found in a separate building out back). The cooking was done on the floor of the hearth at the margin of the fire using trivets, with a pot or two hanging from a metal "crane." In comparison, our cooking options today seem "user-friendly" indeed.*

RANGES

The functions of baking, roasting, rapid cooking, and gentle simmering didn't come together in a single appliance until the introduction of the range stove in the nineteenth century. The development of the closed range, with the fire contained beneath a hotplate, meant that simmering, roasting, baking, and boiling could be carried out using just one piece of equipment – a dramatic improvement on cooking over an open fire. What was more, smoke was drawn through the flue, leaving the kitchen cleaner and fresher. Nevertheless, despite the indisputable convenience of this new invention, traditionalists still preferred meat roasted on a spit!

Ranges, handsome with their glossy black-leaded finish and shining brass controls, were produced to suit all homes and budgets, and remained in common use in rural areas well into the l930s despite the invention of cleaner, controllable gas and electric stoves around the turn of the century.

Simple kitchen units will fit unobtrusively into old houses of any period

A large open-plan kitchen has room for centrally placed working areas

Adapting existing units

Units that are out of style with the age and character of the house can often be adapted, which is generally much less expensive than replacement.

Fitting period-style doors and substituting a more suitable material, such as solid wood, marble, slate, granite, tiles, or synthetic stone, in place of laminate worktops is an effective way to transform modern kitchen units. It is also much less disruptive than refitting the entire kitchen. Manufacturers that specialize in replacement kitchen-unit doors will make period-style doors to order for your existing units.

A relatively modern equivalent of the traditional range suits an old kitchen

WORKING AREAS

I N EARLY KITCHENS, *most of the preparation was carried out at a large central table or in the scullery. Worktops were mostly wooden and had to be scrubbed and scoured daily, making a great deal of work. Shelves and other areas not used for preparation were painted, so they could be wiped clean.*

Until the invention of stoneware and fireclay, sinks were made from stone or wood lined with copper or tin; that is, when there were sinks at all, as portable tubs and barrels were commonplace before running water. Sometimes the sink was located in a scullery, but later large built-in units with multiple sinks were more usual.

Very often kitchen sinks had taps that didn't match, due to hot water pipes being added later.

RESTORING A RANGE

Although many wood or coal cook stoves were removed to make way for gas or electric stoves, such appliances were a part of many American homes for generations. As a result, some owners of Victorian and turn-of-the-century houses have reinstalled such stoves. They are generally available both as rebuilt antiques and in reproduction models.

Cooking only on a range isn't a practical proposition for most families. However, a restored example adds an attractive authentic feature to the kitchen and is useful for heating the room, simmering, and cooking dishes such as stews and casseroles.

If you are lucky enough to discover a range *in situ*, inspect it carefully. You will probably find that the interiors of the oven and boiler are worn out. These can be replaced, although renovating them may not be necessary if the role of the range is to be primarily decorative.

The flues will need to be swept, rusted dampers freed and cleaned, and the entire range wire-brushed to get rid of rust. You will need to replace broken or missing firebricks, too. Finish the exterior of the range with a coat of polish, burnish the oven hinges and handle with emery paper, and polish brass fittings before lighting the fire.

MODERN APPLIANCES

When electric and gas stoves were introduced around the turn of the century, the oven and stove top were housed in one appliance. Although stoves like this are still available, nowadays cooks generally favor a built-in oven, either at eye-level or under a worktop.

Another alternative is the modern equivalent of the traditional range, which can be run on solid fuel, electricity, gas (including bottled gas), or oil. Some ranges also provide central heating and hot water. Most cooks will need a microwave and/or a conventional oven for use during the summer months when running the range may make the kitchen too hot.

POSITIONING A COOKER

If you install an old-fashioned stove in a chimney breast, the vent can be hidden in the chimney, instead of being housed in an artificial chimney unit built to match the kitchen furniture.

Neatly fitted synthetic-stone worktop with a ceramic-tile splashback

WORKTOPS

Today's house restorers have an extensive range of worktop materials to choose from. Worktops used for preparing food should be treated or cleaned only with non-toxic materials.

Wooden worktops

Hardwood worktops made from species such as maple, beech, iroko, or cherry are robust and attractive. They make a good replacement for scratched or out-of-character laminate, and you can have a marble or slate slab inset in the wood for rolling pastry.

Custom-made modern wooden worktops have an oil-resistant, water-repellent surface that can be cleaned by wiping over with a damp cloth. You can remove cuts, scratches, stains, and scorch marks by rubbing them with first medium-grade and then fine-grade sandpaper.

To preserve the surface, the wood should be oiled at intervals (cooking and olive oil are both excellent for the purpose). Sprinkle a few drops of oil onto the wood and continue wiping with a clean absorbent cloth until all the oil has soaked in.

Tiled worktops

Tiled worktops look attractive combined with wood. As tiles are not the ideal surface for all food preparation tasks, you may wish to insert a maple butcher's block or a marble slab. Tiles may craze if you put a very hot pan down on them, so it is advisable to place metal pan stands around the stove.

Granite

Granite is hard-wearing and impervious to stains. It is the best modern alternative to the stone slabs traditionally used in the stillroom. Since it is very heavy, base units may have to be reinforced.

Synthetic stone

An acrylic-based mineral-filled plastic like Corian can be used to create totally seamless work surfaces. The material is made in various finishes, including marble. The worktops have to be made and fitted by a qualified fabricator. They can have carved or chamfered edges, or be edged with synthetic stone of a different color, or with metal or wood.

These worktops are resistant to scratching, heat, household chemicals, and most stains. If surface damage should occur, it can usually be rubbed out with a fine-grade sandpaper.

Laminate

Laminate has been used in kitchens since the l920s. In the early days it was then sold in sheets that were then glued onto blockboard. If old laminate has begun to lift, reglue it using an epoxy adhesive.

Modern laminate comes already bonded to a precut worktop, which can have square or gently rounded edges or may be edged with solid-wood lipping.

A combination of marble, wood, and tiled work surfaces   *Deep fireclay Belfast sink with brass mixer tap*

SINKS AND TAPS

Today's kitchen sinks are almost invariably built into worktops. They are made in a variety of materials and, because of the increasing use of dishwashers, are generally smaller than the sinks of the past.

Freestanding sinks

One alternative to the built-in sink is a freestanding sink supported on stands or brackets. Sometimes referred to as Belfast sinks, these deep fireclay receptacles can be supplied with an integral sloping draining board, but a sloping grooved hardwood drainer edged with metal and fixed beside the sink on brackets was more common.

You are unlikely to find an original Belfast sink that's still in a usable condition, as the glaze will almost certainly have become worn and chipped with age. However, reproduction versions are readily available and are usually built into a grooved wooden draining unit.

To look authentic, this sort of sink should be fitted with brass or brass-effect capstan-head taps. It is possible to

buy restored originals – but make sure that original brass taps or imported reproductions comply with local water regulations.

Stainless steel

Stainless-steel sinks are comparatively inexpensive but are durable and easier on china and dinnerware than porcelain or fireclay sinks.

While not authentic in appearance, in an area in which compromise is common they are a practical solution.

Artificial materials

Sinks that are made from quartz-based artificial materials have the advantage of being light in weight and available in a wide range of colors and sizes. The one drawback is that these materials stain easily and can be difficult to clean. Fireclay is therefore a better option if you want a white sink.

Enamel

Metal sinks with a vitreous-enamel coating were fitted in many homes from the 1930s onward. However, few have survived in good condition, mainly because enamel chips easily. Once the protective enameling has chipped, the metal beneath it rusts and the sink deteriorates. Enamel sinks are still manufactured. However, the chipping problem has not yet been solved.

CHAPTER TWENTY-ONE

BATHROOMS

ONLY 150 YEARS AGO *water for a bath had to be heated then lugged up steep flights of stairs. It is therefore hardly surprising that* in the seventeenth century even the well-to-do considered two baths a year quite sufficient. The Victorians were more hygiene conscious (motivated no doubt by several outbreaks of cholera) and liked frequent baths or showers, preferably taken in front of a roaring fire. The earliest baths were portable, made from copper, zinc, or fireclay, and had to be filled with water brought from downstairs. Cold baths – very much a part of Victorian culture

and believed to subdue "unseemly passions" – were often taken outdoors in a tub sheltered by a lean-to and supplied by rainwater tanks above.

First the geyser (a copper boiler fired by gas, oil, coke or wood that stood behind the tub) freed maids from the chore of filling baths by hand. Then the invention, slightly later, of the circulating hot water system, the availability of ceramic and enameled sanitaryware, and the pioneering work of Crapper, Twyford, and Humpherson on the automatic wash-down toilet helped to move personal hygiene out of the bedroom and into the separate bathroom we know today.

A marble-topped chiffonier is a charming touch in this basic bathroom

Luxurious modern bathroom fitted out in Art Deco style

WASHING FACILITIES

Before there were separate bathrooms, daily washing of hands and face was done in the bedroom with water from an earthenware ewer that formed part of a washstand set. As the Victorians' obsession with health and cleanliness increased, washstands became larger and more elaborate. In 1888, in her compendium of hints for householders *From Kitchen to Garret*, the English writer Mrs Panton recommended that the ideal bedroom should have "two washstands with marble tops and tiled backs, a basin, a jug with a double lip, soap and sponge basins with drainers, tooth and nail brushes, a carafe and glasses, a brass hot water can, a white china foot bath and a slop pail."

But hygiene was still a luxury. Lacking maids to do the heating and carrying of water, or a tub or washstand to put it in, the poor often hardly washed at all.

SANITARY FACILITIES

Sanitary facilities were no less rudimentary, the "earth closet" (literally a seat over a bucket or above a pit dug in the ground) being the norm.

However, in comfortable country houses it was common to have a pot cupboard in the dining room so that gentlemen in difficulties after imbibing too much wine could relieve themselves once the ladies had retired.

Only the rich could afford Joseph Bramah's valve closet invented in 1778, following a patent lodged by Cummings in 1775. This had an earthenware pan fitted with a trap that opened when a handle was pulled. The handle also released water from a cistern above the bowl.

Although it is rare to find a complete suite of original Victorian sanitaryware *in situ*, many houses still boast a turn-of-the-century bath or toilet needing only simple non-specialist restoration. The fashion for Victorian and Edwardian sanitaryware has meant that all sorts of original designs have been revived in reproduction. As a result, creating a period-style bathroom is now both possible and easy.

Folding bathtub with water heater

CONVENIENCE OR INCONVENIENCE?

A BATHROOM THAT IS TOO LARGE *is a waste, especially if you are a bedroom or a closet or two short of your family's needs. A bathrom in the basement or in a back extension (very common in small Victorian town houses) is inconvenient. However, there's no need for the bathroom to stay where it is simply because that's where it has always been.*

Authentic working Victorian bathroom with original fittings

MAKING SPACE FOR A BATHROOM

If your house has a ground-floor or basement bathroom, but none upstairs, you may wish to consider turning what is now an extra bedroom into an upstairs bathroom or partitioning off a portion of a large bedroom for the same purpose

The area for a bathroom doesn't need to be more than 4 square yards (4 square meters) – enough room for a standard-size bath, toilet, and basin. And it can be smaller if, instead of a bath, you have a shower cubicle or a European-style sitz tub (which has much the same area as a shower base but is deep enough for the bather to sit neck deep in water).

Installing a basin or shower stall in a bedroom will help to ease pressure on a family bathroom. Or you can transform a separate toilet into a shower room, moving the toilet into the bathroom if there's space to spare. A sitz tub also saves valuable space if you want to add *en suite* facilities but can't afford to lose a bedroom.

Hot and cold water pipes for a new bathroom can be hidden beneath floorboards or behind paneling. Drainage may be harder to install, as waste from the bath, toilet and basin must empty into large-diameter pipes. The positioning of the toilet in particular – as close to the main vent pipe as possible – is the key decision. Careful planning is especially important when you are trying to shoehorn a lot into a little space. Keep in mind, too that it is essential to check local regulations before starting any work that involves drainage.

BATHS

EARLY BATHS WERE PORTABLE, *made from zinc or copper and filled by hand. Water was poured in over a sheet, so that the user didn't come into direct contact with the hot metal. Fixed baths, which were introduced later, were made either of fireclay or of cast iron coated with vitreous enamel or, less commonly, of wood lined with copper. The roll-top cast-iron bath, introduced around 1880, was mounted on handsome ball-and-claw feet. It was particularly popular because it warmed up quickly (an important consideration when hot water systems were erratic) and was easy to clean both inside and out.*

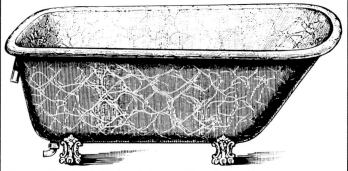

Freestanding steel bathtub with japanned "marble" finish

A Victorian-style bathroom can be a comfortable place to relax in

THE CANOPY BATH

The Rolls-Royce of Victorian baths was the canopy model. This had a canopy or hood equipped with taps that controlled "needle spray" (fine jets of water from tiny holes around the hood), "douche" (overhead cold-water shower supplied by rainwater tanks on the roof), "wave" (a sheet of water that poured from a slit in the canopy and was believed to be beneficial in massaging the kidneys) and "sitz" (bubbles that rose from the bottom of the bath to create a massaging effect).

BATH TRAYS

House-proud Victorians feared that leaking plumbing joints might cause wood rot, so the bath often stood in a zinc or marble tray complete with its own wastepipe. You may possibly find traces of this arrangement where an old bath has been boxed in.

MODERN BATHS

The First World War heralded the demise of houses too large to manage without a staff of servants. As a result, baths became less elaborate to suit smaller houses with plainer bathrooms. Apart from color choice and the introduction of plastics, there is very little difference between modern baths and those installed in the 1920s.

A modern wood-paneled bathtub

RESTORING A CAST-IRON BATH

You may be lucky enough to buy a house with a roll-top or enclosed cast-iron bath still in good condition. But it is much more likely that an old bath will be stained or worn around the drain and below the taps.

Reproduction cast-iron baths are available, but it's cheaper and also less disruptive to restore the existing bath. There are two ways to do this. Admittedly, neither process gives such a long-lasting finish as vitreous enameling – which can only be achieved in the fierce 2000°F (1100°C) temperature of a factory kiln, using glazes too toxic for the inexperienced to handle – but professional resurfacing (see next page) should extend the life of your bath by around ten years.

Do-it-yourself resurfacing

These are fairly new, so it is not yet known how long the coating lasts. First, clean the bath with an abrasive, then rinse and sand the surface. Thorough preparation, plus careful filling of chips, using an epoxy or polyester filler, is essential. Cover the waste and taps with masking tape once the bath is dry.

If the taps drip, fit new washers before applying the coating. Hang a can or plastic container beneath each tap to catch stray drips.

After mixing the coating, brush around taps, drain, and other areas inaccessible to a roller. Use a roller for the rest of the bath, working with smooth, even strokes and as close as possible to edges. Leave to dry for at least two hours before you apply a second coating. The bath should be ready for use about 48 hours later.

Professional resurfacing

A professional resurfacing company will treat and coat the bath on site. Some firms resurface acrylic and fiberglass baths, as well as cast-iron or pressed-steel ones. At the same time, it's usually possible to alter the color of the bath or add decoration.

Professional resurfacers use epoxy resin or a quick-drying acrylic, urethane, or polyurethane finish sometimes described as enamel. The best results are achieved using a chemical bond that helps the finish stick to the bath. With this process, once the bath has been cleaned and degreased, it is heated to encourage the bonding coat to "take." After the bonding has been applied, the enamel is sprayed on to give an even coat. This is left to cure for three hours, then the bath is rinsed and buffed to a shine with an electric polisher. The bath should be ready for use in about three or four days.

Be careful when choosing a bath-resurfacing company. Look for an experienced firm and ask if you can speak to previous customers. Make sure that they have a trained workforce of their own and don't rely on subcontractors.

Caring for a resurfaced bath

Clean the bath with a non-scratch preparation that is recommended for acrylic or fiberglass. Never use abrasive cleaners or bleach.

PRESSED-STEEL BATHS

These are produced in most traditional shapes, including roll-top, and in a wide range of colors. They are a useful cost-saving replacement for cast-iron baths as they are lighter and cheaper. Pressed steel in poor condition can be resurfaced in the same way as cast iron (see above).

Dramatic 1930s bathroom with original fixtures in perfect condition

ACRYLIC BATHS

When they were introduced, acrylic baths had a disturbing tendency to distort and pull away from the wall, which not only made them creak but also caused leaks. However, modern acrylic baths, which are made from material not less than $3/16$in (5mm) thick and sprayed on the outside with strong fiberglass, are supported by a wood-and-metal cradle fitted by the manufacturer.

Although they are a modern innovation, acrylic baths have advantages for house restorers. They are light in weight and, thanks to modern molding technology, are available in a variety of shapes, including corner models and traditional roll-top versions. Water stays hot longer in an acrylic bath, and the material is warm and comfortable to touch.

Unfortunately there's little that can be done to repair a scratched or damaged acrylic bath, so replacement is the only viable option.

ADAPTING A MODERN BATH

A modern bath or one that is out of character can be given an authentic period look.

Replace postwar chrome waste and taps either with reproduction brass fittings or with original ones, which are available from architectural-salvage companies.

Remove plastic side and end panels, and replace them with ready-made period-look mahogany or old-pine panelling, manufactured by companies that specialize in period bathroom fittings.

Tiles with a traditional design are also appropriate. Build a wooden framework around the bath, projecting about 3in (75mm) from the rim, and cover it with marine plywood before tiling.

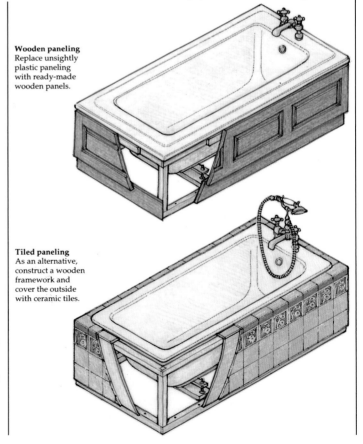

Wooden paneling
Replace unsightly plastic paneling with ready-made wooden panels.

Tiled paneling
As an alternative, construct a wooden framework and cover the outside with ceramic tiles.

WASHBASINS & TOILETS

EARLY BATHROOM FIXTURE *makers allowed their imagination to run riot. Basins and toilets were lavishly decorated with hand-painted flowers, leaves, and fruit. Wood was replaced by ornate cast iron, which was also used for brackets to support the toilet tank. Taps were of polished brass to match those used on the bath.*

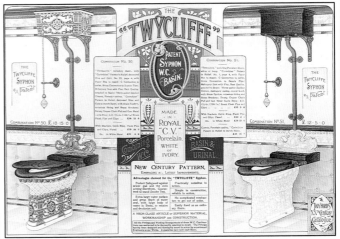

Turn-of-the-century English advertisement for "syphonic water closets"

Elaborate Victorian water closet

WASHBASINS
Victorian washbasins (which were confusingly known as "lavatories") were modeled on bedroom washstands, the great difference being that the basin was set into the top and filled by taps connected to the water supply, instead of being filled by hand.

Gradually the decorative basin was replaced by less ornate designs, such as the "open lavatory," which was simply an elegant elliptical basin supported on metal legs. Accessories, such as a soap dish, shaving mug and toothmug were mounted on a marble splashback. The taps, waste, supply pipes, and towel rail were usually plated with nickel or silver.

Elegance such as this was replaced early in the twentieth century by the pedestal basin that we know today. In tune with fashion, these early pedestal basins were simple rectangular or oval designs – which were much easier to keep clean than the elaborate cast-iron and polished wood fittings of 50 years before.

WATER CLOSETS
The first flush toilets were no less elaborate. Pioneered by Thomas Crapper, the high-level tank, fixed about 6ft 6in (2m) above the bowl, was fitted in almost every late-Victorian house of any size.

Grand houses sometimes had syphonic toilets. With these, the action of the trap drew the contents of the bowl down into the soil pipe as water from the tank flushed it. They were quieter and more costly than Crapper's wash-down design.

Although the high-level tank is associated with Victorian houses, low-level designs were used where it was necessary to fit a toilet below a window. Low-level designs were operated by a push button similar to the type in use today. To compensate for the less forceful flush, the Victorians used a 2½in (63mm) pipe between the tank and the bowl.

Washbasin with cast-iron stand

This type of plumbed washstand is a factory-built modern product

ADAPTING A WASHSTAND
It would be a pity to spoil a valuable antique washstand in good condition, but you can buy a cheap or damaged washstand at an auction or from a second-hand furniture shop and fit a suitable vanity basin and a set of taps yourself.

A wooden top is easy to adapt. Simply cut it with a jigsaw, using the template provided with the basin as a guide. A marble top is much more difficult to cut. It is therefore best to lift it from the washstand and take it, together with the template and taps, to a stonemason who will cut the holes for you using specialist equipment.

It is possible to buy original Victorian washstand basins from antique shops or architectural-salvage companies, or replicas from traditional-bathroom specialists. However, they can be expensive.

Washdown pedestal toilet

RESTORING A TOILET

Many toilets have survived from Victorian times, but very often the original wooden seat has been replaced by a molded-plastic one, the tank and down pipe have been painted over or boxed in, and the bowl has become stained.

Replacement wooden seats, in either mahogany or old pine, are available from bathroom specialists. When buying a replacement, take the plastic seat with you to make sure that the new seat has the right fittings.

Layers of paint on the downpipe and tank can be removed using a chemical stripper that is suitable for use on metal. The tank can then be repainted. The most appropriate colors are black or white, which would have been used in Victorian times. Often, the maker's name was picked out in gold, a nice touch worth attempting if you have a steady hand.

Most people restoring a toilet paint the downpipe. Alternatively, you can apply metal polish to the pipe and buff it till it shines. Several applications of polish may be needed in order to obtain the desired effect. If the chain is rusty, replace it with a new length, fitted with a wooden pull to match the seat. Stains on the bowl can usually be removed by filling it to the brim with dilute bleach and leaving it overnight. To shift limescale, use a proprietary remover.

SHOWERS

CUSTOM-MADE INDEPENDENT SHOWERS *were rare before 1914, but showers were common above bathtubs, either as part of a canopy or as a separate large rose. The forerunner of the modern shower curtain or stall was a device rather like a circular tent. The top part was a tank, the lower part a deep tray. Maids would fill the tank with water, then the user pulled a string and was deluged.*

Wealthy, health-conscious Victorians took invigorating needle-spray showers. Pipes, perforated with tiny holes, were arranged above a tray to make a semi-circular enclosure. When the valves were opened, the user was pounded by a stinging spray of water. Real spartans opted for cold rainwater.

Needle-spray shower over a bathtub

A hand-held showerhead was cheap and effective

An early tiled shower with a modern unit added

MODERN SHOWERS

Although shower stalls are a modern innovation, they offer a solution to lack of space in an old house. If installing one in a bedroom or in the space occupied by a built-in cupboard makes life easier, don't hesitate to do it.

In fact, showers have become such a way of life in the United States that not having one in a house, whether the place is new or old, is regarded by many as a real-estate liability.

Manufacturers now offer replicas of large Victorian shower roses in brass effect and screens and enclosures in etched designs, so shower fittings do not have to be intrusive or out of character.

SHOWER PROBLEMS

An old shower may not perform well for various reasons, ranging from lime deposits to a worn hose or poor pressure.

Limescale

The holes in a showerhead tend to become clogged by limescale. To clear them, disconnect the head from the rose and immerse it in a proprietary descaler, or a strong solution of malt vinegar and water, for two to three hours.

Leaking hose

Performance will be reduced if the flexible hose is leaking. This isn't always easy to see. If the hose is old, replace it. This is a good idea anyway, as it's likely to be clogged by scale. Buy a new hose from a bathroom specialist.

Lack of pressure

Poor water pressure is the most usual cause of a feeble shower. This can be solved by fitting a small pump between the water-supply point and the showerhead.

If you freeze or get scalded whenever taps are turned on elsewhere in the house while you are showering, you may want to consider fitting a temperature stabilizer to the hot-and-cold water-supply pipes leading to the shower.

Since choosing a pump or stabilizer to suit your supply is crucial, consult a plumber before buying either fitting.

GLOSSARY OF TERMS

A

Acanthus
Classical decorative motif based on the large, deeply cut leaves of a plant native to the Mediterranean region.

Aggregate
Particles of sand or stone mixed with cement and water to make concrete or mortar.

Annealing
The process of removing stresses in a material, usually by heating.

Anthemion
Stylized floral motif derived from Greek and Roman architecture, widely used in neo-classical ornamentation. The most common form was based on honeysuckle flowers and leaves.

Applied molding
A wooden molding applied separately.

Architrave
A molding that surrounds a door or window. *or* The lowest horizontal molding of a classical entablature.

Arris
The sharp edge at the meeting of two flat surfaces. *or* The sharp edge of a brick.

Ashlar
Dressed and finely jointed stonework.

Astragal
A molding comprising a half-round raised central spine with a cove or square fillet on each side.

B

Band course
A square-faced horizontal molding in stucco or stone.

Baseboard
A board used to cover the junction between an interior wall and the floor.

Bead
A narrow strip of wood with a half-round profile.

Bevel
A surface that meets another at an angle of less than 90 degrees. See also CHAMFER.

Binding
A term used to describe a door or hinged casement that is rubbing against the surrounding frame.

Blind nailing
A method of securing a component with concealed nail fixings.

Bolection molding
Wooden molding rebated to cover the edge of a frame.

Bonding
A method of interlocking bricks or stone blocks in order to create a stable structure.

Bow
To bend as a result of uneven shrinkage – usually in reference to wood.

Brace
A diagonal member used to prevent a batten door from sagging, or to hold a timber-frame structure square.

Brushing out
Spreading paint or other liquid finishes to avoid runs or uneven coverage.

Burr
A rough raised edge left on metal after cutting or filing.

Butt joint
Joint formed when two pieces are fastened with no overlapping surfaces.

C

Cantilever
A projecting beam that is secured at one end only.

Capital
The topmost part of a column or pilaster.

Caryatid
A supporting column or pilaster in the form of a female figure.

Caulking
Weatherproofing a joint by sealing with a non-setting mastic.

Cement
A gray or white combination of powdered calcined limestone and clay mixed with water and an aggregate to make mortar or concrete.

Chair rail
The cap molding of dado (wainscot) paneling that protected the wall finish from wear and tear by chair backs. After the use of the dado declined, the chair rail was still used as a trim for embossed wallcoverings.

Chamfer
A 45-degree bevel.

Clamp
A primitive kiln for firing, comprising a stack of unbaked bricks and fuel encased in a mound of old bricks and clay.

Compo
A mixture of materials such as whiting and glue used to fashion raised decoration on a frame etc.

Console
A decorative bracket used to support a doorhood, soffit etc.

Coping stones
Stone slabs laid on top of a masonry wall to shed rainwater.

Corbel
A bracket, usually of stone, brick, or plaster.

Corbeling
A projection in masonry, formed by building successive courses outward in a stepped fashion, one above the other.

Cornice
A decorative molding forming a junction between the walls of a room and the ceiling. *or* The uppermost horizontal molding of a classical entablature.

Cove
A concave molding.

Cross grain
Wood grain that deviates from the main axis of a length of timber.

Cup
To bend, usually as a result of shrinkage. Cupping occurs across the width of a piece of wood.

Cutout
A groove cut across the grain of a wooden component, usually to form a joint.

D

Dado
A decorative or protective panel applied to the lower part of an interior wall.

Damp-proof course (DPC)
A layer of impervious material that prevents moisture rising from the ground into the walls of a building.

Dentil
One of a row of small toothlike blocks that form part of a classical cornice.

Distressing
The act of giving something an aged appearance by various measures such as staining and denting.

Dormer
A structure projecting from a roof, usually housing a window.

Dressing
The act of cutting, shaping, and finishing masonry or metal etc.

Drip groove
A groove cut in the underside of a projection such as a molding or sill to cause rainwater to drip to the ground.

Dripstone
A molding placed above a door or window opening to deflect rainwater. Also known as a label or hood mold.

GLOSSARY OF TERMS

E

Edge grain
Grain (growth rings) running at not less than 45 degrees to the faces of a piece of wood. Also known as quarter-sawn timber.

Efflorescence
A white powdery deposit on masonry or plaster caused by mineral salts migrating to the surface as a result of evaporation.

Elevation
A geometrical drawing showing a vertical plane of a building's surface.

End grain
The surface of wood exposed after cutting across the fibers.

Engaged
Attached to a wall (e.g. an engaged column).

Enrichments
Decorative features, usually added separately to a cornice, frieze etc.

Entablature
The band of moldings near the top of a façade, divided into cornice, frieze, and architrave.

Expanded metal
A type of lathing for plasterwork made by slitting and stretching metal sheet.

F

Façade
The exterior face of a building.

Facings
Weather-resistant bricks used for constructing exterior brickwork.

Faience
Glazed terracotta.

Feathering
Brushing out the edge of paint or other finishes.

Festoon
See SWAG.

Fillet
Strip of mortar used to seal the junction between two surfaces such as a roof and a wall.

Finial
A decorative spike or post set at the apex of a gable or on the point of a spire, tower etc.

Flashing
A weatherproof strip (usually of metal) used to cover the junction between a roof and a wall or chimney, or between one part of a roof and another.

Frieze
The strip of wall between a ceiling cornice and a picture rail. *or* The central panel of a classical entablature.

Frog
The recess in the top face of a brick. Some bricks have a frog in the bedding face, too.

G

Gable
The triangular section of wall at the end of a gable roof. Also known as a gable end.

Gable roof
The most common form of pitched roof, in which the front and rear slopes are pitched.

Galvanized
Protected with an electroplated or dipped zinc coating.

Gauging
The mixing of a little cement or gypsum with lime mortar or plaster to hasten setting time.

Gesso
A mixture of plaster and size used as a base coat for gilding or painting.

Glazing point
Small triangular fixing used to hold window glass in a rebate.

H

Hardwood
Wood cut from broadleaved (mostly deciduous) trees belonging to the botanical group *Angiospermae.*

Head
The topmost horizontal component of a casement-window.

Header
A brick or stone block laid so that the end is visible. *or* Another term for the topmost horizontal component of an exterior door frame.

Hingebound
A term used to describe a door or casement that cannot be closed properly due to a misaligned or poorly fitted hinge.

Hip
The external sloping corner formed by two angled faces of a pitched roof.

Hipped roof
A form of pitched roof in which one or both ends are pitched as well as the front and rear slopes.

Horn
An extension of a sliding-sash stile that strengthens the joint between it and the meeting rail. *or* The extension of a door stile, designed to protect a new door from accidental damage during transportation.

I

Indenting
Patching damaged masonry by cutting out a worn area and inserting new stone.

J

Jamb
The vertical side member of a doorframe or casement-window frame.

K

Keying
Abrading or incising a surface to provide a better grip for gluing or plastering etc.

Knapping
The process of shaping a flint by chipping flakes from its edges.

L

Laying off
Finishing an application of paint or varnish etc. with upward brush strokes.

Lintel
A beam supporting the masonry above a door or window

M

Mansard roof
A variation of the pitched roof incorporating two angles on each side.

Miter
A joint between two pieces of wood formed by cutting bevels of equal angle (usually 45 degrees) at the ends of both pieces.

Modillion
One of a row of brackets, usually decorated with acanthus leaves, forming part of a cornice.

Mortar
A mixture of cement or lime with an aggregate and water for bonding bricks or blocks of stone.

Mullion
A vertical member separating two windows.

Muntin
A vertical member between panels (e.g. of a door or wall paneling). *or* Another term for glazing bar.

N

Nailers
Rough strips of wood attached to masonry as fixing points for paneling, baseboards etc.

Newel
A substantial post at either end of a balustrade.

O

Orders
The five classical architectural styles that provided the basis for the proportions and detailing of neo-classical buildings.

GLOSSARY OF TERMS

Overmantel
A framed mirror surmounting a fireplace.

Ovolo
A quarter-round convex molding.

Oxidize
To form a layer of metal oxide, as in rusting.

P

Pallets
Wooden plugs built into masonry joints on each side of a door or window opening to serve as fixing points for the frame.

Parapet
A low wall at the edge of a roof or balcony.

Parging
The interior lining of a flue.

Paterae
Floral motifs, often alternating with modillions when used to decorate cornices.

Pediment
A triangular structure forming a gable on a Greek or Roman temple. Neo-classical doors and windows were often surmounted by a pediment.

Pilaster
A shallow square-section engaged column.

Pilot hole
A small-diameter hole drilled before inserting a screw to act as a guide for its thread.

Pin holes
Small holes caused by cutting into voids made by gas bubbles formed in cast metal during the casting process.

Pitch
The slope of a roof.

Plan
Top view of a building, room etc.

Pointing
The act of shaping the mortar joints between bricks or stone blocks. *or* The mortar joints themselves.

Pontil
Iron rod used for spinning glass.

Poultice
An absorbent paste applied to masonry to draw out stains.

Pugging
The act of mixing and kneading clay with water to produce an even consistency.

Purlin
A horizontal beam providing intermediate support for rafters or sheet roofing.

Q

Quarry
A square or diamond-shape pane of glass for a leaded light.

Quirk
A V-shaped groove cut into a molding profile that separates one element from another. *or* The groove cut along the top of a picture rail to take picture hooks.

Quoin
A masonry reinforcement at the corner of a wall.

R

Rafter
One of a set of parallel sloping beams that form the main structural element of a roof.

Raised grain
Roughening of the surface of a piece of wood, caused by the fibers swelling due to the presence of water.

Rebate
A stepped recess along the edge of a workpiece or component. Also known as a rabbet.

Relieving arch
A masonry arch built above a door or window to deflect the load away from a lintel.

Repoussé work
Thin decorative metalwork raised in relief by hammering the metal from behind.

Reveal
The vertical side of a door or window opening, between the frame and the face of the wall.

Ridge
The horizontal joint line at the apex of a pitched roof.

Ridge board
The horizontal beam to which the rafters are joined at the apex of a roof.

Roof cresting
A decorative ceramic or metal strip running along the ridge of a roof.

Rose plate
A backing plate for a door knob.

Roundel
A small circular piece of crown glass containing the pontil mark, used as a decorative element in leaded lights.

Rub joint
A joint made by sliding one glued component from side to side on another until suction causes the joint to stick.

Running mold
A template used for shaping stucco or plaster moldings. Also known as a horse.

Rustication
Beveled or chaneled joints between blocks of masonry.

S

Saddle bar
A metal bar used to reinforce a leaded light.

Sandblasting
The process of cleaning a surface (usually metal or masonry) with a jet of abrasive grit or sand. See also SHOT BLASTING.

Sapwood
New wood surrounding the denser heartwood of a tree.

Sash
A glazed frame forming part of a window, sometimes fixed but more often made to slide or to pivot on hinges.

Scribe
To mark and shape the edge of a workpiece so that it will fit exactly against another surface. *or* To mark by scratching with a pointed tool.

Scrim
Open-weave fabric used for reinforcing plasterwork.

Seasoning
Reducing the moisture content of wood.

Selvage
The irregular, untrimmed edge on each side of a length or roll of wallcovering.

Setting in
Making vertical cuts with a chisel or gouge to establish the outline of a motif carved in relief.

Sherardized
Covered with a protective coating produced by heating iron or steel in a container together with zinc dust.

Shim
A thin packing piece.

Short grain
This occurs where the general direction of the wood fibers runs across a narrow section of timber.

Shot blasting
A similar process to sandblasting but using iron or steel particles instead of sand or grit.

Show wood
Wood intended to be seen, often coated with a clear finish.

Sill
The lowest horizontal member of a window.

Soffit
The underside of a structure such as an arch, stair, or cornice.

Softwood
Wood cut from coniferous trees belonging to the botanical group *Gymnospermae*.

Soldiers
Vertical wooden grounds to which a baseboard is fixed. *or* bricks laid standing on end.

Spalling
Flaking of the outer face of masonry, often caused by expanding moisture in freezing conditions.

GLOSSARY OF TERMS

Spandrel
Paneling used to fill the triangular shape below a stair stringer.

Sprig
Small cut nail used for fixing a window pane in a rebate.

Sprue
Excess metal left on a casting due to the metal solidifying in the channel through which it was introduced into the mold.

Stile
The vertical member on each side of a door or window sash.

Stippling
Applying paint or other finishes as spots, using the tip of a brush.

Straight grain
Grain (wood fibers) that aligns with the main axis of a length of timber.

Straightedge
A length of timber or metal with at least one true edge for drawing straight lines or scraping a surface level.

Stretcher
A brick or stone block laid so that one of its long faces is visible.

Stringer
A board running from one floor level to another, into which the treads and risers of a staircase are jointed. Also known as a string or stringboard.

String course
A horizontal strip of molded stone or stucco (similar to a cornice but smaller in scale) that extends across a façade.

Stucco
A mixture of cement, lime, and sand used for coating the exterior of a wall. *or* To coat a wall with stucco.

Stuck molding
A molding that is cut into a piece of wood. Also known as a struck or integral molding.

Stud wall
An interior wood-frame wall sheathed with lath and plaster or plasterboard.

Studs
The vertical wooden members within a timber-frame wall.

Swag
An ornamental motif depicting a hanging garland of flowers and leaves etc. Also known as a festoon.

T

Template
A cut-out pattern used to help shape a workpiece accurately.

Thixotropic
A term used to describe paints that have a gel-like consistency until stirred or applied, at which point they liquefy.

Throat
The narrow aperture at the base of a flue.

Transom
A horizontal rail separating a fan-light from a door. *or* A horizontal window-frame member.

U

Undercutting
Cutting away material from the edges of a recess to form a dovetail-shape cavity.

V

Valley
Trough formed by the convergence of two sloping roof surfaces.

Vapor barrier
A layer of impervious material that prevents the passage of moisture-laden air.

Vermiculation
A form of carved surface dressing for stonework, composed of closely packed shallow recesses separated by wavy ridges. It is said to resemble worm tracks.

Volute
A decorative spiral scroll found on column capitals, consoles etc.

Voussoir
A wedge-shape member of a brick or stone arch.

W

Wainscoting
Paneling extending up the chair rail; also called wainscot or dado.

Wall plate
A horizontal wooden member placed along the top of a wall to support the ends of joists and rafters, thus spreading their load.

Wet-and-dry paper
A sandpaper consisting of silicon-carbide particles glued to a waterproof backing, used to smooth new paintwork or varnish between coats.

Window guard
A low metal panel, grill, or railing placed across a window at sill level on the outside.

Withe
A masonry partition dividing one flue from another in a chimney. Also known as a midfeather.

Work hardening
Increasing the strength or hardness of a metal workpiece by manipulation such as stretching, bending, hammering etc.

INDEX

INDEX

ACKNOWLEDGMENTS

Inklink are grateful to the following companies, organizations and individuals
for their assistance in the production of this book:

Acquisitions Fireplaces Ltd., London, NW1
Hélène Alexander, The Fan Museum, London, SE10
The Antique Hardware Store, Kintnerville, PA, USA
Aristocast Originals Ltd., Sheffield, S. Yorkshire
Art Directions, St Louis, MO, USA
Artisan, Lindfield, Sussex
Ball & Ball, Exton, PA, USA
The Bath Wizard, Greenford, Middlesex
BCM Contracts Ltd., Whitchurch, Shropshire
S. A. Bendheim Co. Inc., Passaic, NJ, USA
Geoff Bennett, Conservation Dept., Brighton Borough Council, Sussex
Chris Blanchett
Charles Brooking, The Brooking Collection Trust, Guildford, Surrey
R. Bleasdale (Spirals), London, N1
Phillip Bradbury Glass, London, N4
Brickmatch Ltd., Chesterfield, Derbyshire
Britannia Architectural Metalwork & Restoration, Alton, Hampshire
British Gypsum Ltd., Sidcup, Kent
British Society of Master Glass Painters
R. W. Brunskill
Building Adhesives Ltd., Stoke-on-Trent, Staffordshire
The Building Conservation Trust, East Molesey, Surrey
Richard Burbidge Ltd., Oswestry, Shropshire
Barbara & Tony Burrough
C. D. (UK) Ltd., Leeds, W. Yorkshire
Constance & Jack Cairns
Capricorn Architectural Ironwork Ltd., London, W6
The Carving Workshop, Cambridge, Cambridgeshire
Cattles Precision Woodwork, Milton Keynes, Buckinghamshire
Cement & Plaster Mouldings Ltd., Ipswich, Suffolk
Cico Chimney Linings Ltd., Saxmundham, Suffolk
Pat & Jim Clark
Classic Designs, Coventry, W. Midlands
Classical Concrete Ltd., Bath, Avon
Clayton-Munroe Ltd., Totnes, Devon
Clean Walls Ltd., Manchester
Comyn Ching Ltd., London, EC1
Conklin Metal Industries, Atlanta, GA, USA
Cookson Industrial Materials Ltd., Reading, Berkshire
Peter Cornish
County Forge Ltd., Frome, Somerset
The Country Iron Foundary, Paoli, PA, USA
Crawford's Old House Store, Waukesha, WI, USA
Crittal Windows Ltd., Braintree, Essex
Anthony Cross
Crown Berger Ltd., Darwen, Lancashire
Department of the Environment, London, SW1
Barbara Doig
John Dorrington Ward
The End of Day Lighting Co., Ltd., London, NW1
English Heritage, London, W1
Exchem Mining & Construction Ltd., London, WC1
Feltham Glass Works, Feltham, Middlesex
Fine Homebuilding Magazine, Newtown, CT, USA
Geoff & Mareszka Fleming
Focal Point Architectural Products, Atlanta, GA, USA
Forgeries Ltd., Winchester, Hampshire
Fourth Bay, Garrettsville, OH, USA
The Georgian Group, London, E1
Golden Age Glassworks, New York, USA
Gray & McDonnell Ltd., London, E2
The Hardwood Flooring Co. Ltd., London, NW6
E. J. Harmer & Co. Ltd., London, SE21
Harrison Thompson & Co. Ltd., Leeds, W. Yorkshire
Haslemere Design Ltd., London, WC2
Hayes & Howe, Bristol, Avon
Tony Herbert
James Hetley & Co. Ltd., London, W4
Allen Charles Hill, AIA
Hodkin & Jones Ltd., Sheffield, S. Yorkshire
Ibstock Building Products Ltd., Ibstock, Leicestershire
ICI Chemicals & Polymers Ltd., Buxton, Derbyshire

Jackfield Tile Museum, Ironbridge, Shropshire
Jackson & Cox Architectural Restoration Ltd., London, W10
H. & R. Johnson Tiles Ltd., London, W9
Kirby Millworks, Ignacio, KY, USA
Lamont Antiques Ltd., London, SE10
Langlow Products Ltd., Chesham, Buckinghamshire
Lead Development Association, London, W1
Warwick Leadlay, London, SE10
J. Legge & Co. Ltd., Willenhall, W. Midlands
Ludowici Celadon, New Lexington, OH, USA
Luminaries Stained Glass Studio, London, SE10
Marflex International Ltd., Cowbridge, South Glamorgan
Marston & Langinger Ltd., London, W9
Memphis Hardwood Flooring Co., Memphis, TN, USA
The Metalock Organisation, Belvedere, Kent
The Michelmersh Brick & Tile Co. Ltd., Michelmersh, Hampshire
E. G. Millar (Plastering) Ltd., London, E4
Mr & Mrs Scovell
Mumford & Wood Ltd., Braintree, Essex
National Corrosion Service, Teddington, Middlesex
National Park Service, US Dept of the Interior, Washington, DC, USA
National Trust for Historic Preservation, Washington, DC, USA
Nero Designs, London, SW9
Old House Journal, New York, USA
Old Jefferson Tile Co., Jefferson, TX, USA
The Original Box Sash Window Co., Windsor, Berkshire
The Paint Research Association, Teddington, Middlesex
Mr & Mrs Pery-Knox-Gore
Pilkington Glass Ltd., St Helens, Merseyside
Plantation Shutters, London W4
Post Office Archives, London, SE1
Protim Services Ltd., Hayes, Middlesex
The Rainbow Glass Co., Bristol, Avon
The Readybuilt Products Co., Baltimore, MD, USA
Red Bank Manufacturing Co. Ltd., Burton-on-Trent, Staffordshire
Rejuvenation Lamp & Fixture Co., Portland, OR, USA
Rentokil Ltd., East Grinstead, Sussex
Ridout Associates Ltd., Stourbridge, W. Midlands
Dennis Ruabon Ltd., Wrexham, Clywd
John Sambrook, Northiam, E. Sussex
B. C. Sanitan Ltd., Reading, Berkshire
The Society for the Protection of Ancient Buildings, London, E1
Solaglass Technical Advisory Service, Coventry, W. Midlands
St Joseph's Academy (De La Salle Brothers), London, SE3
Stag Polymer & Sealants Ltd., West Drayton, Middlesex
Stained Glass Supplies, London, E2
Staircase Solutions, London, N22
Sterling Roncraft, Barnsley, S. Yorkshire
The Stewart Iron Works Co., Covington, KY, USA
The Stone Federation
Stovax Ltd., Exeter, Devon
Superior Clay Corporation, Uhrichsville, OH, USA
Peter Tew, London Regional Planning, DOE, London, SW1
Thames Moulding Co., Purley, Surrey
Tiles & Architectural Ceramics Society
Joseph Tipper Ltd., Darlaston, W. Midlands
Jenny Todd
Top Knobs Ltd., Bovey Tracey, Devon
Townsends (London) Ltd., London, NW3
The Universal Railings Co. Ltd., Nottingham, Nottinghamshire
Hans van Lemmen, Leeds, W. Yorkshire
Vermont Castings, Derby, Derbyshire
Vintage Wood Works, Fredericksburg, TX, USA
Jack Wallis Doors, Murray, KY, USA
Webb & Kempf Ltd., Ilminster, Somerset
Wellington Tile Co., Wellington, Somerset
Westcombe Antiques, London, SE3
John Williams & Co. Ltd., London, SE16
Tony Wimble, K.C.C. Planning Department
Winther Browne & Co. Ltd., London, N18
Woodstock Soapstone Co. Inc., West Lebanon, NH, USA
Worthington Group Ltd., Atlanta, GA, USA